BUSTED!

Also by Jerry Scott and Jim Borgman

Zits: Sketchbook 1
Growth Spurt: Zits Sketchbook 2
Don't Roll Your Eyes at Me, Young Man!: Zits Sketchbook 3
Are We an "Us?": Zits Sketchbook 4
Zits Unzipped: Zits Sketchbook 5

Humongous Zits: A Zits Treasury
Big Honkin' Zits: A Zits Treasury

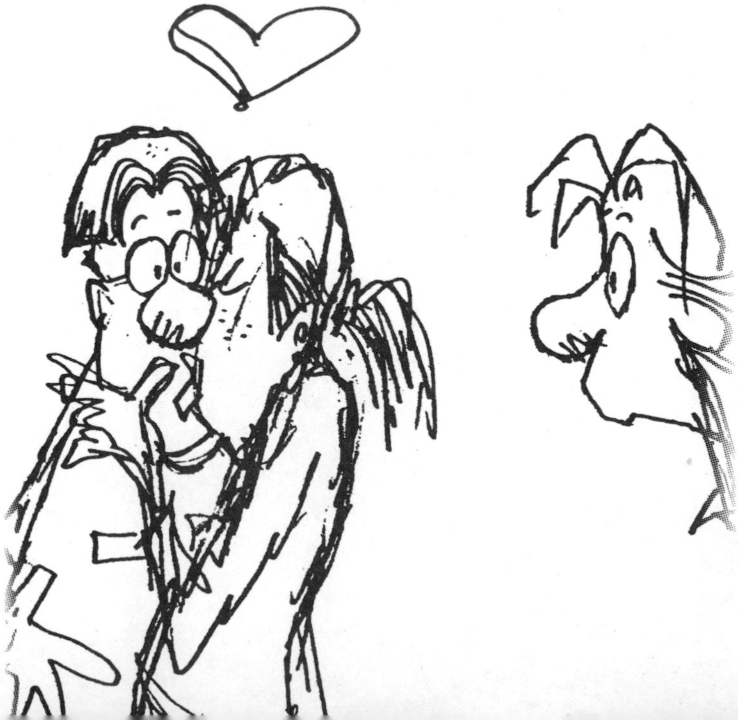

Zits®

BUSTED!

A ZITS® Collection
Sketchbook 6

by JERRY SCOTT and JIM BORGMAN

Andrews McMeel Publishing

Kansas City

Zits® is syndicated internationally by King Features Syndicate, Inc. For information, write King Features Syndicate, Inc., 888 Seventh Avenue, New York, New York 10019.

03 04 05 06 BAH 10 9 8 7 6 5 4 3

ISBN: 0-7407-2675-7

Library of Congress Control Number: 2002103766

Zits® may be viewed online at:
www.kingfeatures.com

To my goddaughters Alix, Nancy, and Cady Lane—Big adventures ahead!

—J.B.

To Heavy C—Love to my Malibu brother.

—J.S.

Zits
by JERRY SCOTT and JIM BORGMAN

YOU'RE UP LATE, JEREMY... WHAT'S THE PROBLEM?
THIS PAPER IS DUE TOMORROW AND I'M STUCK.
HMM...
WELL, THIS DOESN'T FLOW.
AND THIS POINT SHOULD BE AT THE BEGINNING.
THIS NEEDS A REWRITE.
HERE, LET'S MOVE THIS UP...
...AND REWORK THIS.
CLICK CLICK
IS THERE MORE WE COULD SAY HERE?
HOW ABOUT...
THERE'S STILL A LOT OF CLEANING UP TO DO.
DO YOU SEE WHAT I'M DOING HERE?
TYPE TYPE
OKAY, NOW WATCH THIS.
TYPE TYPETTY TYPE TYPE TYPE TYPE TYPE
SCOTT and BORGMAN
I DIDN'T SEE WHY WE SHOULD BOTH BE UP ALL NIGHT.

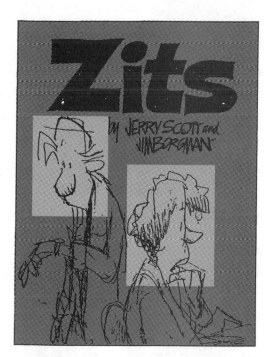

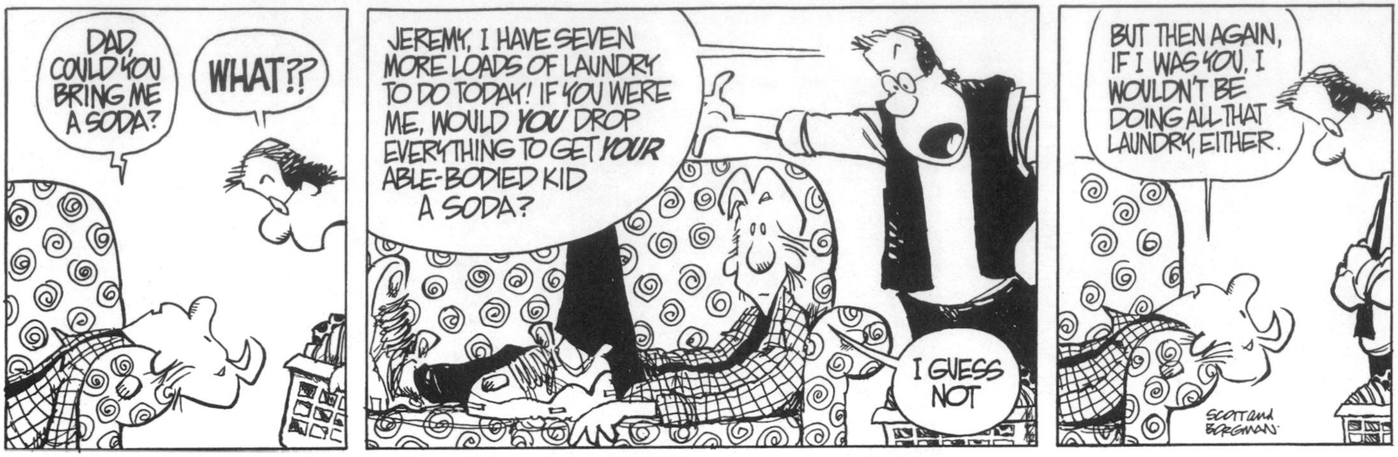
DAD, COULD YOU BRING ME A SODA?
WHAT??
JEREMY, I HAVE SEVEN MORE LOADS OF LAUNDRY TO DO TODAY! IF YOU WERE ME, WOULD YOU DROP EVERYTHING TO GET YOUR ABLE-BODIED KID A SODA?
I GUESS NOT
BUT THEN AGAIN, IF I WAS YOU, I WOULDN'T BE DOING ALL THAT LAUNDRY, EITHER.
SCOTT AND BORGMAN

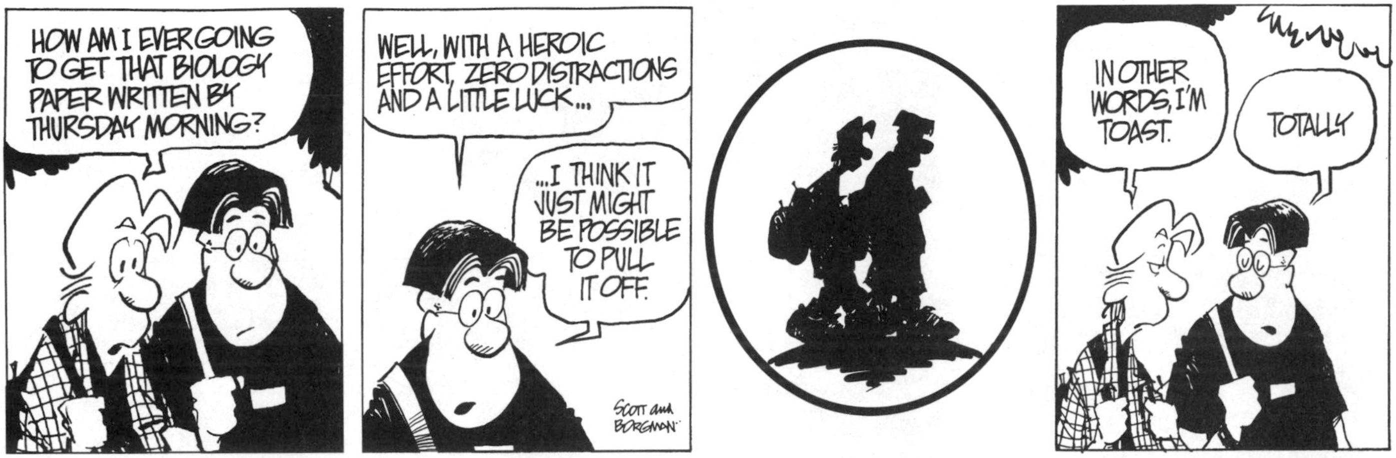
HOW AM I EVER GOING TO GET THAT BIOLOGY PAPER WRITTEN BY THURSDAY MORNING?
WELL, WITH A HEROIC EFFORT, ZERO DISTRACTIONS AND A LITTLE LUCK...
...I THINK IT JUST MIGHT BE POSSIBLE TO PULL IT OFF.
SCOTT AND BORGMAN
IN OTHER WORDS, I'M TOAST.
TOTALLY

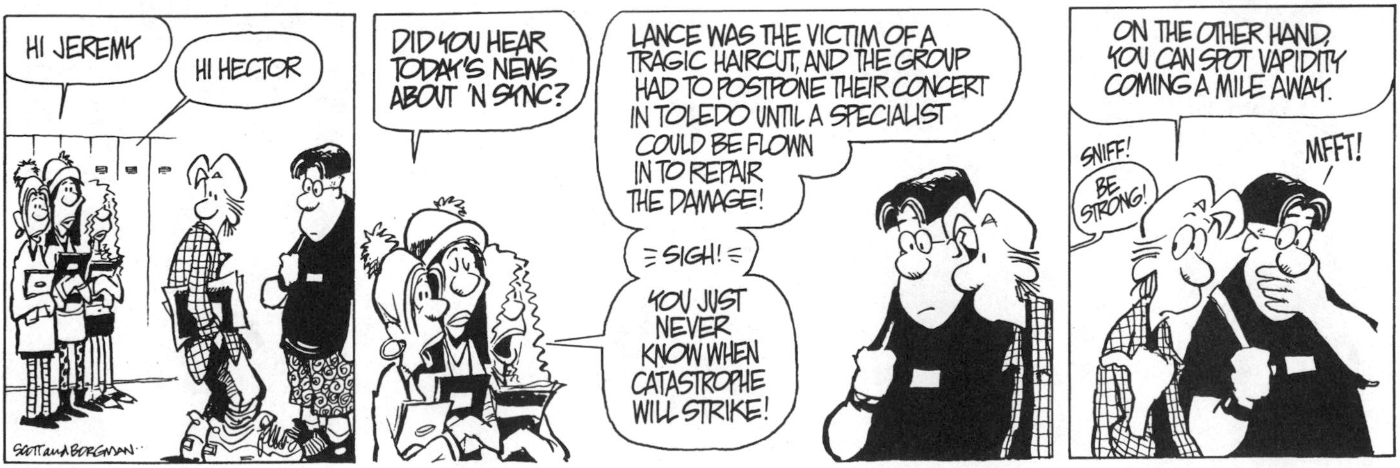
HI JEREMY
HI HECTOR
SCOTT AND BORGMAN
DID YOU HEAR TODAY'S NEWS ABOUT 'N SYNC?
LANCE WAS THE VICTIM OF A TRAGIC HAIRCUT, AND THE GROUP HAD TO POSTPONE THEIR CONCERT IN TOLEDO UNTIL A SPECIALIST COULD BE FLOWN IN TO REPAIR THE DAMAGE!
SIGH!
YOU JUST NEVER KNOW WHEN CATASTROPHE WILL STRIKE!
ON THE OTHER HAND, YOU CAN SPOT VAPIDITY COMING A MILE AWAY.
SNIFF!
BE STRONG!
MFFT!

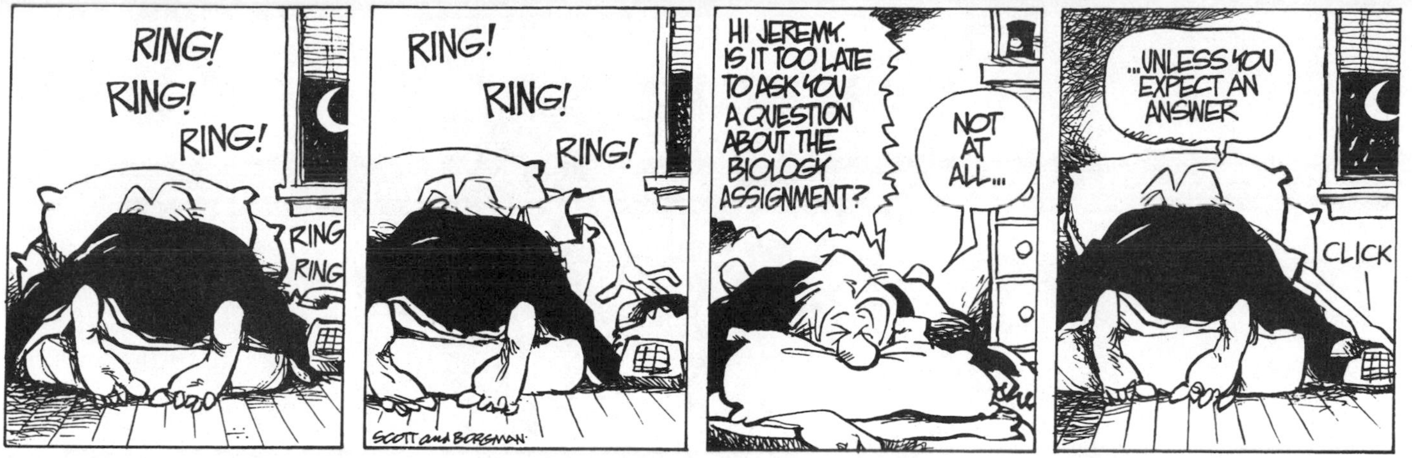
RING!
RING!
RING!
RING
RING
SCOTT and BORGMAN
RING!
RING!
RING!
HI JEREMY. IS IT TOO LATE TO ASK YOU A QUESTION ABOUT THE BIOLOGY ASSIGNMENT?
NOT AT ALL...
...UNLESS YOU EXPECT AN ANSWER
CLICK

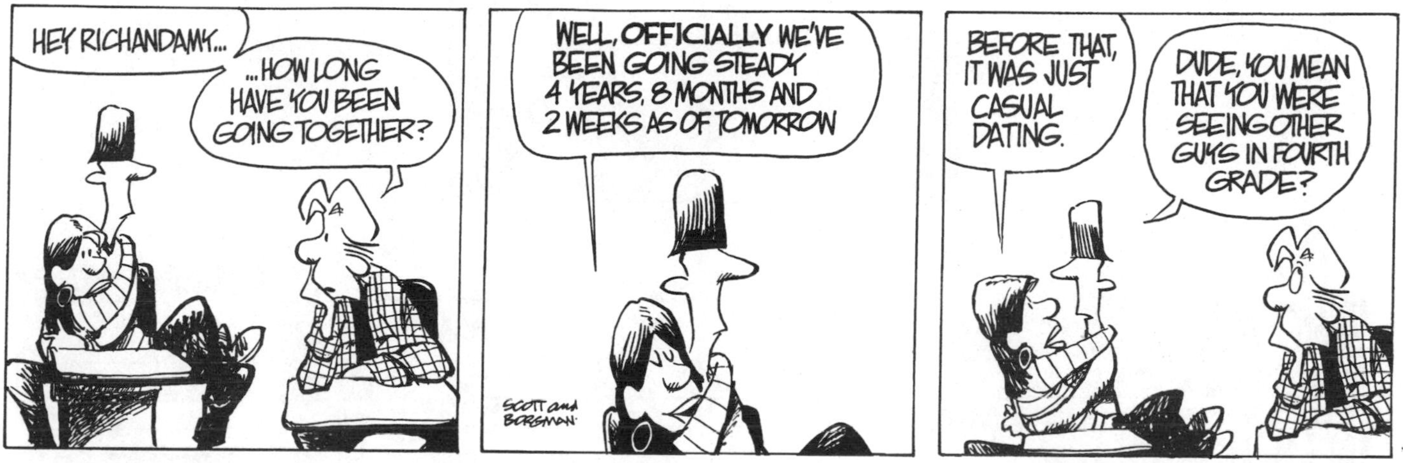
HEY RICHANDAMY...
...HOW LONG HAVE YOU BEEN GOING TOGETHER?
WELL, OFFICIALLY WE'VE BEEN GOING STEADY 4 YEARS, 8 MONTHS AND 2 WEEKS AS OF TOMORROW
SCOTT and BORGMAN
BEFORE THAT, IT WAS JUST CASUAL DATING.
DUDE, YOU MEAN THAT YOU WERE SEEING OTHER GUYS IN FOURTH GRADE?

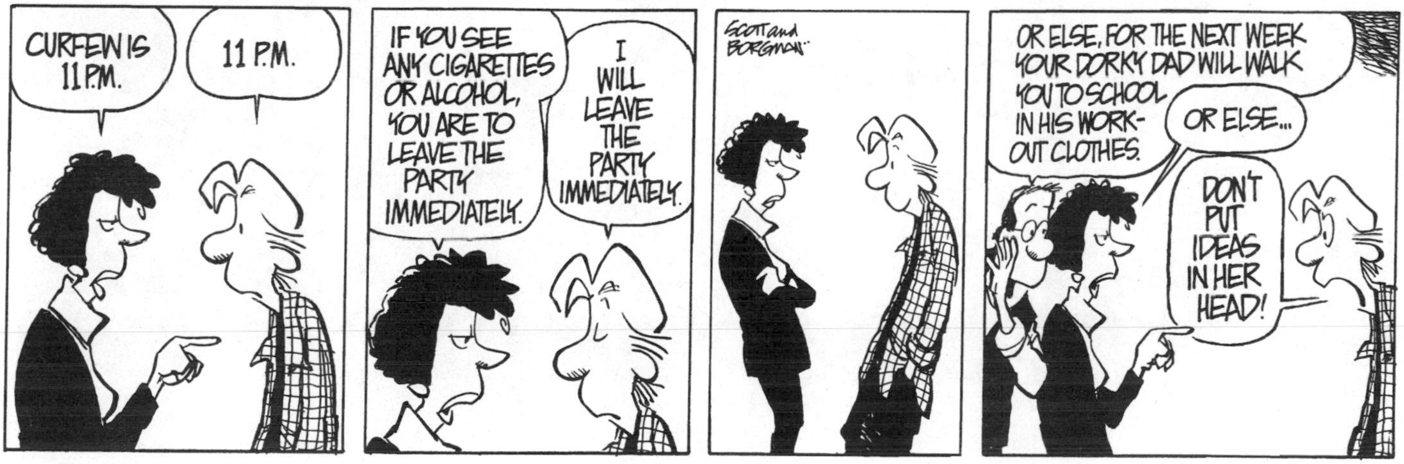
CURFEW IS 11 P.M.
11 P.M.
IF YOU SEE ANY CIGARETTES OR ALCOHOL, YOU ARE TO LEAVE THE PARTY IMMEDIATELY.
I WILL LEAVE THE PARTY IMMEDIATELY.
SCOTT and BORGMAN
OR ELSE, FOR THE NEXT WEEK YOUR DORKY DAD WILL WALK YOU TO SCHOOL IN HIS WORK-OUT CLOTHES.
OR ELSE...
DON'T PUT IDEAS IN HER HEAD!

Zits
by JERRY SCOTT and JIM BORGMAN

WHO MADE THIS MESS IN HERE?
SLAM!
WAIT A MINUTE...
WHAT AM I DOING?
MOM HOLLERS, AND MY FIRST REACTION IS TO RUN AND HIDE?
THAT'S SO IMMATURE!
WHY DO I IMMEDIATELY ASSUME THAT SHE'S YELLING AT ME?
AND EVEN IF SHE WAS, SHOULDN'T I HAVE THE COURAGE TO TAKE RESPONSIBILITY FOR MY ACTIONS?
DON'T BE TOO HARD ON YOURSELF.

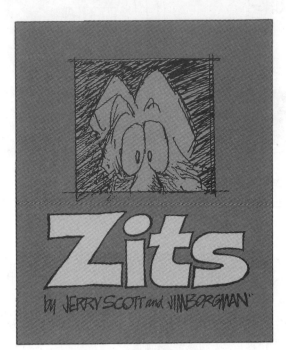

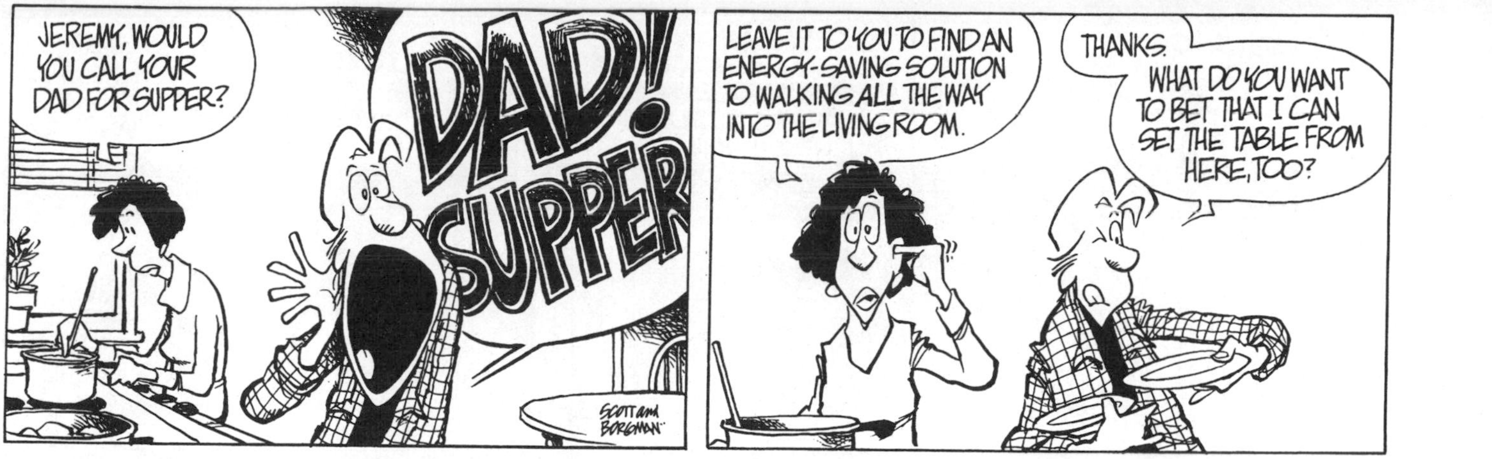
JEREMY, WOULD YOU CALL YOUR DAD FOR SUPPER?
DAD! SUPPER
SCOTT and BORGMAN
LEAVE IT TO YOU TO FIND AN ENERGY-SAVING SOLUTION TO WALKING ALL THE WAY INTO THE LIVING ROOM.
THANKS.
WHAT DO YOU WANT TO BET THAT I CAN SET THE TABLE FROM HERE, TOO?

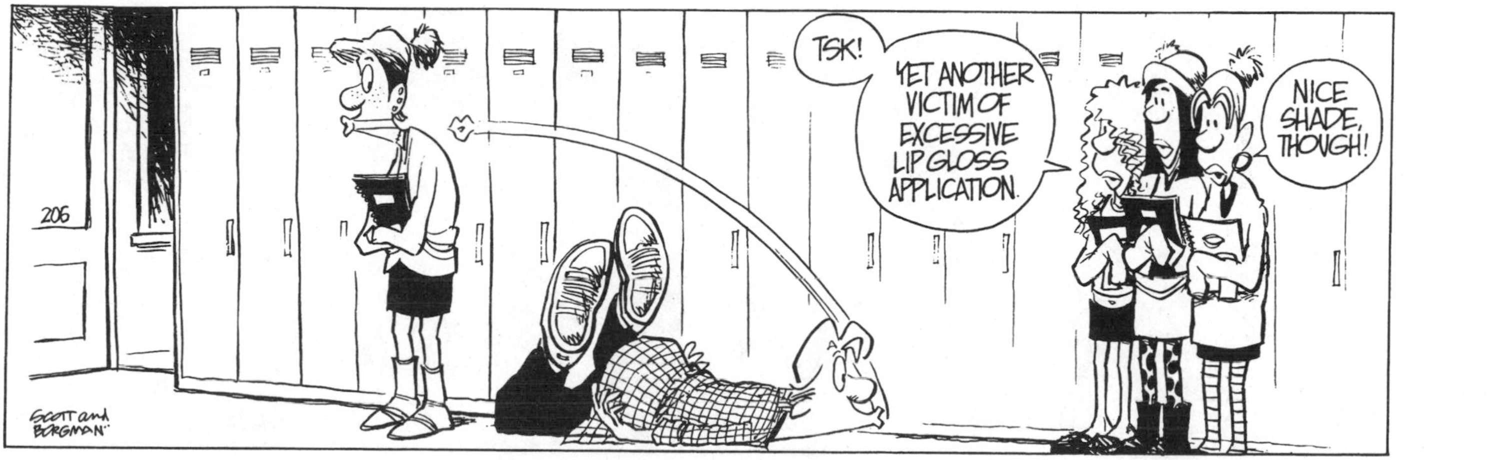
206
SCOTT and BORGMAN
TSK!
YET ANOTHER VICTIM OF EXCESSIVE LIP GLOSS APPLICATION.
NICE SHADE, THOUGH!

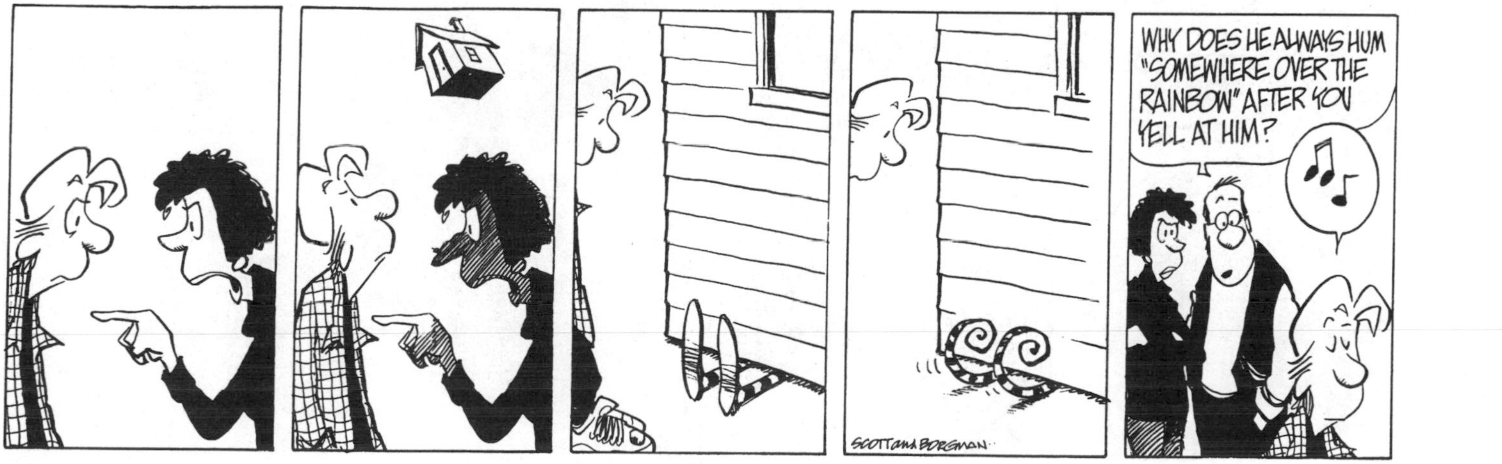
SCOTT and BORGMAN
WHY DOES HE ALWAYS HUM "SOMEWHERE OVER THE RAINBOW" AFTER YOU YELL AT HIM?

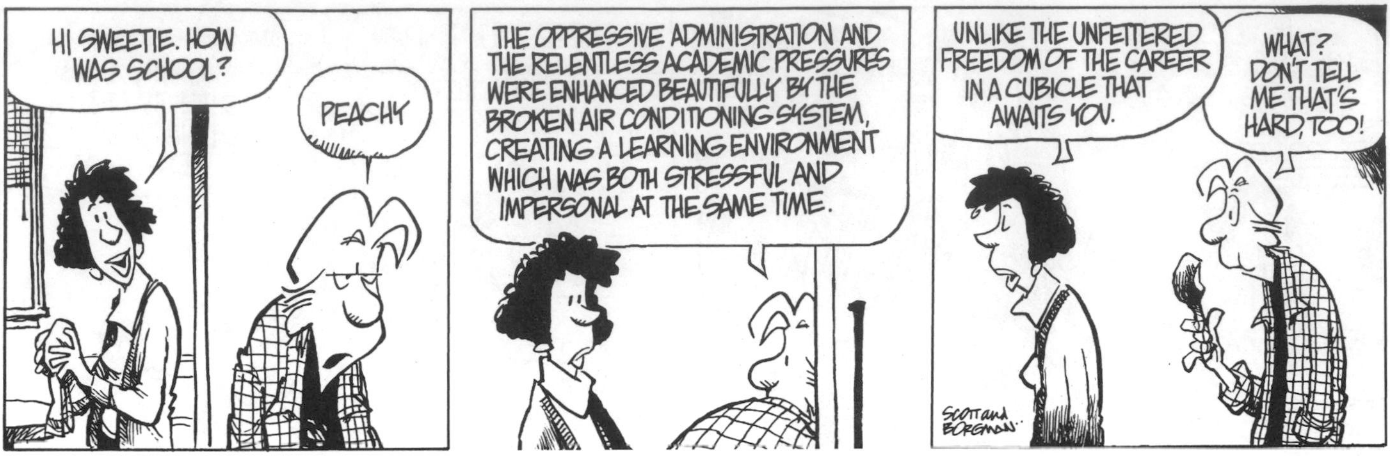
HI SWEETIE. HOW WAS SCHOOL?
PEACHY
THE OPPRESSIVE ADMINISTRATION AND THE RELENTLESS ACADEMIC PRESSURES WERE ENHANCED BEAUTIFULLY BY THE BROKEN AIR CONDITIONING SYSTEM, CREATING A LEARNING ENVIRONMENT WHICH WAS BOTH STRESSFUL AND IMPERSONAL AT THE SAME TIME.
UNLIKE THE UNFETTERED FREEDOM OF THE CAREER IN A CUBICLE THAT AWAITS YOU.
WHAT? DON'T TELL ME THAT'S HARD, TOO!
SCOTT AND BORGMAN

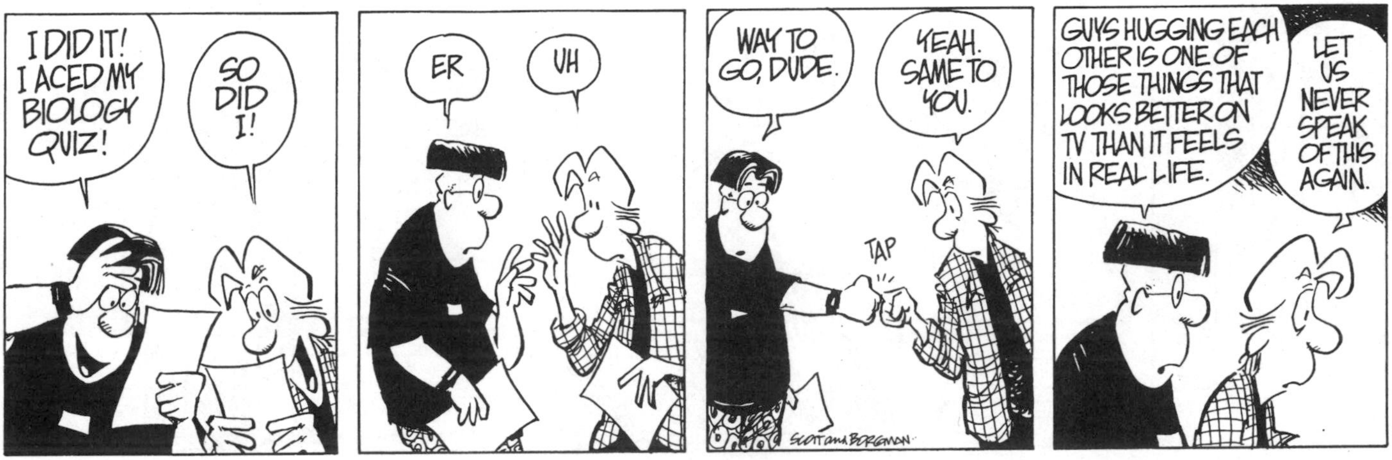
I DID IT! I ACED MY BIOLOGY QUIZ!
SO DID I!
ER
UH
WAY TO GO, DUDE.
YEAH. SAME TO YOU.
TAP
SCOTT AND BORGMAN
GUYS HUGGING EACH OTHER IS ONE OF THOSE THINGS THAT LOOKS BETTER ON TV THAN IT FEELS IN REAL LIFE.
LET US NEVER SPEAK OF THIS AGAIN.

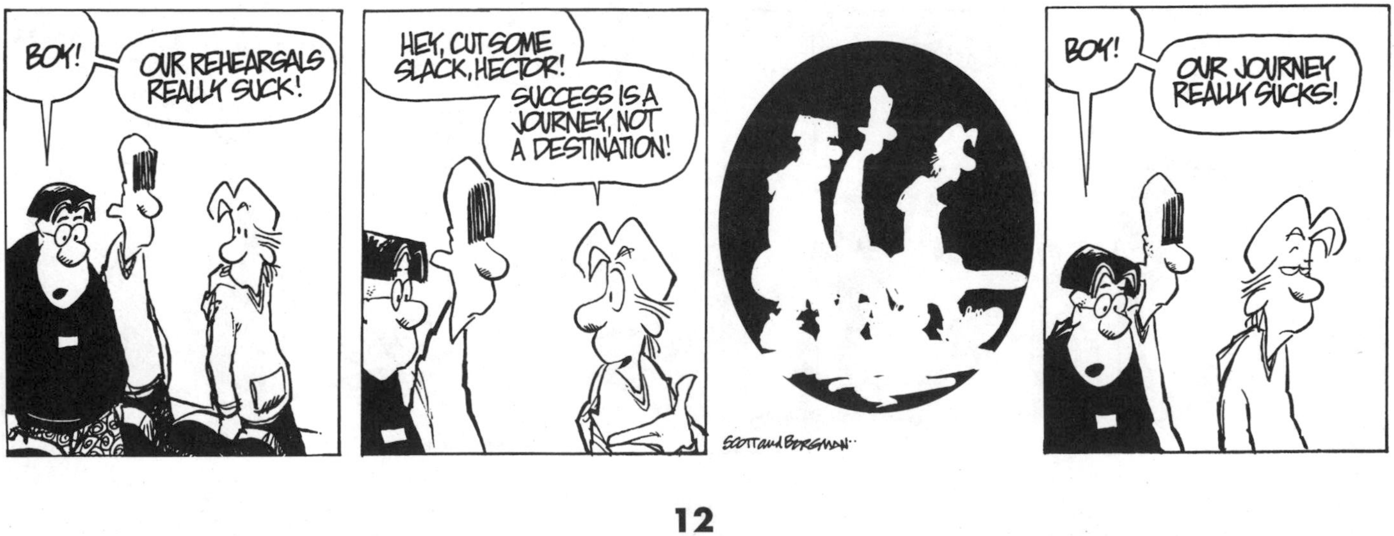
BOY!
OUR REHEARSALS REALLY SUCK!
HEY, CUT SOME SLACK, HECTOR!
SUCCESS IS A JOURNEY, NOT A DESTINATION!
SCOTT AND BORGMAN
BOY!
OUR JOURNEY REALLY SUCKS!

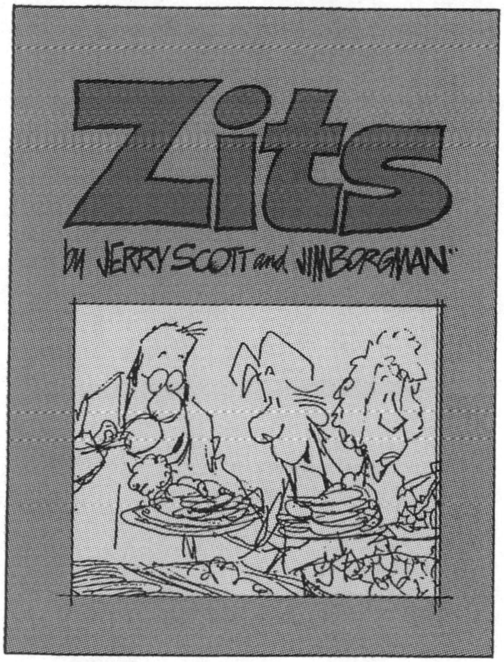
Zits
by JERRY SCOTT and JIM BORGMAN

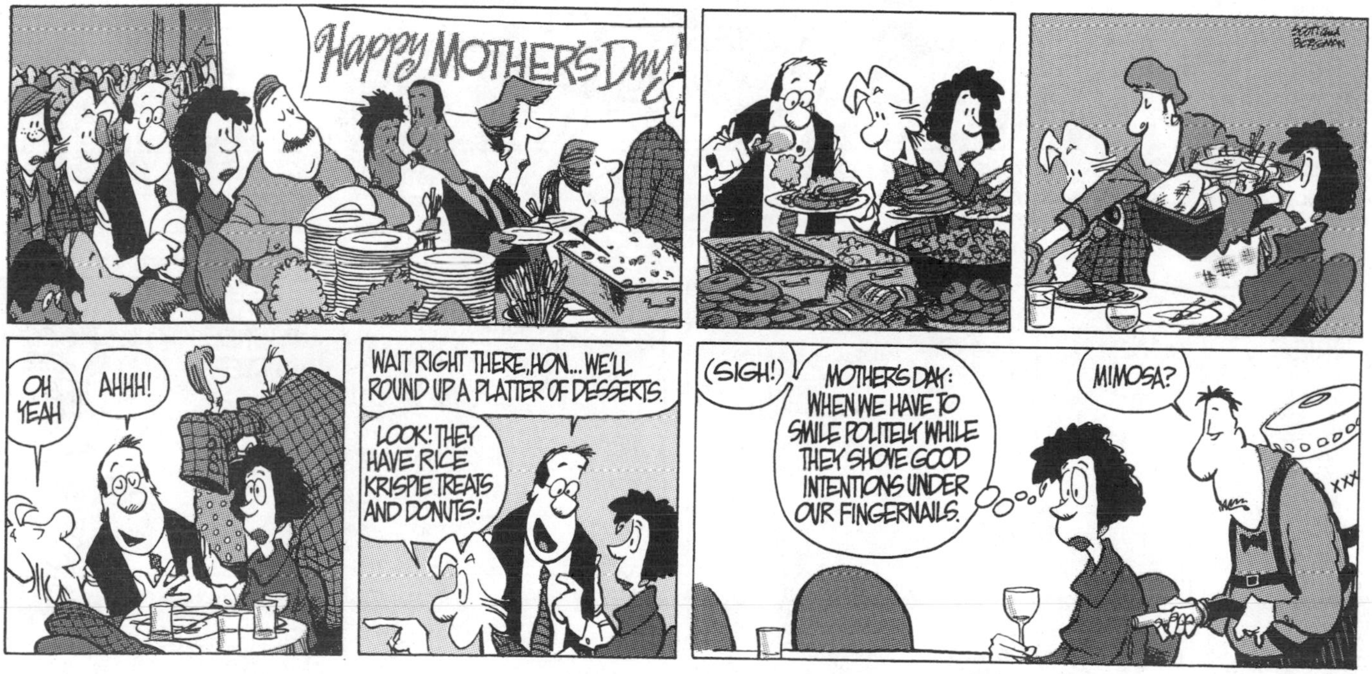
Happy MOTHER'S Day!
OH YEAH
AHHH!
WAIT RIGHT THERE, HON... WE'LL ROUND UP A PLATTER OF DESSERTS.
LOOK! THEY HAVE RICE KRISPIE TREATS AND DONUTS!
(SIGH!)
MOTHER'S DAY: WHEN WE HAVE TO SMILE POLITELY WHILE THEY SHOVE GOOD INTENTIONS UNDER OUR FINGERNAILS.
MIMOSA?

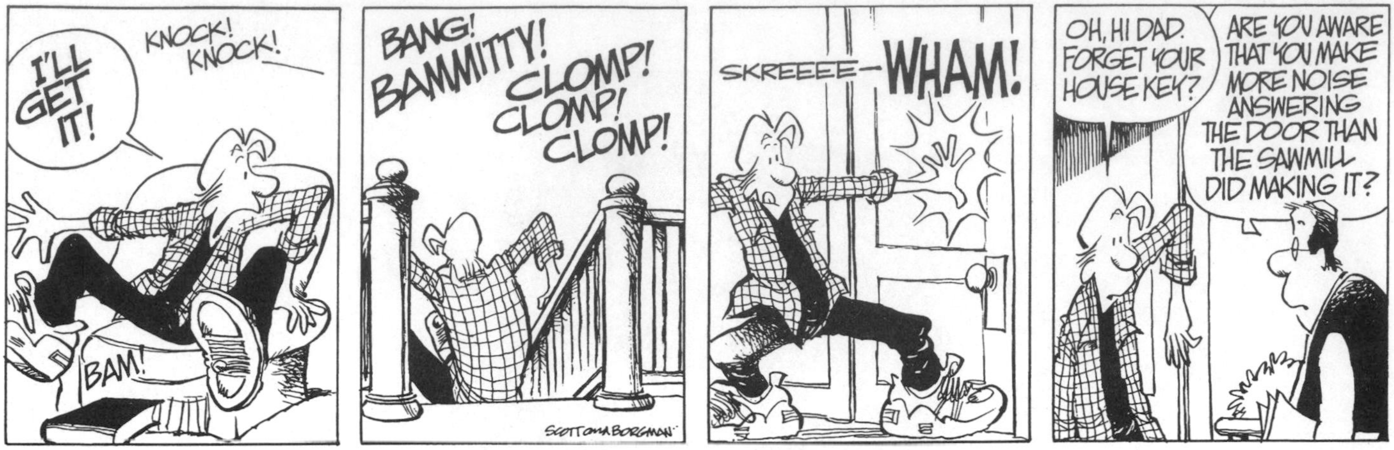
I'LL GET IT!
KNOCK! KNOCK!
BAM!
BANG! BAMMITTY! CLOMP! CLOMP! CLOMP!
SKREEEEE-WHAM!
OH, HI DAD. FORGET YOUR HOUSE KEY?
ARE YOU AWARE THAT YOU MAKE MORE NOISE ANSWERING THE DOOR THAN THE SAWMILL DID MAKING IT?

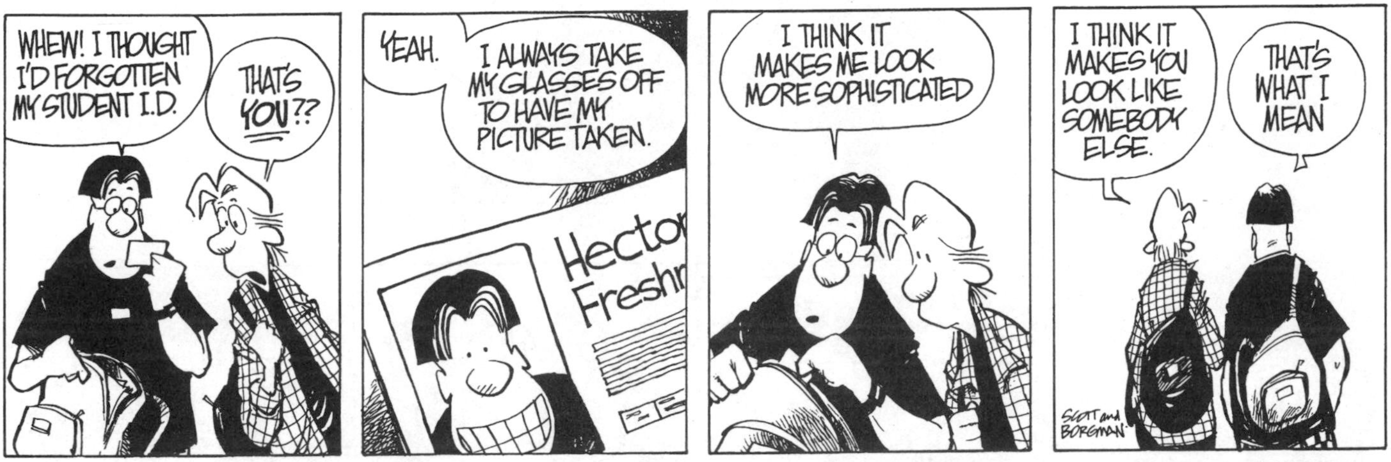
WHEW! I THOUGHT I'D FORGOTTEN MY STUDENT I.D.
THAT'S YOU??
YEAH.
I ALWAYS TAKE MY GLASSES OFF TO HAVE MY PICTURE TAKEN.
I THINK IT MAKES ME LOOK MORE SOPHISTICATED
I THINK IT MAKES YOU LOOK LIKE SOMEBODY ELSE.
THAT'S WHAT I MEAN

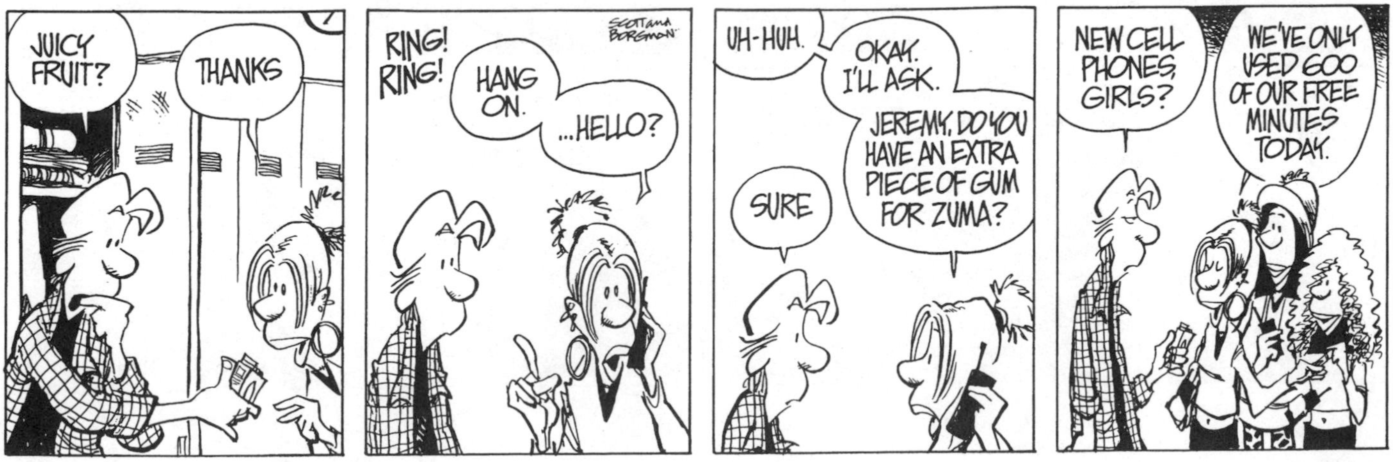
JUICY FRUIT?
THANKS
RING! RING!
HANG ON.
...HELLO?
UH-HUH.
OKAY. I'LL ASK.
JEREMY, DO YOU HAVE AN EXTRA PIECE OF GUM FOR ZUMA?
SURE
NEW CELL PHONES, GIRLS?
WE'VE ONLY USED 600 OF OUR FREE MINUTES TODAY.

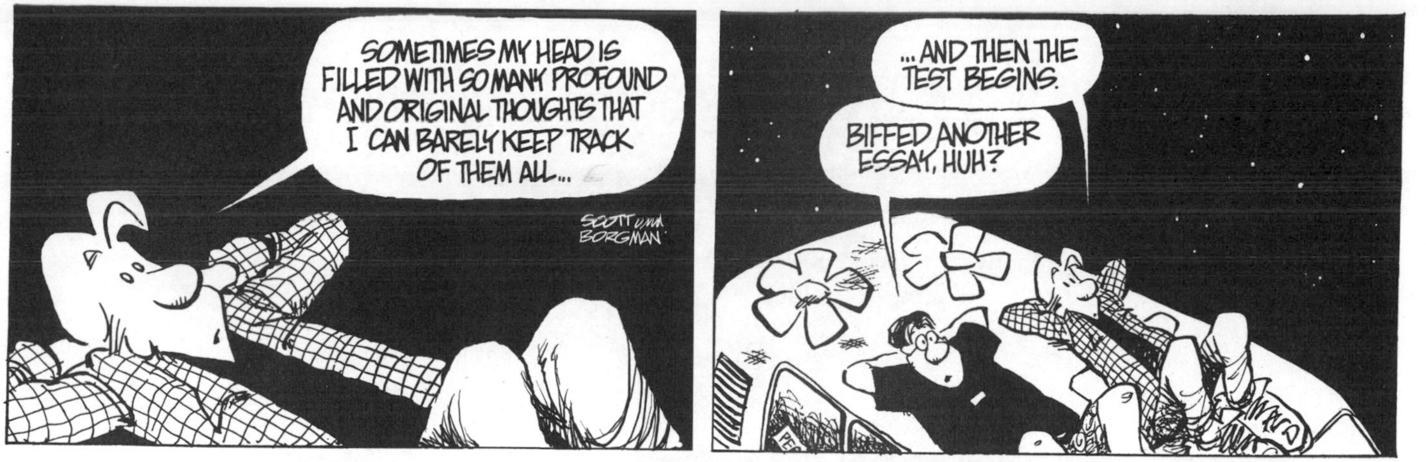
SOMETIMES MY HEAD IS FILLED WITH SO MANY PROFOUND AND ORIGINAL THOUGHTS THAT I CAN BARELY KEEP TRACK OF THEM ALL...
SCOTT and BORGMAN
...AND THEN THE TEST BEGINS.
BIFFED ANOTHER ESSAY, HUH?

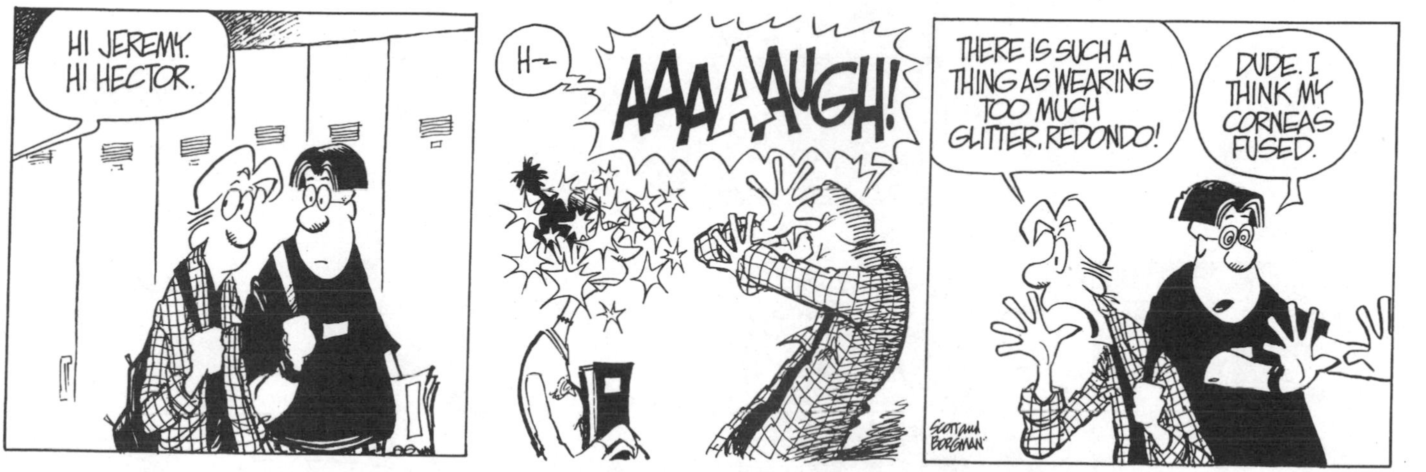
HI JEREMY. HI HECTOR.
H--
AAAAAUGH!
THERE IS SUCH A THING AS WEARING TOO MUCH GLITTER, REDONDO!
DUDE. I THINK MY CORNEAS FUSED.
SCOTT and BORGMAN

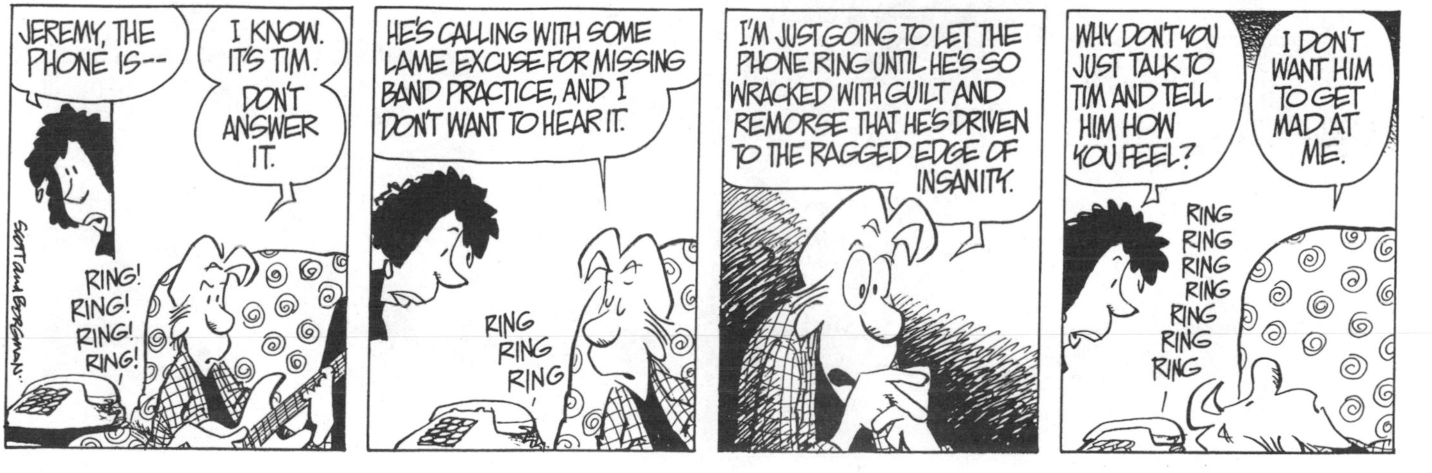
JEREMY, THE PHONE IS--
I KNOW. IT'S TIM.
DON'T ANSWER IT.
RING! RING! RING! RING!
SCOTT and BORGMAN
HE'S CALLING WITH SOME LAME EXCUSE FOR MISSING BAND PRACTICE, AND I DON'T WANT TO HEAR IT.
RING RING RING
I'M JUST GOING TO LET THE PHONE RING UNTIL HE'S SO WRACKED WITH GUILT AND REMORSE THAT HE'S DRIVEN TO THE RAGGED EDGE OF INSANITY.
WHY DON'T YOU JUST TALK TO TIM AND TELL HIM HOW YOU FEEL?
I DON'T WANT HIM TO GET MAD AT ME.
RING RING RING RING RING RING RING

Zits
by
JERRY SCOTT and
JIM BORGMAN

HI MOM. WHAT'S COOKING?
SPAGHETTI SAUCE
LET ME HAVE A TASTE
IN YOUR DREAMS
NOW GET LOST!
SEE YOU AT DINNER!
WHAP!
I'LL BET IT'S TERRIBLE
HEY! GET OUT OF THERE!
PUT ME DOWN!
MMMM
YOU LOOK FRAZZLED.
YEAH, WELL, JEREMY'S IN A GOOD MOOD.
SCOTT and BORGMAN

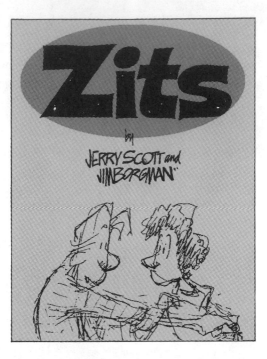

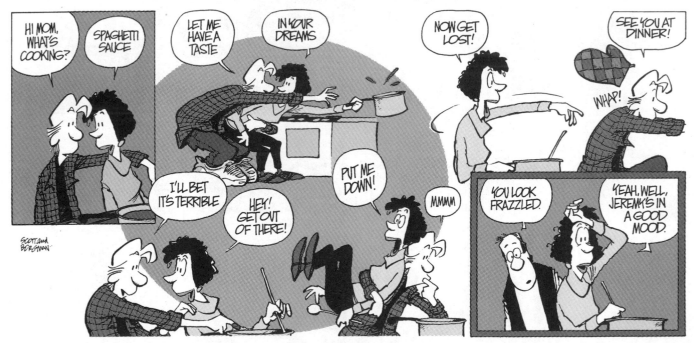

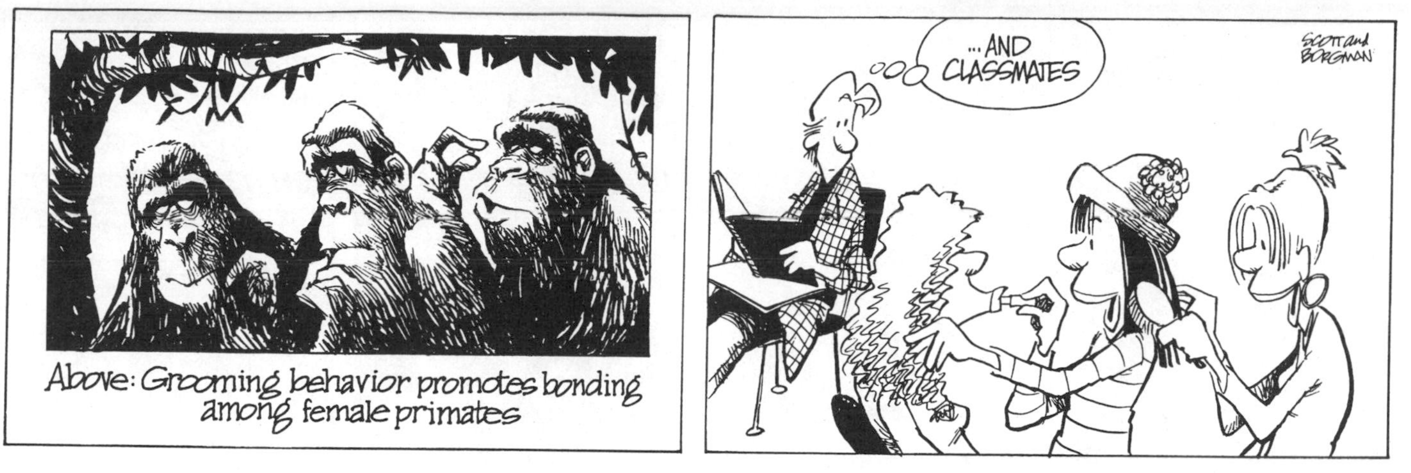
Above: Grooming behavior promotes bonding among female primates
...AND CLASSMATES
SCOTT and BORGMAN

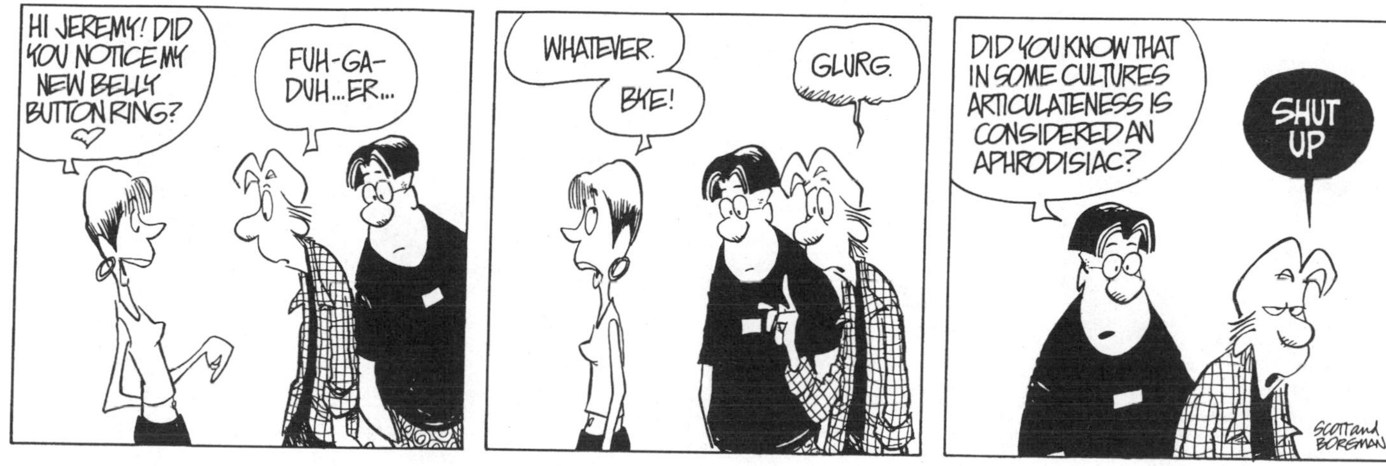
HI JEREMY! DID YOU NOTICE MY NEW BELLY BUTTON RING?
FUH-GA-DUH...ER...
WHATEVER.
BYE!
GLURG.
DID YOU KNOW THAT IN SOME CULTURES ARTICULATENESS IS CONSIDERED AN APHRODISIAC?
SHUT UP
SCOTT and BORGMAN

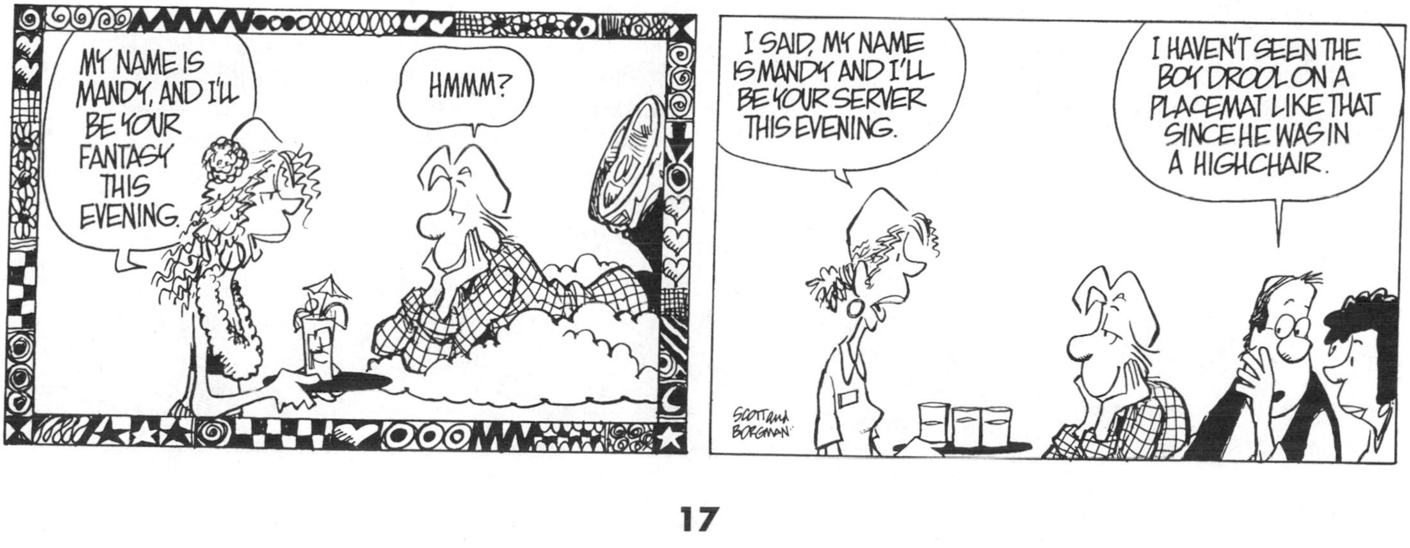
MY NAME IS MANDY, AND I'LL BE YOUR FANTASY THIS EVENING.
HMMM?
SCOTT and BORGMAN
I SAID, MY NAME IS MANDY AND I'LL BE YOUR SERVER THIS EVENING.
I HAVEN'T SEEN THE BOY DROOL ON A PLACEMAT LIKE THAT SINCE HE WAS IN A HIGHCHAIR.

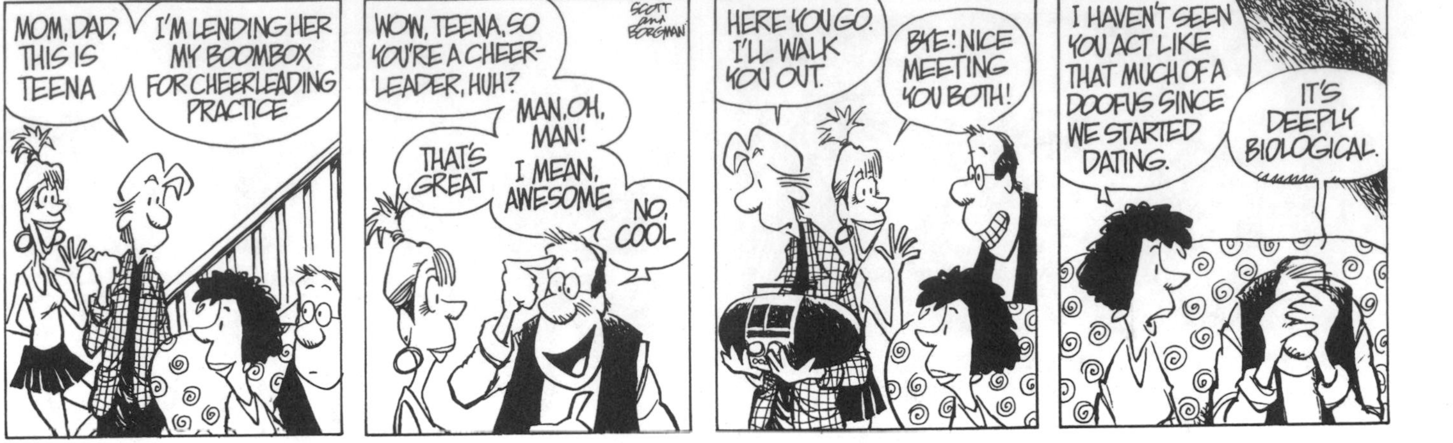
MOM, DAD, THIS IS TEENA
I'M LENDING HER MY BOOMBOX FOR CHEERLEADING PRACTICE
WOW, TEENA, SO YOU'RE A CHEERLEADER, HUH?
THAT'S GREAT
MAN, OH, MAN! I MEAN, AWESOME
NO, COOL
SCOTT and BORGMAN
HERE YOU GO. I'LL WALK YOU OUT.
BYE! NICE MEETING YOU BOTH!
I HAVEN'T SEEN YOU ACT LIKE THAT MUCH OF A DOOFUS SINCE WE STARTED DATING.
IT'S DEEPLY BIOLOGICAL.

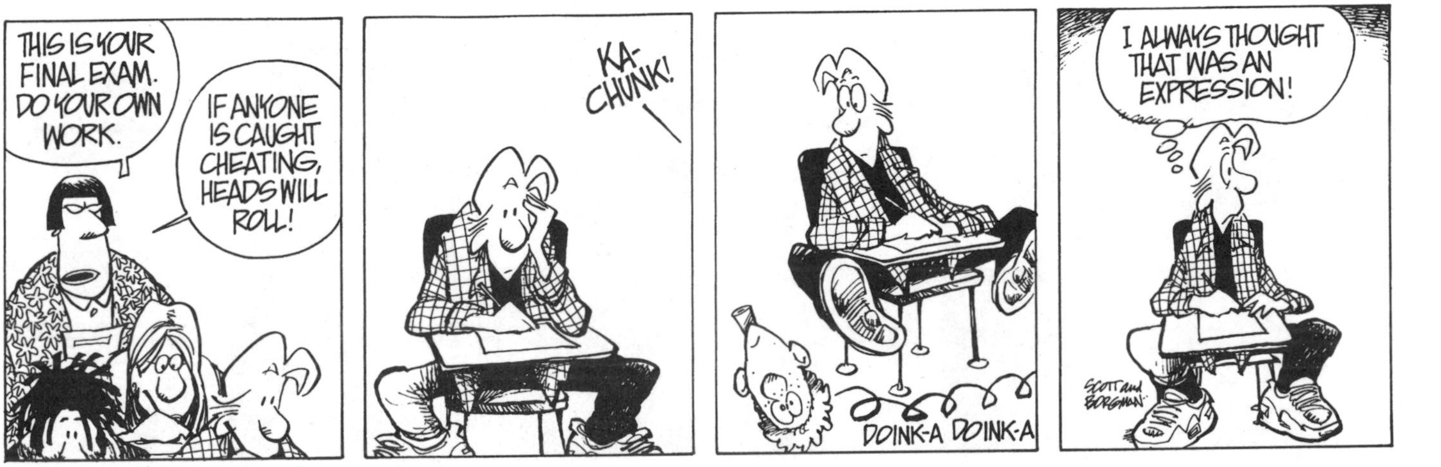
THIS IS YOUR FINAL EXAM. DO YOUR OWN WORK.
IF ANYONE IS CAUGHT CHEATING, HEADS WILL ROLL!
KA-CHUNK!
DOINK-A DOINK-A
I ALWAYS THOUGHT THAT WAS AN EXPRESSION!
SCOTT and BORGMAN

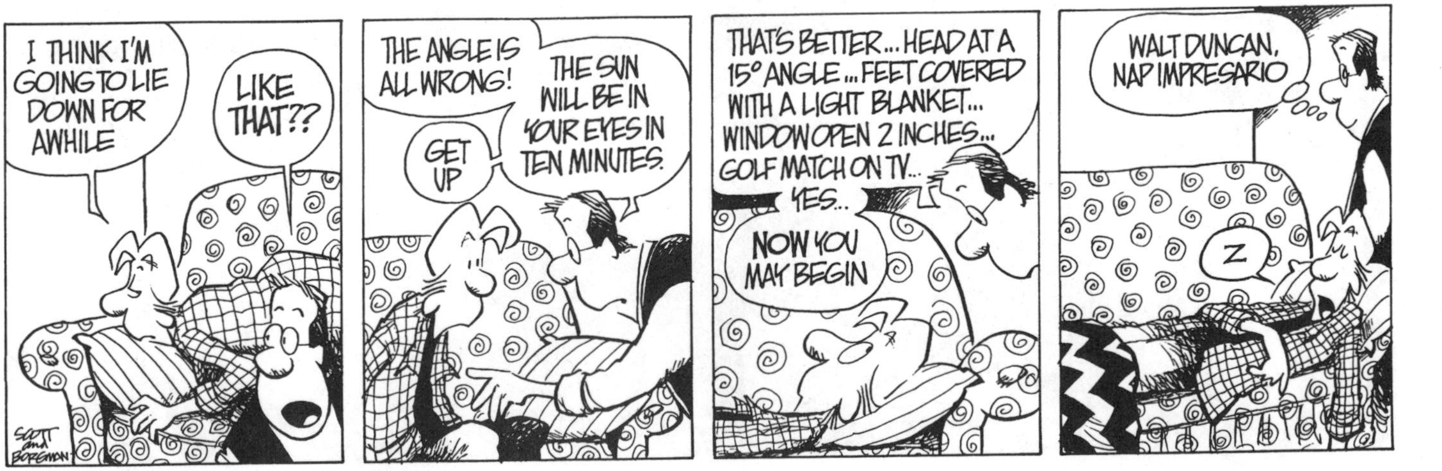
I THINK I'M GOING TO LIE DOWN FOR AWHILE
LIKE THAT??
SCOTT and BORGMAN
THE ANGLE IS ALL WRONG!
GET UP
THE SUN WILL BE IN YOUR EYES IN TEN MINUTES.
THAT'S BETTER... HEAD AT A 15° ANGLE... FEET COVERED WITH A LIGHT BLANKET... WINDOW OPEN 2 INCHES... GOLF MATCH ON TV...
YES...
NOW YOU MAY BEGIN
WALT DUNCAN, NAP IMPRESARIO
Z

Zits

JERRY SCOTT and JIM BORGMAN

WHAT DO YOU WANT TO DO TODAY?

MAYBE WE SHOULD WORK ON THE VAN.

WE HAVEN'T TOUCHED IT SINCE LAST FALL.

TRUE DAT

AFTER A WINTER LIKE THE ONE WE JUST HAD, THERE ARE BOUND TO BE A FEW BASIC MAINTENANCE ISSUES TO ADDRESS.

SCOTT and BORGMAN

YOU GET THE FAMILY OF SQUIRRELS OUT OF THE ENGINE COMPARTMENT, AND I'LL MOW THE INTERIOR.

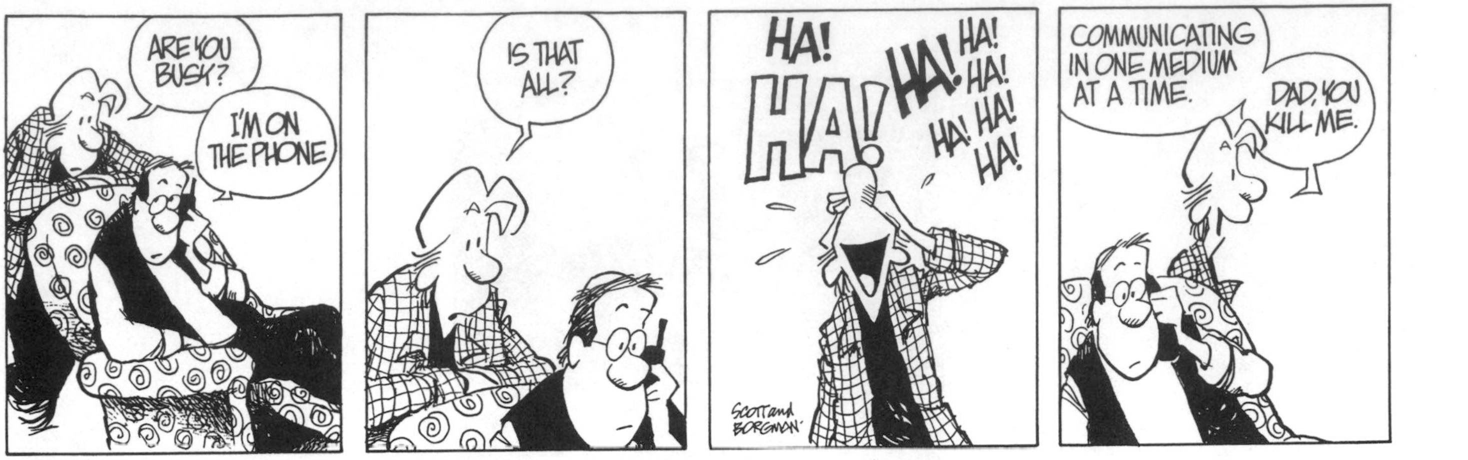
ARE YOU BUSY?
I'M ON THE PHONE
IS THAT ALL?
HA! HA! HA! HA! HA! HA! HA! HA!
SCOTT and BORGMAN
COMMUNICATING IN ONE MEDIUM AT A TIME.
DAD, YOU KILL ME.

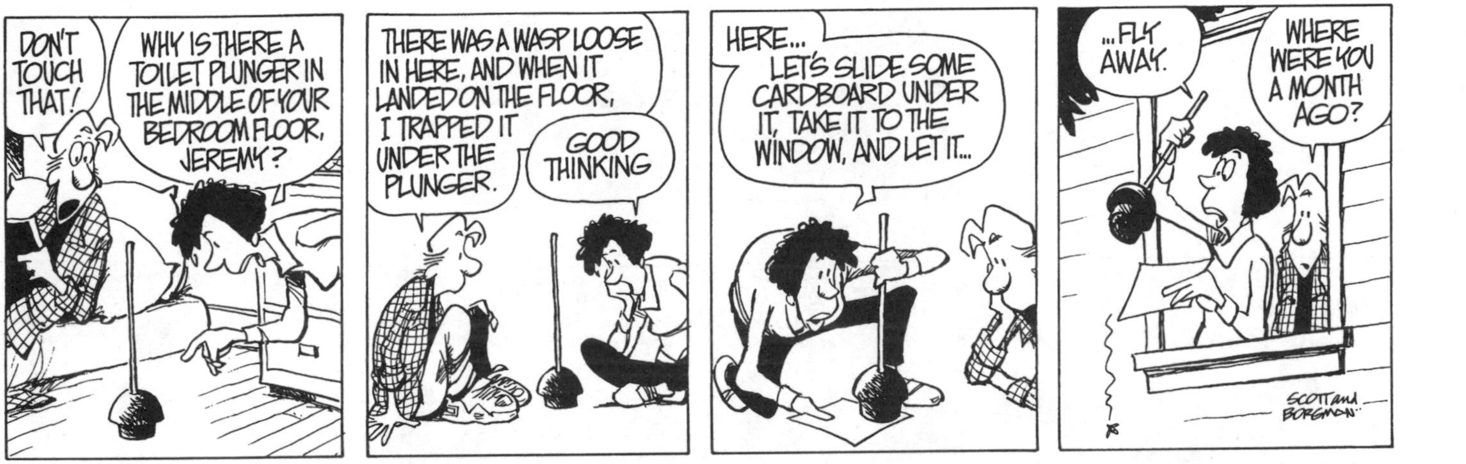
DON'T TOUCH THAT!
WHY IS THERE A TOILET PLUNGER IN THE MIDDLE OF YOUR BEDROOM FLOOR, JEREMY?
THERE WAS A WASP LOOSE IN HERE, AND WHEN IT LANDED ON THE FLOOR, I TRAPPED IT UNDER THE PLUNGER.
GOOD THINKING
HERE...
LET'S SLIDE SOME CARDBOARD UNDER IT, TAKE IT TO THE WINDOW, AND LET IT...
...FLY AWAY.
WHERE WERE YOU A MONTH AGO?
SCOTT and BORGMAN

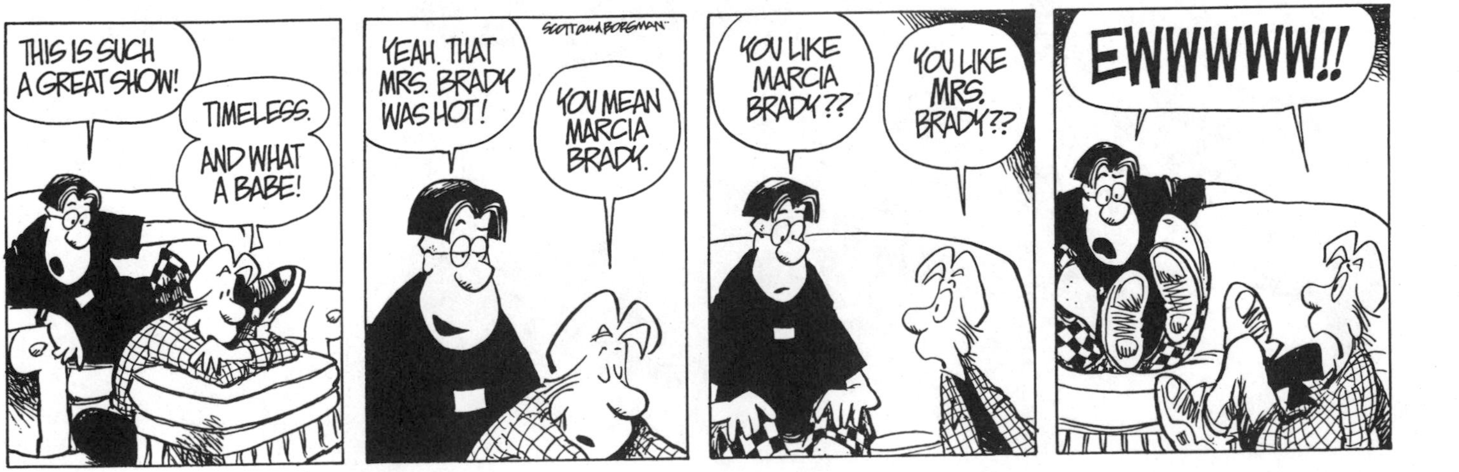
THIS IS SUCH A GREAT SHOW!
TIMELESS.
AND WHAT A BABE!
SCOTT and BORGMAN
YEAH. THAT MRS. BRADY WAS HOT!
YOU MEAN MARCIA BRADY.
YOU LIKE MARCIA BRADY??
YOU LIKE MRS. BRADY??
EWWWWW!!

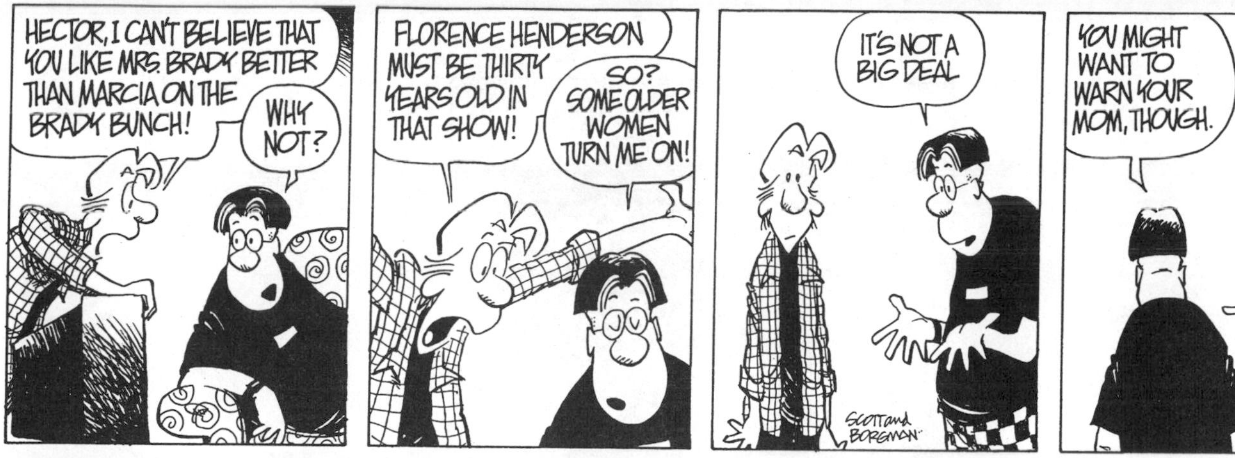
HECTOR, I CAN'T BELIEVE THAT YOU LIKE MRS. BRADY BETTER THAN MARCIA ON THE BRADY BUNCH!
WHY NOT?
FLORENCE HENDERSON MUST BE THIRTY YEARS OLD IN THAT SHOW!
SO? SOME OLDER WOMEN TURN ME ON!
IT'S NOT A BIG DEAL
SCOTT and BORGMAN
YOU MIGHT WANT TO WARN YOUR MOM, THOUGH.
DON'T EVEN JOKE ABOUT THAT!

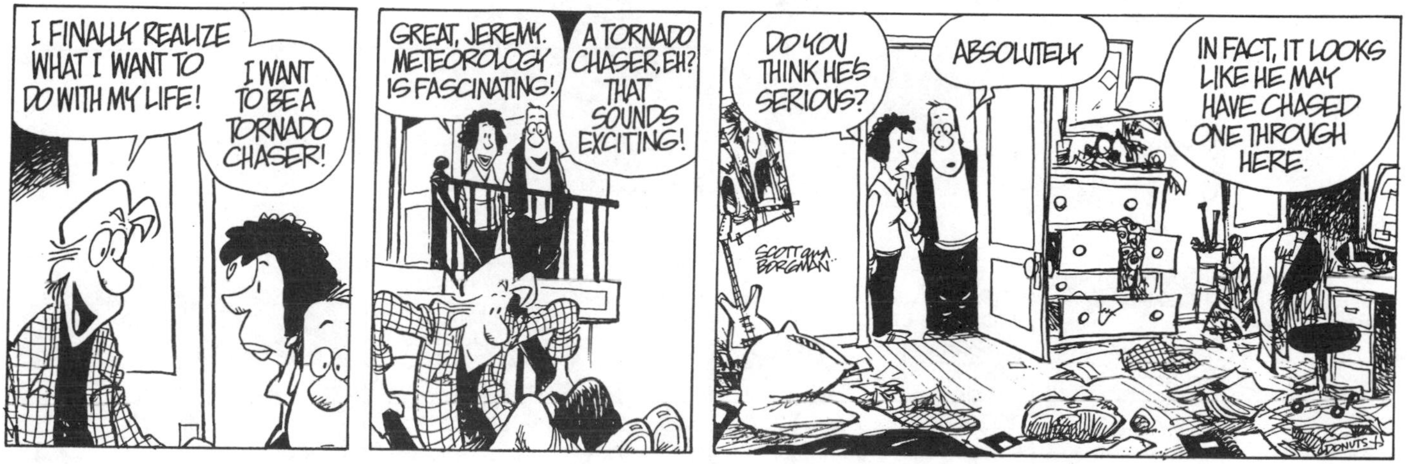
I FINALLY REALIZE WHAT I WANT TO DO WITH MY LIFE!
I WANT TO BE A TORNADO CHASER!
GREAT, JEREMY. METEOROLOGY IS FASCINATING!
A TORNADO CHASER, EH? THAT SOUNDS EXCITING!
DO YOU THINK HE'S SERIOUS?
ABSOLUTELY
IN FACT, IT LOOKS LIKE HE MAY HAVE CHASED ONE THROUGH HERE.
SCOTT and BORGMAN

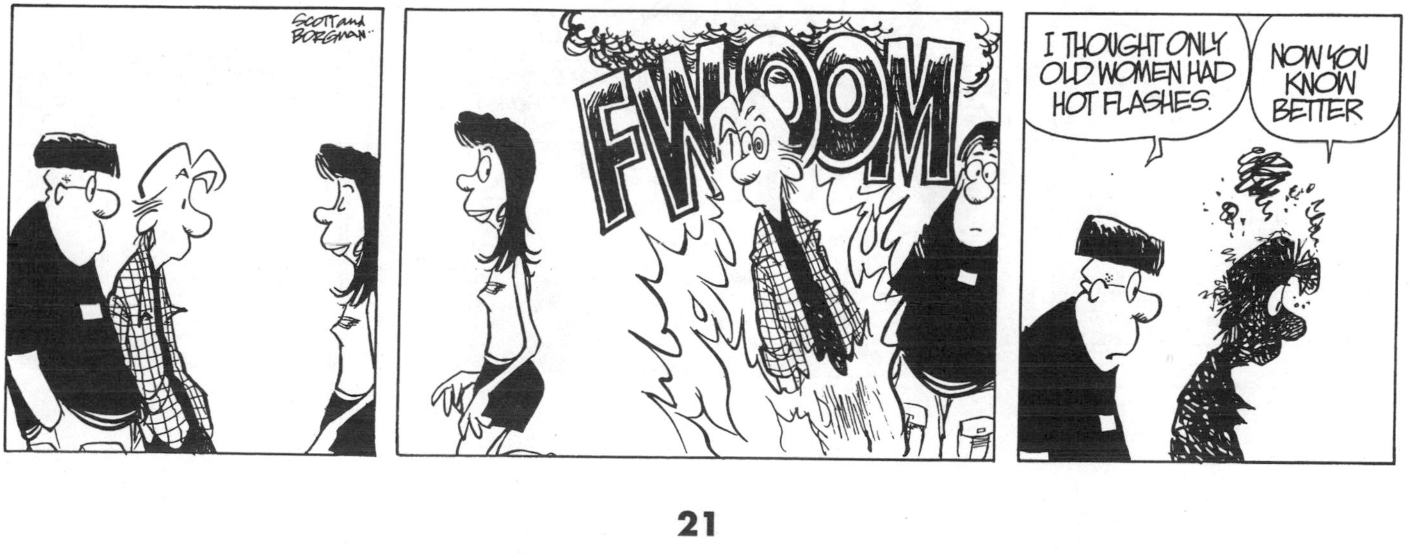
SCOTT and BORGMAN
FWOOM
I THOUGHT ONLY OLD WOMEN HAD HOT FLASHES.
NOW YOU KNOW BETTER

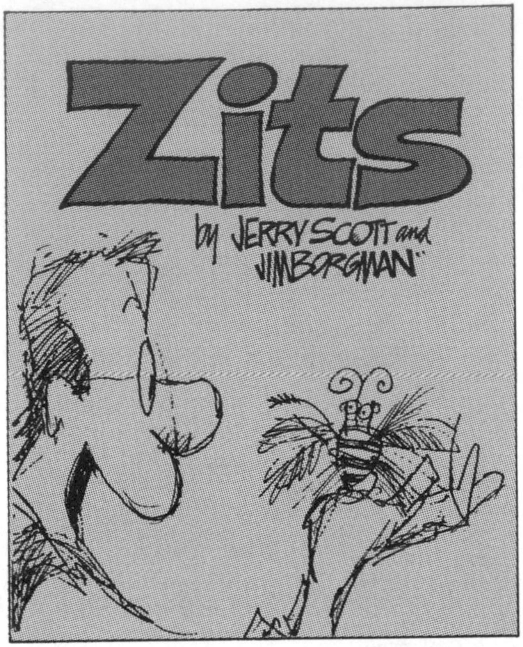
Zits
by JERRY SCOTT and JIM BORGMAN

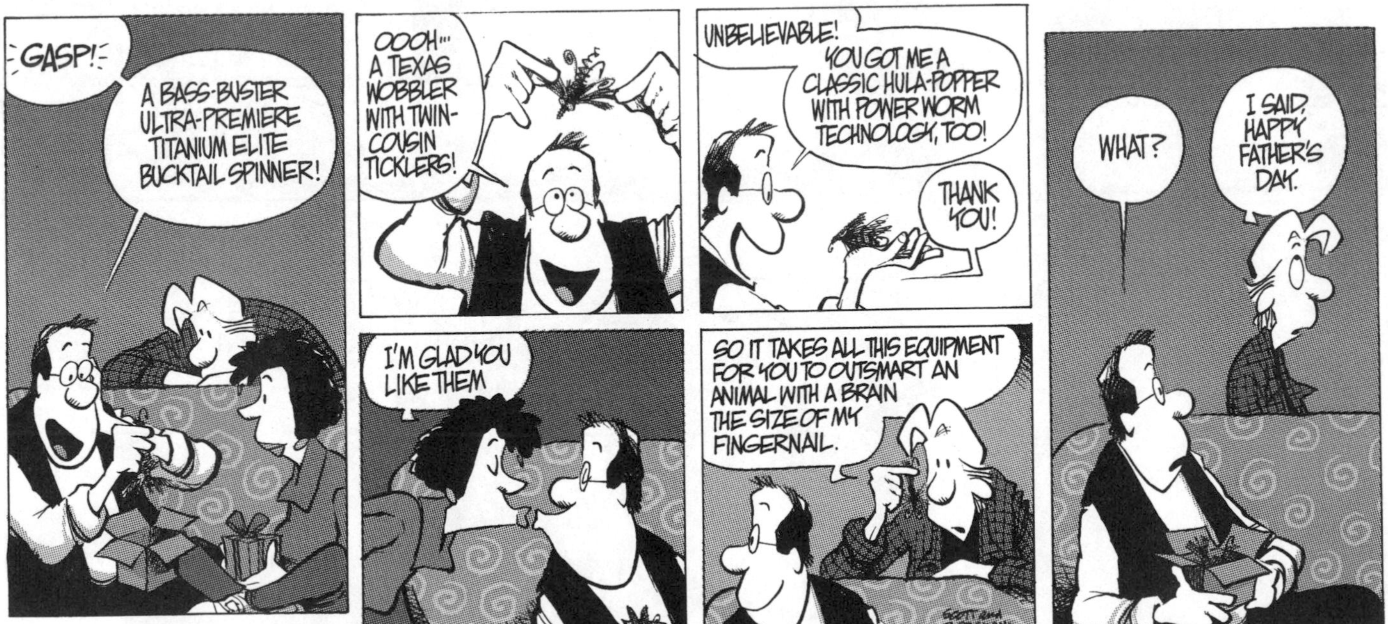
GASP!
A BASS-BUSTER ULTRA-PREMIERE TITANIUM ELITE BUCKTAIL SPINNER!
OOOH... A TEXAS WOBBLER WITH TWIN-COUSIN TICKLERS!
UNBELIEVABLE!
YOU GOT ME A CLASSIC HULA-POPPER WITH POWER WORM TECHNOLOGY, TOO!
THANK YOU!
I'M GLAD YOU LIKE THEM
SO IT TAKES ALL THIS EQUIPMENT FOR YOU TO OUTSMART AN ANIMAL WITH A BRAIN THE SIZE OF MY FINGERNAIL.
SCOTT and BORGMAN
WHAT?
I SAID, HAPPY FATHER'S DAY.

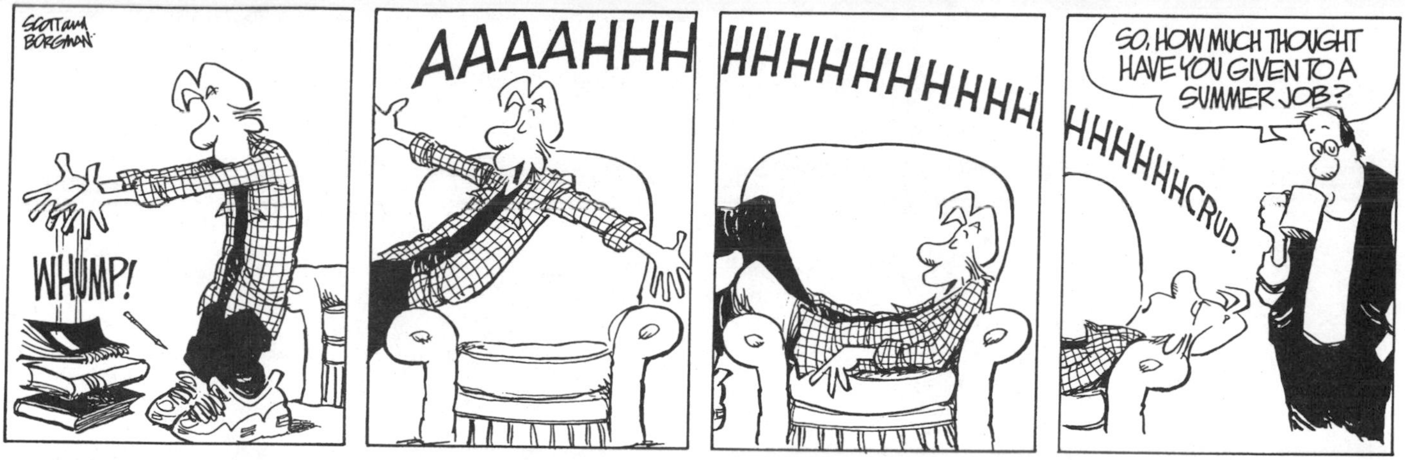
SCOTT and BORGMAN
WHUMP!
AAAAHHH
HHHHHHHHHHH
HHHHHHHCRUD.
SO, HOW MUCH THOUGHT HAVE YOU GIVEN TO A SUMMER JOB?

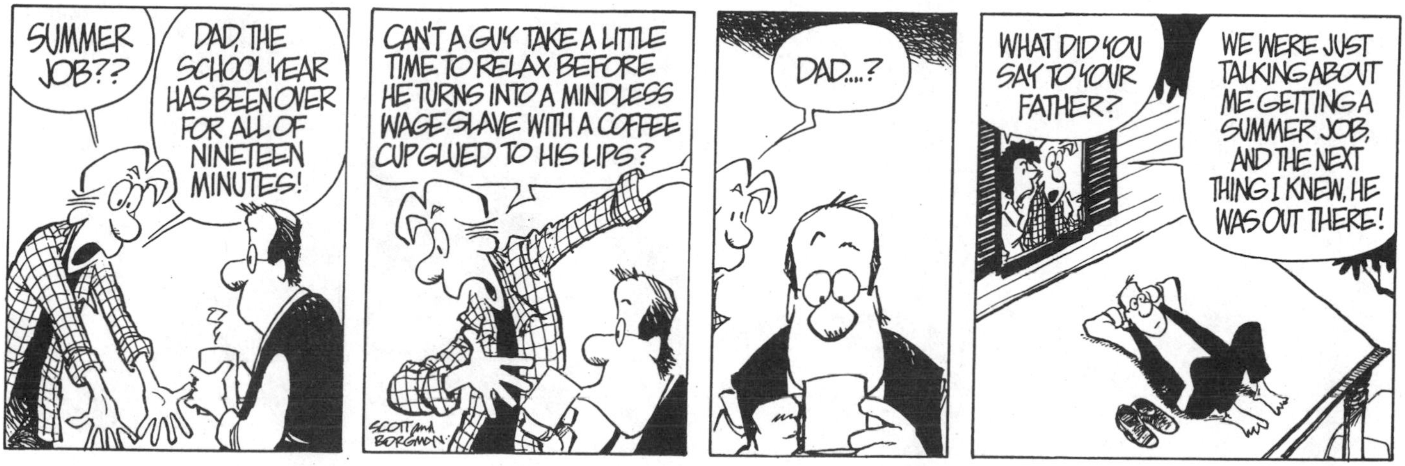
SUMMER JOB??
DAD, THE SCHOOL YEAR HAS BEEN OVER FOR ALL OF NINETEEN MINUTES!
CAN'T A GUY TAKE A LITTLE TIME TO RELAX BEFORE HE TURNS INTO A MINDLESS WAGE SLAVE WITH A COFFEE CUP GLUED TO HIS LIPS?
SCOTT and BORGMAN
DAD....?
WHAT DID YOU SAY TO YOUR FATHER?
WE WERE JUST TALKING ABOUT ME GETTING A SUMMER JOB, AND THE NEXT THING I KNEW, HE WAS OUT THERE!

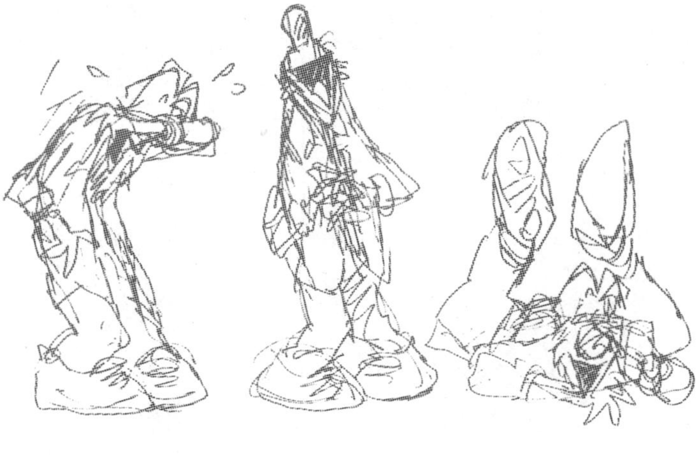

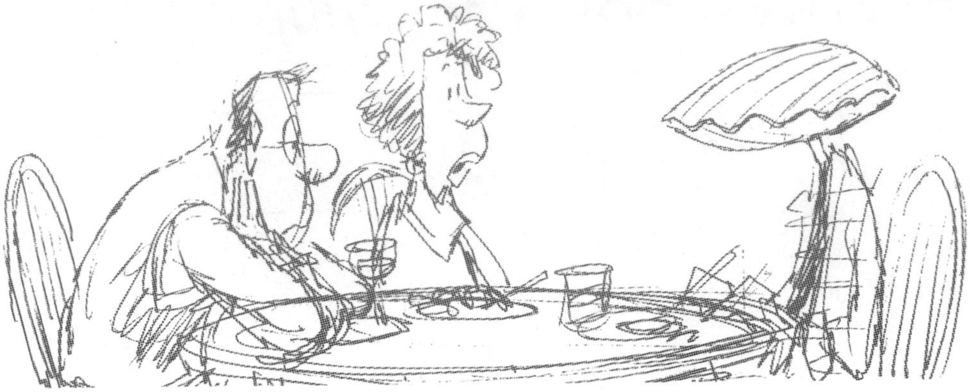

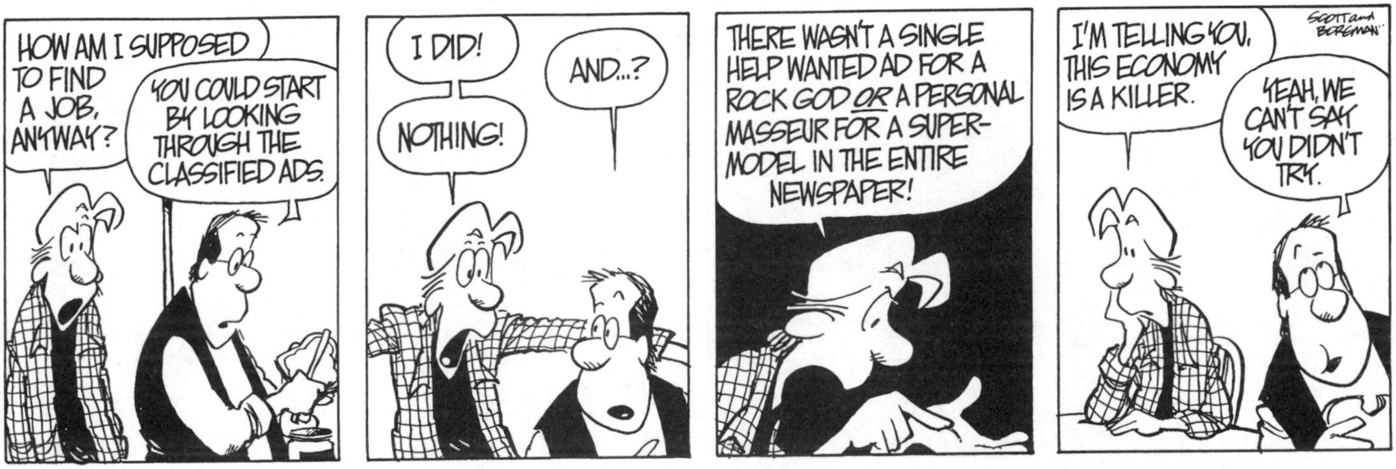
HOW AM I SUPPOSED TO FIND A JOB, ANYWAY?
YOU COULD START BY LOOKING THROUGH THE CLASSIFIED ADS.
I DID!
NOTHING!
AND...?
THERE WASN'T A SINGLE HELP WANTED AD FOR A ROCK GOD OR A PERSONAL MASSEUR FOR A SUPER-MODEL IN THE ENTIRE NEWSPAPER!
SCOTT and BORGMAN
I'M TELLING YOU, THIS ECONOMY IS A KILLER.
YEAH, WE CAN'T SAY YOU DIDN'T TRY.

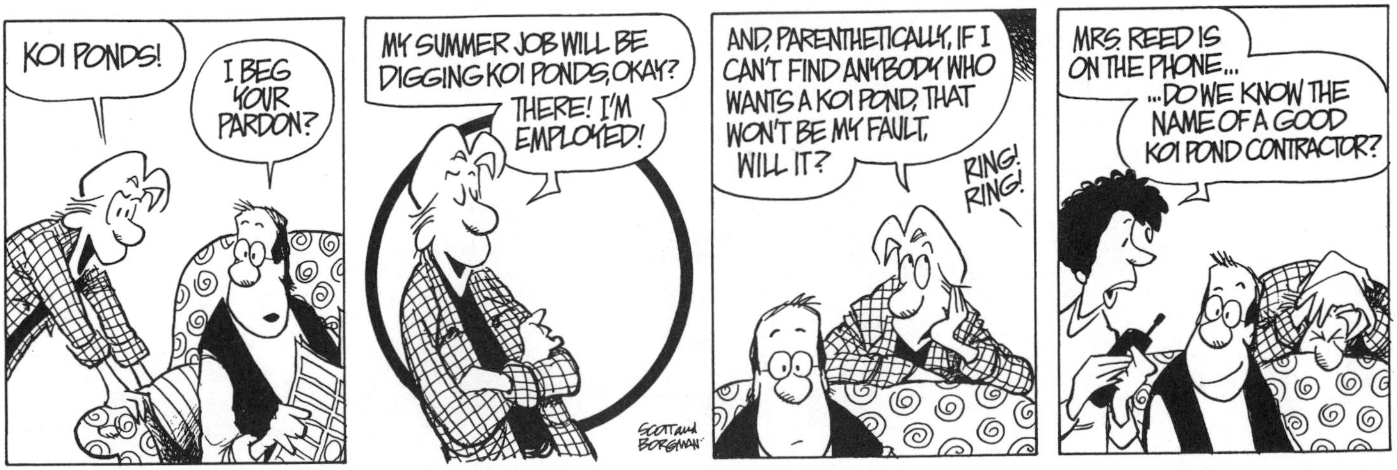
KOI PONDS!
I BEG YOUR PARDON?
MY SUMMER JOB WILL BE DIGGING KOI PONDS, OKAY?
THERE! I'M EMPLOYED!
SCOTT and BORGMAN
AND, PARENTHETICALLY, IF I CAN'T FIND ANYBODY WHO WANTS A KOI POND, THAT WON'T BE MY FAULT, WILL IT?
RING! RING!
MRS. REED IS ON THE PHONE...
...DO WE KNOW THE NAME OF A GOOD KOI POND CONTRACTOR?

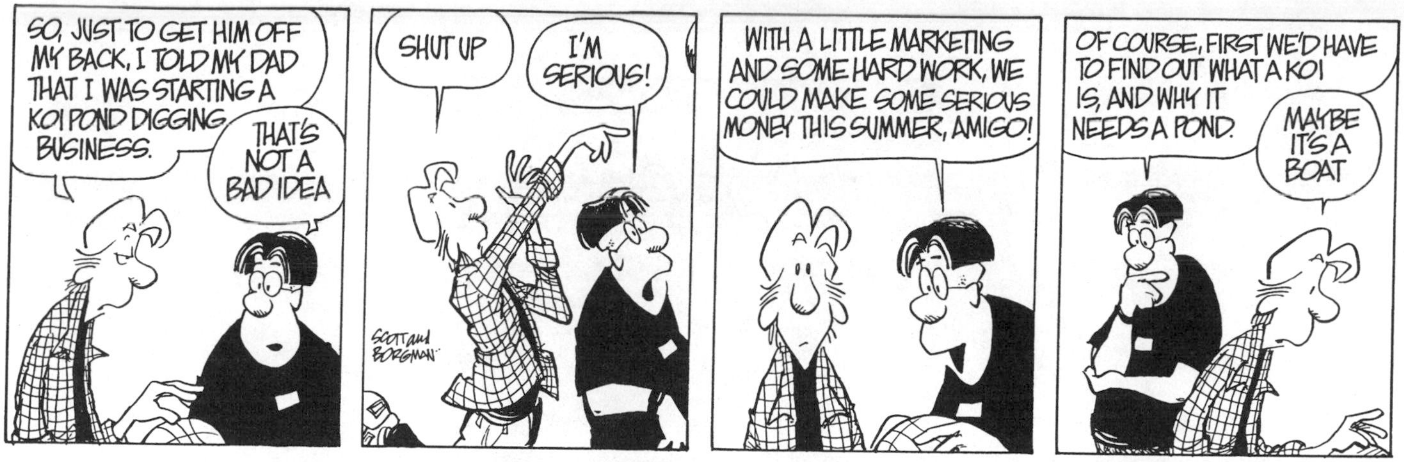
SO, JUST TO GET HIM OFF MY BACK, I TOLD MY DAD THAT I WAS STARTING A KOI POND DIGGING BUSINESS.
THAT'S NOT A BAD IDEA
SHUT UP
I'M SERIOUS!
SCOTT and BORGMAN
WITH A LITTLE MARKETING AND SOME HARD WORK, WE COULD MAKE SOME SERIOUS MONEY THIS SUMMER, AMIGO!
OF COURSE, FIRST WE'D HAVE TO FIND OUT WHAT A KOI IS, AND WHY IT NEEDS A POND.
MAYBE IT'S A BOAT

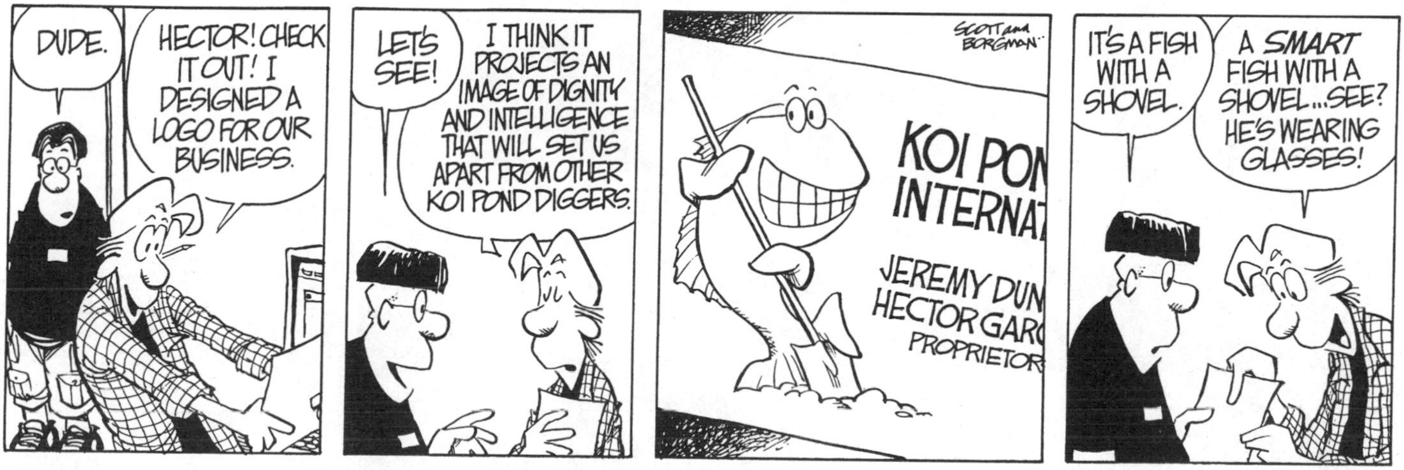
DUDE.
HECTOR! CHECK IT OUT! I DESIGNED A LOGO FOR OUR BUSINESS.
LET'S SEE!
I THINK IT PROJECTS AN IMAGE OF DIGNITY AND INTELLIGENCE THAT WILL SET US APART FROM OTHER KOI POND DIGGERS.
SCOTT and BORGMAN
KOI PON
INTERNAT
JEREMY DUN
HECTOR GARC
PROPRIETOR
IT'S A FISH WITH A SHOVEL.
A SMART FISH WITH A SHOVEL... SEE? HE'S WEARING GLASSES!

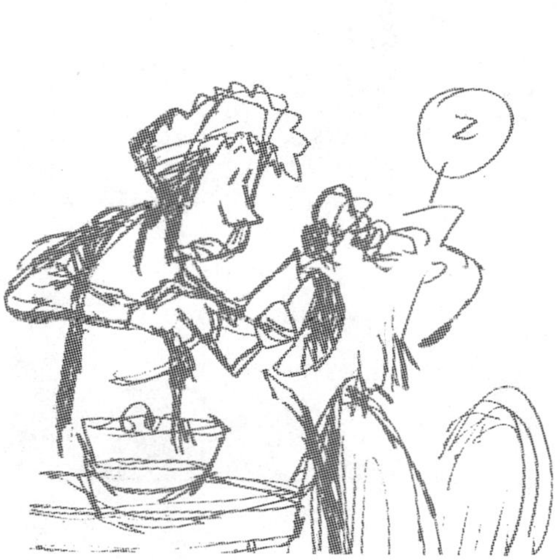

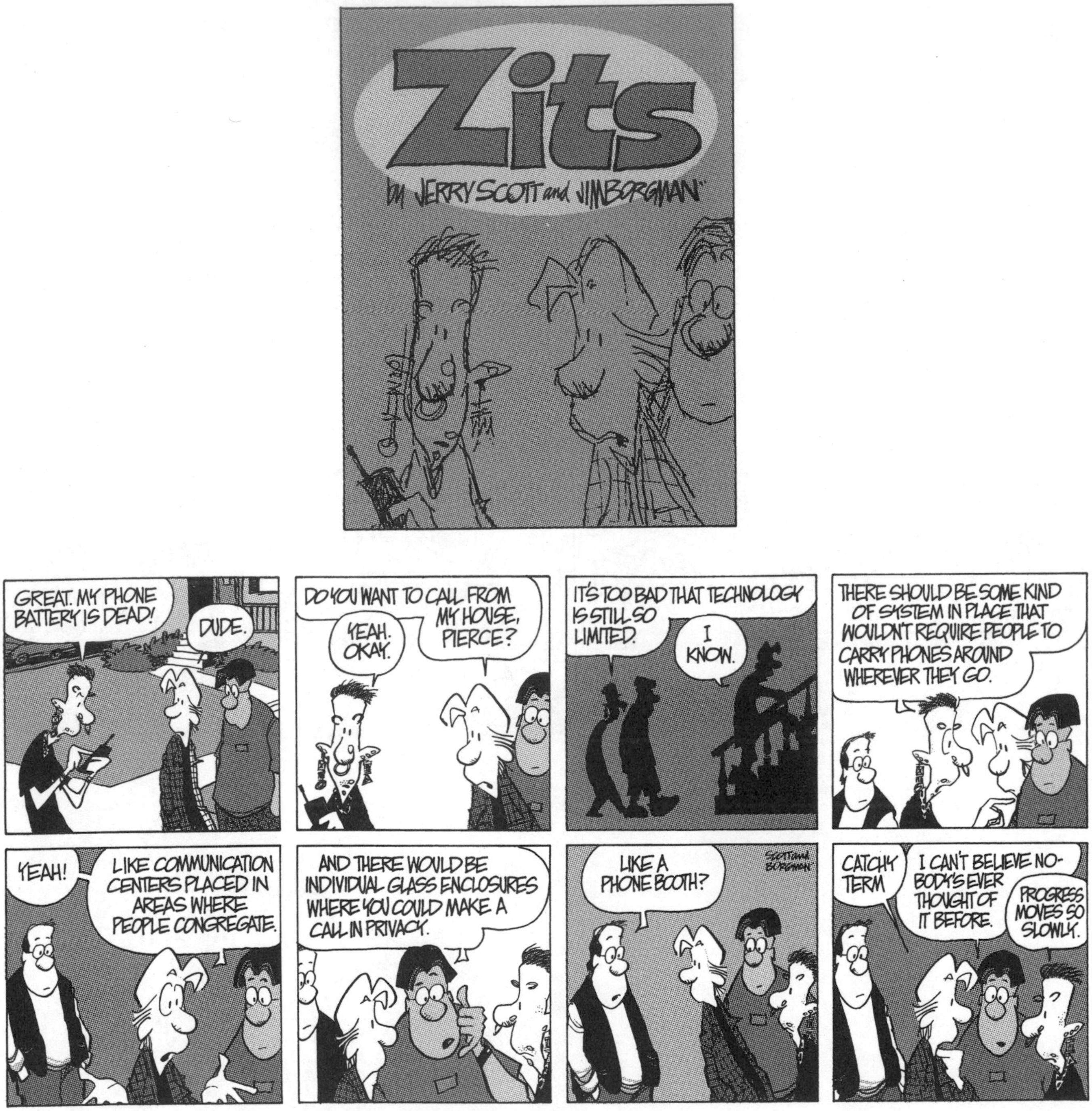
Zits
by JERRY SCOTT and JIM BORGMAN
GREAT. MY PHONE BATTERY IS DEAD!
DUDE.
DO YOU WANT TO CALL FROM MY HOUSE, PIERCE?
YEAH. OKAY.
IT'S TOO BAD THAT TECHNOLOGY IS STILL SO LIMITED.
I KNOW.
THERE SHOULD BE SOME KIND OF SYSTEM IN PLACE THAT WOULDN'T REQUIRE PEOPLE TO CARRY PHONES AROUND WHEREVER THEY GO.
YEAH!
LIKE COMMUNICATION CENTERS PLACED IN AREAS WHERE PEOPLE CONGREGATE.
AND THERE WOULD BE INDIVIDUAL GLASS ENCLOSURES WHERE YOU COULD MAKE A CALL IN PRIVACY.
LIKE A PHONE BOOTH?
SCOTT and BORGMAN
CATCHY TERM
I CAN'T BELIEVE NOBODY'S EVER THOUGHT OF IT BEFORE.
PROGRESS MOVES SO SLOWLY.

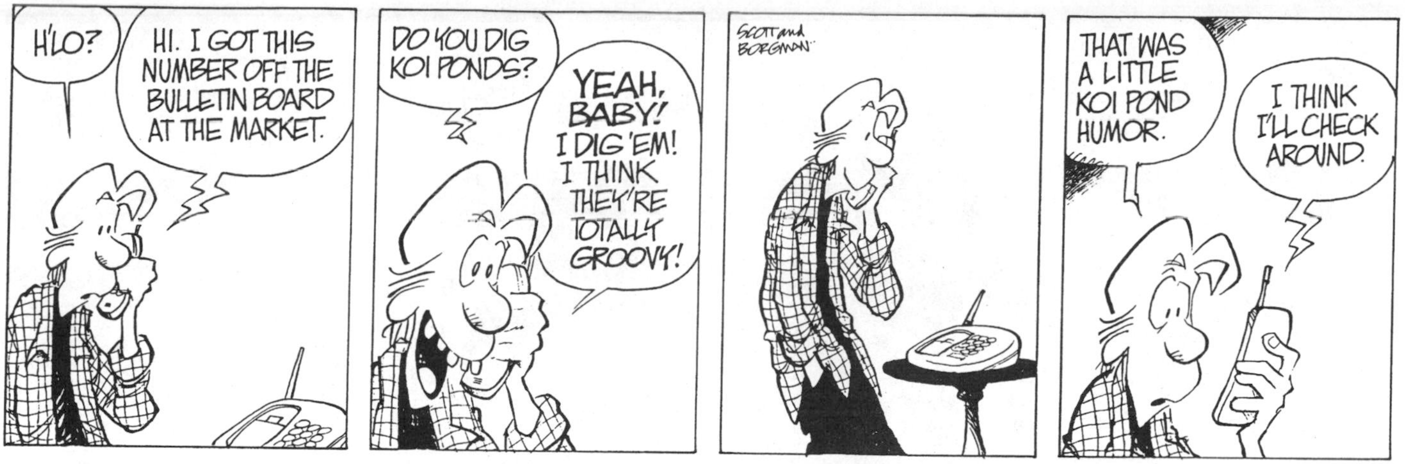
H'LO?
HI. I GOT THIS NUMBER OFF THE BULLETIN BOARD AT THE MARKET.
DO YOU DIG KOI PONDS?
YEAH, BABY! I DIG 'EM! I THINK THEY'RE TOTALLY GROOVY!
SCOTT and BORGMAN
THAT WAS A LITTLE KOI POND HUMOR.
I THINK I'LL CHECK AROUND.

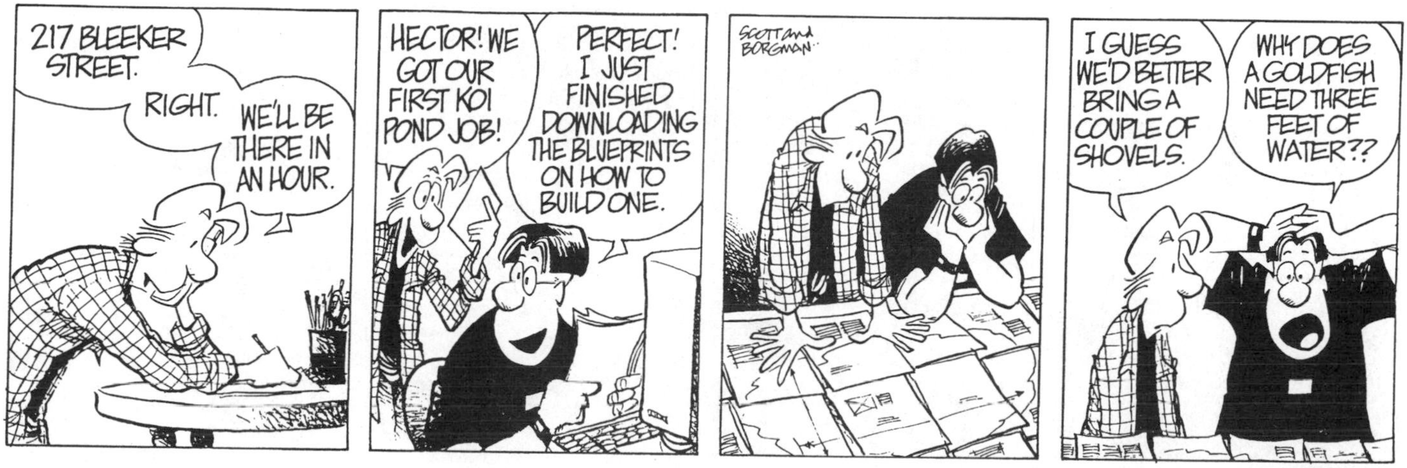
217 BLEEKER STREET.
RIGHT.
WE'LL BE THERE IN AN HOUR.
HECTOR! WE GOT OUR FIRST KOI POND JOB!
PERFECT! I JUST FINISHED DOWNLOADING THE BLUEPRINTS ON HOW TO BUILD ONE.
SCOTT and BORGMAN
I GUESS WE'D BETTER BRING A COUPLE OF SHOVELS.
WHY DOES A GOLDFISH NEED THREE FEET OF WATER??

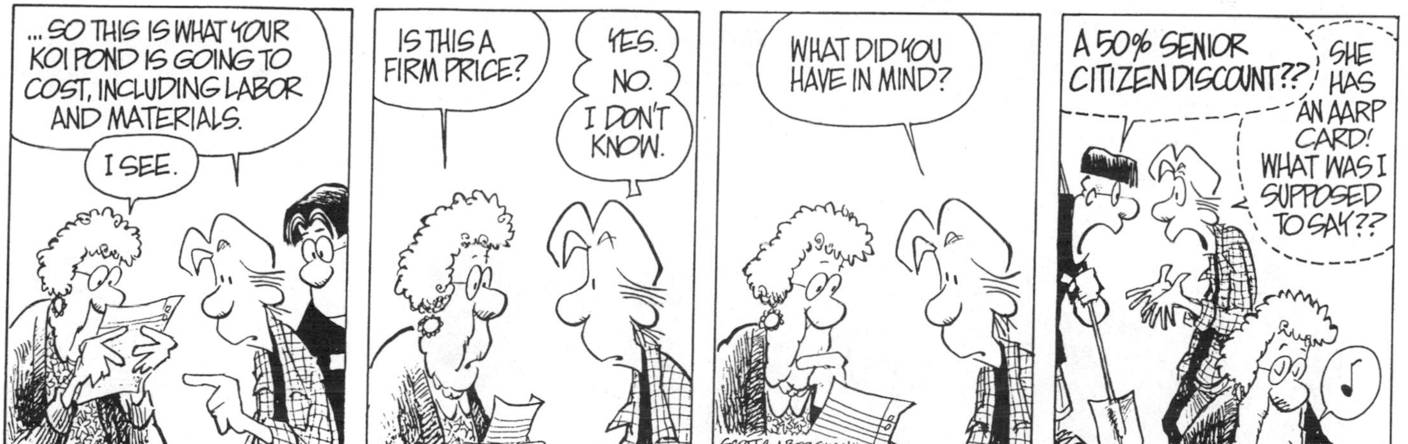
...SO THIS IS WHAT YOUR KOI POND IS GOING TO COST, INCLUDING LABOR AND MATERIALS.
I SEE.
IS THIS A FIRM PRICE?
YES.
NO.
I DON'T KNOW.
WHAT DID YOU HAVE IN MIND?
SCOTT and BORGMAN
A 50% SENIOR CITIZEN DISCOUNT??
SHE HAS AN AARP CARD! WHAT WAS I SUPPOSED TO SAY??

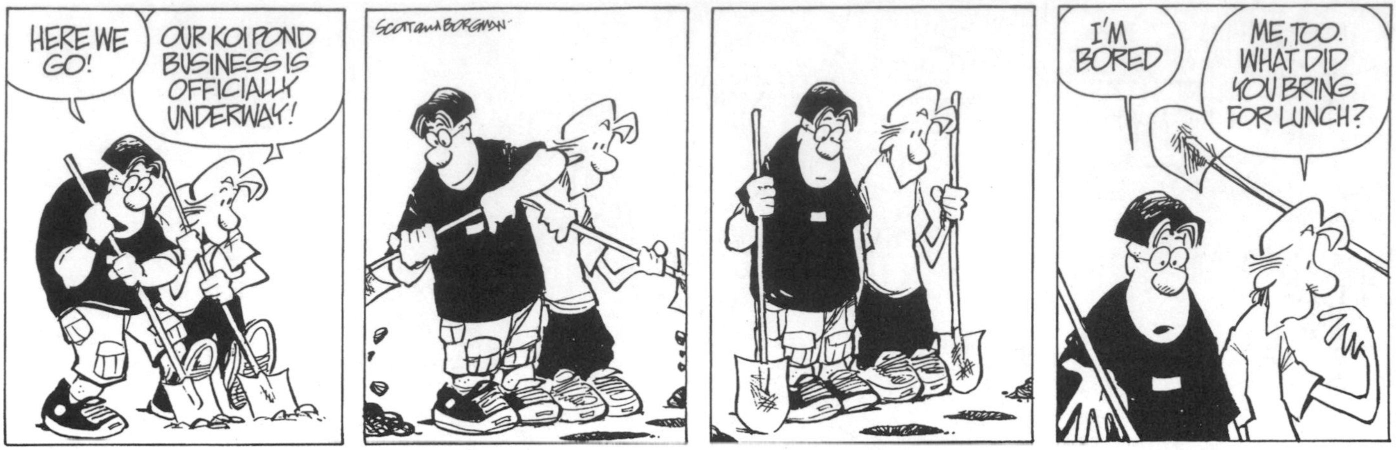
HERE WE GO!
OUR KOI POND BUSINESS IS OFFICIALLY UNDERWAY!
SCOTT and BORGMAN
I'M BORED
ME, TOO. WHAT DID YOU BRING FOR LUNCH?

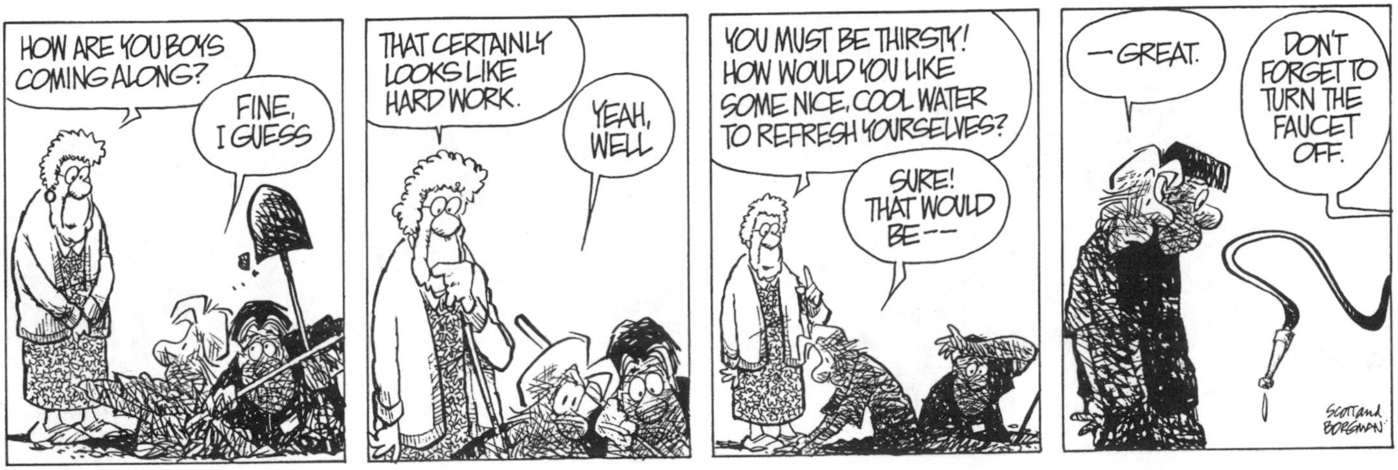
HOW ARE YOU BOYS COMING ALONG?
FINE, I GUESS
THAT CERTAINLY LOOKS LIKE HARD WORK.
YEAH, WELL
YOU MUST BE THIRSTY! HOW WOULD YOU LIKE SOME NICE, COOL WATER TO REFRESH YOURSELVES?
SURE! THAT WOULD BE--
—GREAT.
DON'T FORGET TO TURN THE FAUCET OFF.
SCOTT and BORGMAN

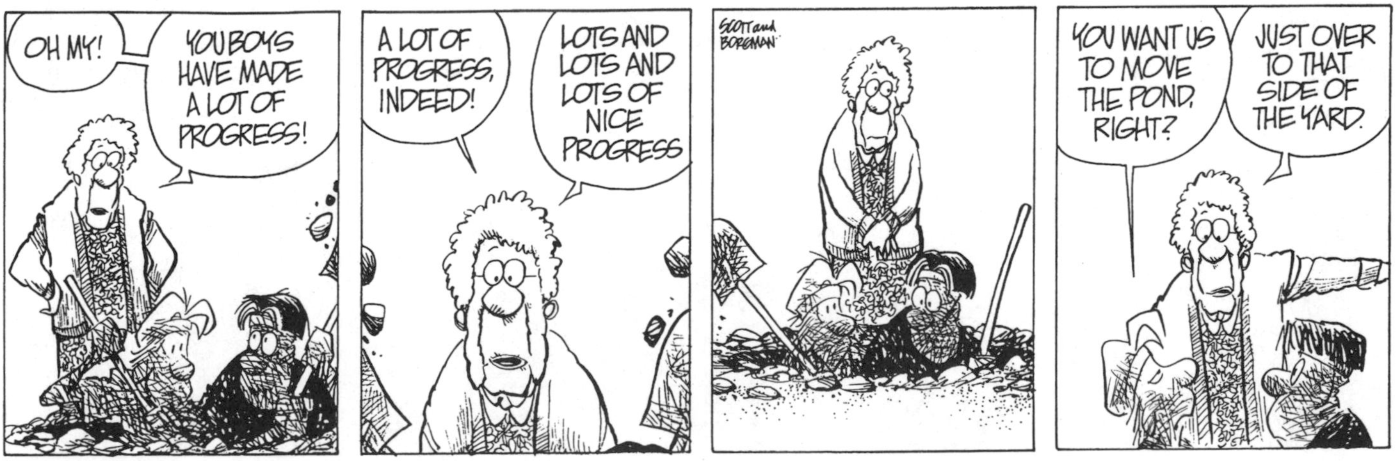
OH MY!
YOU BOYS HAVE MADE A LOT OF PROGRESS!
A LOT OF PROGRESS, INDEED!
LOTS AND LOTS AND LOTS OF NICE PROGRESS
SCOTT and BORGMAN
YOU WANT US TO MOVE THE POND, RIGHT?
JUST OVER TO THAT SIDE OF THE YARD.

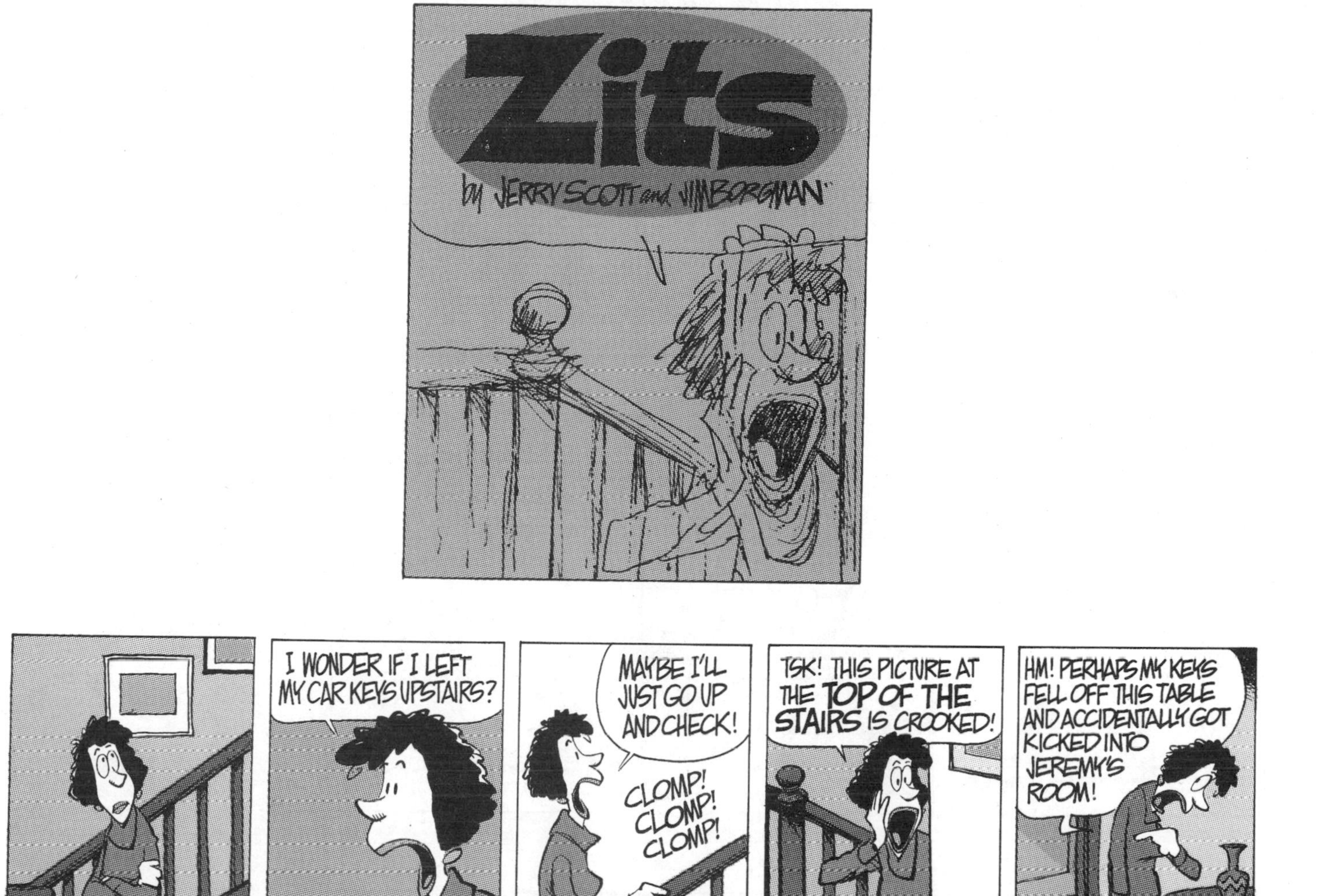
Zits
by JERRY SCOTT and JIM BORGMAN
I WONDER IF I LEFT MY CAR KEYS UPSTAIRS?
MAYBE I'LL JUST GO UP AND CHECK!
CLOMP! CLOMP! CLOMP!
TSK! THIS PICTURE AT THE TOP OF THE STAIRS IS CROOKED!
HM! PERHAPS MY KEYS FELL OFF THIS TABLE AND ACCIDENTALLY GOT KICKED INTO JEREMY'S ROOM!
I THINK I'LL TAKE A LOOK...
...AROUND!
RELAX, MOM. WE'RE JUST TALKING.
WHY CAN'T THEY TALK SOMEPLACE WHERE I CAN SEE THEIR HANDS?
NICE ACTING, THOUGH.

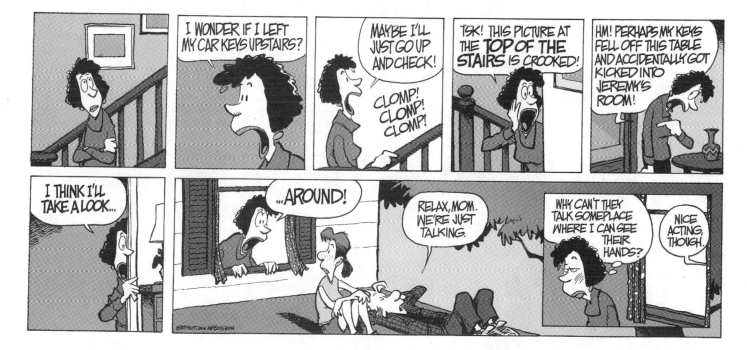

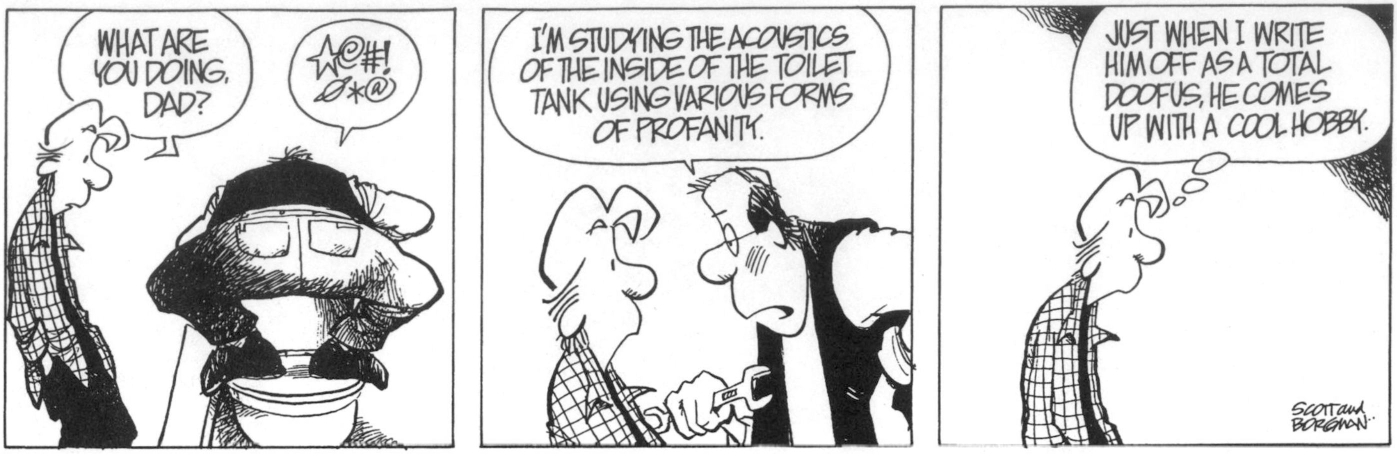
WHAT ARE YOU DOING, DAD?
I'M STUDYING THE ACOUSTICS OF THE INSIDE OF THE TOILET TANK USING VARIOUS FORMS OF PROFANITY.
JUST WHEN I WRITE HIM OFF AS A TOTAL DOOFUS, HE COMES UP WITH A COOL HOBBY.

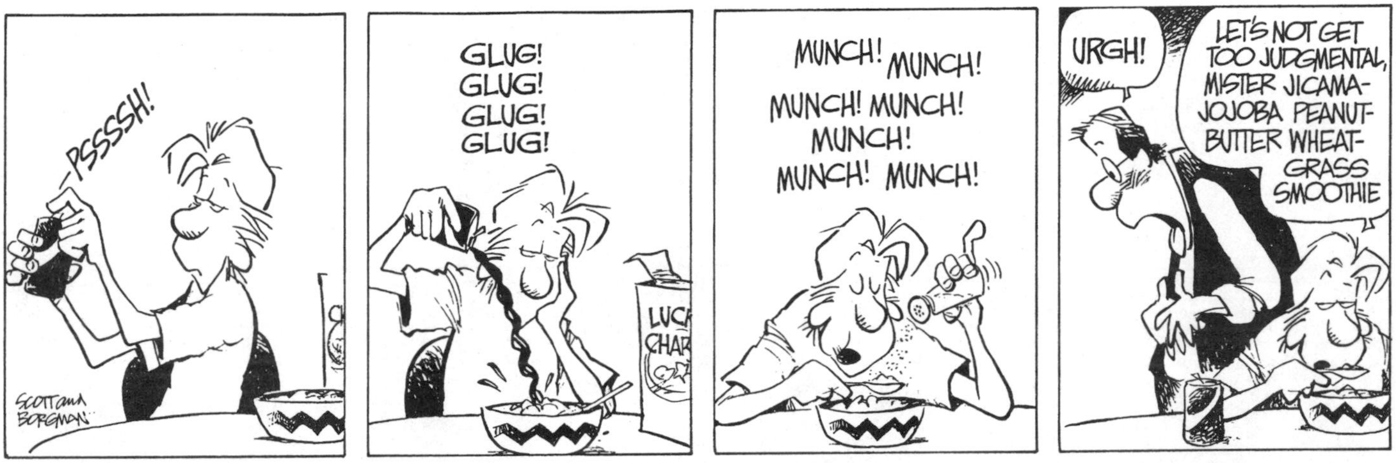
PSSSSH!
GLUG! GLUG! GLUG! GLUG!
MUNCH! MUNCH! MUNCH! MUNCH! MUNCH! MUNCH! MUNCH!
URGH!
LET'S NOT GET TOO JUDGMENTAL, MISTER JICAMA-JOJOBA PEANUT-BUTTER WHEAT-GRASS SMOOTHIE

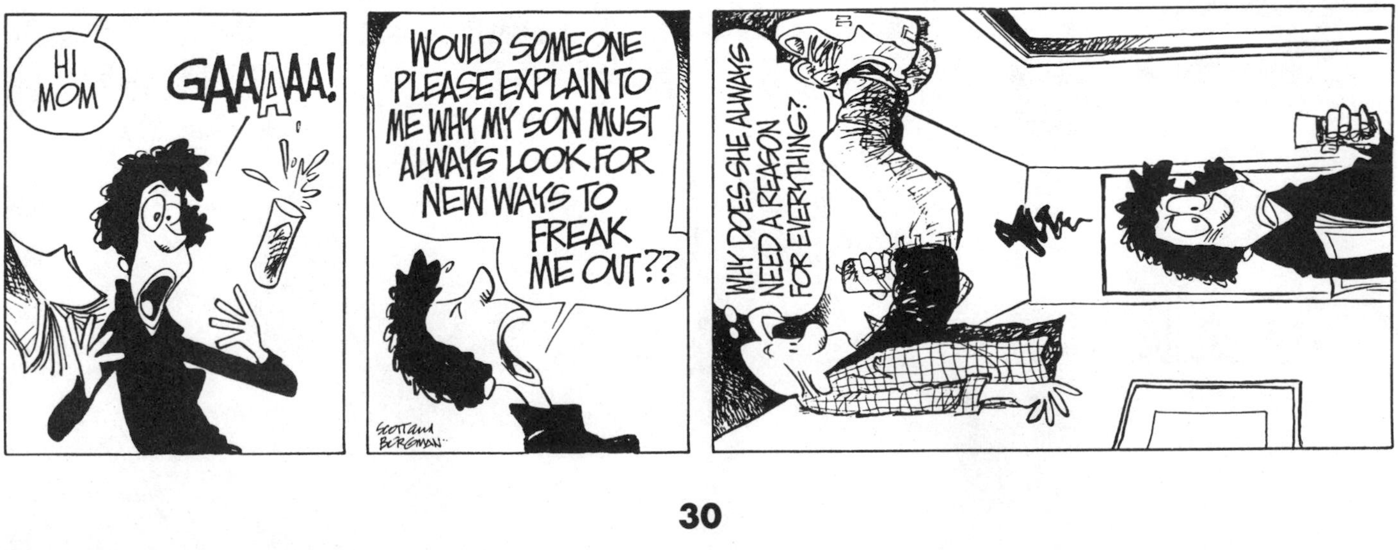
HI MOM
GAAAAA!
WOULD SOMEONE PLEASE EXPLAIN TO ME WHY MY SON MUST ALWAYS LOOK FOR NEW WAYS TO FREAK ME OUT??
WHY DOES SHE ALWAYS NEED A REASON FOR EVERYTHING?

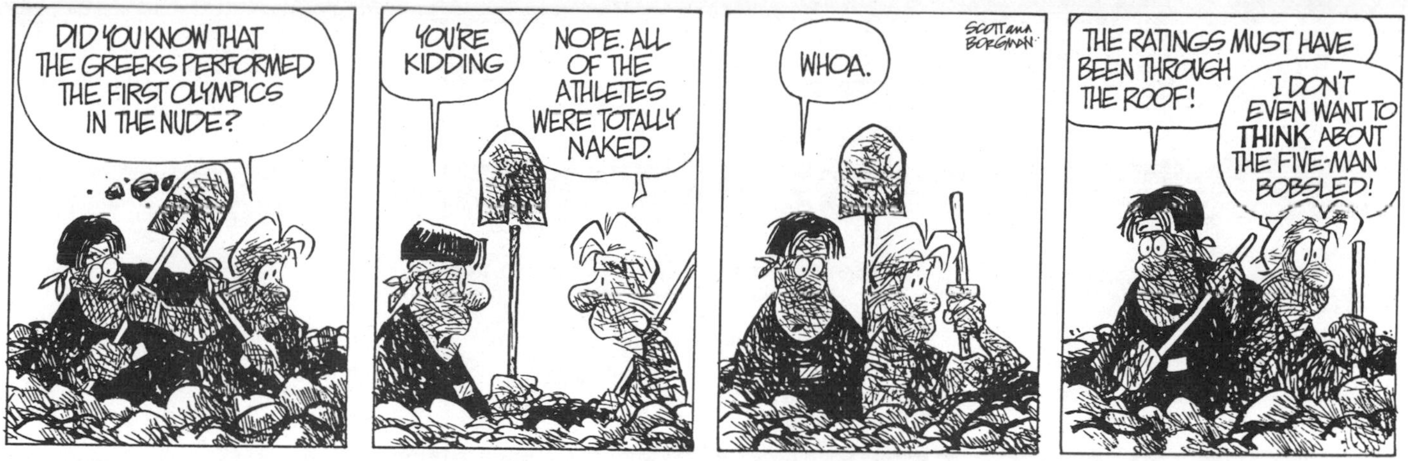
DID YOU KNOW THAT THE GREEKS PERFORMED THE FIRST OLYMPICS IN THE NUDE?
YOU'RE KIDDING
NOPE. ALL OF THE ATHLETES WERE TOTALLY NAKED.
WHOA.
SCOTT and BORGMAN
THE RATINGS MUST HAVE BEEN THROUGH THE ROOF!
I DON'T EVEN WANT TO THINK ABOUT THE FIVE-MAN BOBSLED!

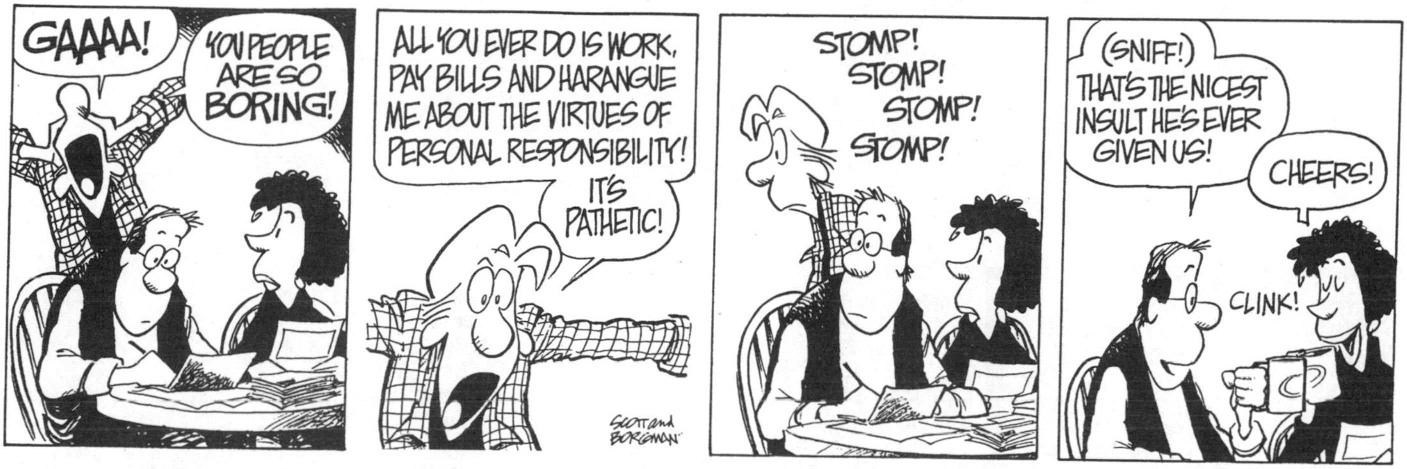
GAAAA!
YOU PEOPLE ARE SO BORING!
ALL YOU EVER DO IS WORK, PAY BILLS AND HARANGUE ME ABOUT THE VIRTUES OF PERSONAL RESPONSIBILITY!
IT'S PATHETIC!
SCOTT and BORGMAN
STOMP! STOMP! STOMP! STOMP!
(SNIFF!) THAT'S THE NICEST INSULT HE'S EVER GIVEN US!
CHEERS!
CLINK!

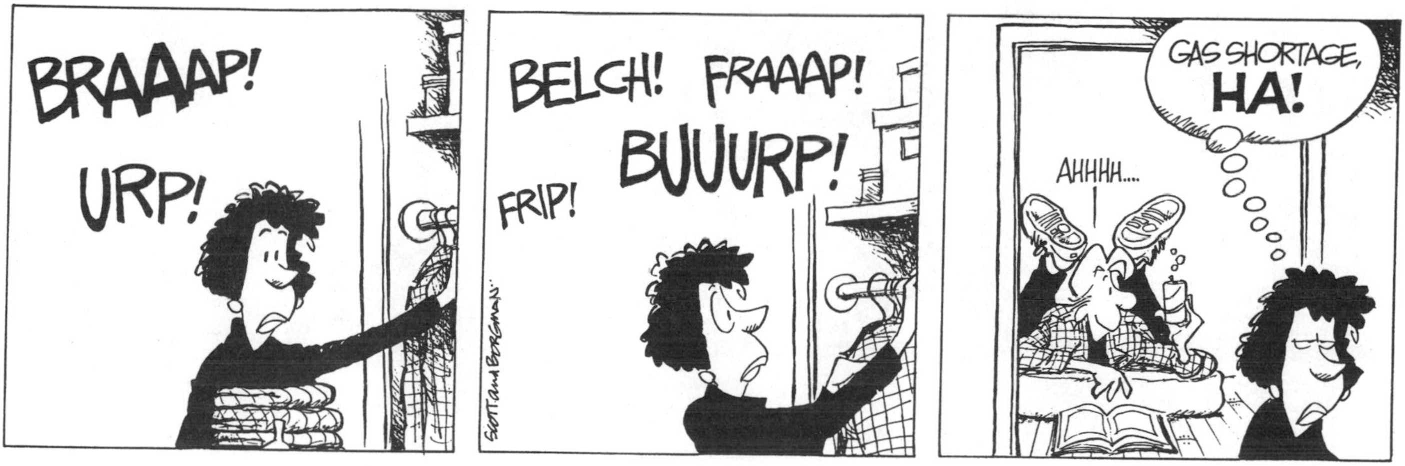
BRAAAP!
URP!
SCOTT and BORGMAN
BELCH!
FRAAAP!
BUUURP!
FRIP!
GAS SHORTAGE, HA!
AHHHH....

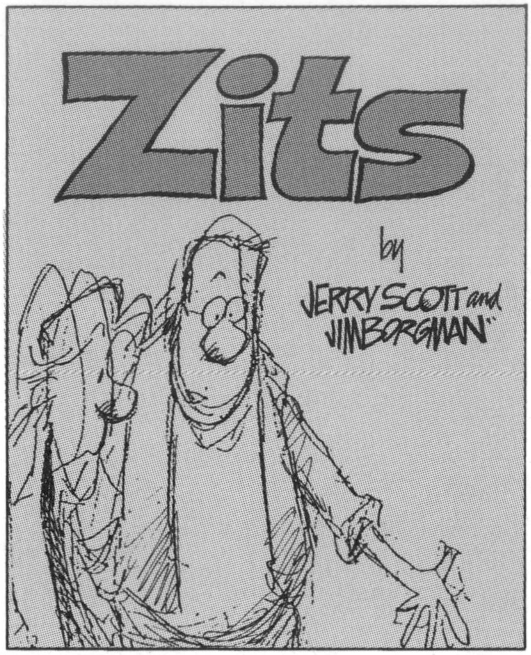
Zits
by
JERRY SCOTT and
JIM BORGMAN

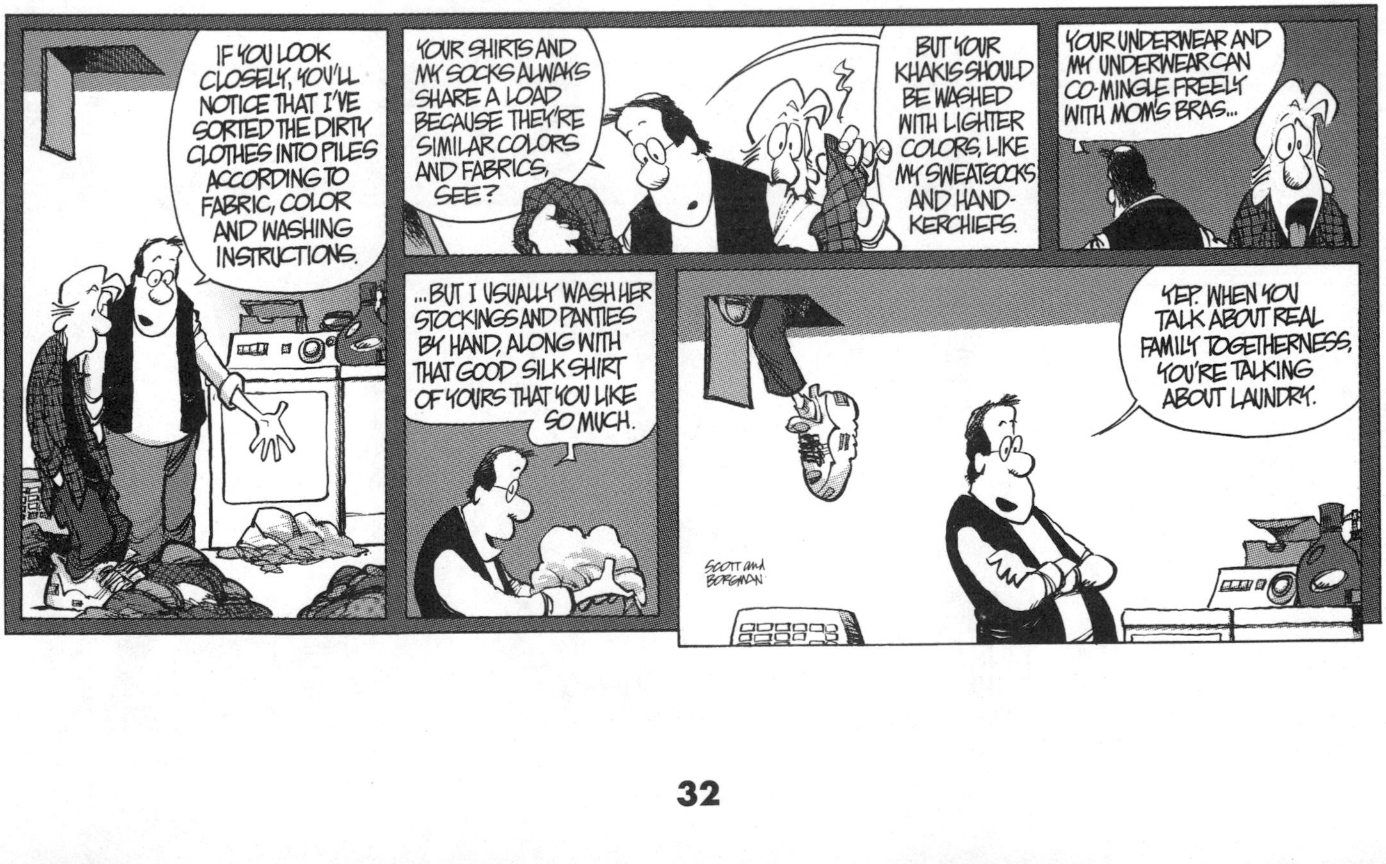
IF YOU LOOK CLOSELY, YOU'LL NOTICE THAT I'VE SORTED THE DIRTY CLOTHES INTO PILES ACCORDING TO FABRIC, COLOR AND WASHING INSTRUCTIONS.
YOUR SHIRTS AND MY SOCKS ALWAYS SHARE A LOAD BECAUSE THEY'RE SIMILAR COLORS AND FABRICS, SEE?
BUT YOUR KHAKIS SHOULD BE WASHED WITH LIGHTER COLORS, LIKE MY SWEATSOCKS AND HAND-KERCHIEFS.
YOUR UNDERWEAR AND MY UNDERWEAR CAN CO-MINGLE FREELY WITH MOM'S BRAS...
...BUT I USUALLY WASH HER STOCKINGS AND PANTIES BY HAND, ALONG WITH THAT GOOD SILK SHIRT OF YOURS THAT YOU LIKE SO MUCH.
YEP. WHEN YOU TALK ABOUT REAL FAMILY TOGETHERNESS, YOU'RE TALKING ABOUT LAUNDRY.
SCOTT AND BORGMAN

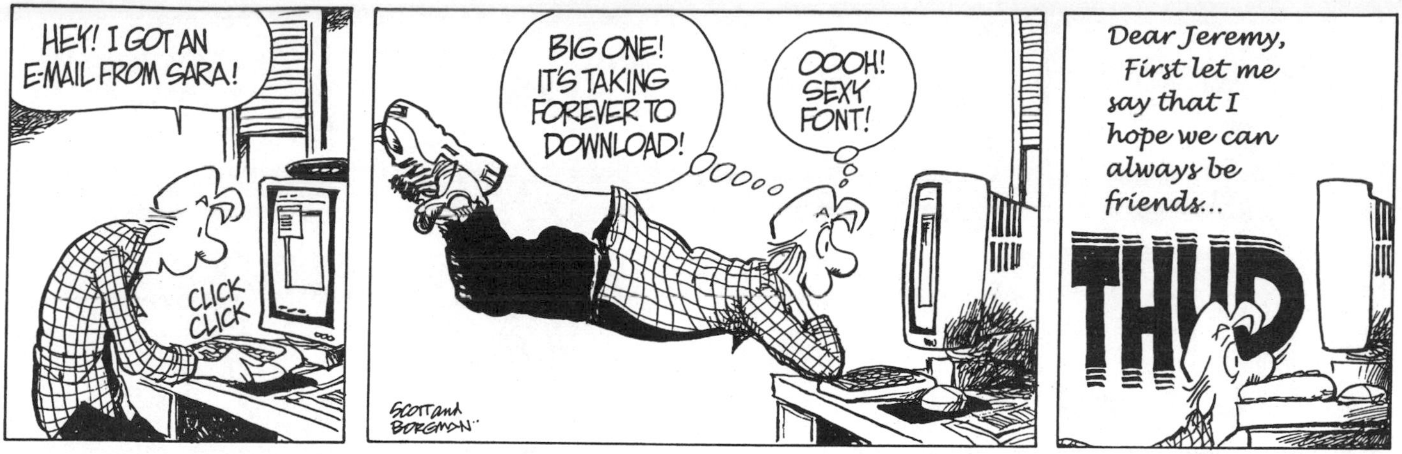
HEY! I GOT AN E-MAIL FROM SARA!
CLICK CLICK
BIG ONE! IT'S TAKING FOREVER TO DOWNLOAD!
OOOH! SEXY FONT!
SCOTT and BORGMAN
Dear Jeremy, First let me say that I hope we can always be friends...
THUD

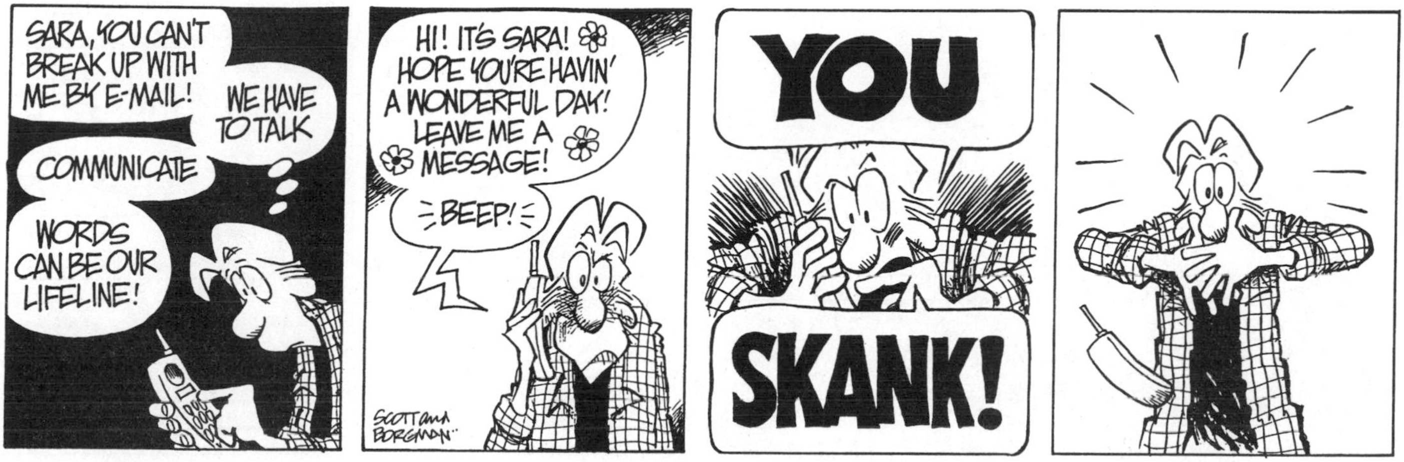
SARA, YOU CAN'T BREAK UP WITH ME BY E-MAIL!
WE HAVE TO TALK
COMMUNICATE
WORDS CAN BE OUR LIFELINE!
HI! IT'S SARA! HOPE YOU'RE HAVIN' A WONDERFUL DAY! LEAVE ME A MESSAGE!
BEEP!
SCOTT and BORGMAN
YOU
SKANK!

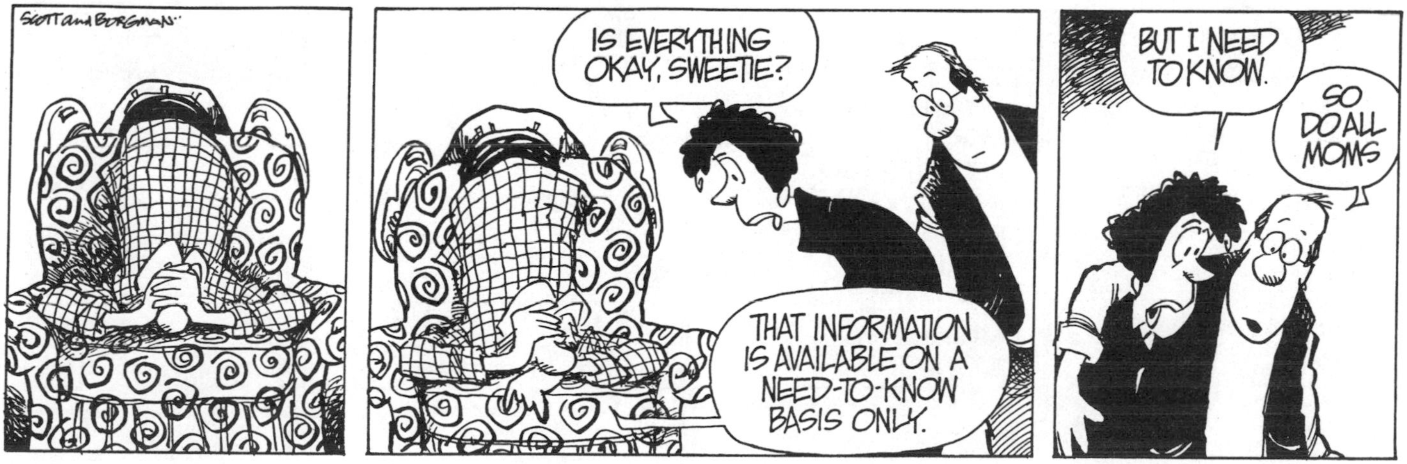
SCOTT and BORGMAN
IS EVERYTHING OKAY, SWEETIE?
THAT INFORMATION IS AVAILABLE ON A NEED-TO-KNOW BASIS ONLY.
BUT I NEED TO KNOW.
SO DO ALL MOMS

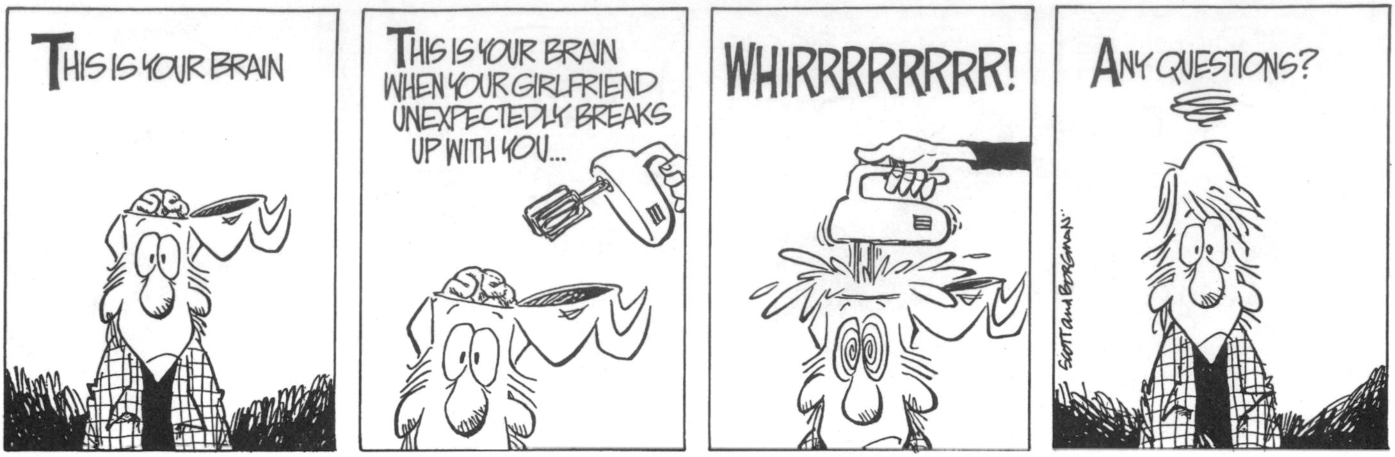
THIS IS YOUR BRAIN
THIS IS YOUR BRAIN WHEN YOUR GIRLFRIEND UNEXPECTEDLY BREAKS UP WITH YOU...
WHIRRRRRRRR!
ANY QUESTIONS?
SCOTT and BORGMAN

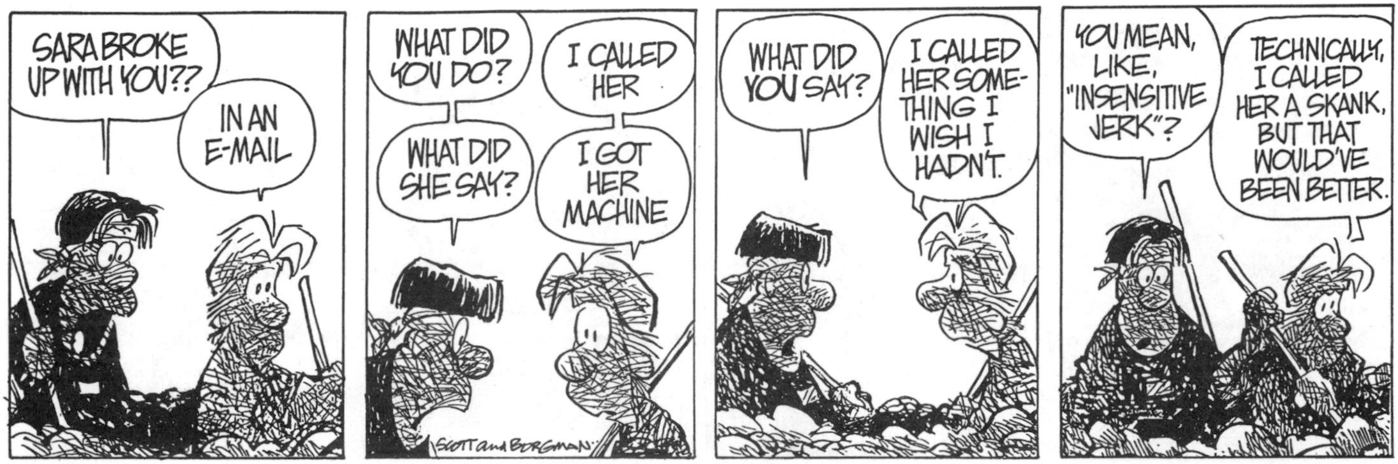
SARA BROKE UP WITH YOU??
IN AN E-MAIL
WHAT DID YOU DO?
I CALLED HER
WHAT DID SHE SAY?
I GOT HER MACHINE
SCOTT and BORGMAN
WHAT DID YOU SAY?
I CALLED HER SOMETHING I WISH I HADN'T.
YOU MEAN, LIKE, "INSENSITIVE JERK"?
TECHNICALLY, I CALLED HER A SKANK, BUT THAT WOULD'VE BEEN BETTER.

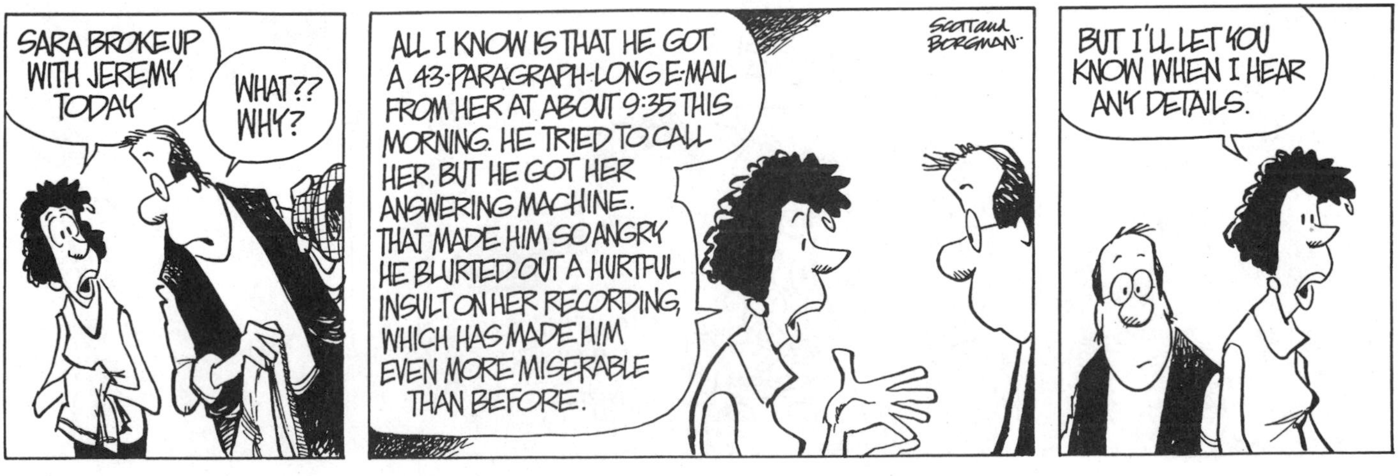
SARA BROKE UP WITH JEREMY TODAY
WHAT?? WHY?
ALL I KNOW IS THAT HE GOT A 43-PARAGRAPH-LONG E-MAIL FROM HER AT ABOUT 9:35 THIS MORNING. HE TRIED TO CALL HER, BUT HE GOT HER ANSWERING MACHINE. THAT MADE HIM SO ANGRY HE BLURTED OUT A HURTFUL INSULT ON HER RECORDING, WHICH HAS MADE HIM EVEN MORE MISERABLE THAN BEFORE.
SCOTT and BORGMAN
BUT I'LL LET YOU KNOW WHEN I HEAR ANY DETAILS.

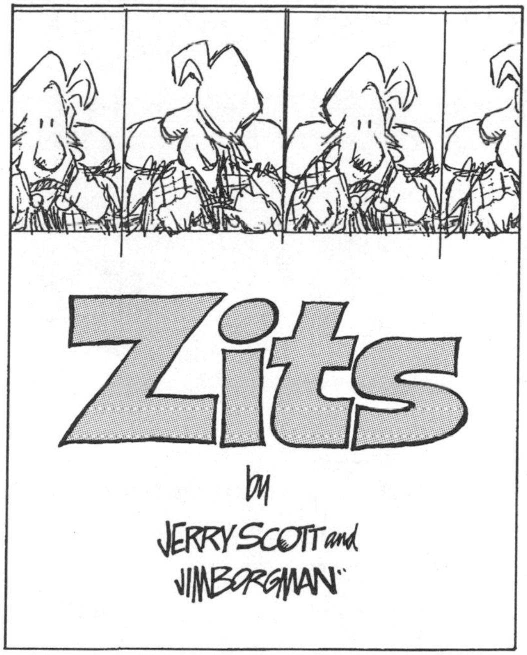
Zits
by
JERRY SCOTT and
JIM BORGMAN

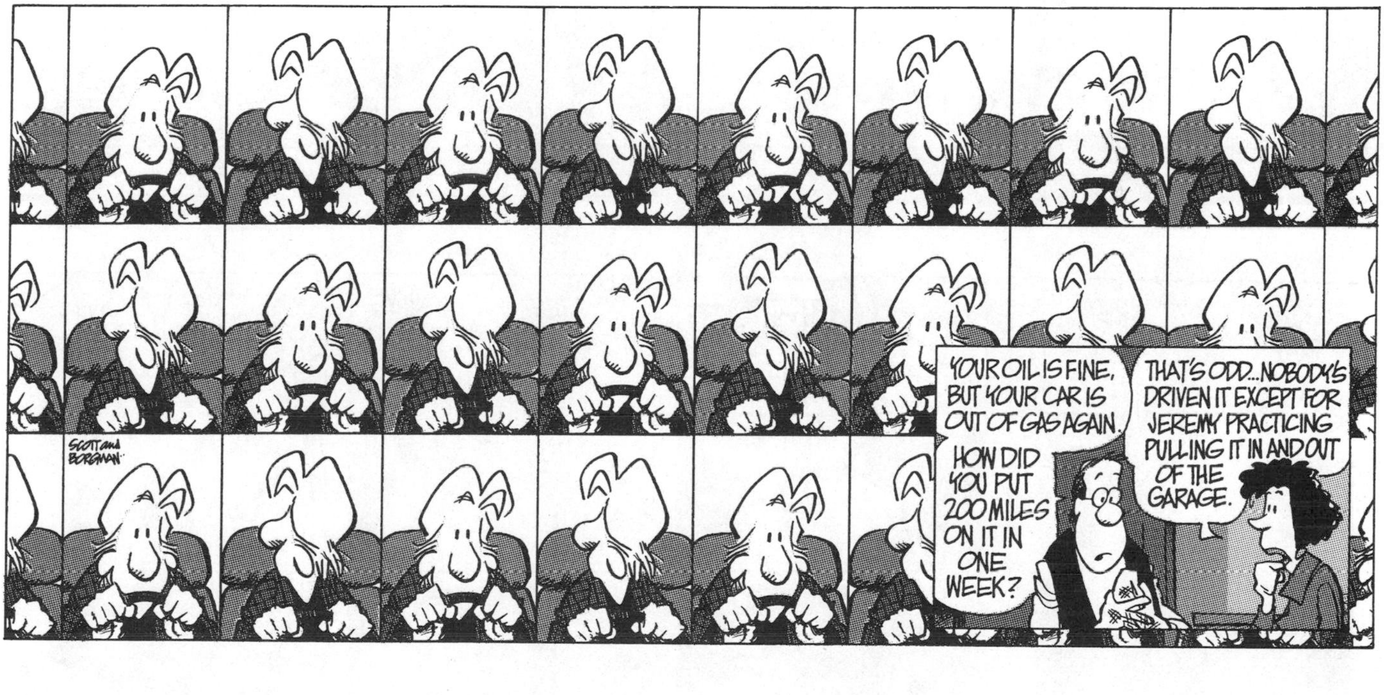
SCOTT and BORGMAN
YOUR OIL IS FINE, BUT YOUR CAR IS OUT OF GAS AGAIN.
HOW DID YOU PUT 200 MILES ON IT IN ONE WEEK?
THAT'S ODD...NOBODY'S DRIVEN IT EXCEPT FOR JEREMY PRACTICING PULLING IT IN AND OUT OF THE GARAGE.

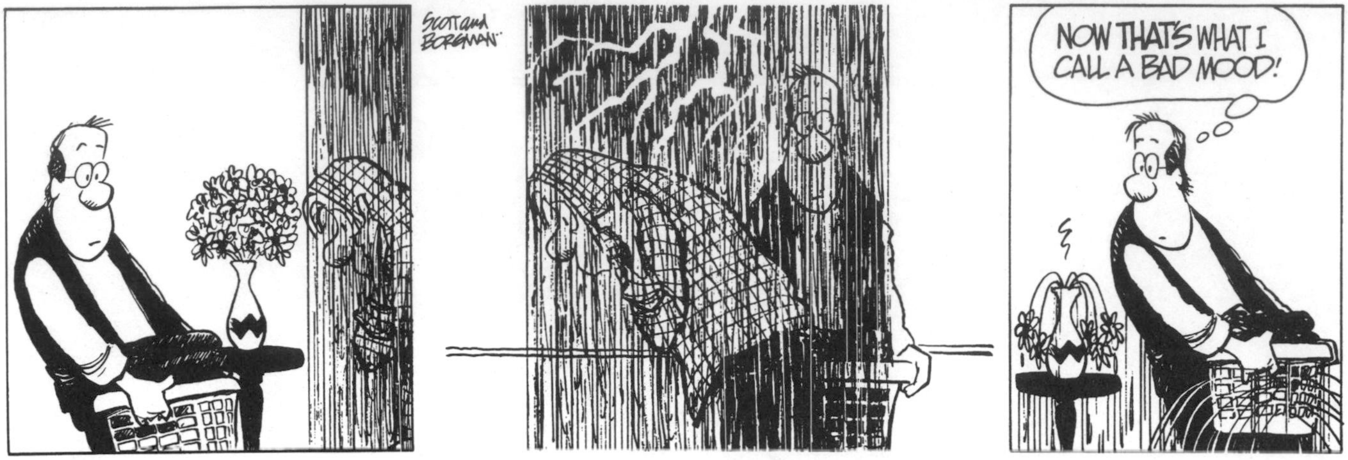
NOW THAT'S WHAT I CALL A BAD MOOD!

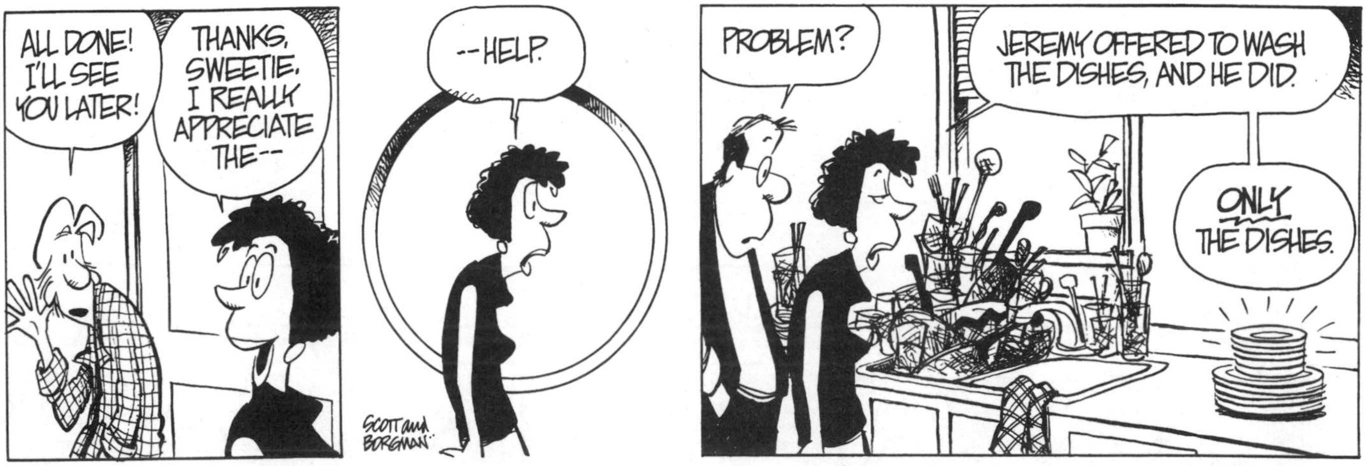
ALL DONE! I'LL SEE YOU LATER!
THANKS, SWEETIE. I REALLY APPRECIATE THE--
--HELP.
PROBLEM?
JEREMY OFFERED TO WASH THE DISHES, AND HE DID.
ONLY THE DISHES.

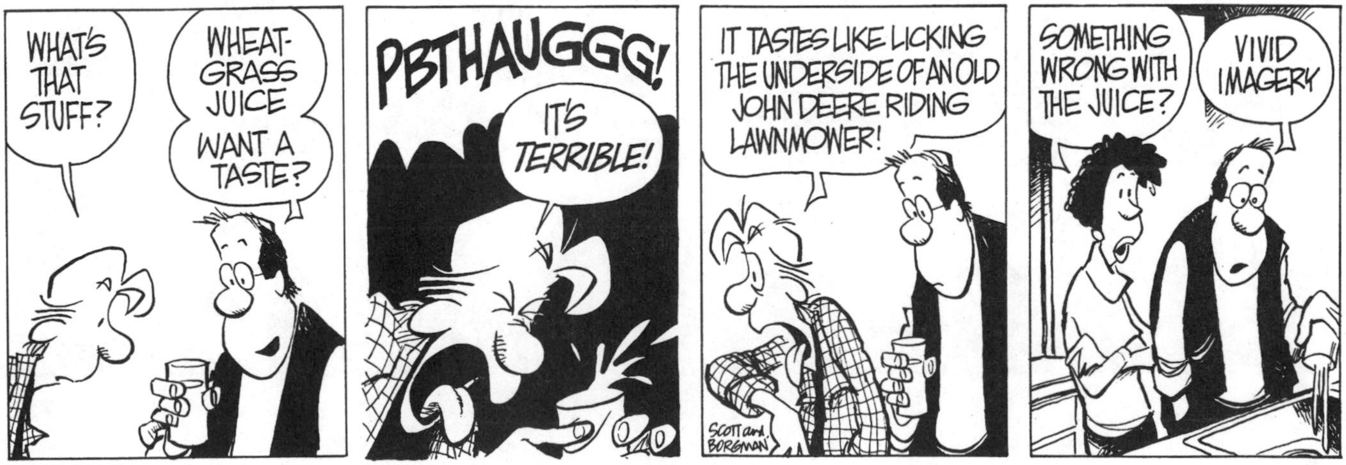
WHAT'S THAT STUFF?
WHEAT-GRASS JUICE
WANT A TASTE?
PBTHAUGGG!
IT'S TERRIBLE!
IT TASTES LIKE LICKING THE UNDERSIDE OF AN OLD JOHN DEERE RIDING LAWNMOWER!
SOMETHING WRONG WITH THE JUICE?
VIVID IMAGERY

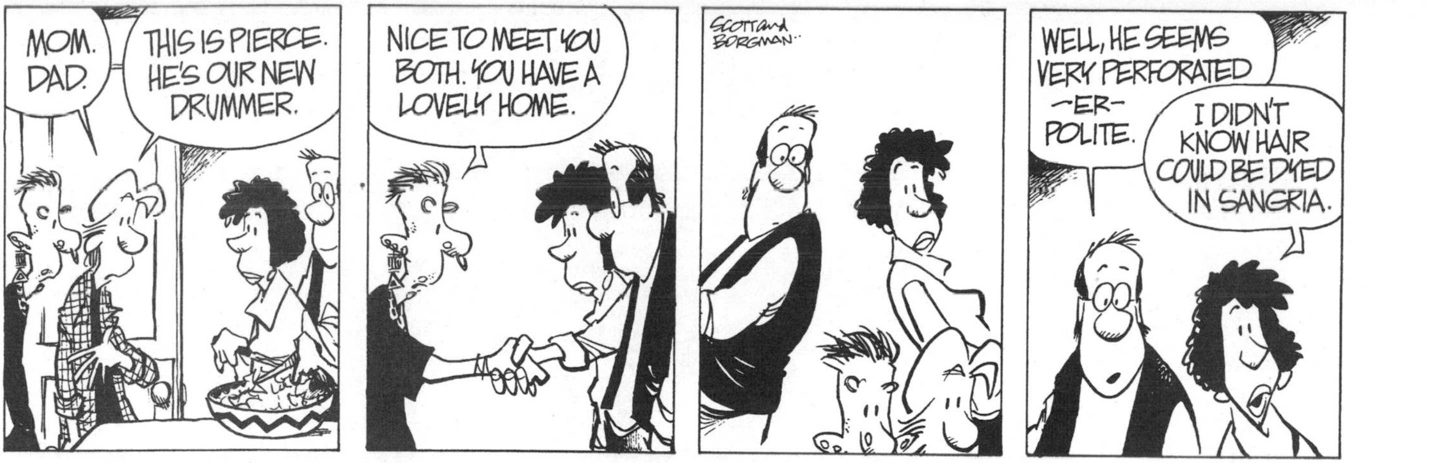
MOM. DAD.
THIS IS PIERCE. HE'S OUR NEW DRUMMER.
NICE TO MEET YOU BOTH. YOU HAVE A LOVELY HOME.
WELL, HE SEEMS VERY PERFORATED —ER— POLITE.
I DIDN'T KNOW HAIR COULD BE DYED IN SANGRIA.

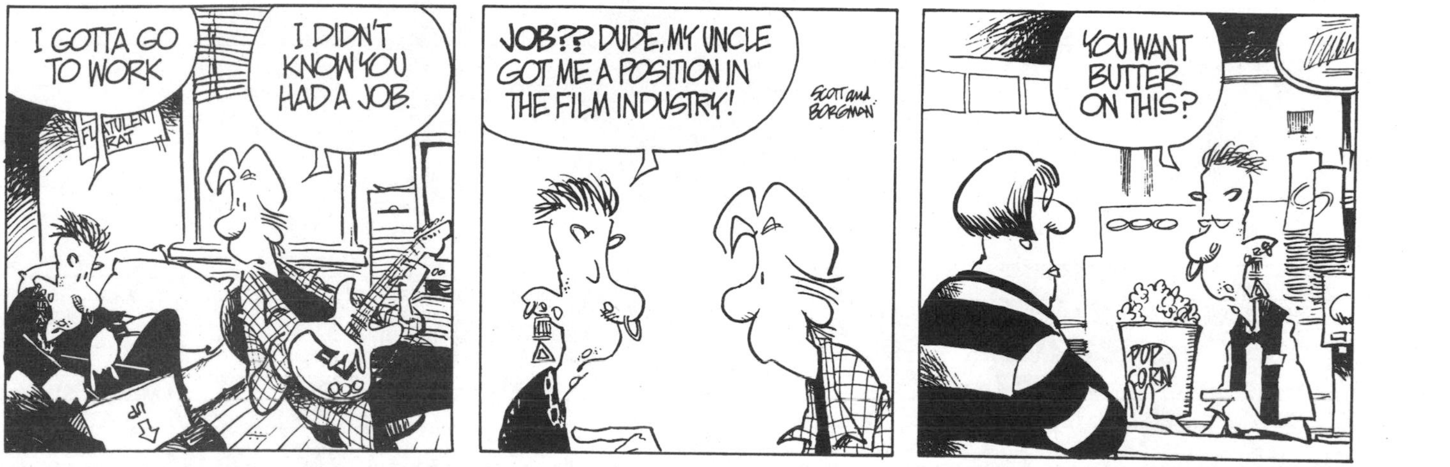
I GOTTA GO TO WORK
FLATULENT RAT
UP
I DIDN'T KNOW YOU HAD A JOB.
JOB?? DUDE, MY UNCLE GOT ME A POSITION IN THE FILM INDUSTRY!
YOU WANT BUTTER ON THIS?
POP CORN

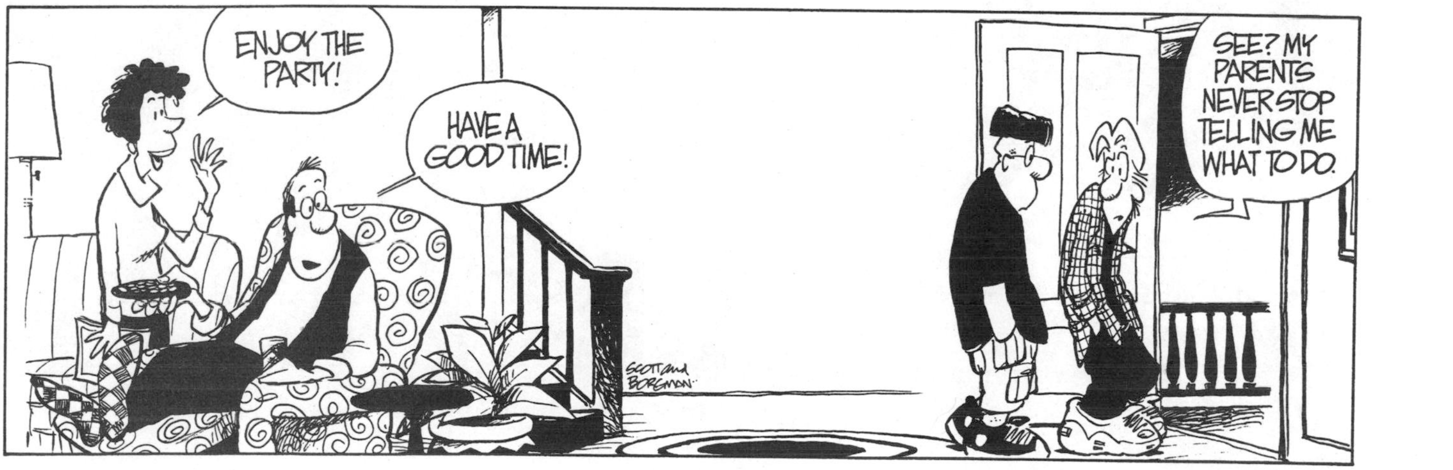
ENJOY THE PARTY!
HAVE A GOOD TIME!
SEE? MY PARENTS NEVER STOP TELLING ME WHAT TO DO.

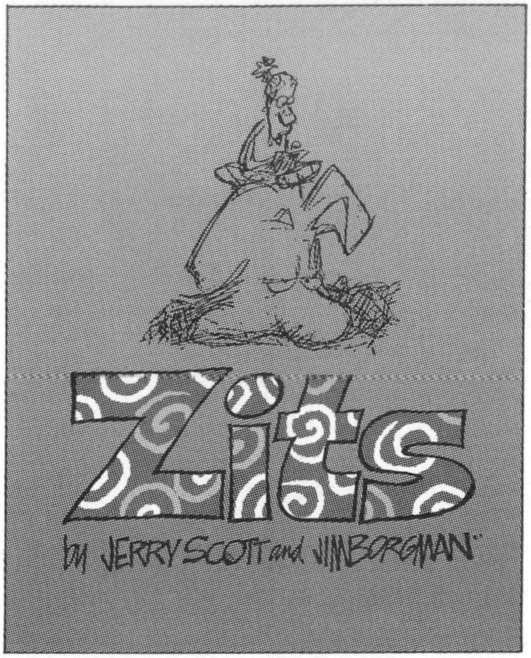
Zits
by JERRY SCOTT and JIM BORGMAN

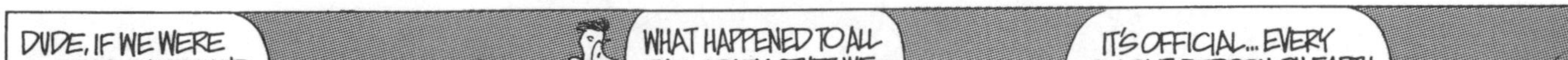
DUDE, IF WE WERE A *REAL* BAND, WE'D BE DOING *TWO* PRACTICES A DAY!
MAYBE MY MOM IS RIGHT—WE SHOULD SEE OTHER PEOPLE.
WHAT HAPPENED TO ALL THE CRAZY STUFF WE WERE GOING TO DO TO MAKE THIS A TRULY COOL SUMMER?
SHOULDN'T YOU BE DOING SOME VOLUNTEER WORK TO HELP WITH YOUR COLLEGE RESUMÉ?
WHEN I WAS YOUR AGE, A SUMMER JOB MEANT THAT YOU WORKED EIGHT HOURS A DAY, FIVE DAYS A WEEK, AND WERE GRATEFUL FOR THE OPPORTUNITY!
IT'S OFFICIAL... EVERY SINGLE PERSON ON EARTH IS HAVING A BETTER VACATION THAN YOU ARE.
A Midsummer's DAYDREAM
AGE 15

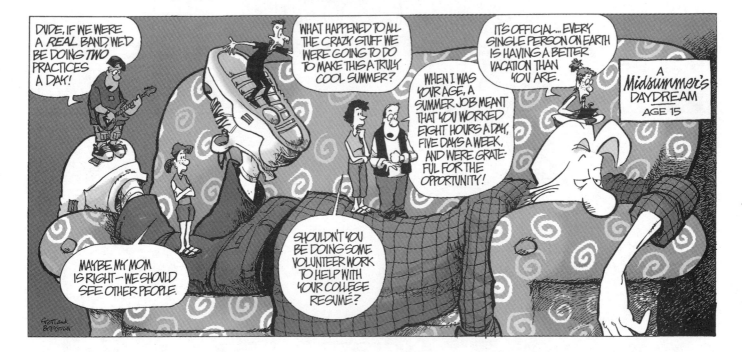

Zits
by JERRY SCOTT and JIM BORGMAN

"The best way to give advice to your children is to find out what they want, and then advise them to do it."
-Harry Truman
SCOTT and BORGMAN
SO YOU REALLY THINK I SHOULD SPEND MY SUMMER JOB MONEY ON SKYDIVING LESSONS?
ABSOLU
WALT!

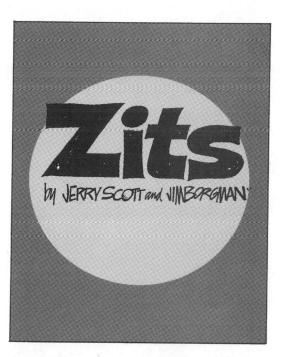

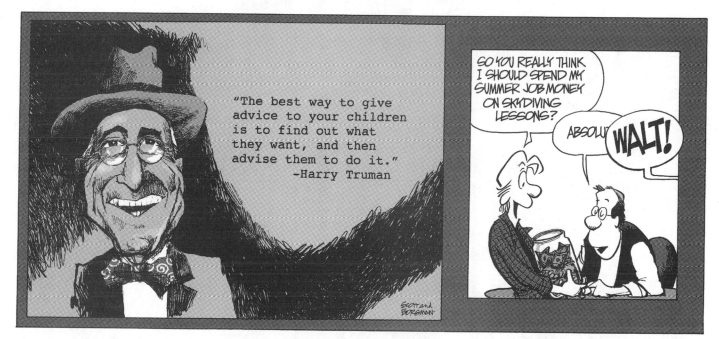

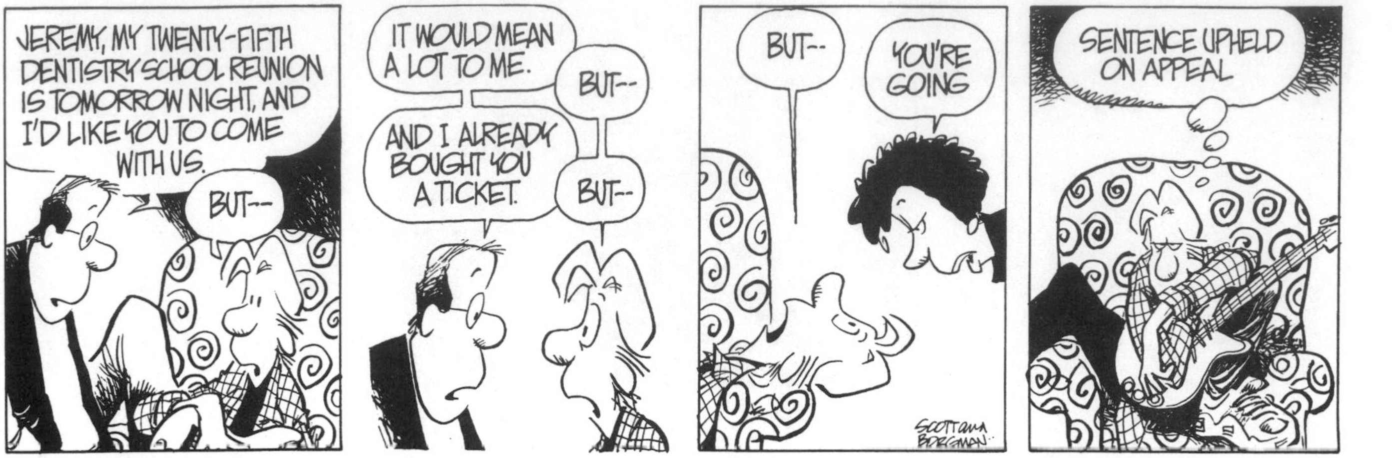
JEREMY, MY TWENTY-FIFTH DENTISTRY SCHOOL REUNION IS TOMORROW NIGHT, AND I'D LIKE YOU TO COME WITH US.
BUT--
IT WOULD MEAN A LOT TO ME.
BUT--
AND I ALREADY BOUGHT YOU A TICKET.
BUT--
BUT--
YOU'RE GOING
SENTENCE UPHELD ON APPEAL
SCOTT and BORGMAN

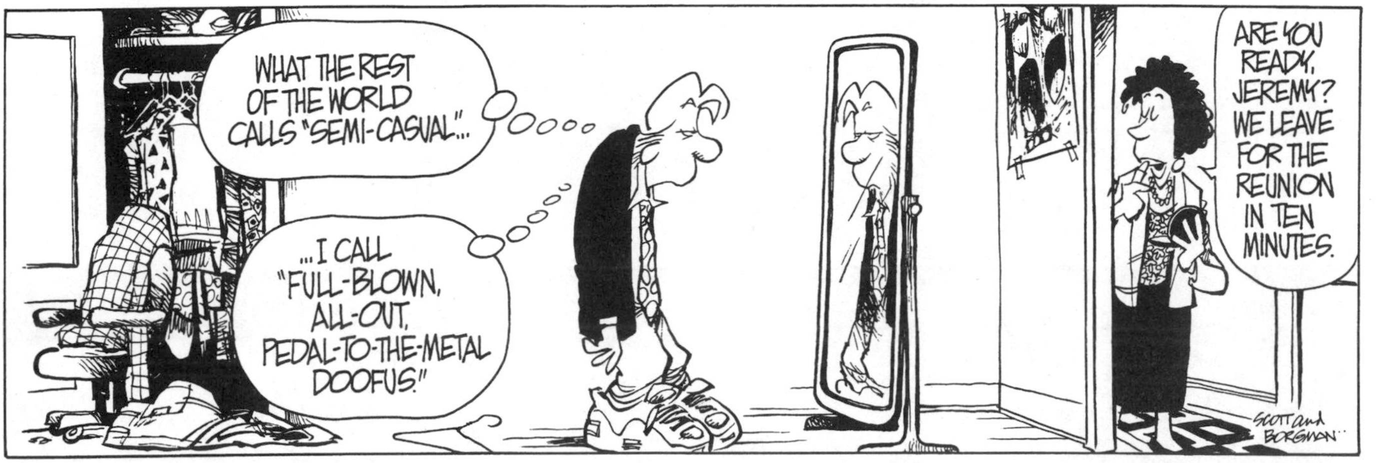
WHAT THE REST OF THE WORLD CALLS "SEMI-CASUAL"...
...I CALL "FULL-BLOWN, ALL-OUT, PEDAL-TO-THE-METAL DOOFUS."
ARE YOU READY, JEREMY? WE LEAVE FOR THE REUNION IN TEN MINUTES.
SCOTT and BORGMAN

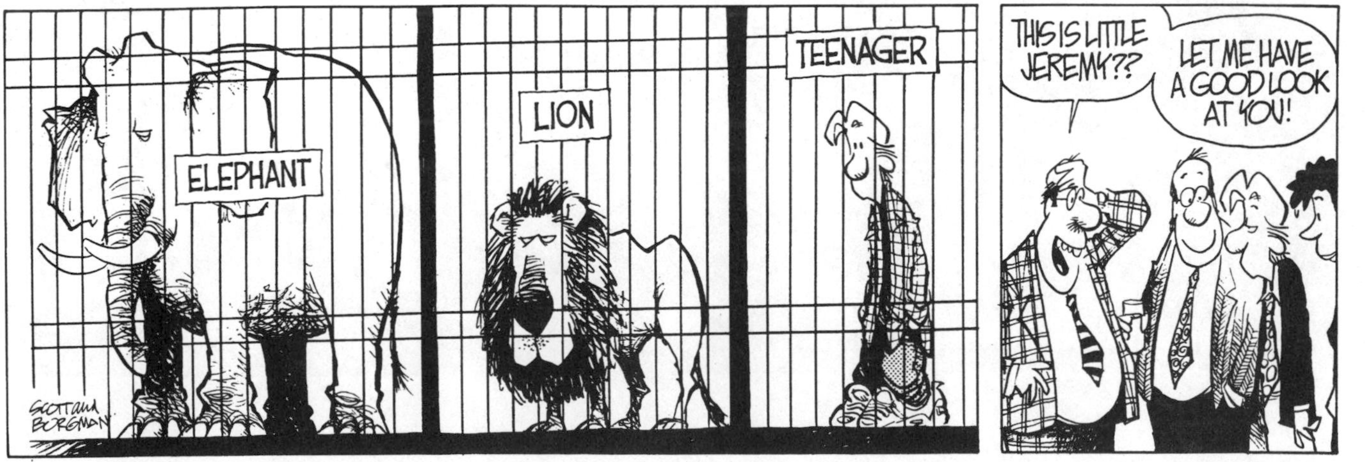
ELEPHANT
LION
TEENAGER
SCOTT and BORGMAN
THIS IS LITTLE JEREMY??
LET ME HAVE A GOOD LOOK AT YOU!

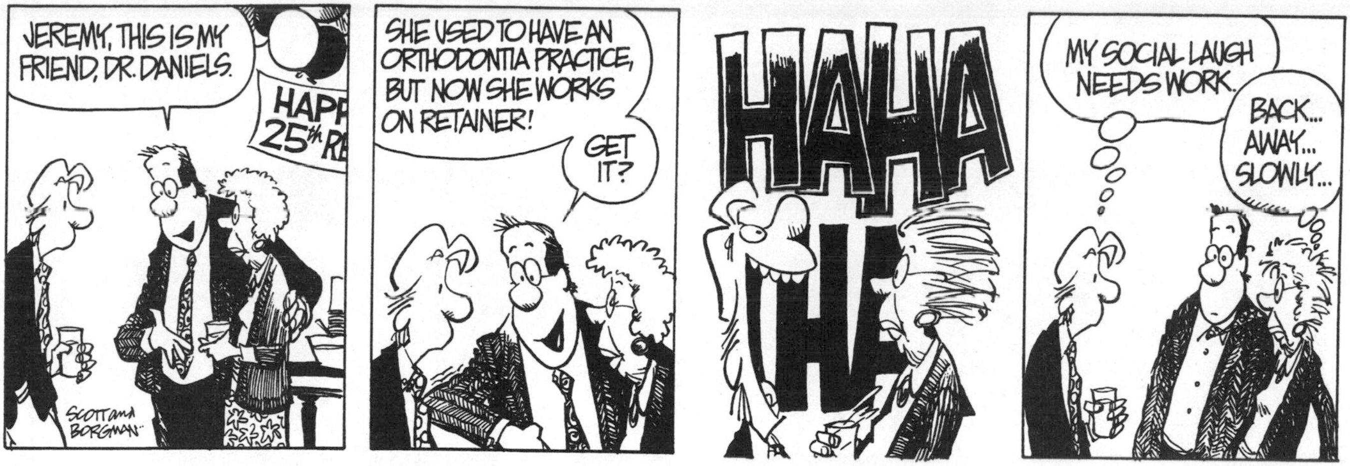
JEREMY, THIS IS MY FRIEND, DR. DANIELS.
HAPP
25th RE
SCOTT and BORGMAN
SHE USED TO HAVE AN ORTHODONTIA PRACTICE, BUT NOW SHE WORKS ON RETAINER!
GET IT?
HAHA
HA
MY SOCIAL LAUGH NEEDS WORK.
BACK... AWAY... SLOWLY...

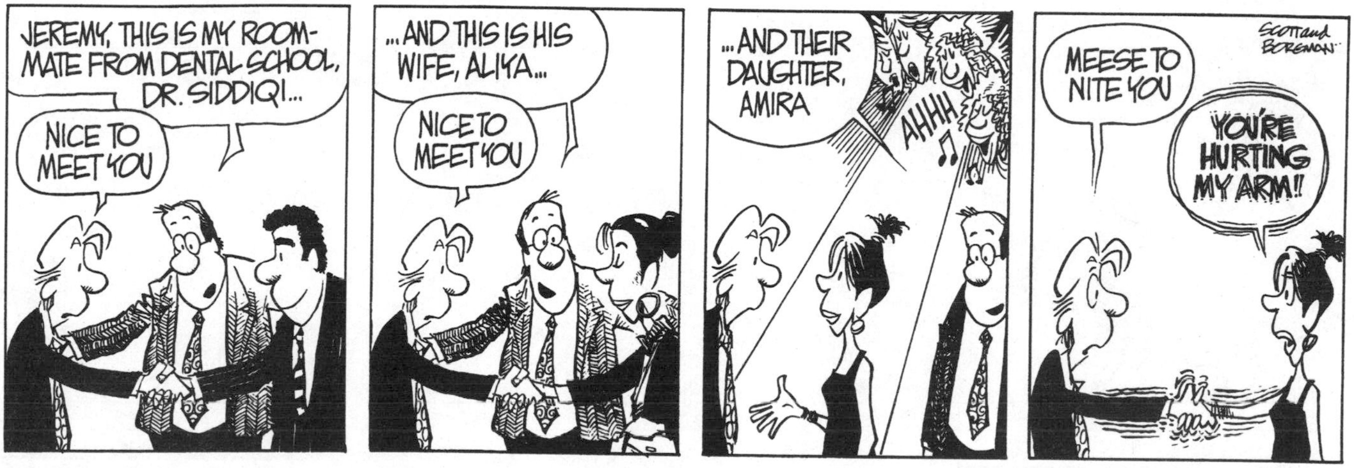
JEREMY, THIS IS MY ROOM-MATE FROM DENTAL SCHOOL, DR. SIDDIQI...
NICE TO MEET YOU
...AND THIS IS HIS WIFE, ALIYA...
NICE TO MEET YOU
...AND THEIR DAUGHTER, AMIRA
AHHH
SCOTT and BORGMAN
MEESE TO NITE YOU
YOU'RE HURTING MY ARM!!

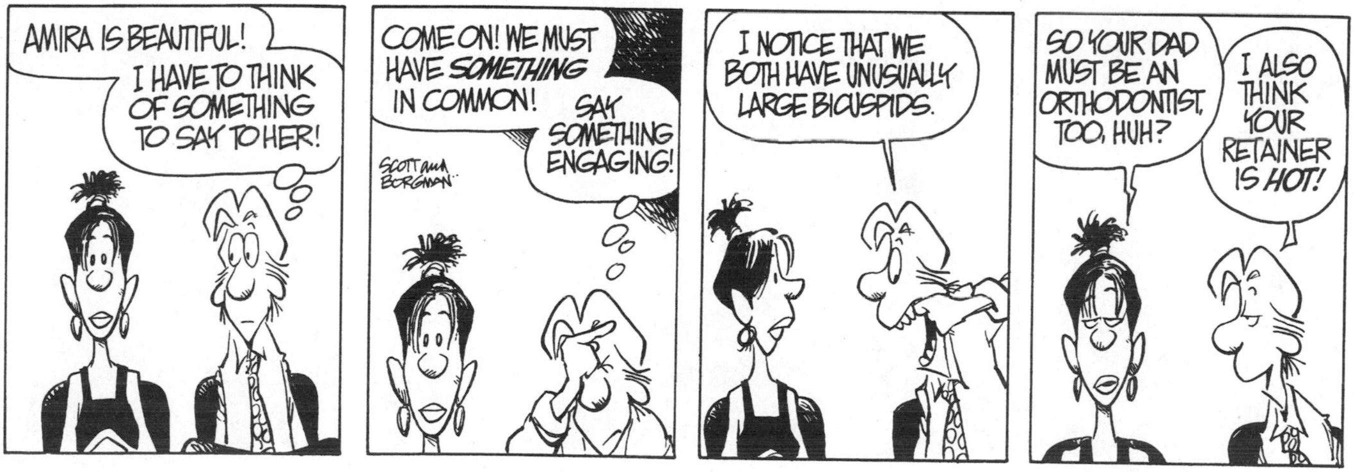
AMIRA IS BEAUTIFUL!
I HAVE TO THINK OF SOMETHING TO SAY TO HER!
COME ON! WE MUST HAVE *SOMETHING* IN COMMON!
SAY SOMETHING ENGAGING!
SCOTT and BORGMAN
I NOTICE THAT WE BOTH HAVE UNUSUALLY LARGE BICUSPIDS.
SO YOUR DAD MUST BE AN ORTHODONTIST, TOO, HUH?
I ALSO THINK YOUR RETAINER IS *HOT*!

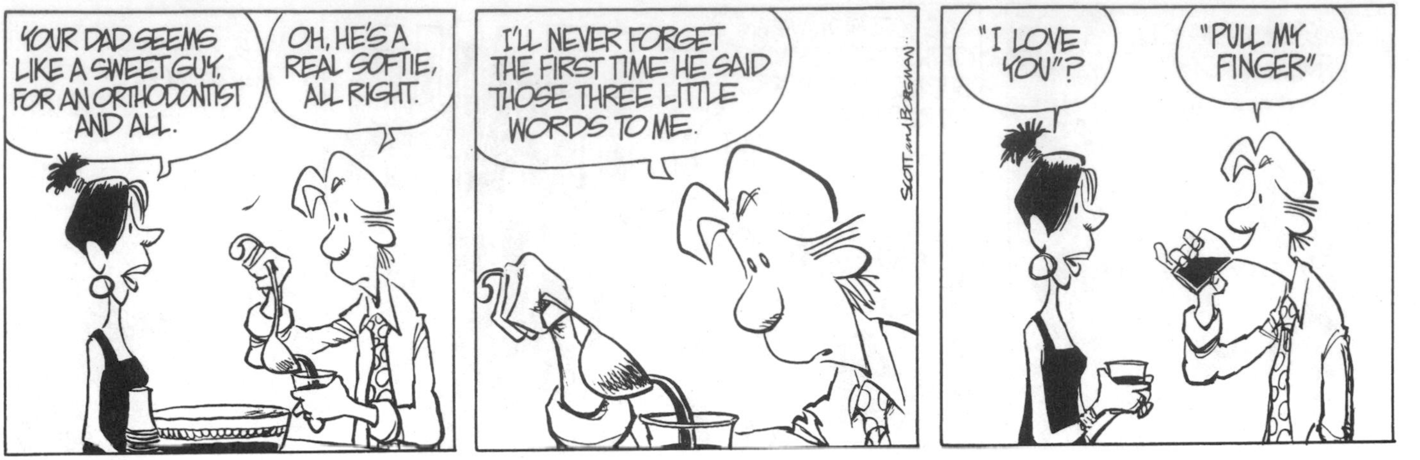
YOUR DAD SEEMS LIKE A SWEET GUY, FOR AN ORTHODONTIST AND ALL.
OH, HE'S A REAL SOFTIE, ALL RIGHT.
I'LL NEVER FORGET THE FIRST TIME HE SAID THOSE THREE LITTLE WORDS TO ME.
SCOTT and BORGMAN
"I LOVE YOU"?
"PULL MY FINGER"

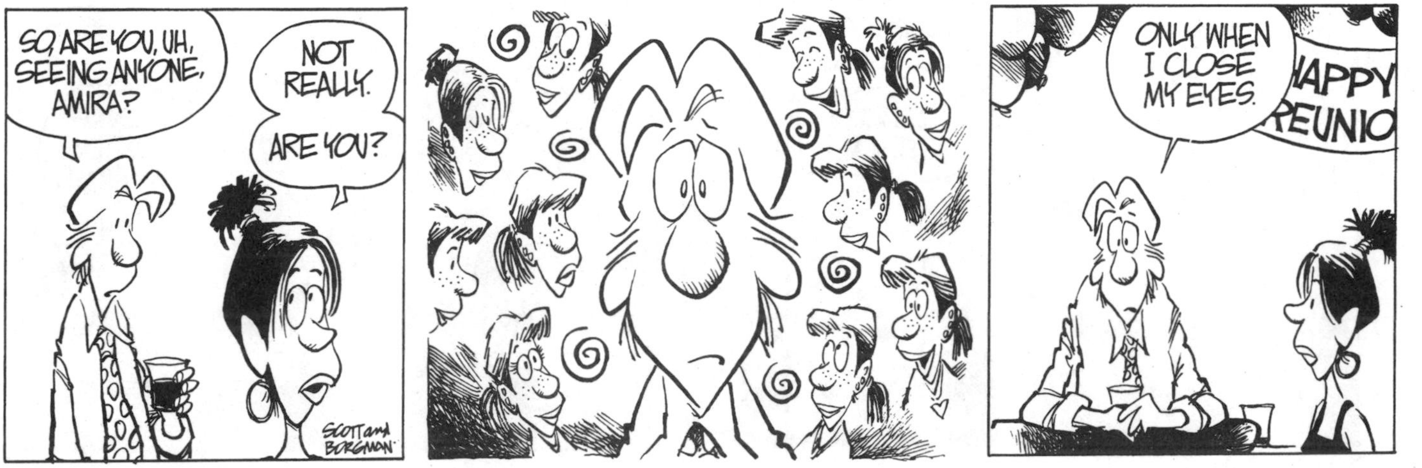
SO, ARE YOU, UH, SEEING ANYONE, AMIRA?
NOT REALLY.
ARE YOU?
SCOTT and BORGMAN
ONLY WHEN I CLOSE MY EYES.
HAPPY REUNIO

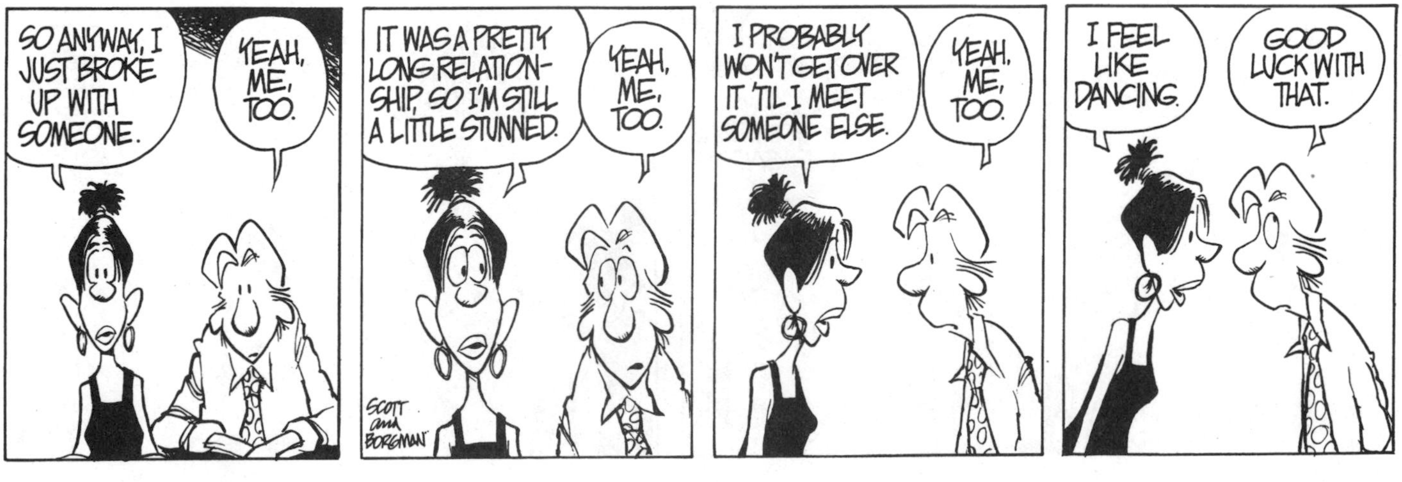
SO ANYWAY, I JUST BROKE UP WITH SOMEONE.
YEAH, ME, TOO.
IT WAS A PRETTY LONG RELATIONSHIP, SO I'M STILL A LITTLE STUNNED.
YEAH, ME, TOO.
SCOTT and BORGMAN
I PROBABLY WON'T GET OVER IT 'TIL I MEET SOMEONE ELSE.
YEAH, ME, TOO.
I FEEL LIKE DANCING.
GOOD LUCK WITH THAT.

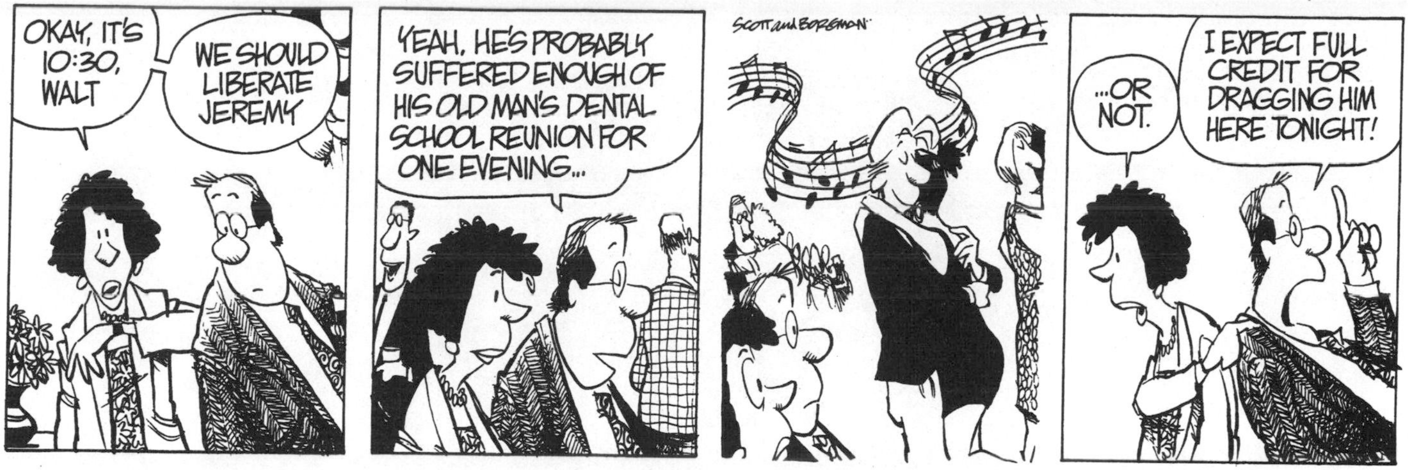
OKAY, IT'S 10:30, WALT
WE SHOULD LIBERATE JEREMY
YEAH, HE'S PROBABLY SUFFERED ENOUGH OF HIS OLD MAN'S DENTAL SCHOOL REUNION FOR ONE EVENING...
SCOTT and BORGMAN
...OR NOT.
I EXPECT FULL CREDIT FOR DRAGGING HIM HERE TONIGHT!

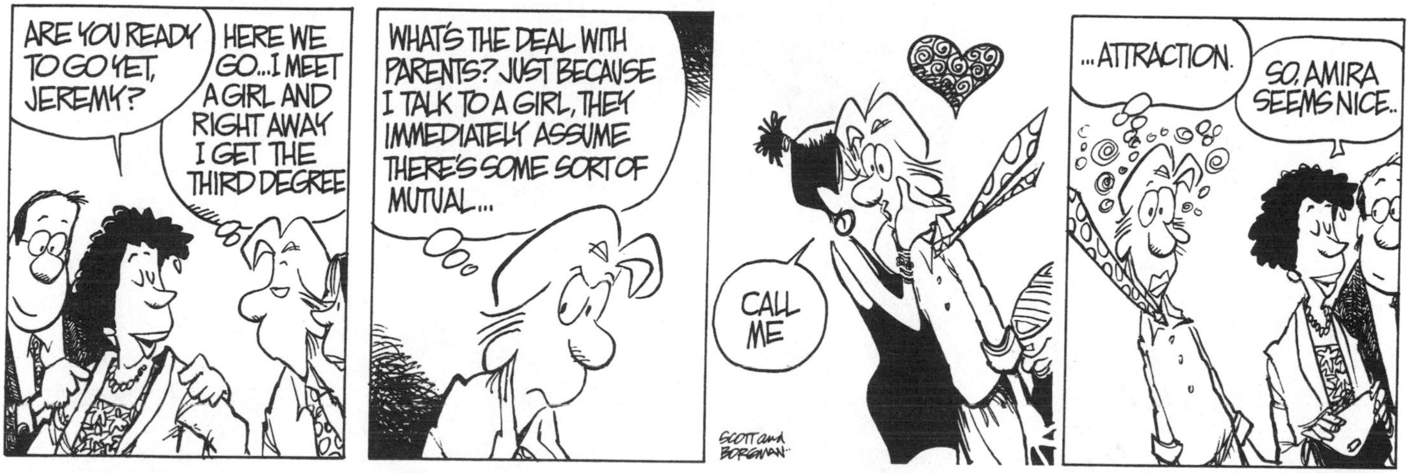
ARE YOU READY TO GO YET, JEREMY?
HERE WE GO...I MEET A GIRL AND RIGHT AWAY I GET THE THIRD DEGREE
WHAT'S THE DEAL WITH PARENTS? JUST BECAUSE I TALK TO A GIRL, THEY IMMEDIATELY ASSUME THERE'S SOME SORT OF MUTUAL...
CALL ME
SCOTT and BORGMAN
...ATTRACTION.
SO, AMIRA SEEMS NICE..

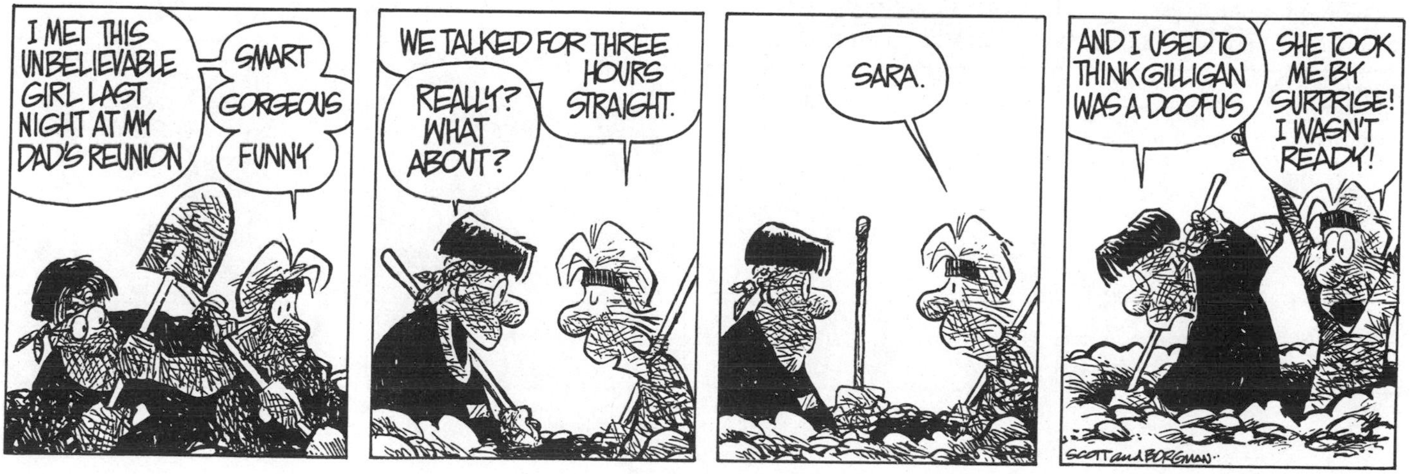
I MET THIS UNBELIEVABLE GIRL LAST NIGHT AT MY DAD'S REUNION
SMART
GORGEOUS
FUNNY
WE TALKED FOR THREE HOURS STRAIGHT.
REALLY? WHAT ABOUT?
SARA.
AND I USED TO THINK GILLIGAN WAS A DOOFUS
SHE TOOK ME BY SURPRISE! I WASN'T READY!
SCOTT and BORGMAN

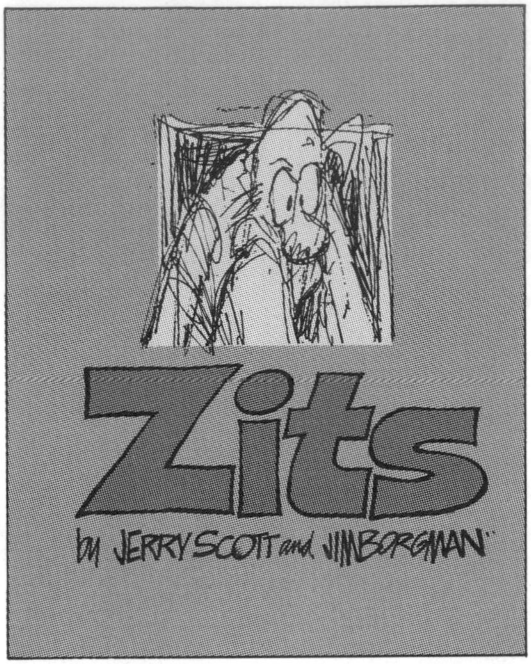
Zits
by JERRY SCOTT and JIM BORGMAN

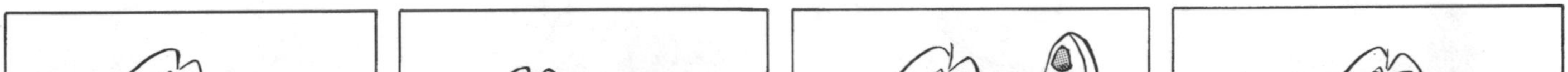
SCOTT and BORGMAN
WHAT ON EARTH?!?
DON'T JUST STAND THERE, DO SOMETHING, MOM!
FLASH!
NICE!
I THINK WE HAVE OUR NEXT CHRISTMAS CARD!

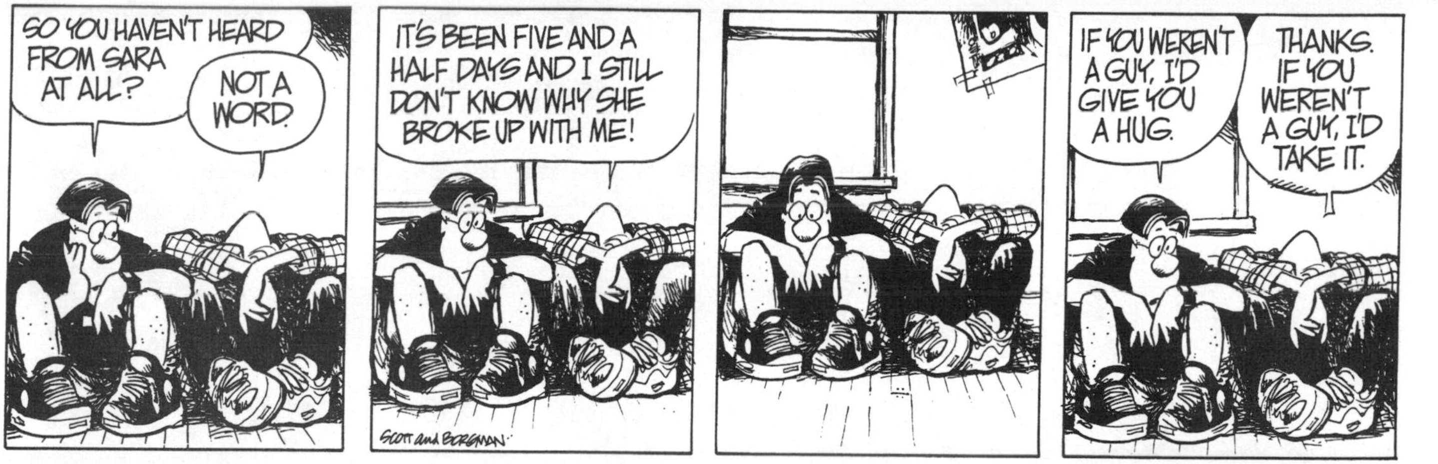
SO YOU HAVEN'T HEARD FROM SARA AT ALL?
NOT A WORD.
IT'S BEEN FIVE AND A HALF DAYS AND I STILL DON'T KNOW WHY SHE BROKE UP WITH ME!
IF YOU WEREN'T A GUY, I'D GIVE YOU A HUG.
THANKS. IF YOU WEREN'T A GUY, I'D TAKE IT.

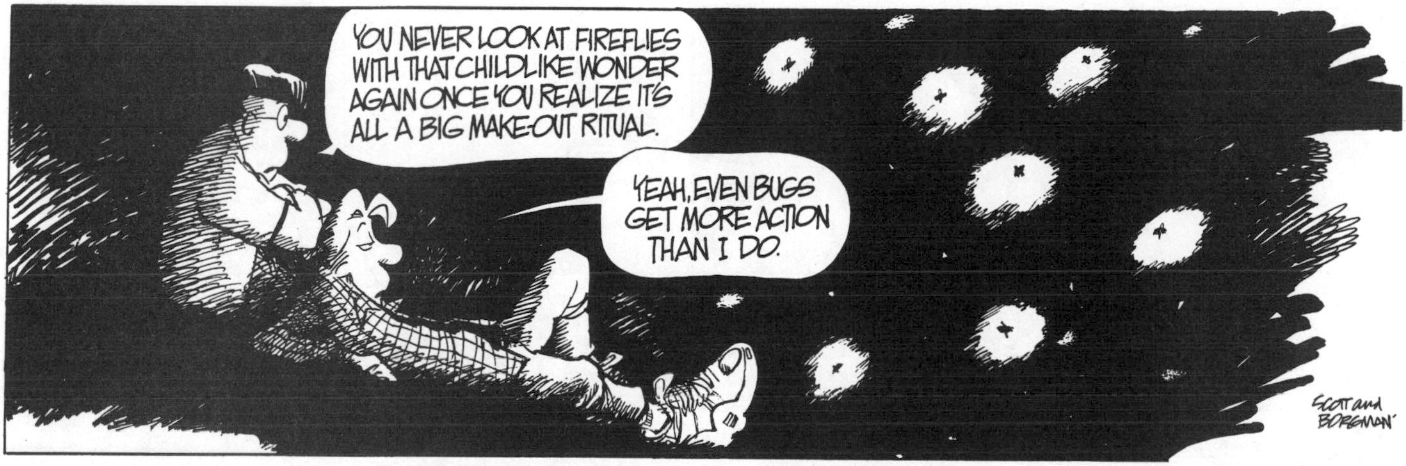
YOU NEVER LOOK AT FIREFLIES WITH THAT CHILDLIKE WONDER AGAIN ONCE YOU REALIZE IT'S ALL A BIG MAKE-OUT RITUAL.
YEAH, EVEN BUGS GET MORE ACTION THAN I DO.

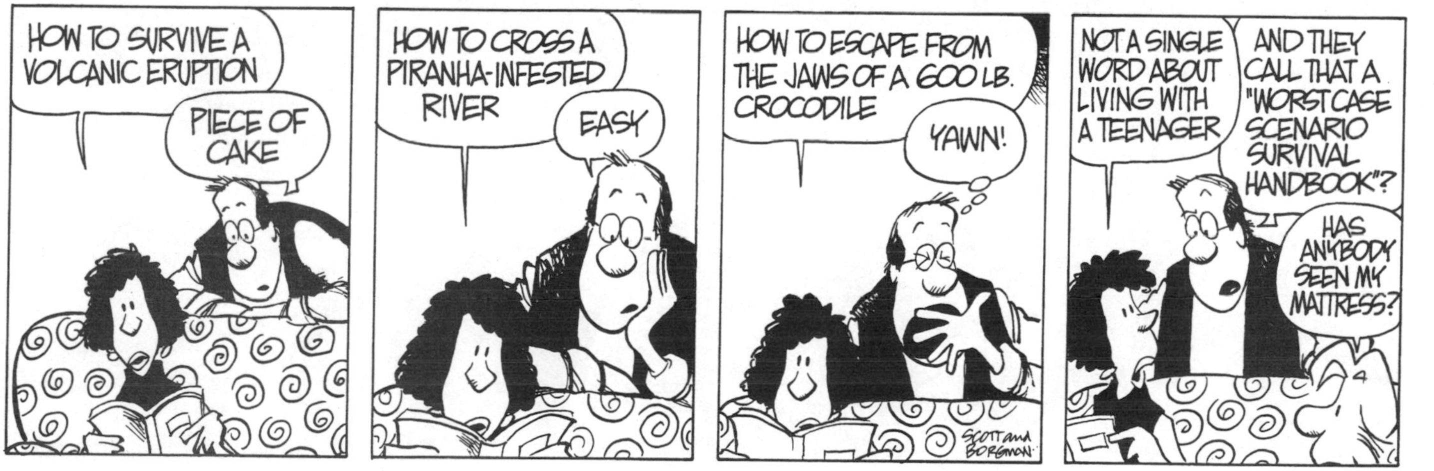
HOW TO SURVIVE A VOLCANIC ERUPTION
PIECE OF CAKE
HOW TO CROSS A PIRANHA-INFESTED RIVER
EASY
HOW TO ESCAPE FROM THE JAWS OF A 600 LB. CROCODILE
YAWN!
NOT A SINGLE WORD ABOUT LIVING WITH A TEENAGER
AND THEY CALL THAT A "WORST CASE SCENARIO SURVIVAL HANDBOOK"?
HAS ANYBODY SEEN MY MATTRESS?

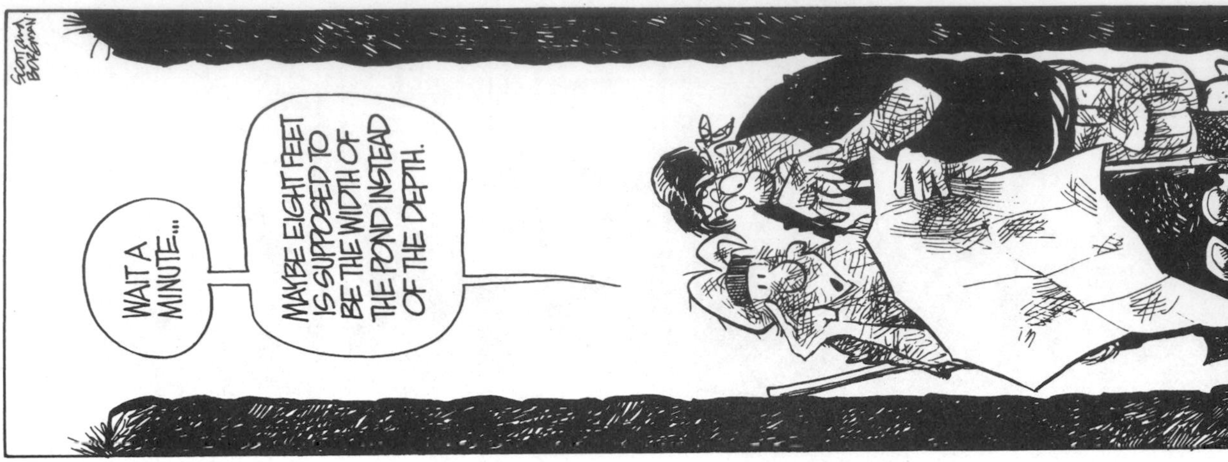

SCOTT and BORGMAN
WAIT A MINUTE...
MAYBE EIGHT FEET IS SUPPOSED TO BE THE WIDTH OF THE POND INSTEAD OF THE DEPTH.

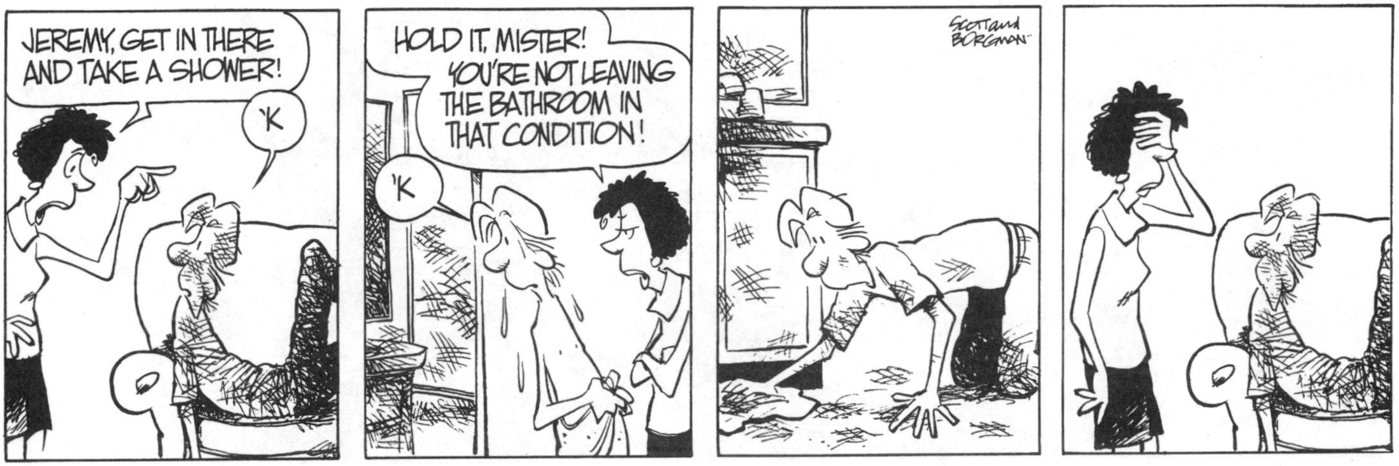

JEREMY, GET IN THERE AND TAKE A SHOWER!
'K
HOLD IT, MISTER! YOU'RE NOT LEAVING THE BATHROOM IN THAT CONDITION!
'K
SCOTT and BORGMAN

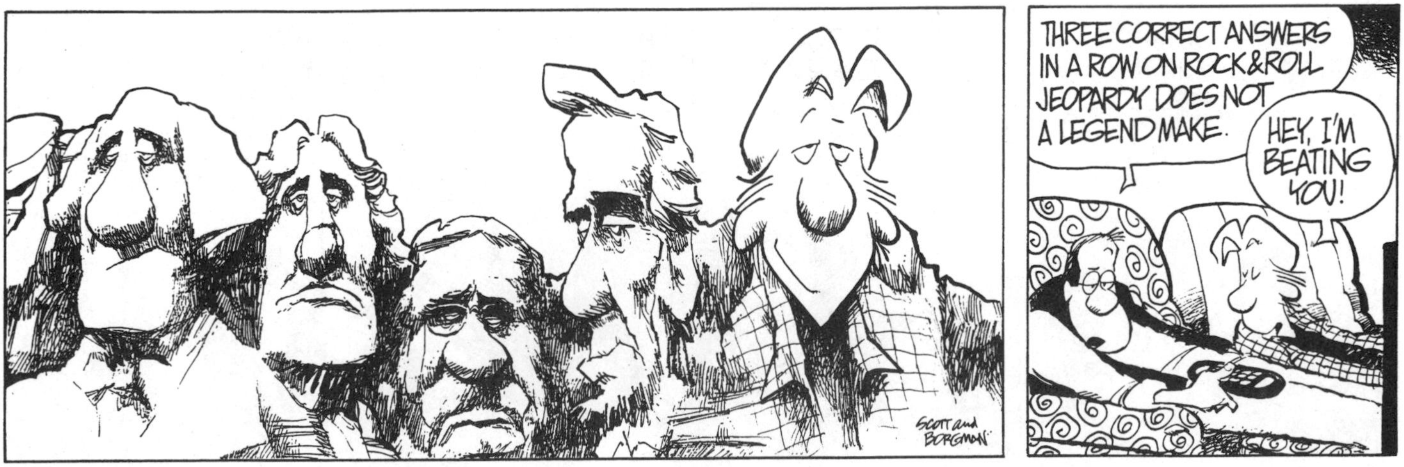

SCOTT and BORGMAN
THREE CORRECT ANSWERS IN A ROW ON ROCK&ROLL JEOPARDY DOES NOT A LEGEND MAKE.
HEY, I'M BEATING YOU!

Zits
by
JERRY SCOTT and
JIM BORGMAN

YAWN!
I HAVE NO RECOLLECTION OF THE REAGAN ERA.
BLACK AND WHITE TV? WHAT'S THAT?
SCOTT and BORGMAN
CDs HAVE BEEN AROUND SINCE BEFORE I WAS BORN
IS IT TRUE THAT THE TONIGHT SHOW WASN'T ALWAYS HOSTED BY JAY LENO?
DO YOU THINK JEREMY REMEMBERED THAT IT'S YOUR BIRTHDAY TODAY?
MORNIN', OLD TIMER!
HE REMEMBERED.

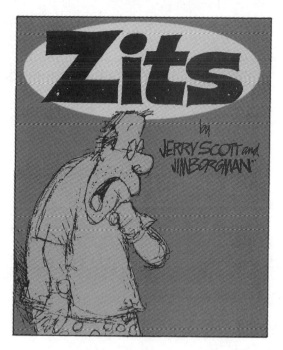

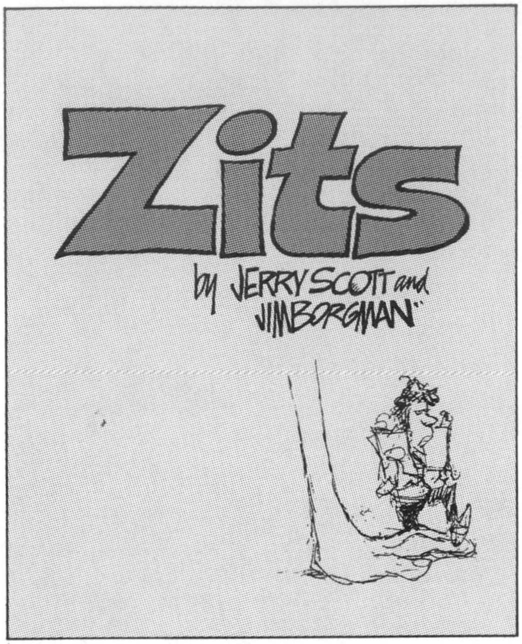
Zits
by JERRY SCOTT and
JIM BORGMAN

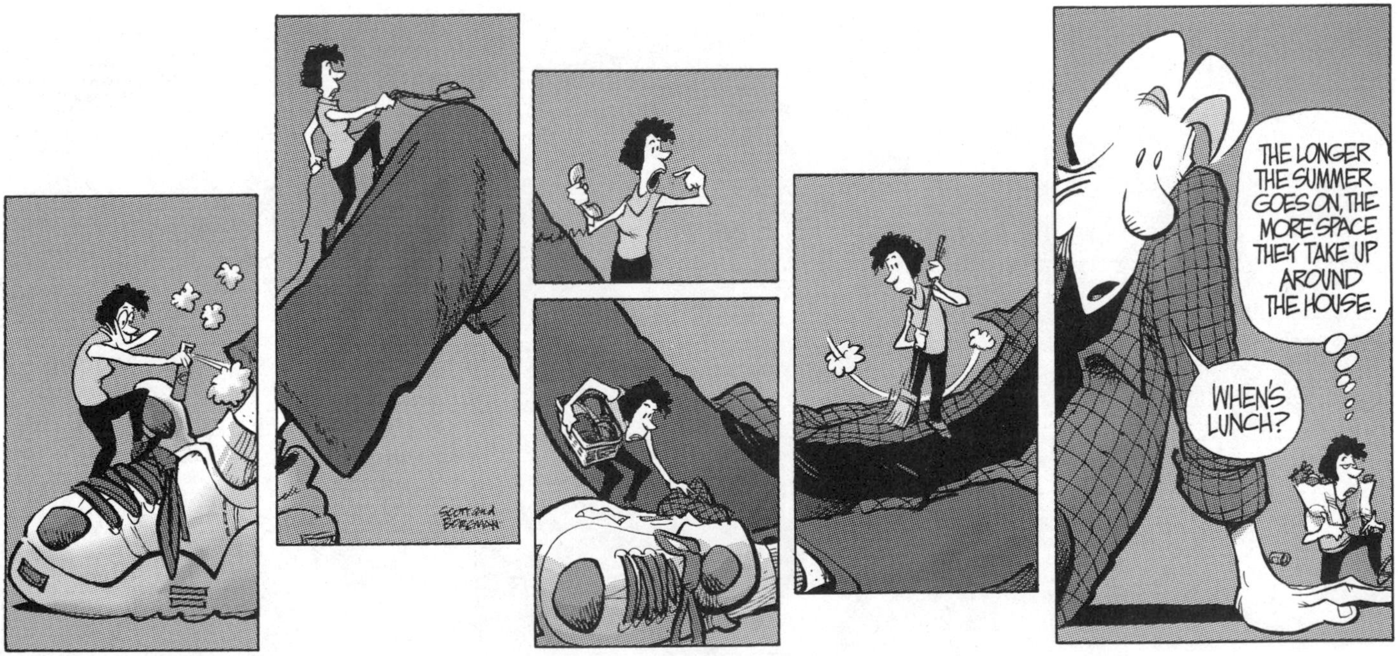
SCOTT and BORGMAN
THE LONGER THE SUMMER GOES ON, THE MORE SPACE THEY TAKE UP AROUND THE HOUSE.
WHEN'S LUNCH?

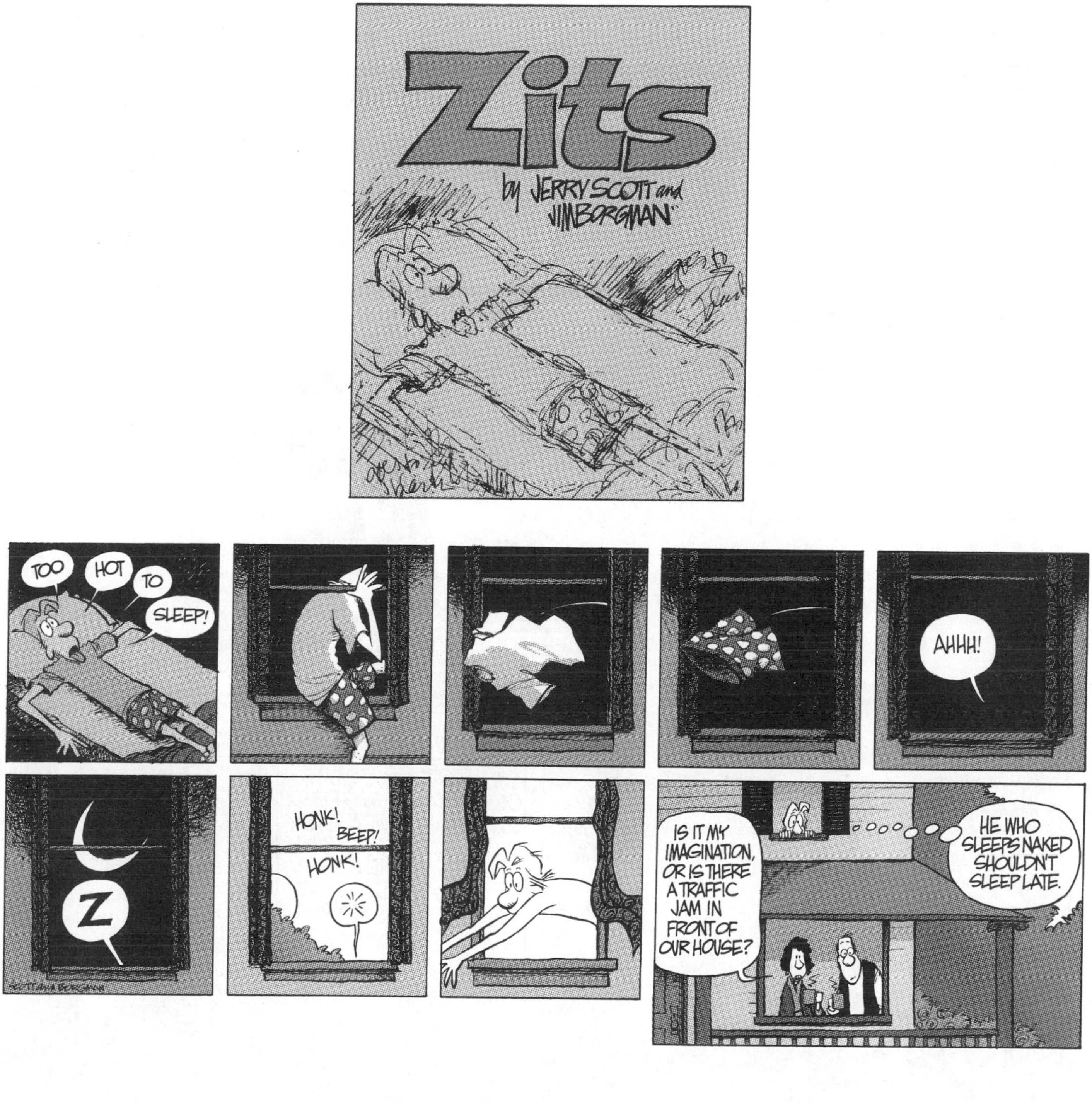
Zits
by JERRY SCOTT and JIM BORGMAN
TOO
HOT
TO
SLEEP!
AHHH!
Z
HONK!
BEEP!
HONK!
IS IT MY IMAGINATION, OR IS THERE A TRAFFIC JAM IN FRONT OF OUR HOUSE?
HE WHO SLEEPS NAKED SHOULDN'T SLEEP LATE.

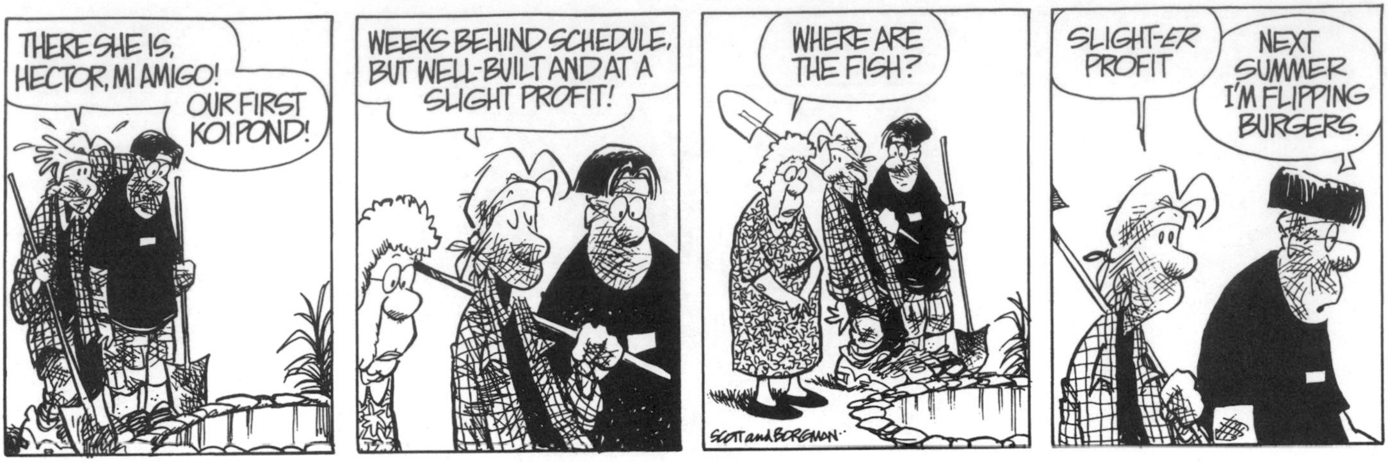
THERE SHE IS, HECTOR, MI AMIGO!
OUR FIRST KOI POND!
WEEKS BEHIND SCHEDULE, BUT WELL-BUILT AND AT A SLIGHT PROFIT!
WHERE ARE THE FISH?
SLIGHT-ER PROFIT
NEXT SUMMER I'M FLIPPING BURGERS.
SCOTT and BORGMAN

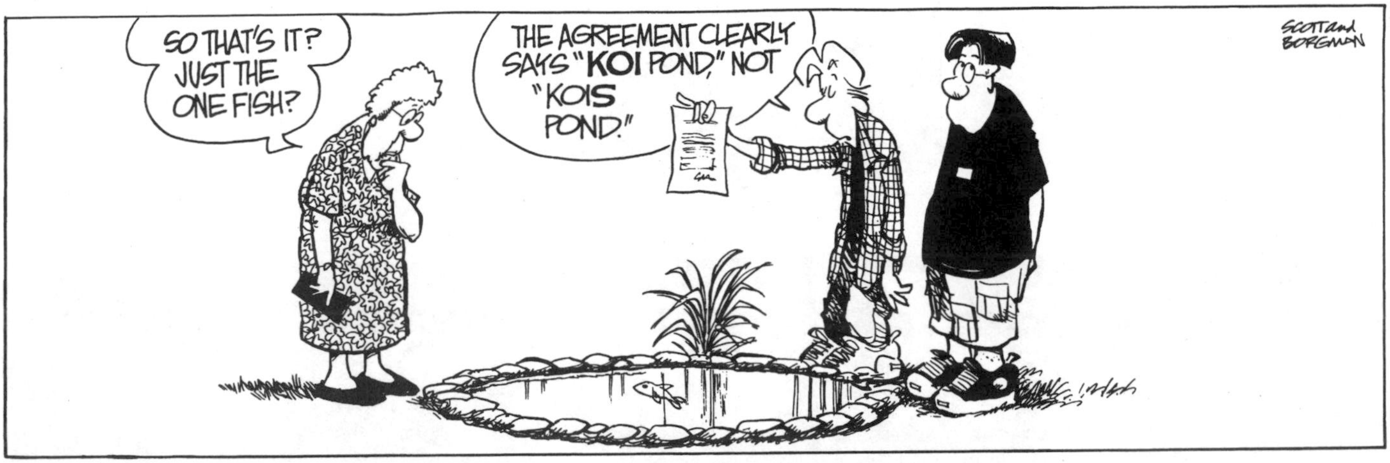
SO THAT'S IT? JUST THE ONE FISH?
THE AGREEMENT CLEARLY SAYS "KOI POND," NOT "KOIS POND."
SCOTT and BORGMAN

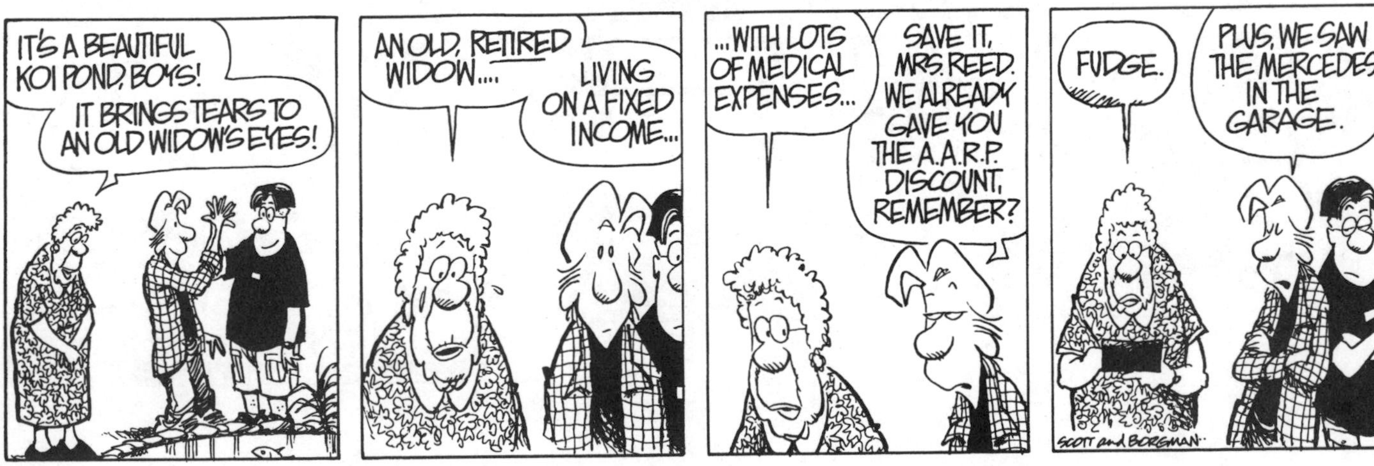
IT'S A BEAUTIFUL KOI POND, BOYS!
IT BRINGS TEARS TO AN OLD WIDOW'S EYES!
AN OLD, RETIRED WIDOW....
LIVING ON A FIXED INCOME...
...WITH LOTS OF MEDICAL EXPENSES...
SAVE IT, MRS. REED. WE ALREADY GAVE YOU THE A.A.R.P. DISCOUNT, REMEMBER?
FUDGE.
PLUS, WE SAW THE MERCEDES IN THE GARAGE.
SCOTT and BORGMAN

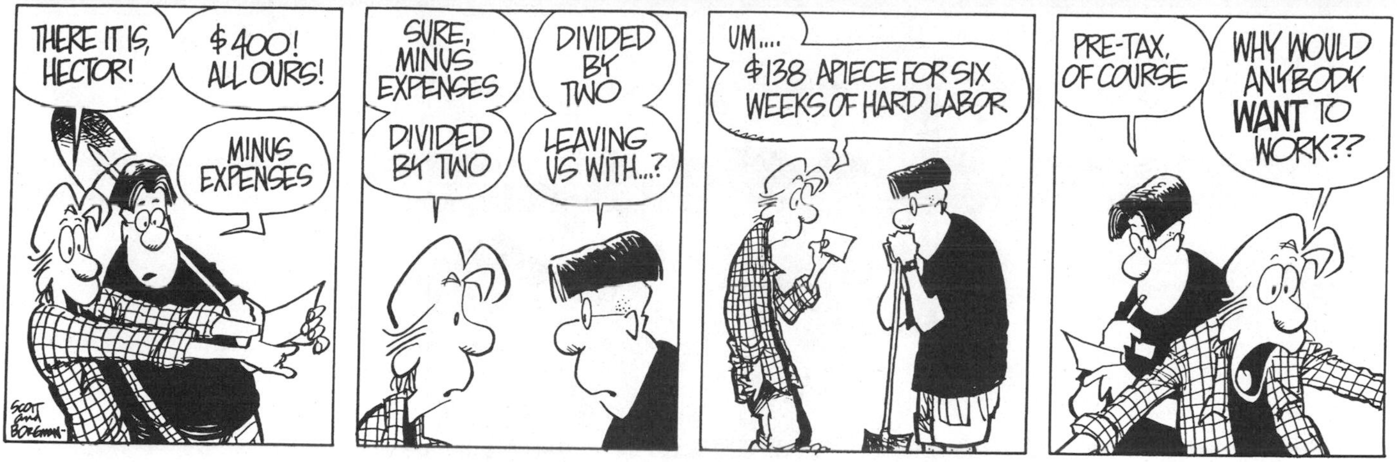
THERE IT IS, HECTOR!
$400! ALL OURS!
MINUS EXPENSES
SURE, MINUS EXPENSES
DIVIDED BY TWO
DIVIDED BY TWO
LEAVING US WITH...?
UM....
$138 APIECE FOR SIX WEEKS OF HARD LABOR
PRE-TAX, OF COURSE
WHY WOULD ANYBODY WANT TO WORK??
SCOTT and BORGMAN

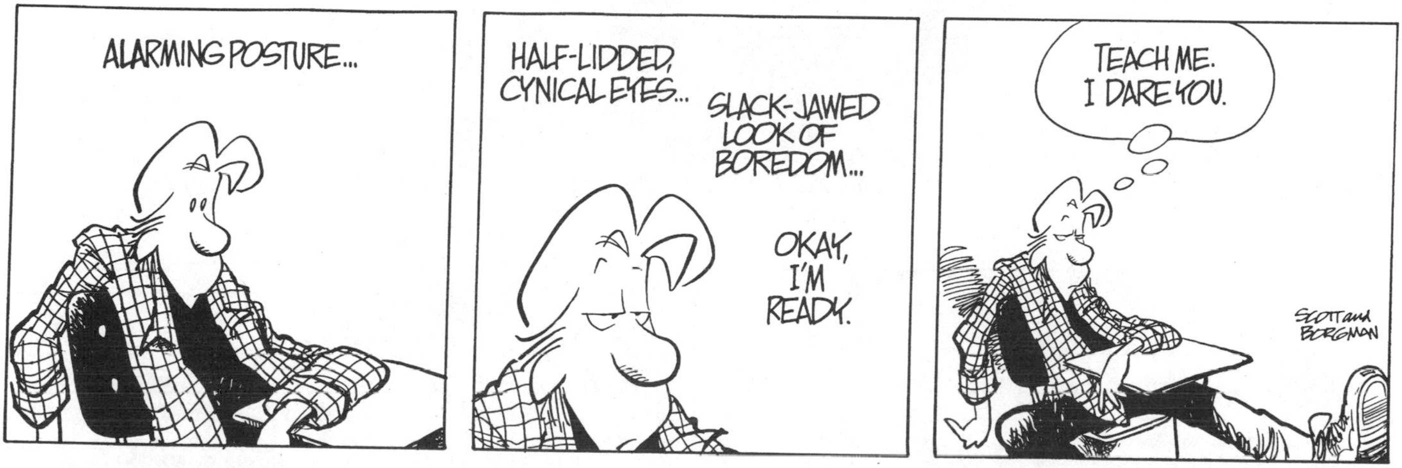
ALARMING POSTURE...
HALF-LIDDED, CYNICAL EYES...
SLACK-JAWED LOOK OF BOREDOM...
OKAY, I'M READY.
TEACH ME. I DARE YOU.
SCOTT and BORGMAN

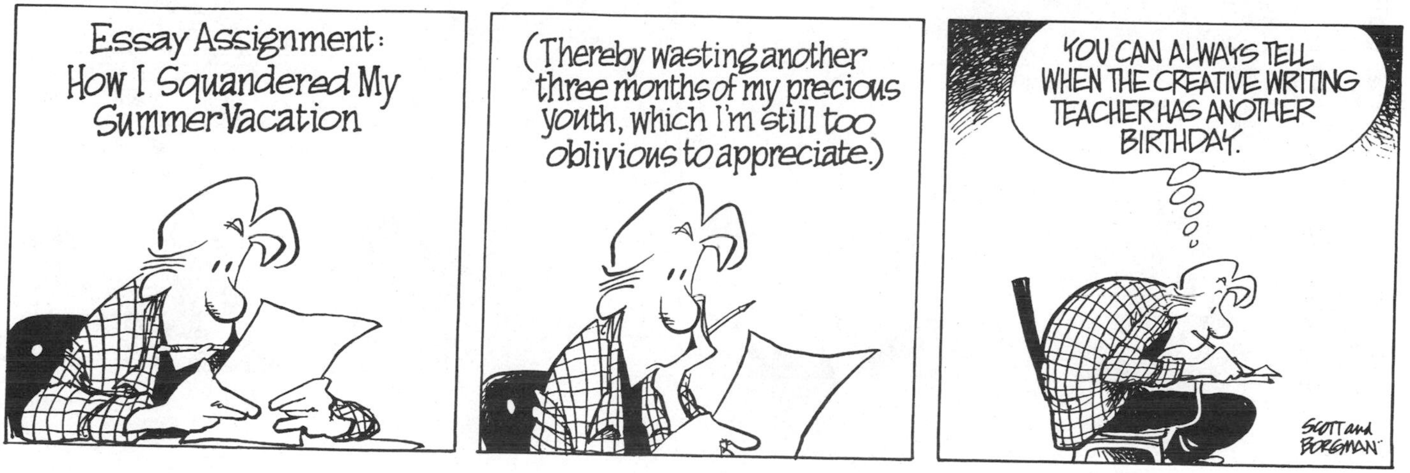
Essay Assignment: How I Squandered My Summer Vacation
(Thereby wasting another three months of my precious youth, which I'm still too oblivious to appreciate.)
YOU CAN ALWAYS TELL WHEN THE CREATIVE WRITING TEACHER HAS ANOTHER BIRTHDAY.
SCOTT and BORGMAN

Zits
by
JERRY SCOTT and JIM BORGMAN

SCOTT and BORGMAN
HOW COME JEREMY IS THE ONLY ONE WHO GETS A CLOSE-UP IN THIS VIDEO?
HEY, IF YOU WANT A CLOSE-UP, YOU HOLD THE CAMERA DURING THE NEXT SONG!

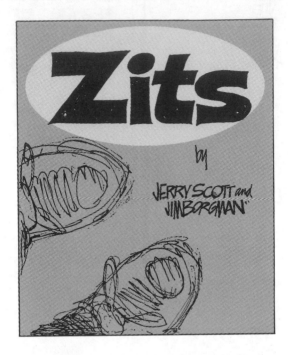

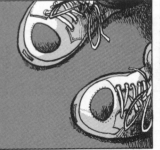

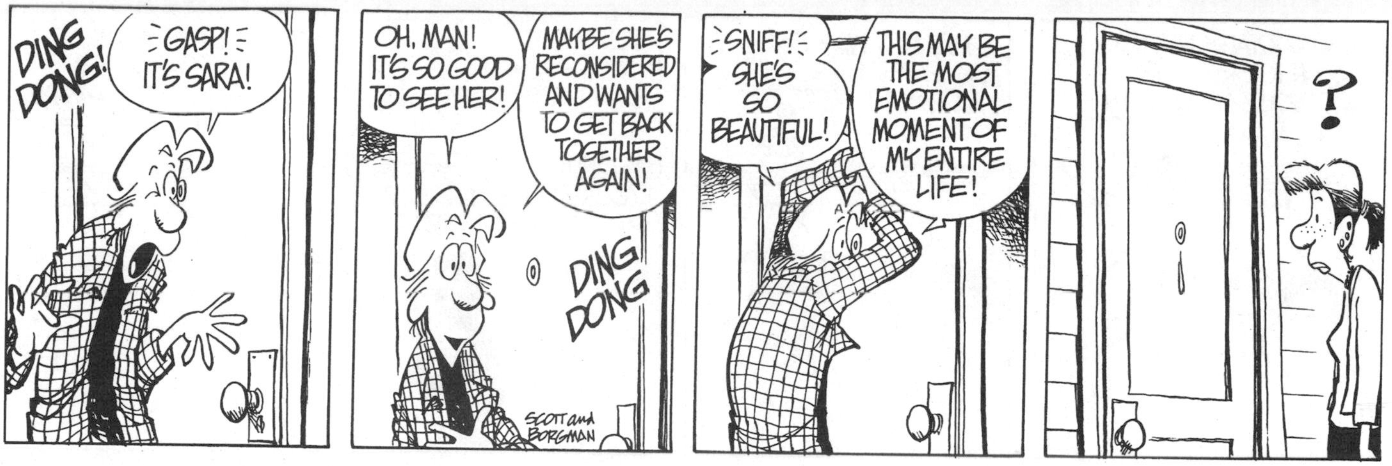
DING DONG!
GASP! IT'S SARA!
OH, MAN! IT'S SO GOOD TO SEE HER!
MAYBE SHE'S RECONSIDERED AND WANTS TO GET BACK TOGETHER AGAIN!
DING DONG
SCOTT and BORGMAN
SNIFF! SHE'S SO BEAUTIFUL!
THIS MAY BE THE MOST EMOTIONAL MOMENT OF MY ENTIRE LIFE!
?

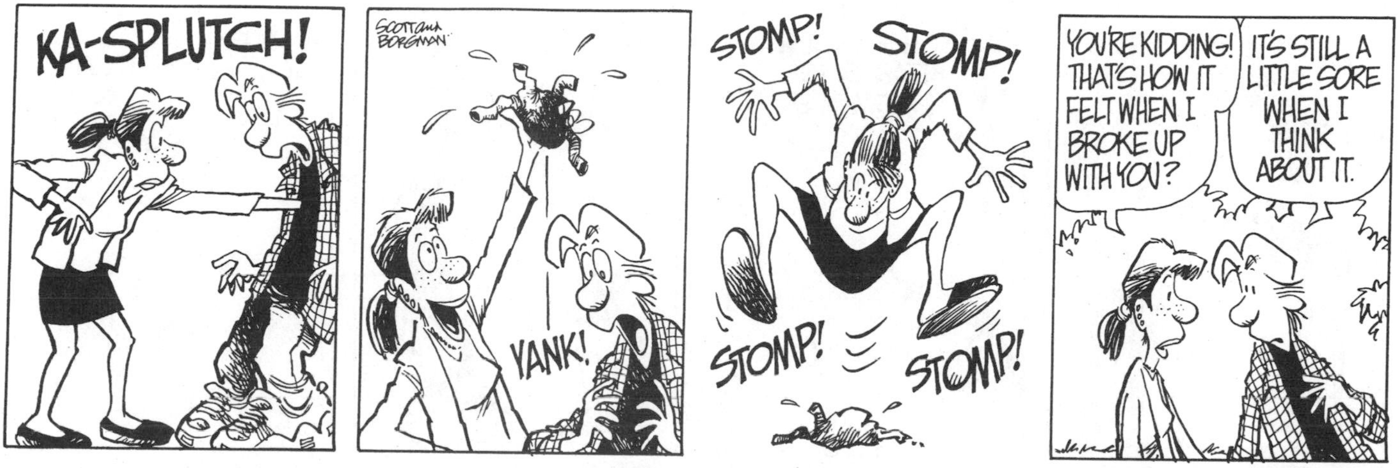
KA-SPLUTCH!
SCOTT and BORGMAN
YANK!
STOMP!
STOMP!
STOMP!
STOMP!
YOU'RE KIDDING! THAT'S HOW IT FELT WHEN I BROKE UP WITH YOU?
IT'S STILL A LITTLE SORE WHEN I THINK ABOUT IT.

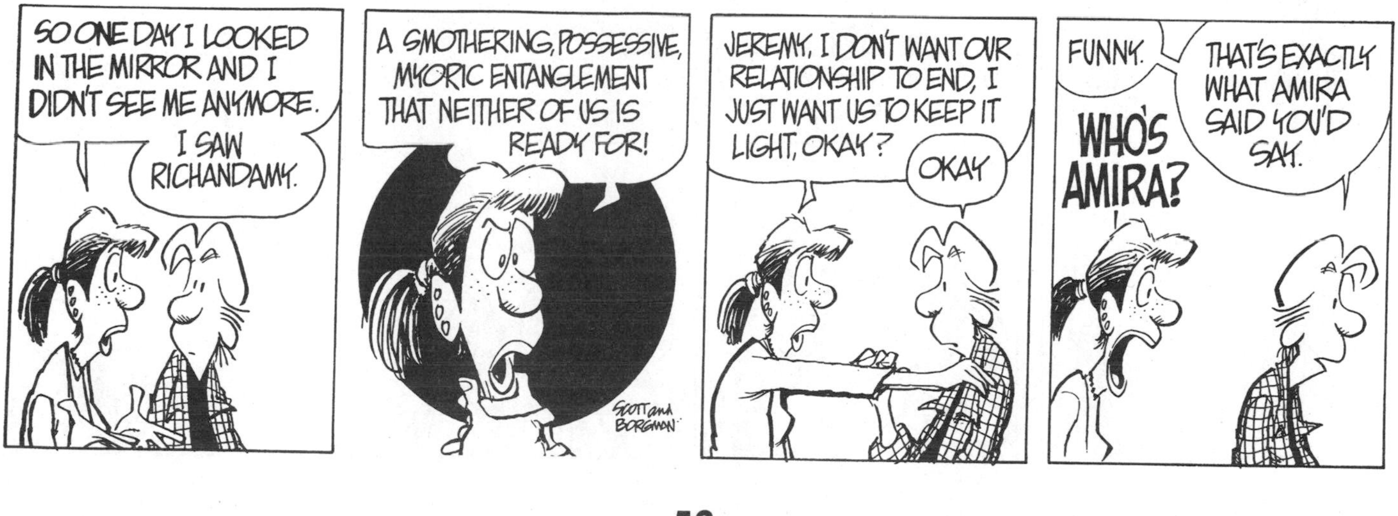
SO ONE DAY I LOOKED IN THE MIRROR AND I DIDN'T SEE ME ANYMORE.
I SAW RICHANDAMY.
A SMOTHERING, POSSESSIVE, MYORIC ENTANGLEMENT THAT NEITHER OF US IS READY FOR!
SCOTT and BORGMAN
JEREMY, I DON'T WANT OUR RELATIONSHIP TO END, I JUST WANT US TO KEEP IT LIGHT, OKAY?
OKAY
FUNNY.
THAT'S EXACTLY WHAT AMIRA SAID YOU'D SAY.
WHO'S AMIRA?

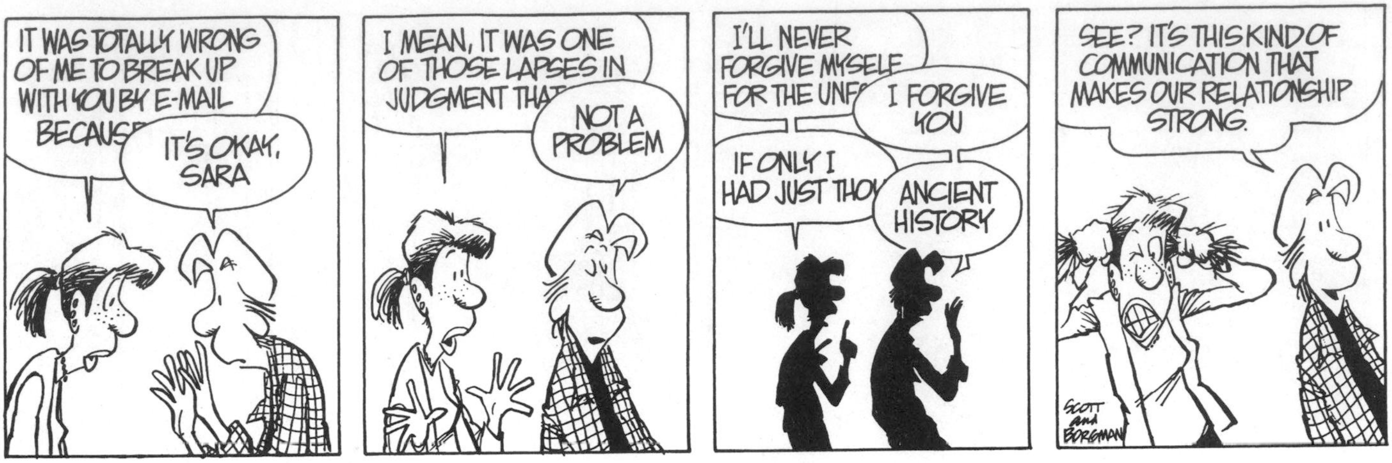
IT WAS TOTALLY WRONG OF ME TO BREAK UP WITH YOU BY E-MAIL BECAUS
IT'S OKAY, SARA
I MEAN, IT WAS ONE OF THOSE LAPSES IN JUDGMENT THAT
NOT A PROBLEM
I'LL NEVER FORGIVE MYSELF FOR THE UNF
I FORGIVE YOU
IF ONLY I HAD JUST THO
ANCIENT HISTORY
SEE? IT'S THIS KIND OF COMMUNICATION THAT MAKES OUR RELATIONSHIP STRONG.
SCOTT and BORGMAN

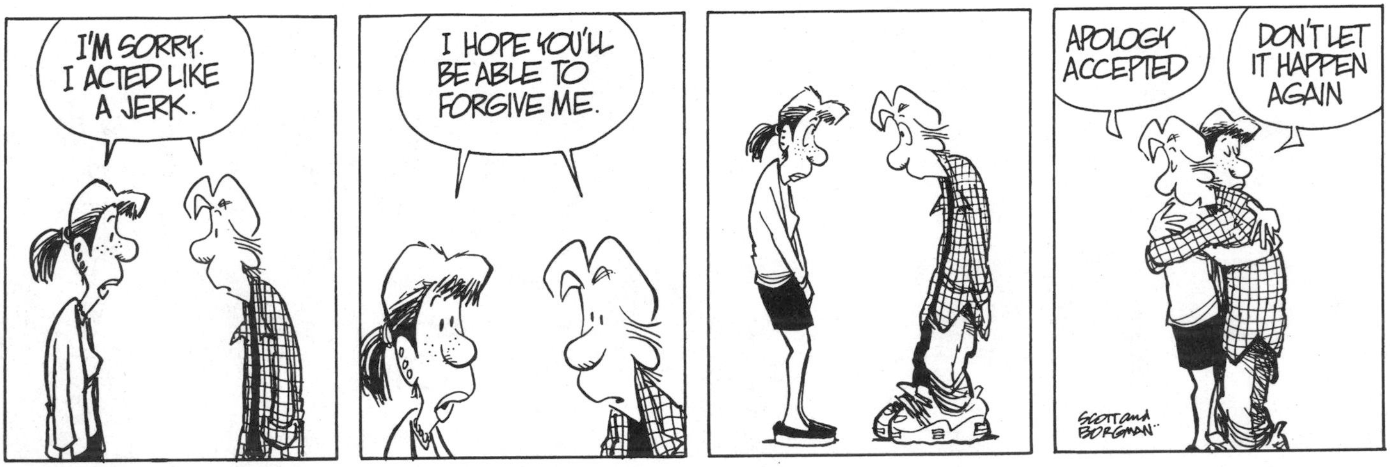
I'M SORRY. I ACTED LIKE A JERK.
I HOPE YOU'LL BE ABLE TO FORGIVE ME.
APOLOGY ACCEPTED
DON'T LET IT HAPPEN AGAIN
SCOTT and BORGMAN

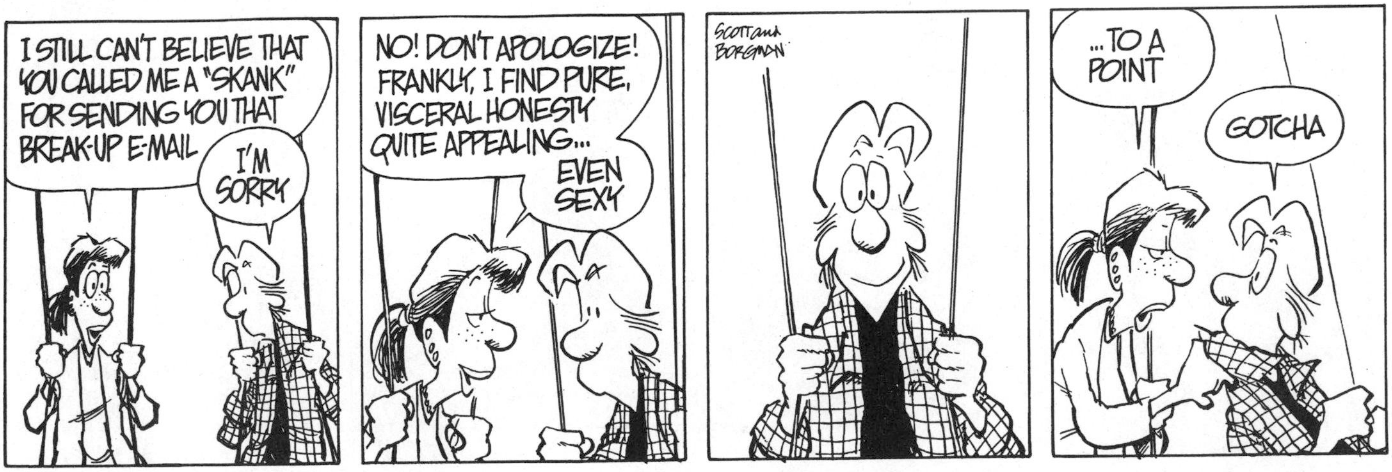
I STILL CAN'T BELIEVE THAT YOU CALLED ME A "SKANK" FOR SENDING YOU THAT BREAK-UP E-MAIL
I'M SORRY
NO! DON'T APOLOGIZE! FRANKLY, I FIND PURE, VISCERAL HONESTY QUITE APPEALING...
EVEN SEXY
SCOTT and BORGMAN
...TO A POINT
GOTCHA

Zits
by JERRY SCOTT and JIM BORGMAN

LOOK AT THAT SKY! WHAT A GREAT NIGHT FOR STAR-GAZING!
WHAT'S WRONG? NO STARS?
LET'S JUST SAY THAT THE HEAVENLY BODIES ARE OTHERWISE OCCUPIED.

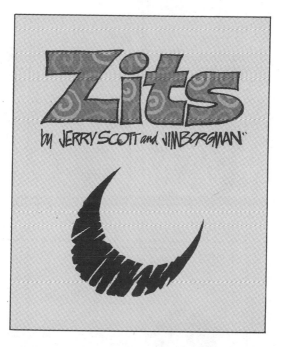

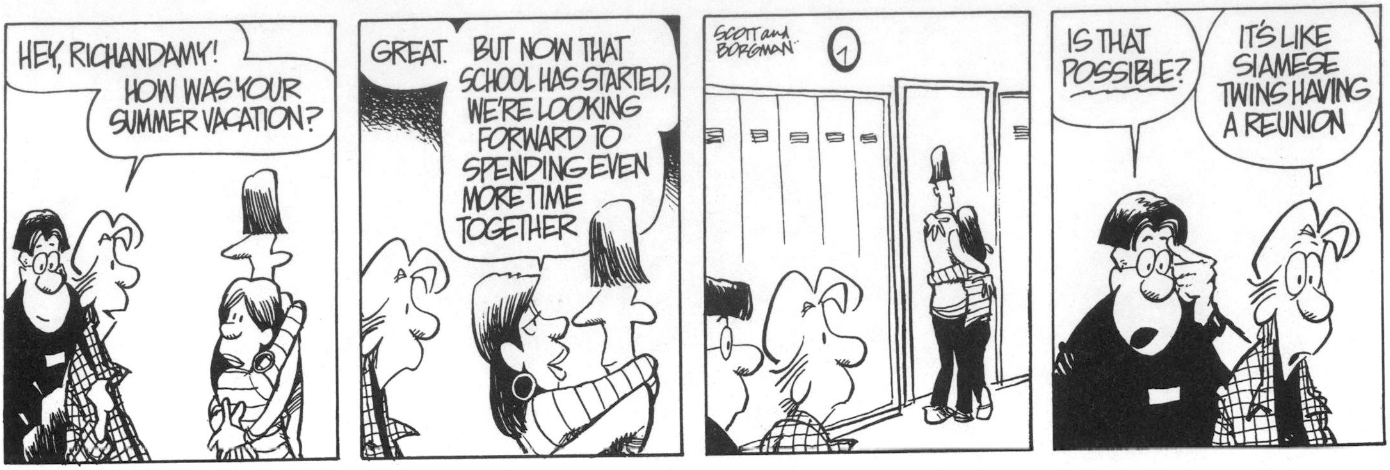
HEY, RICHANDAMY!
HOW WAS YOUR SUMMER VACATION?
GREAT.
BUT NOW THAT SCHOOL HAS STARTED, WE'RE LOOKING FORWARD TO SPENDING EVEN MORE TIME TOGETHER
SCOTT and BORGMAN
IS THAT POSSIBLE?
IT'S LIKE SIAMESE TWINS HAVING A REUNION

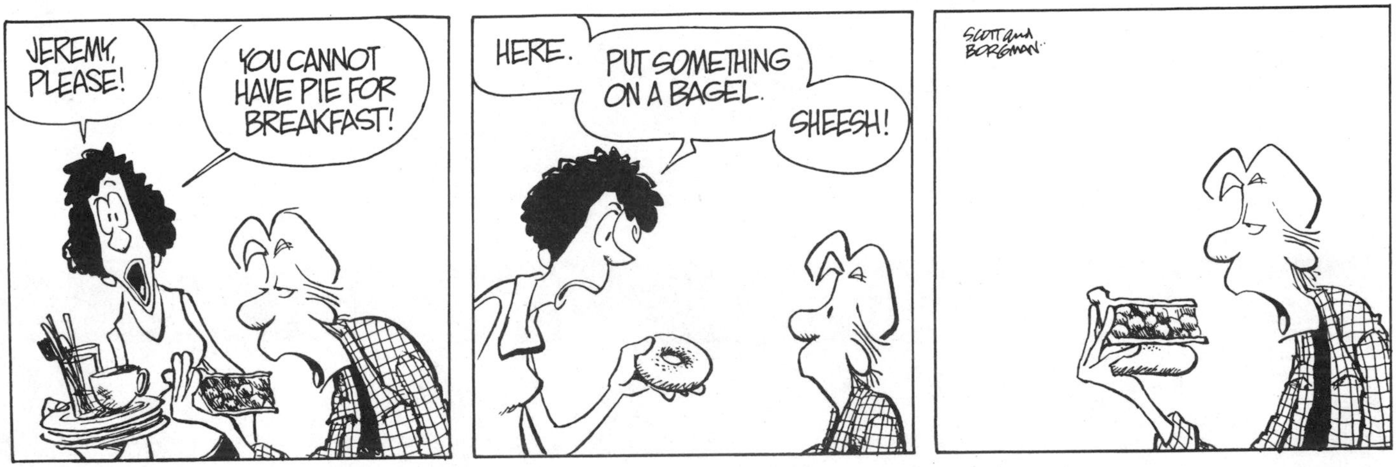
JEREMY, PLEASE!
YOU CANNOT HAVE PIE FOR BREAKFAST!
HERE.
PUT SOMETHING ON A BAGEL.
SHEESH!
SCOTT and BORGMAN

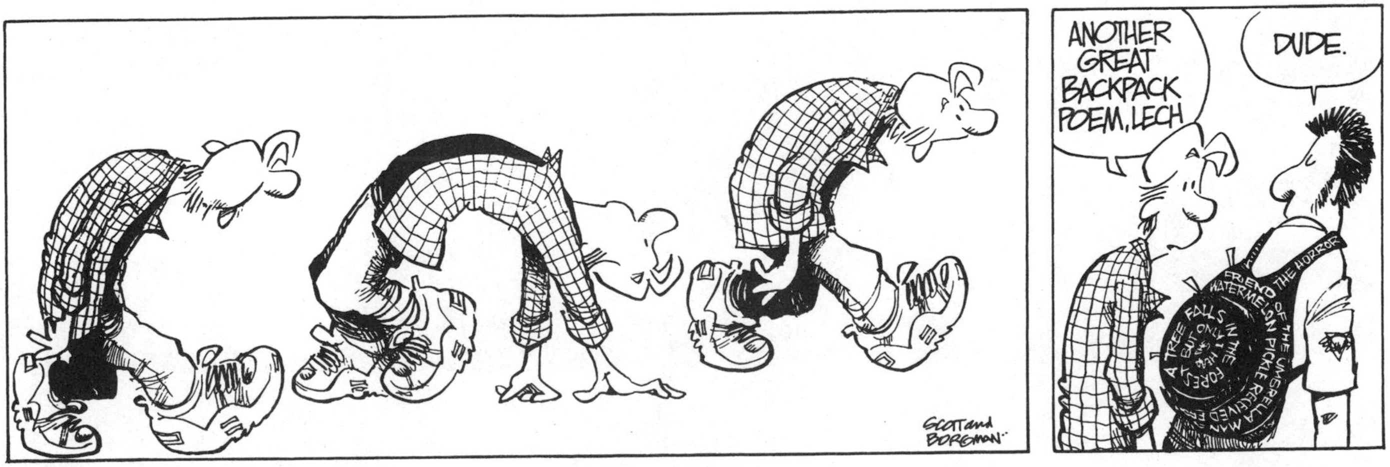
SCOTT and BORGMAN
ANOTHER GREAT BACKPACK POEM, LECH
DUDE.

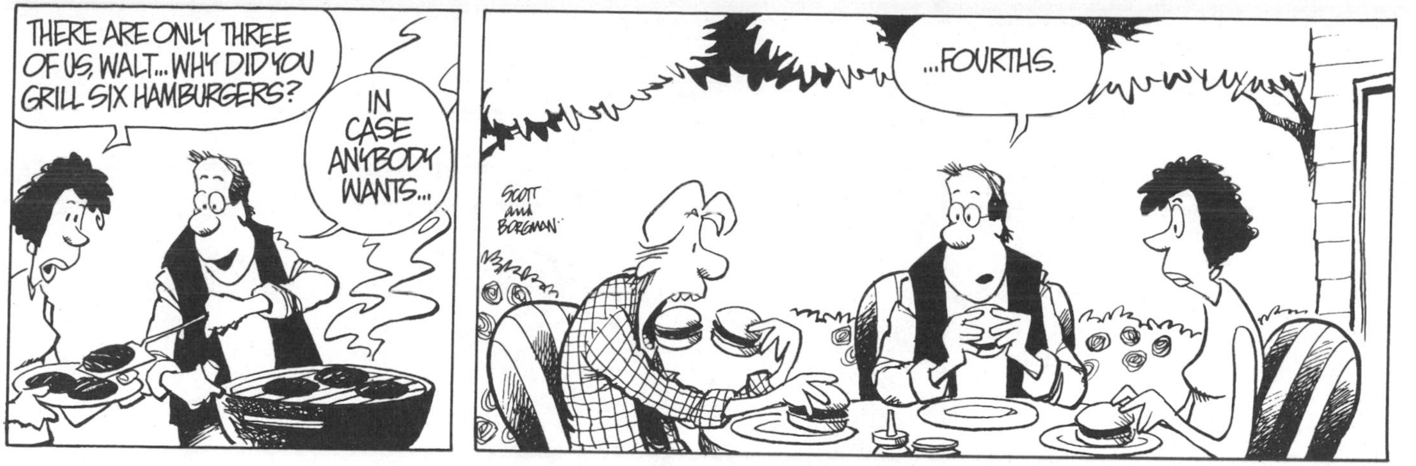
THERE ARE ONLY THREE OF US, WALT... WHY DID YOU GRILL SIX HAMBURGERS?
IN CASE ANYBODY WANTS...
...FOURTHS.
SCOTT AND BORGMAN

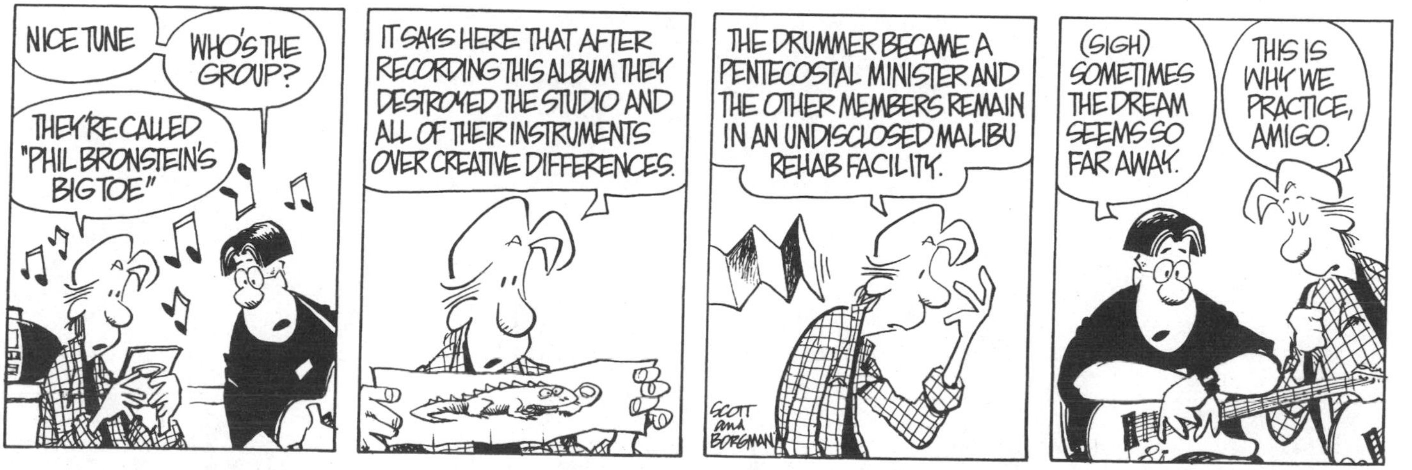
NICE TUNE
WHO'S THE GROUP?
THEY'RE CALLED "PHIL BRONSTEIN'S BIG TOE"
IT SAYS HERE THAT AFTER RECORDING THIS ALBUM THEY DESTROYED THE STUDIO AND ALL OF THEIR INSTRUMENTS OVER CREATIVE DIFFERENCES.
THE DRUMMER BECAME A PENTECOSTAL MINISTER AND THE OTHER MEMBERS REMAIN IN AN UNDISCLOSED MALIBU REHAB FACILITY.
SCOTT AND BORGMAN
(SIGH) SOMETIMES THE DREAM SEEMS SO FAR AWAY.
THIS IS WHY WE PRACTICE, AMIGO.

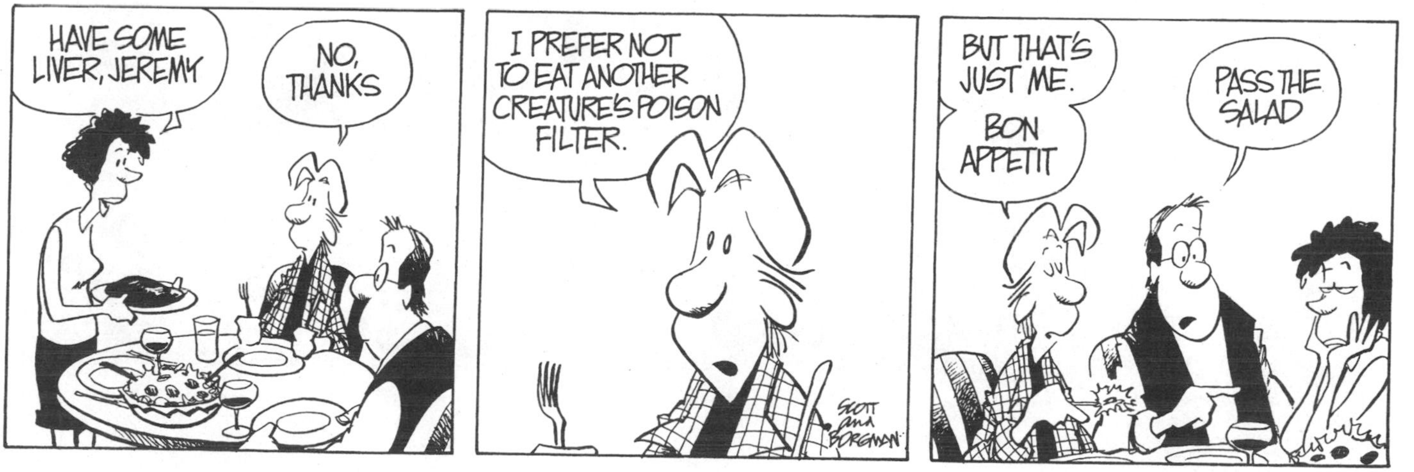
HAVE SOME LIVER, JEREMY
NO, THANKS
I PREFER NOT TO EAT ANOTHER CREATURE'S POISON FILTER.
SCOTT AND BORGMAN
BUT THAT'S JUST ME.
BON APPETIT
PASS THE SALAD

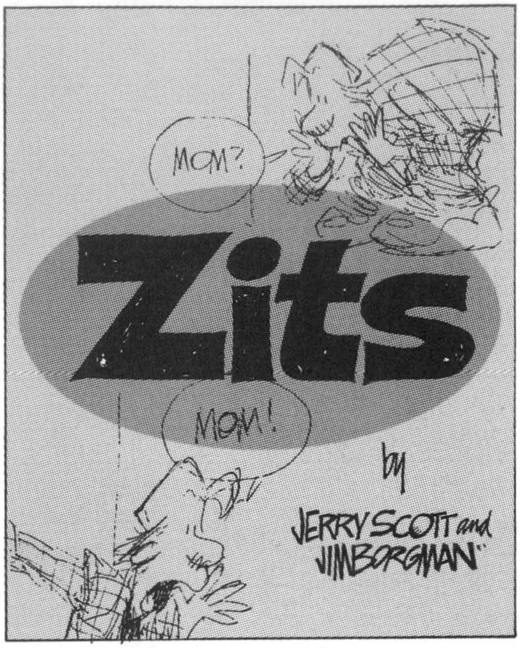
MOM?
Zits
MOM!
by
JERRY SCOTT and
JIM BORGMAN

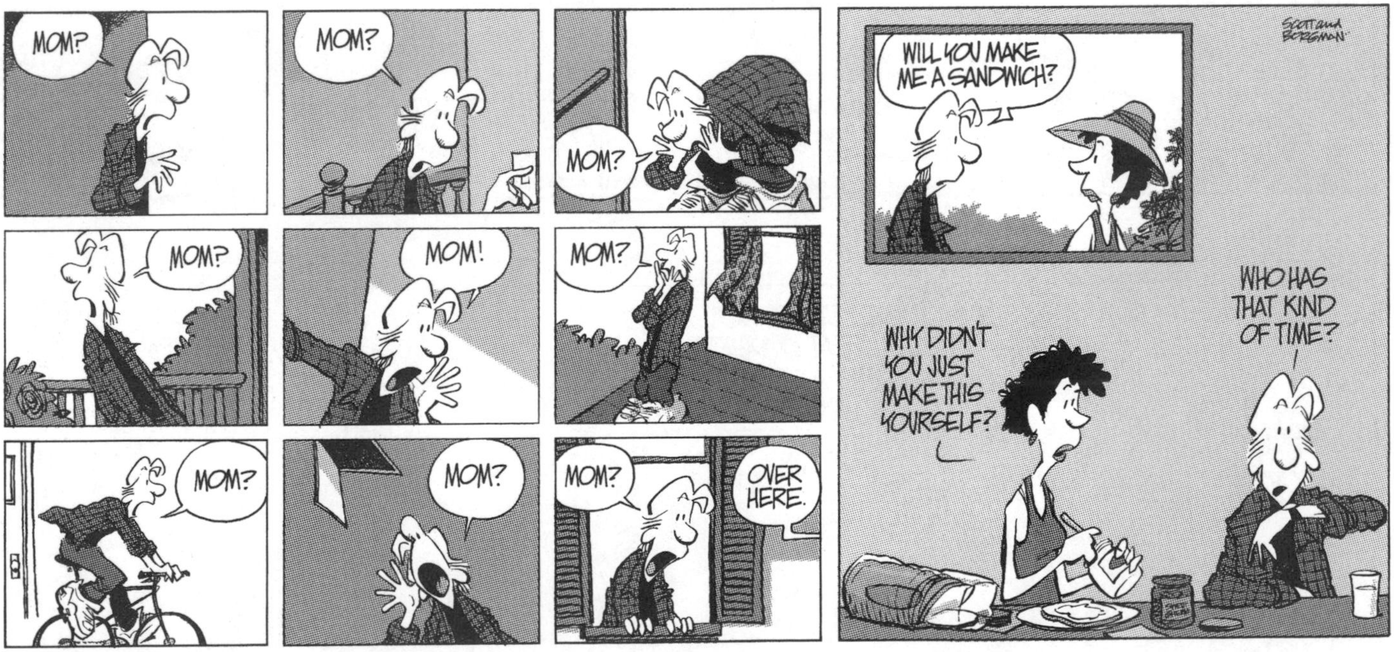
MOM?
MOM?
MOM?
MOM?
MOM!
MOM?
MOM?
MOM?
MOM?
OVER HERE.
SCOTT and BORGMAN
WILL YOU MAKE ME A SANDWICH?
WHY DIDN'T YOU JUST MAKE THIS YOURSELF?
WHO HAS THAT KIND OF TIME?

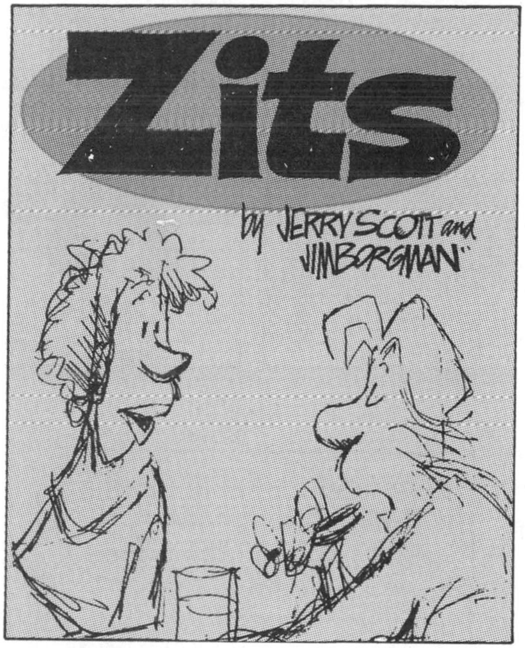
Zits
by JERRY SCOTT and JIM BORGMAN

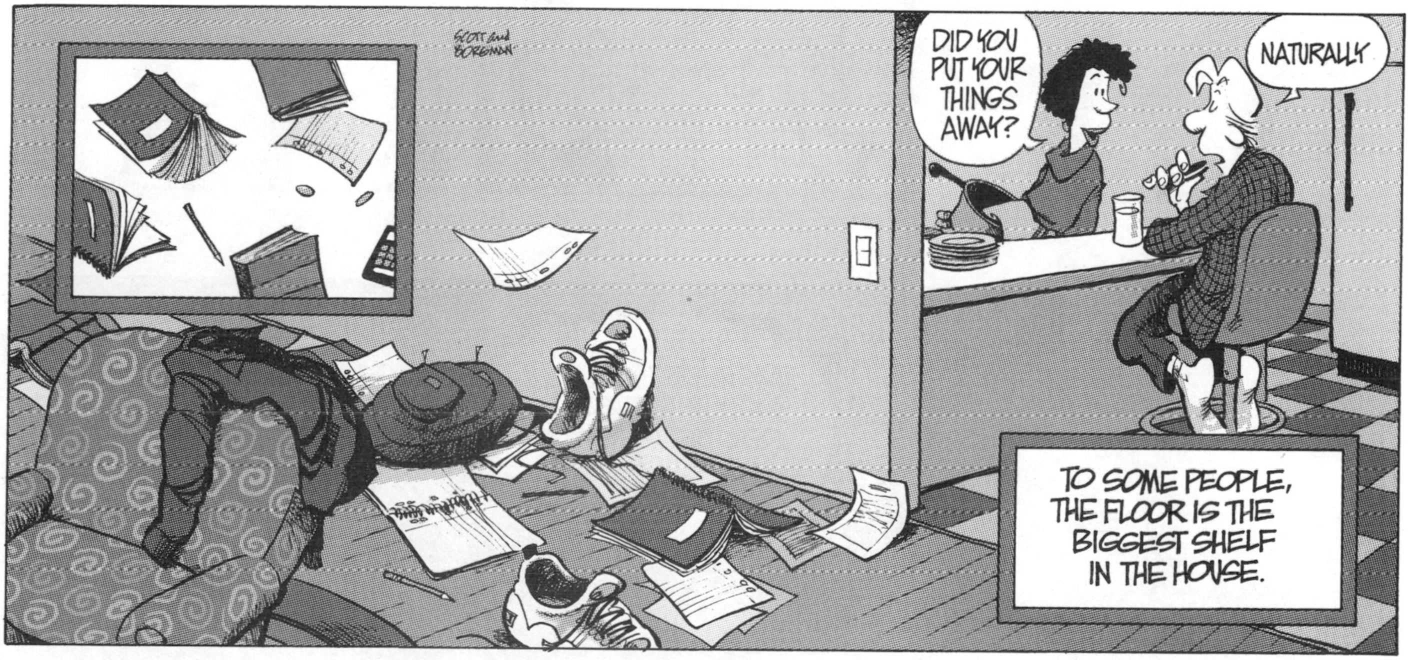
SCOTT and BORGMAN
DID YOU PUT YOUR THINGS AWAY?
NATURALLY
TO SOME PEOPLE, THE FLOOR IS THE BIGGEST SHELF IN THE HOUSE.

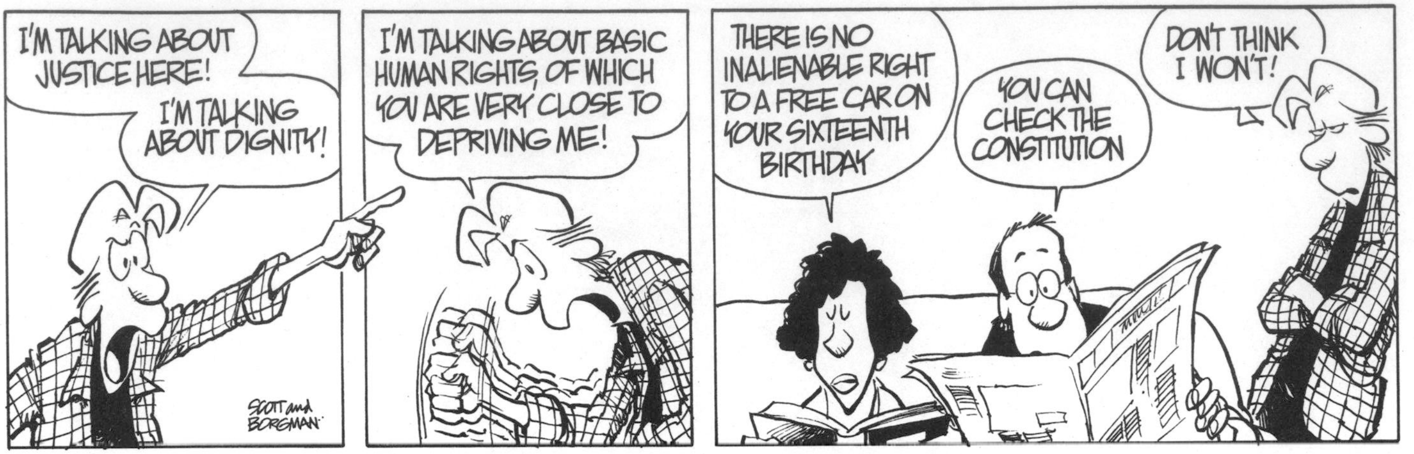
I'M TALKING ABOUT JUSTICE HERE!
I'M TALKING ABOUT DIGNITY!
SCOTT and BORGMAN
I'M TALKING ABOUT BASIC HUMAN RIGHTS, OF WHICH YOU ARE VERY CLOSE TO DEPRIVING ME!
THERE IS NO INALIENABLE RIGHT TO A FREE CAR ON YOUR SIXTEENTH BIRTHDAY
YOU CAN CHECK THE CONSTITUTION
DON'T THINK I WON'T!

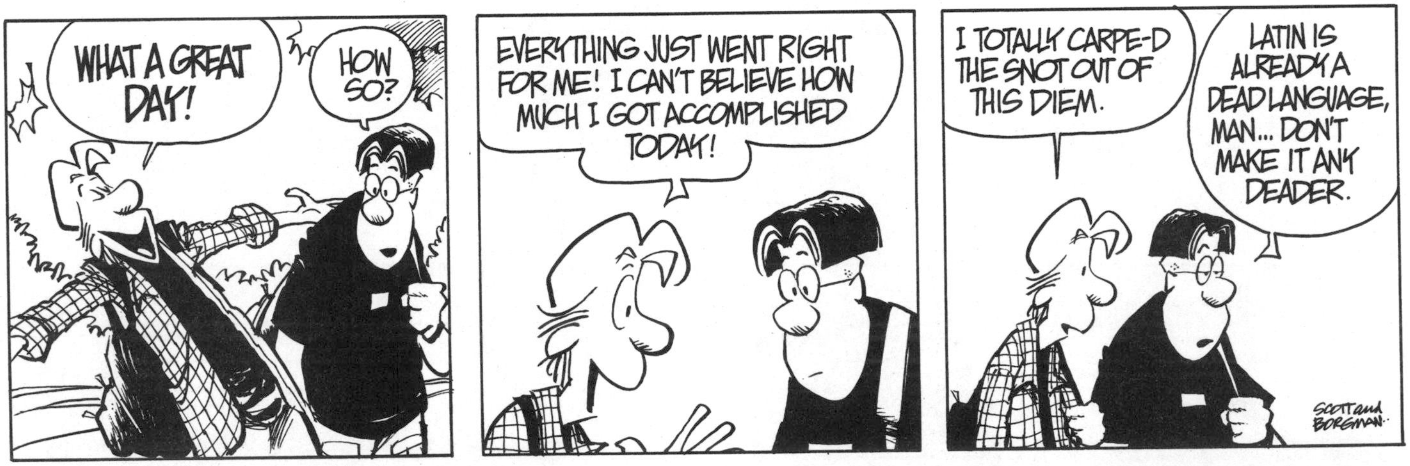
WHAT A GREAT DAY!
HOW SO?
EVERYTHING JUST WENT RIGHT FOR ME! I CAN'T BELIEVE HOW MUCH I GOT ACCOMPLISHED TODAY!
I TOTALLY CARPE-D THE SNOT OUT OF THIS DIEM.
LATIN IS ALREADY A DEAD LANGUAGE, MAN... DON'T MAKE IT ANY DEADER.
SCOTT and BORGMAN

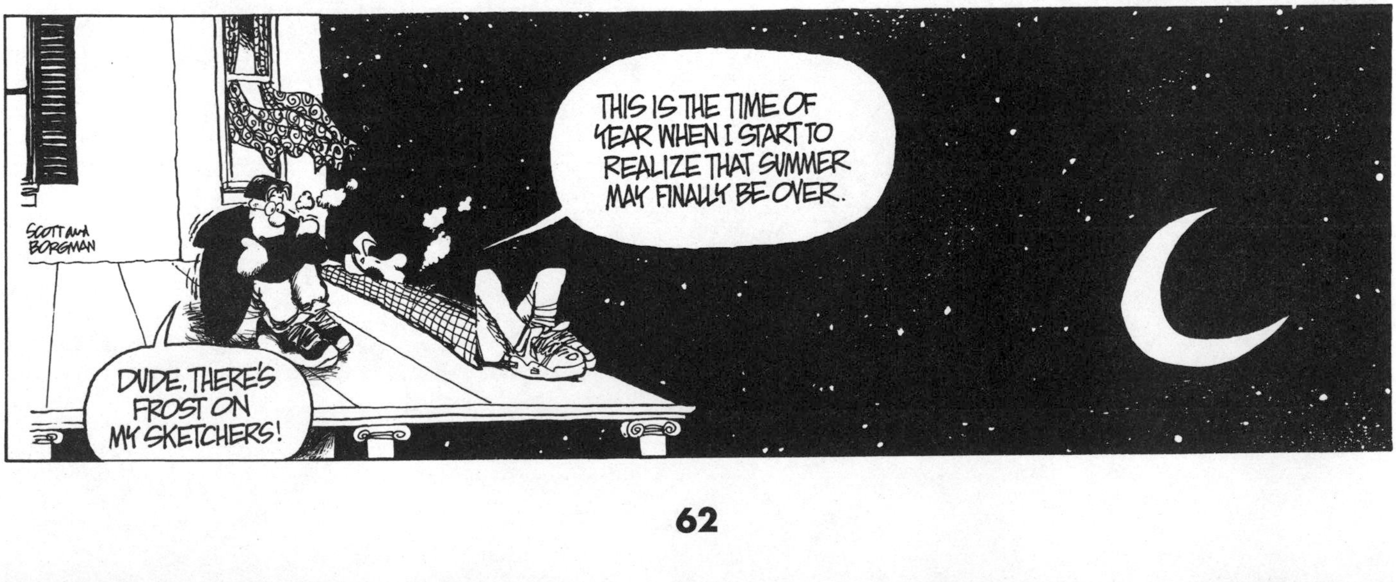
SCOTT and BORGMAN
THIS IS THE TIME OF YEAR WHEN I START TO REALIZE THAT SUMMER MAY FINALLY BE OVER.
DUDE, THERE'S FROST ON MY SKETCHERS!

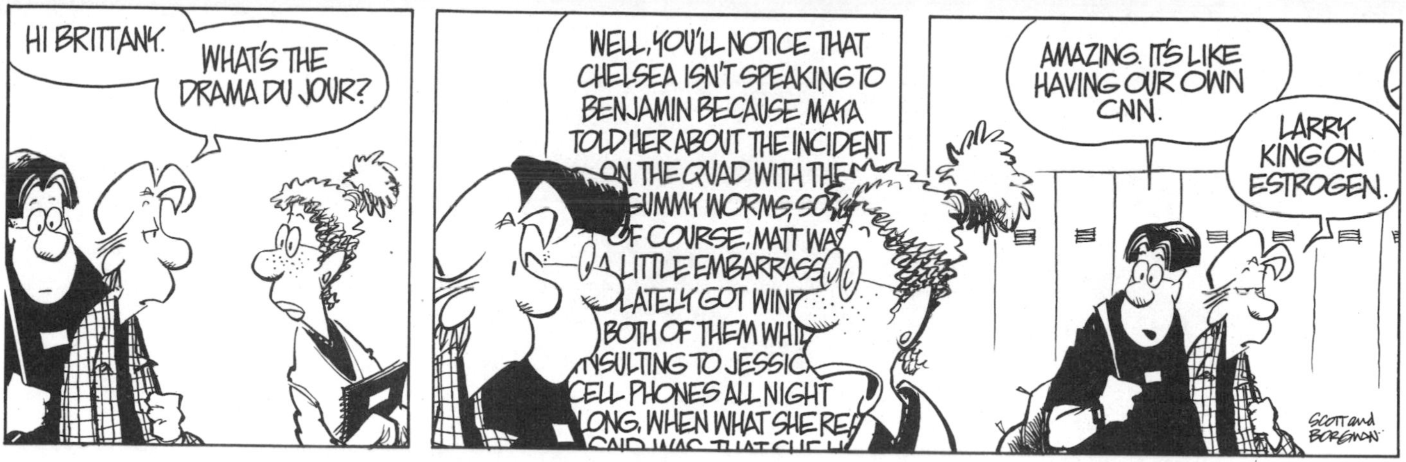
HI BRITTANY.
WHAT'S THE DRAMA DU JOUR?
WELL, YOU'LL NOTICE THAT CHELSEA ISN'T SPEAKING TO BENJAMIN BECAUSE MAYA TOLD HER ABOUT THE INCIDENT ON THE QUAD WITH THE GUMMY WORMS, SO OF COURSE, MATT WAS A LITTLE EMBARRASS LATELY GOT WIN BOTH OF THEM WHI NSULTING TO JESSIC CELL PHONES ALL NIGHT LONG, WHEN WHAT SHE RE
AMAZING. IT'S LIKE HAVING OUR OWN CNN.
LARRY KING ON ESTROGEN.
SCOTT and BORGMAN

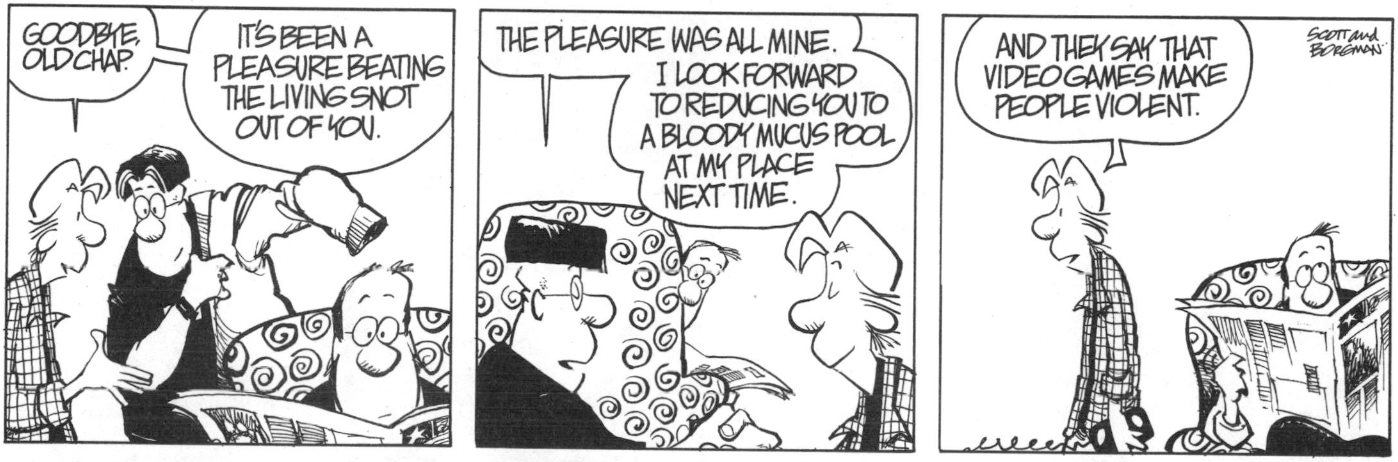
GOODBYE, OLD CHAP.
IT'S BEEN A PLEASURE BEATING THE LIVING SNOT OUT OF YOU.
THE PLEASURE WAS ALL MINE.
I LOOK FORWARD TO REDUCING YOU TO A BLOODY MUCUS POOL AT MY PLACE NEXT TIME.
AND THEY SAY THAT VIDEO GAMES MAKE PEOPLE VIOLENT.
SCOTT and BORGMAN

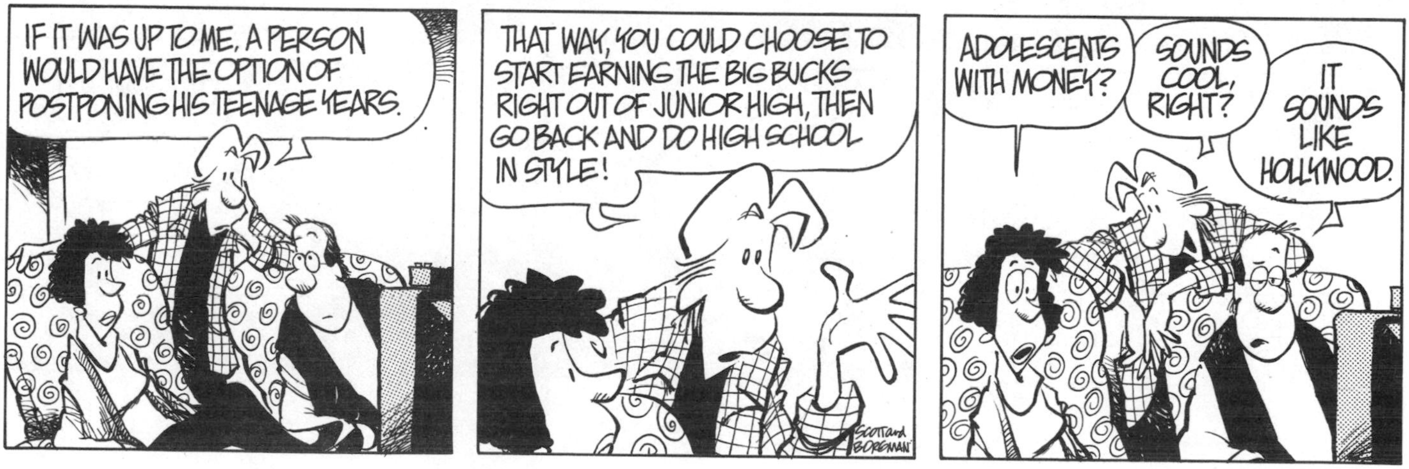
IF IT WAS UP TO ME, A PERSON WOULD HAVE THE OPTION OF POSTPONING HIS TEENAGE YEARS.
THAT WAY, YOU COULD CHOOSE TO START EARNING THE BIG BUCKS RIGHT OUT OF JUNIOR HIGH, THEN GO BACK AND DO HIGH SCHOOL IN STYLE!
SCOTT and BORGMAN
ADOLESCENTS WITH MONEY?
SOUNDS COOL, RIGHT?
IT SOUNDS LIKE HOLLYWOOD.

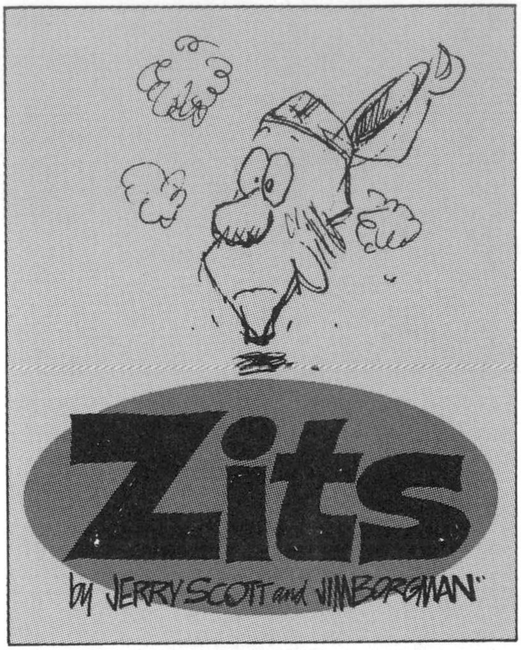
Zits
by JERRY SCOTT and JIM BORGMAN

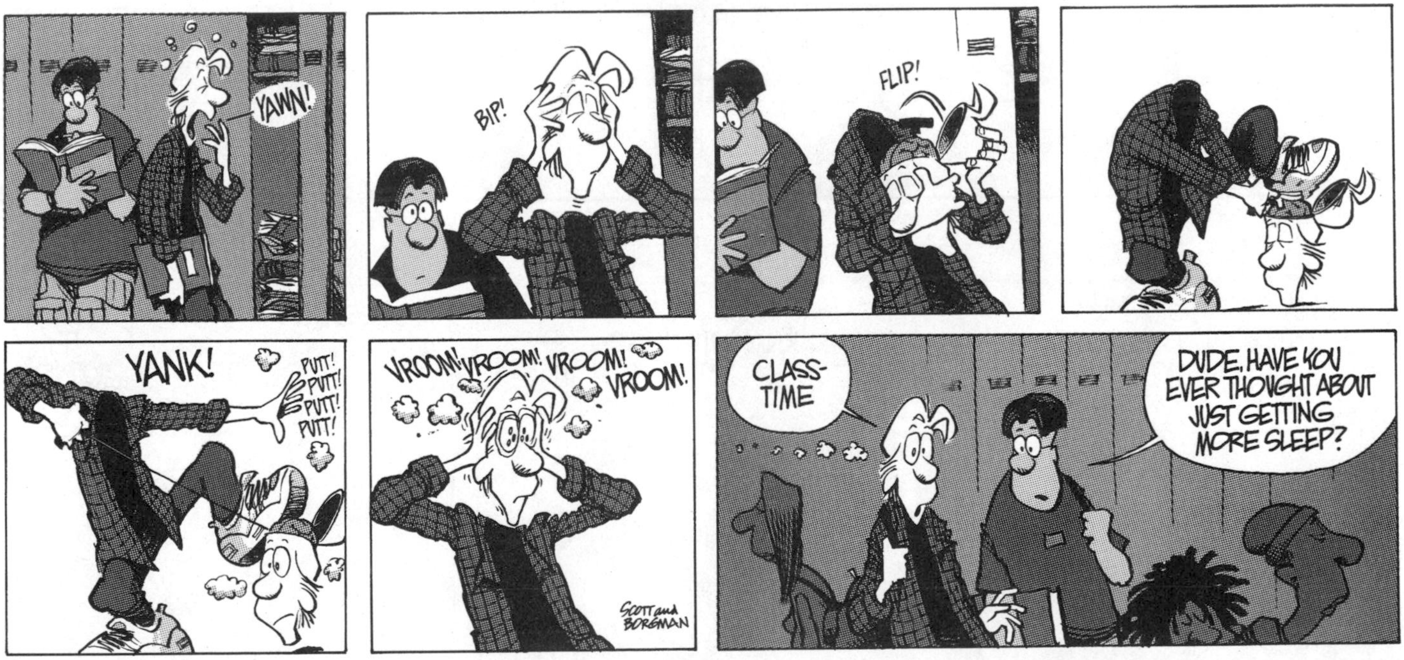
YAWN!
BIP!
FLIP!
YANK!
PUTT! PUTT! PUTT! PUTT!
VROOM! VROOM! VROOM! VROOM!
SCOTT and BORGMAN
CLASS-TIME
DUDE, HAVE YOU EVER THOUGHT ABOUT JUST GETTING MORE SLEEP?

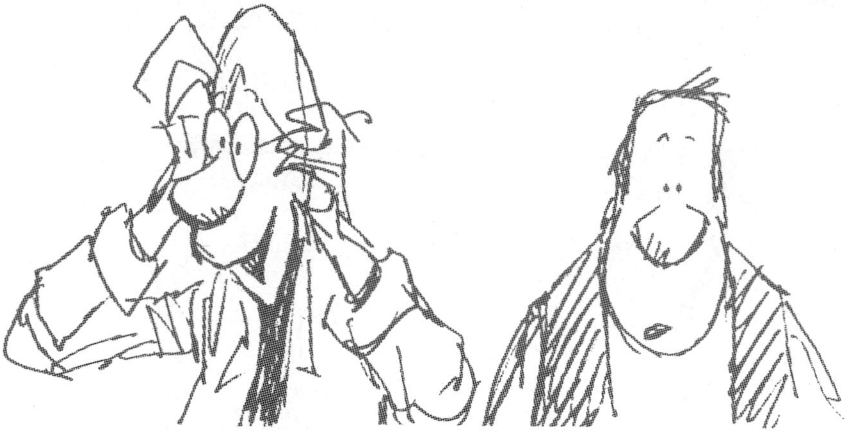

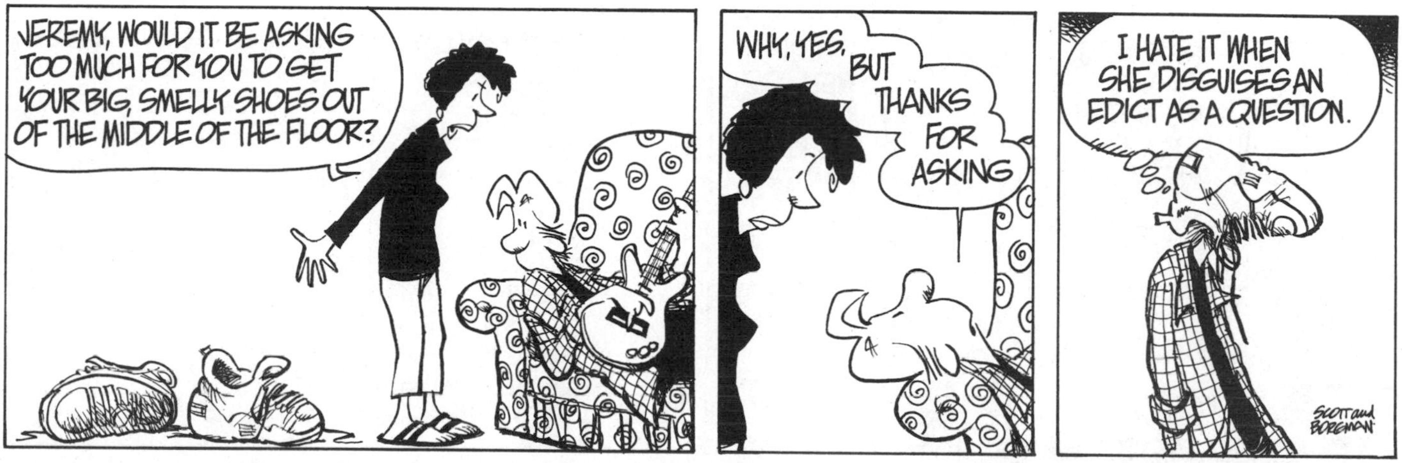

JEREMY, WOULD IT BE ASKING TOO MUCH FOR YOU TO GET YOUR BIG, SMELLY SHOES OUT OF THE MIDDLE OF THE FLOOR?
WHY, YES,
BUT THANKS FOR ASKING
I HATE IT WHEN SHE DISGUISES AN EDICT AS A QUESTION.
SCOTT and BORGMAN

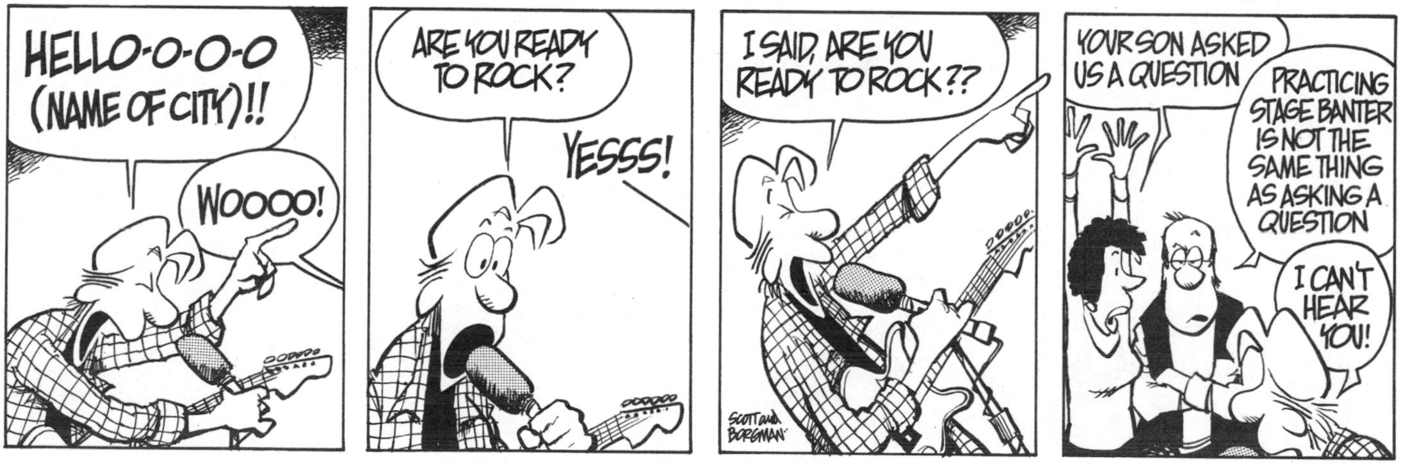

HELLO-O-O-O (NAME OF CITY)!!
WOOOO!
ARE YOU READY TO ROCK?
YESSS!
I SAID, ARE YOU READY TO ROCK??
SCOTT and BORGMAN
YOUR SON ASKED US A QUESTION
PRACTICING STAGE BANTER IS NOT THE SAME THING AS ASKING A QUESTION
I CAN'T HEAR YOU!

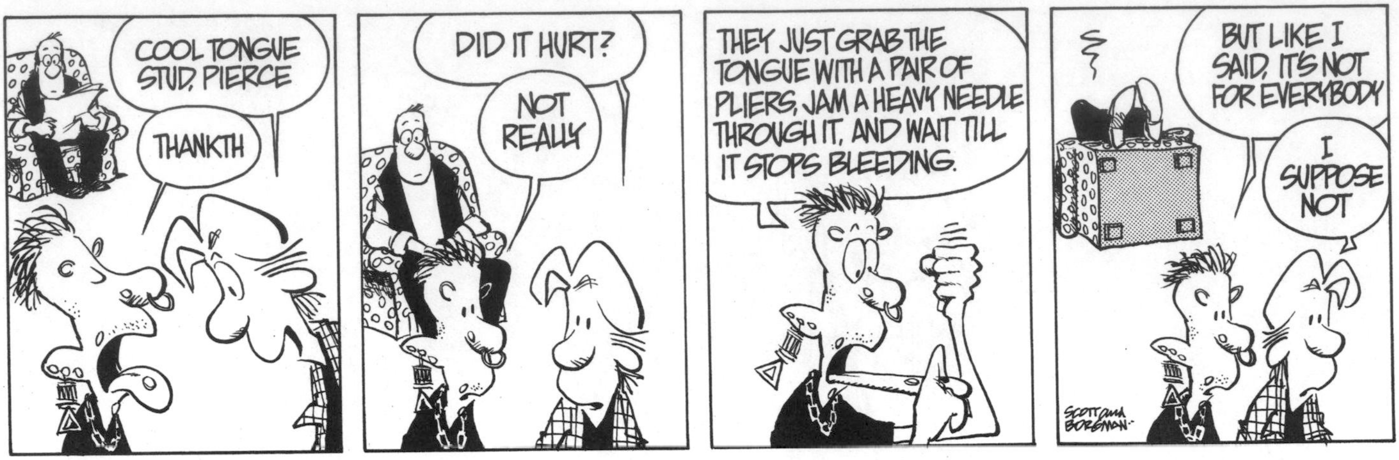
COOL TONGUE STUD, PIERCE
THANKTH
DID IT HURT?
NOT REALLY
THEY JUST GRAB THE TONGUE WITH A PAIR OF PLIERS, JAM A HEAVY NEEDLE THROUGH IT, AND WAIT TILL IT STOPS BLEEDING.
BUT LIKE I SAID, IT'S NOT FOR EVERYBODY
I SUPPOSE NOT

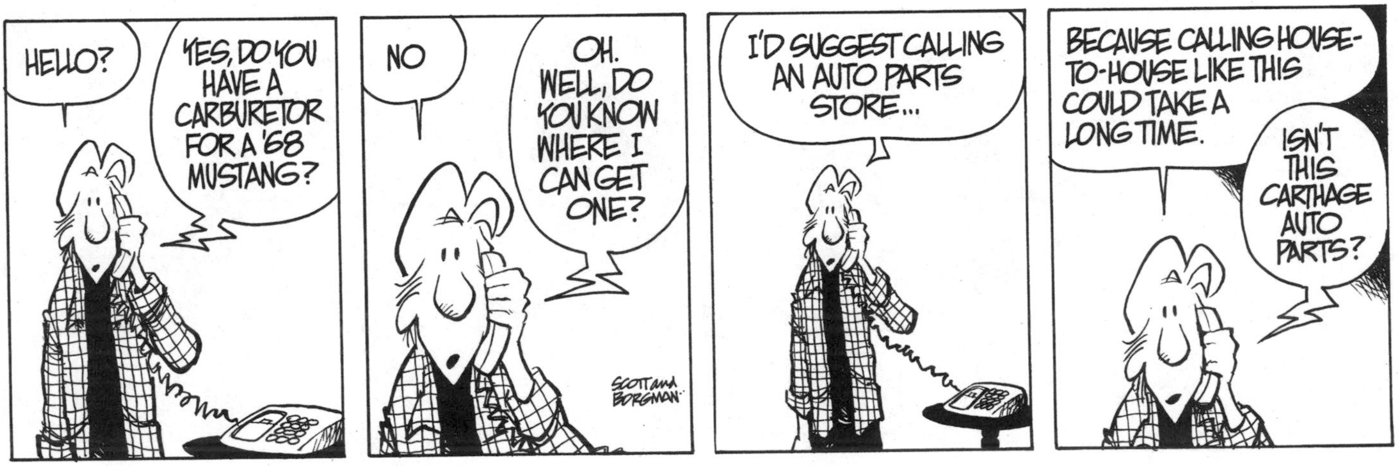
HELLO?
YES, DO YOU HAVE A CARBURETOR FOR A '68 MUSTANG?
NO
OH. WELL, DO YOU KNOW WHERE I CAN GET ONE?
I'D SUGGEST CALLING AN AUTO PARTS STORE...
BECAUSE CALLING HOUSE-TO-HOUSE LIKE THIS COULD TAKE A LONG TIME.
ISN'T THIS CARTHAGE AUTO PARTS?

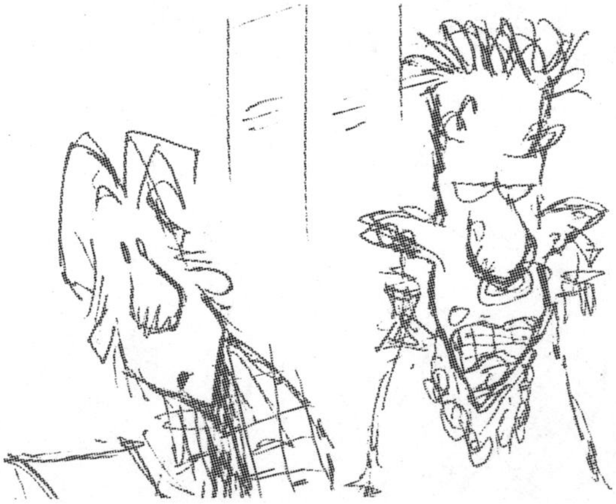

OKAY, MISTER, LET'S HAVE IT!
I WANT THE TRUTH, THE WHOLE TRUTH...
...AND MORE TRUTH THAN IS JUST TECHNICALLY NECESSARY TO AVOID TELLING A LIE.
UH-OH

PEOPLE
PEOPLE
PEOPLE!
YOU'RE IN YOUR PAJAMAS BY 8, YOU WATCH TV UNTIL 9:30 AND YOU GO TO BED AT 10!
WHAT'S WRONG WITH THIS PICTURE?
TOO MUCH TV?
I COULD STAND TO TURN IN EARLIER IF YOU COULD
SOMEBODY PLEASE TELL ME I'M ADOPTED!!!
NOPE. I CAN PROVE IT IF YOU WANT TO SEE THE SCAR.
'NITE

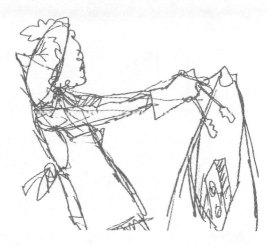

Zits
by JERRY SCOTT and JIM BORGMAN

GOOD MORNING, JEREMY
WHAT'S GOOD ABOUT IT?
TSK! YOU'RE ALWAYS SO GLOOMY IN THE MORNING!
MAYBE YOU'D FEEL BETTER IF YOU TRIED LOOKING ON THE BRIGHT SIDE FOR A CHANGE.
"THE BRIGHT SIDE"
GOLLY!
WHY DIDN'T I THINK OF THAT? I CAN SOLVE ALL OF MY PROBLEMS BY SIMPLY HAVING HAPPY THOUGHTS!
I SEE THAT THE SUN ROSE RIGHT ON SCHEDULE AGAIN!
DON'T YOU LOVE HOW PAINT STICKS TO WALLS ALL BY ITSELF?
SNIFF! AHH! GOOD OLD OXYGEN!
WELL, I'M OFF TO TAKE ADVANTAGE OF ANOTHER DAY OF FREE, TAXPAYER-SUPPORTED PUBLIC EDUCATION!
LUCKY ME!
CRUD.
I DO FEEL BETTER.
SCOTT and BORGMAN

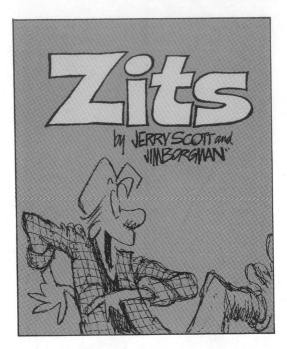

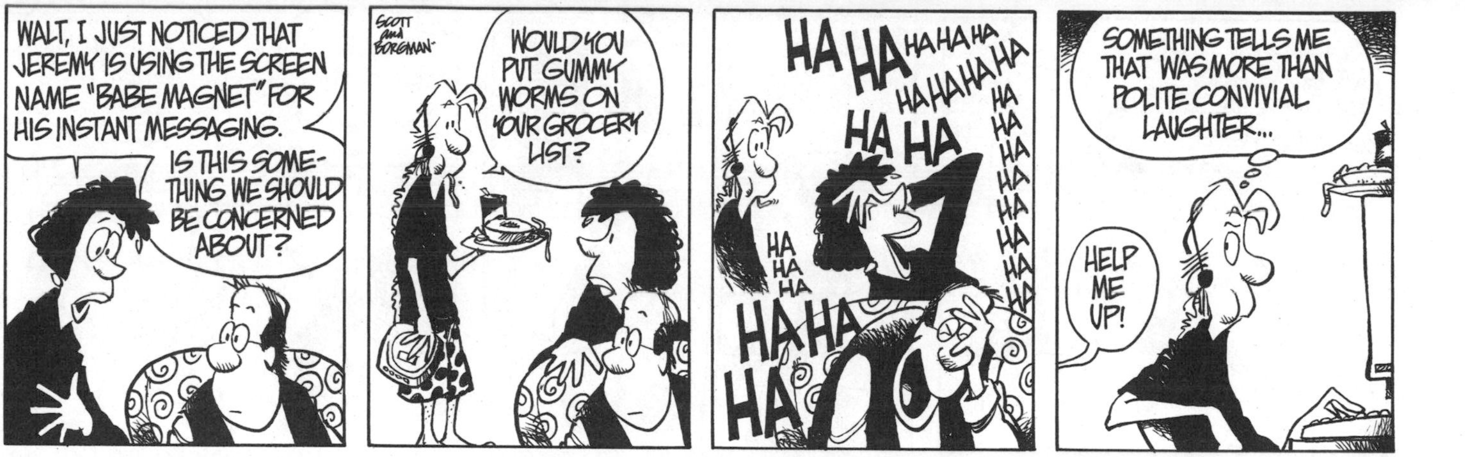
WALT, I JUST NOTICED THAT JEREMY IS USING THE SCREEN NAME "BABE MAGNET" FOR HIS INSTANT MESSAGING.
IS THIS SOMETHING WE SHOULD BE CONCERNED ABOUT?
SCOTT AND BORGMAN
WOULD YOU PUT GUMMY WORMS ON YOUR GROCERY LIST?
HA HA HA HA HA HA HA HA HA HA HA
HA HA
HA HA HA HA HA HA HA HA HA HA
HA HA HA
HA HA HA
SOMETHING TELLS ME THAT WAS MORE THAN POLITE CONVIVIAL LAUGHTER...
HELP ME UP!

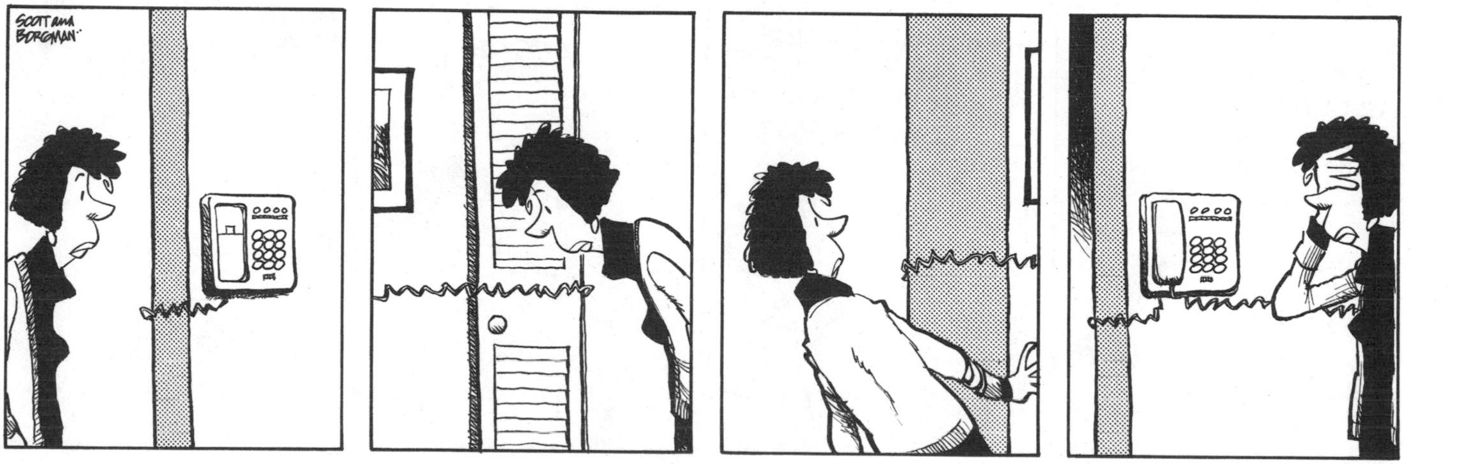
SCOTT AND BORGMAN

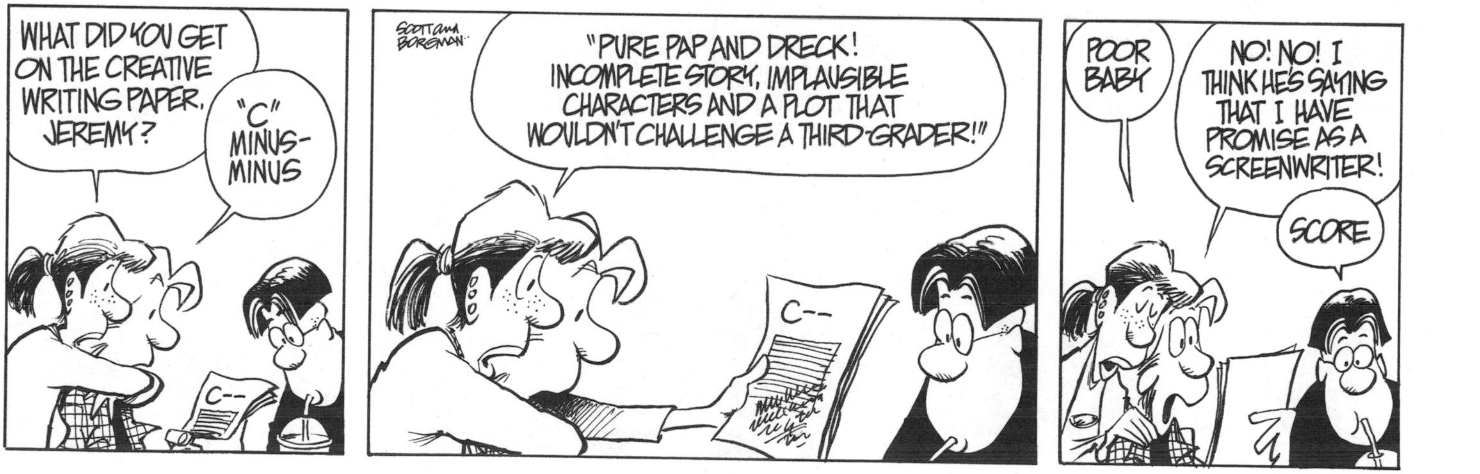
WHAT DID YOU GET ON THE CREATIVE WRITING PAPER, JEREMY?
"C" MINUS-MINUS
C--
SCOTT AND BORGMAN
"PURE PAP AND DRECK! INCOMPLETE STORY, IMPLAUSIBLE CHARACTERS AND A PLOT THAT WOULDN'T CHALLENGE A THIRD-GRADER!"
C--
POOR BABY
NO! NO! I THINK HE'S SAYING THAT I HAVE PROMISE AS A SCREENWRITER!
SCORE

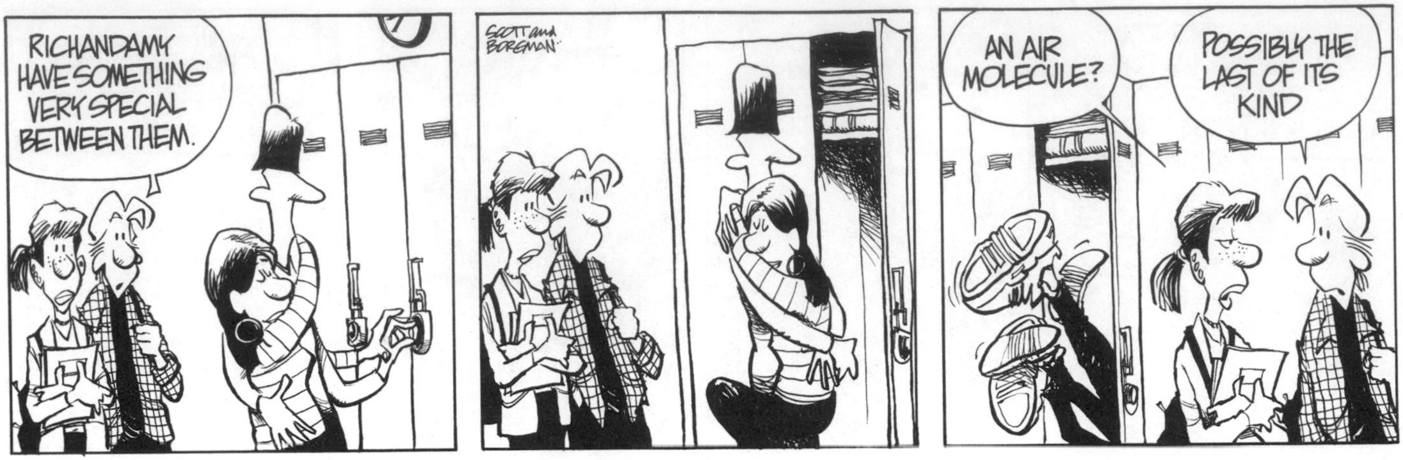
RICH AND AMY HAVE SOMETHING VERY SPECIAL BETWEEN THEM.
SCOTT and BORGMAN
AN AIR MOLECULE?
POSSIBLY THE LAST OF ITS KIND

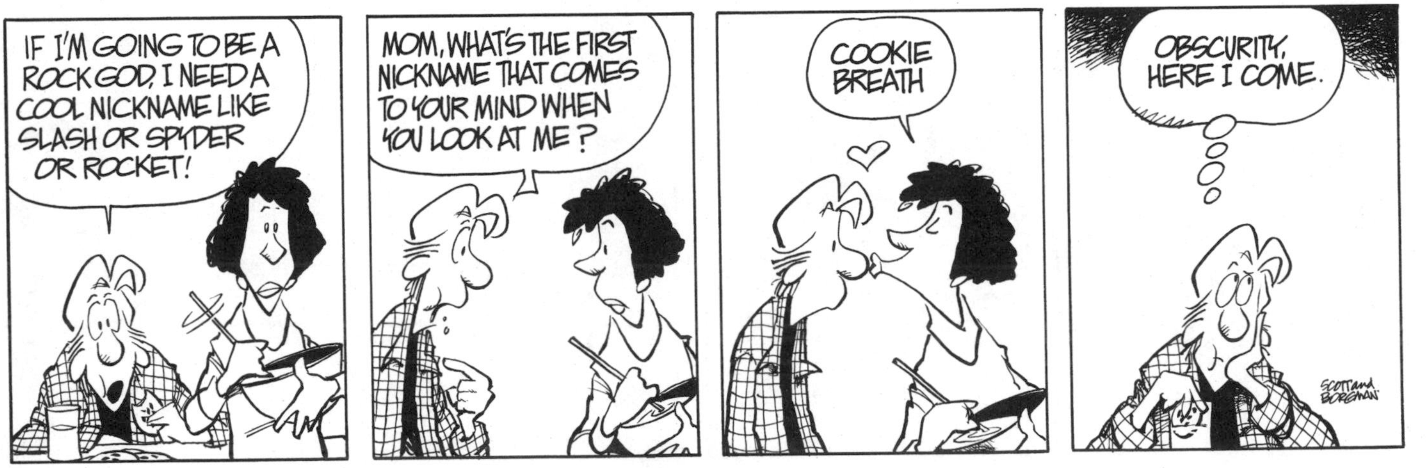
IF I'M GOING TO BE A ROCK GOD, I NEED A COOL NICKNAME LIKE SLASH OR SPYDER OR ROCKET!
MOM, WHAT'S THE FIRST NICKNAME THAT COMES TO YOUR MIND WHEN YOU LOOK AT ME?
COOKIE BREATH
OBSCURITY, HERE I COME.
SCOTT and BORGMAN

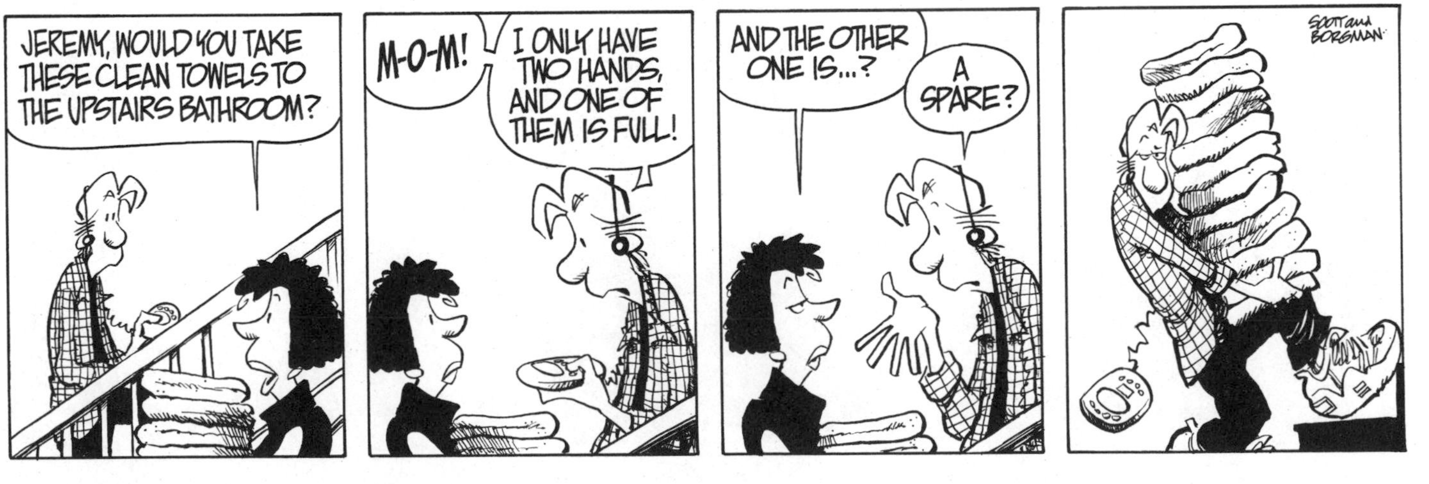
JEREMY, WOULD YOU TAKE THESE CLEAN TOWELS TO THE UPSTAIRS BATHROOM?
M-O-M!
I ONLY HAVE TWO HANDS, AND ONE OF THEM IS FULL!
AND THE OTHER ONE IS...?
A SPARE?
SCOTT and BORGMAN

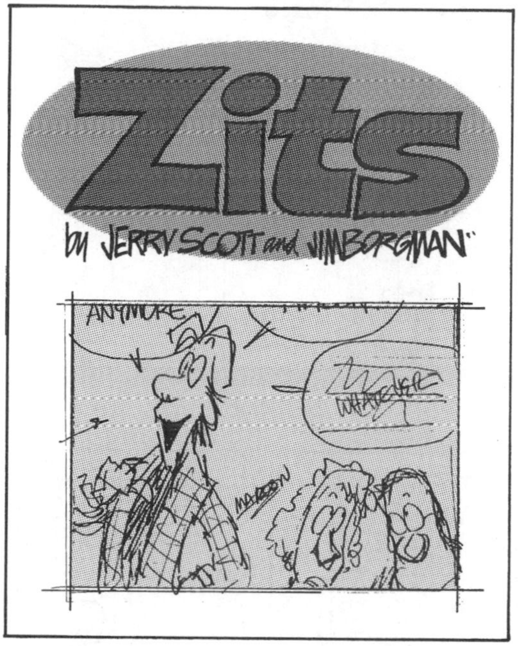
Zits
by JERRY SCOTT and JIM BORGMAN
ANYMORE

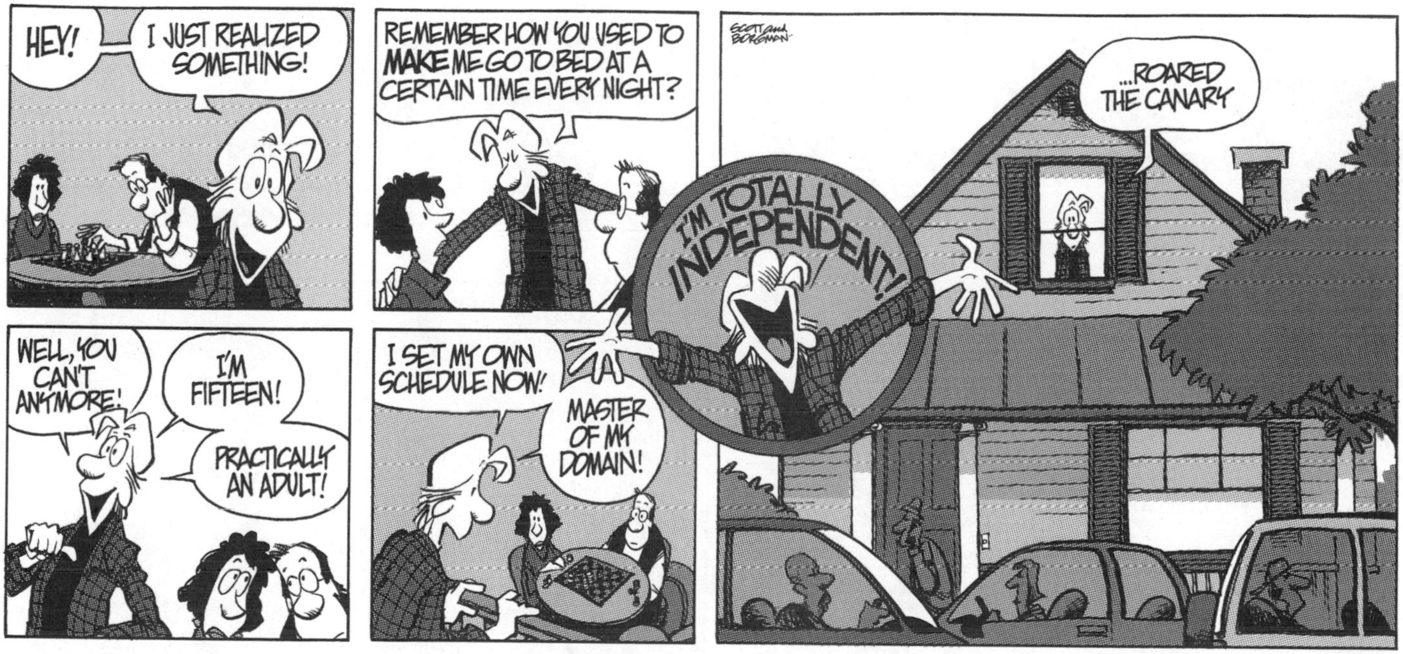
HEY!
I JUST REALIZED SOMETHING!
REMEMBER HOW YOU USED TO **MAKE** ME GO TO BED AT A CERTAIN TIME EVERY NIGHT?
WELL, YOU CAN'T ANYMORE!
I'M FIFTEEN!
PRACTICALLY AN ADULT!
I SET MY OWN SCHEDULE NOW!
MASTER OF MY DOMAIN!
SCOTT and BORGMAN
I'M TOTALLY INDEPENDENT!
...ROARED THE CANARY

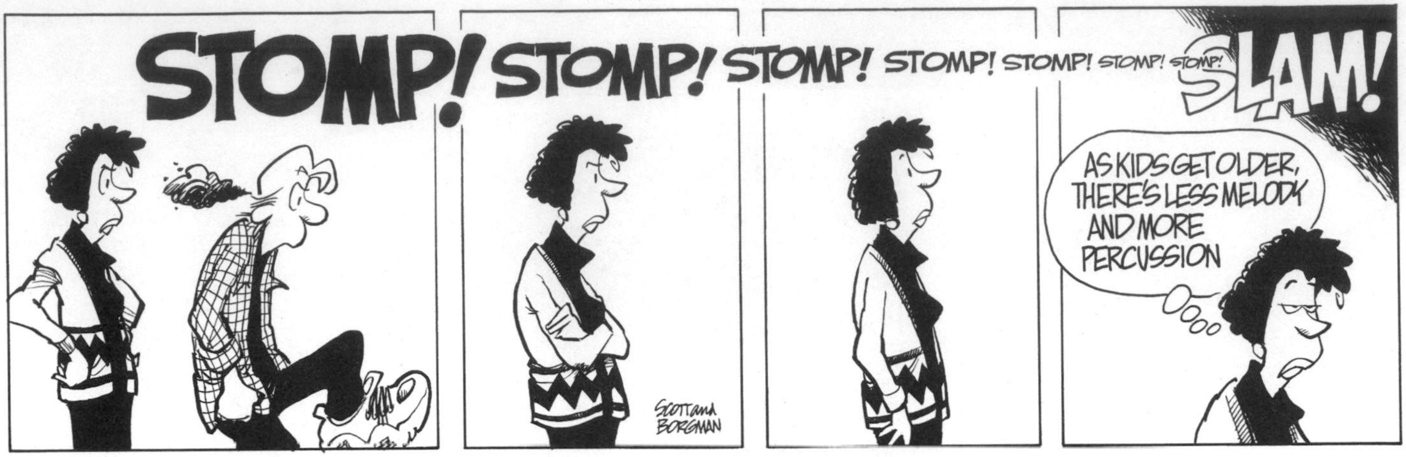
STOMP! STOMP! STOMP! STOMP! STOMP! STOMP! STOMP!
SLAM!
SCOTT and BORGMAN
AS KIDS GET OLDER, THERE'S LESS MELODY AND MORE PERCUSSION

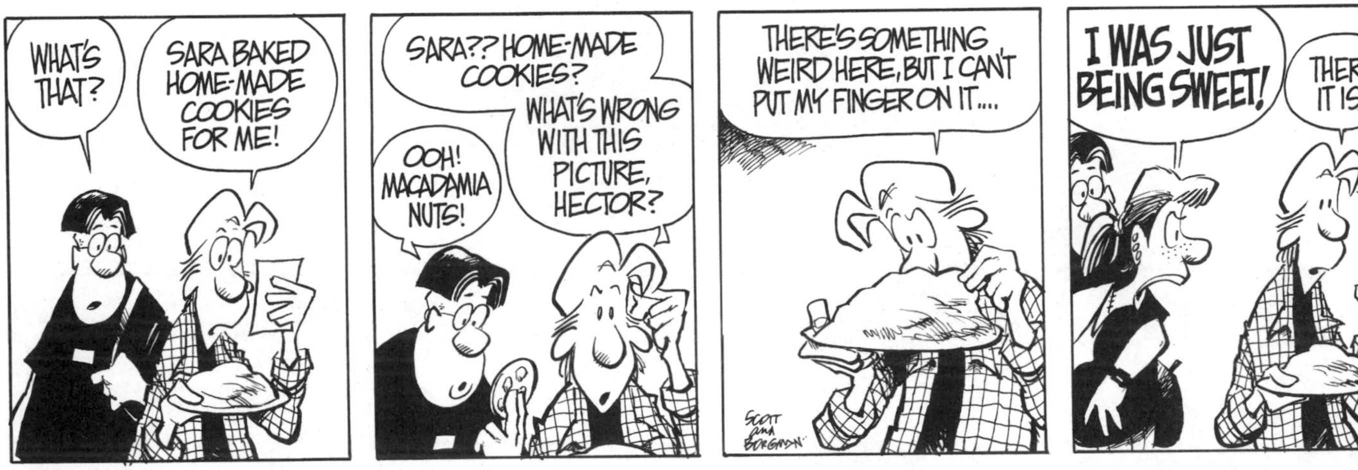
WHAT'S THAT?
SARA BAKED HOME-MADE COOKIES FOR ME!
SARA?? HOME-MADE COOKIES?
WHAT'S WRONG WITH THIS PICTURE, HECTOR?
OOH! MACADAMIA NUTS!
THERE'S SOMETHING WEIRD HERE, BUT I CAN'T PUT MY FINGER ON IT....
SCOTT and BORGMAN
I WAS JUST BEING SWEET!
THERE IT IS!

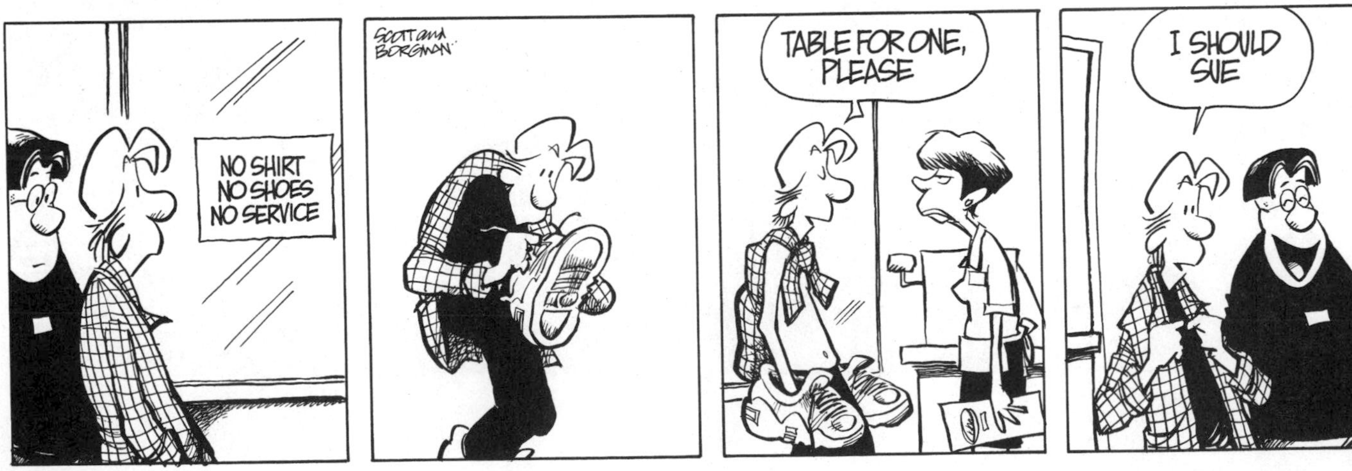
NO SHIRT NO SHOES NO SERVICE
SCOTT and BORGMAN
TABLE FOR ONE, PLEASE
I SHOULD SUE

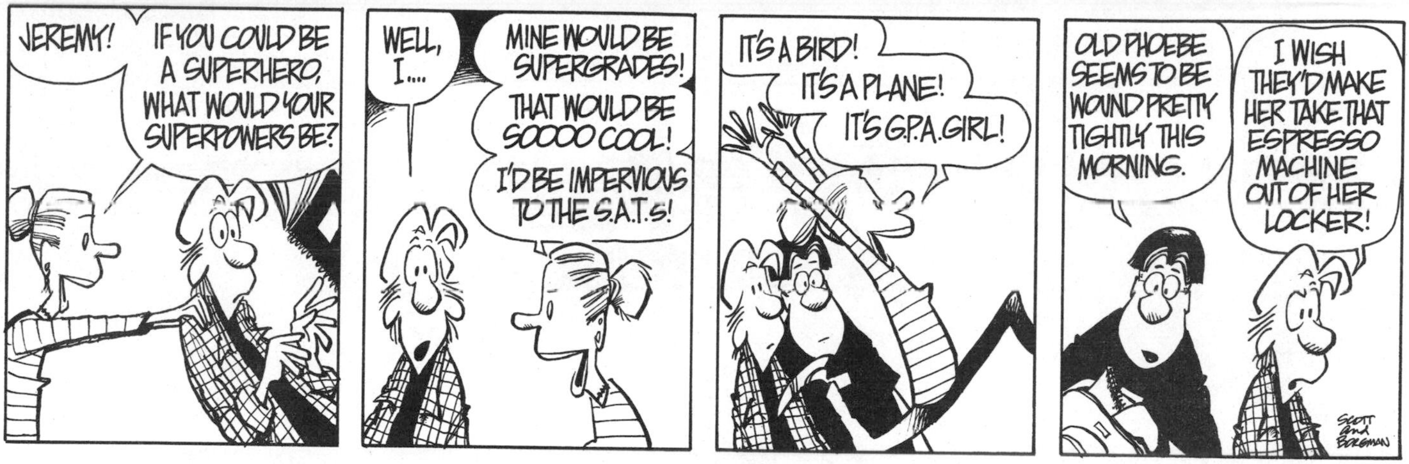
JEREMY!
IF YOU COULD BE A SUPERHERO, WHAT WOULD YOUR SUPERPOWERS BE?
WELL, I....
MINE WOULD BE SUPERGRADES!
THAT WOULD BE SOOOO COOL!
I'D BE IMPERVIOUS TO THE S.A.T.s!
IT'S A BIRD!
IT'S A PLANE!
IT'S G.P.A. GIRL!
OLD PHOEBE SEEMS TO BE WOUND PRETTY TIGHTLY THIS MORNING.
I WISH THEY'D MAKE HER TAKE THAT ESPRESSO MACHINE OUT OF HER LOCKER!
SCOTT and BORGMAN

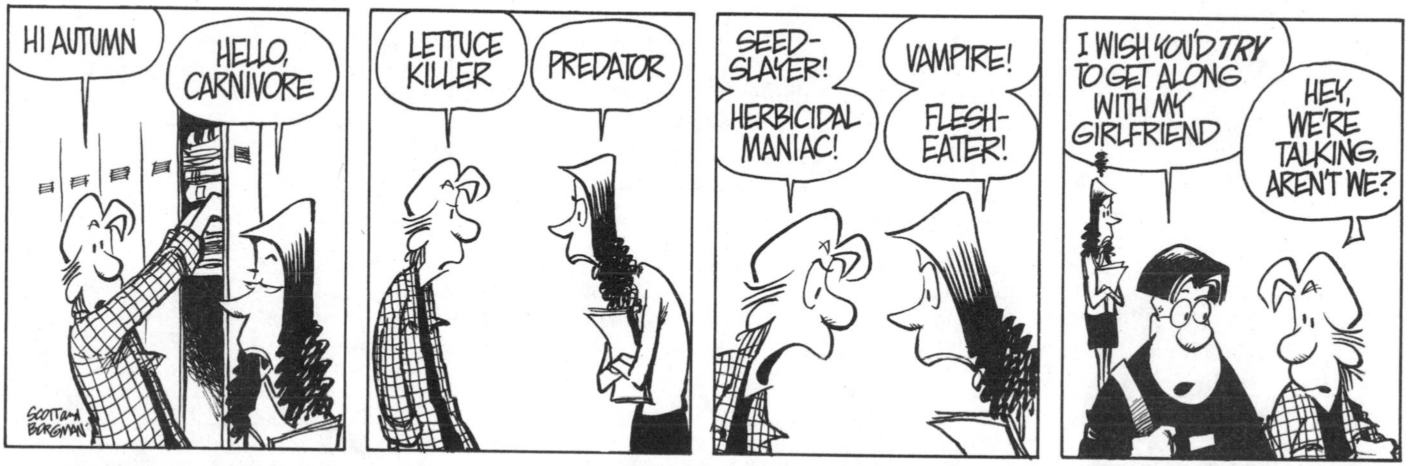
HI AUTUMN
HELLO, CARNIVORE
SCOTT and BORGMAN
LETTUCE KILLER
PREDATOR
SEED-SLAYER!
HERBICIDAL MANIAC!
VAMPIRE!
FLESH-EATER!
I WISH YOU'D TRY TO GET ALONG WITH MY GIRLFRIEND
HEY, WE'RE TALKING, AREN'T WE?

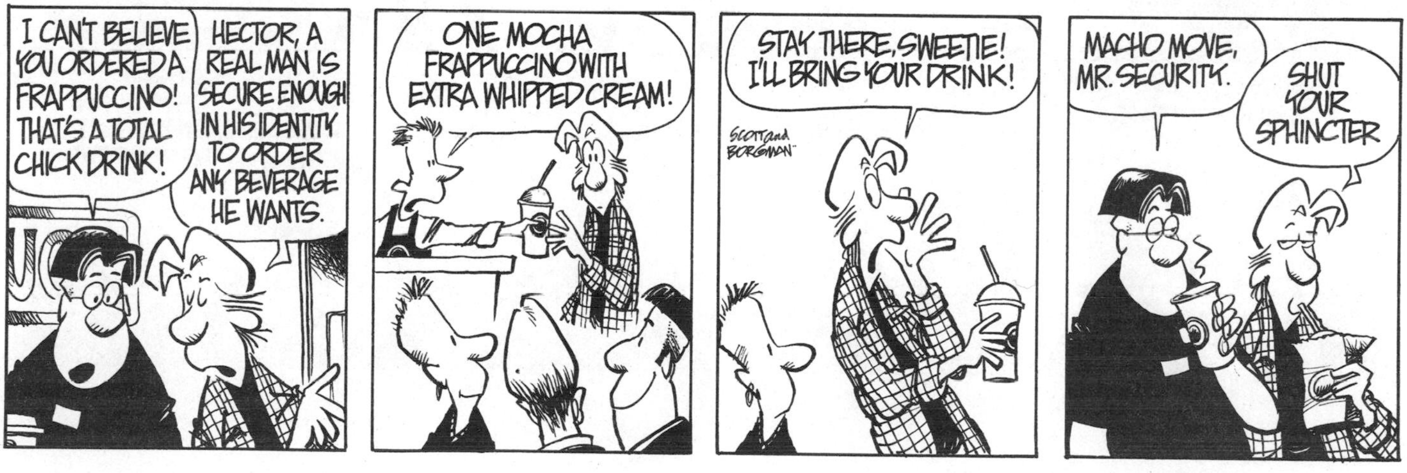
I CAN'T BELIEVE YOU ORDERED A FRAPPUCCINO! THAT'S A TOTAL CHICK DRINK!
HECTOR, A REAL MAN IS SECURE ENOUGH IN HIS IDENTITY TO ORDER ANY BEVERAGE HE WANTS.
ONE MOCHA FRAPPUCCINO WITH EXTRA WHIPPED CREAM!
STAY THERE, SWEETIE! I'LL BRING YOUR DRINK!
SCOTT and BORGMAN
MACHO MOVE, MR. SECURITY.
SHUT YOUR SPHINCTER

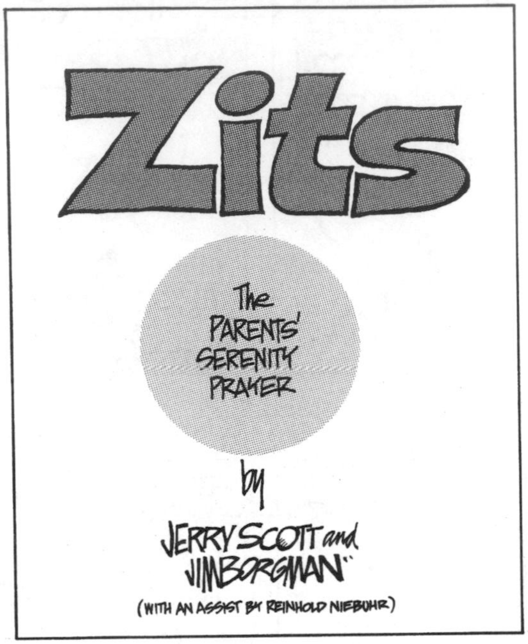
Zits
The Parents' Serenity Prayer
by
Jerry Scott and Jim Borgman
(with an assist by Reinhold Niebuhr)

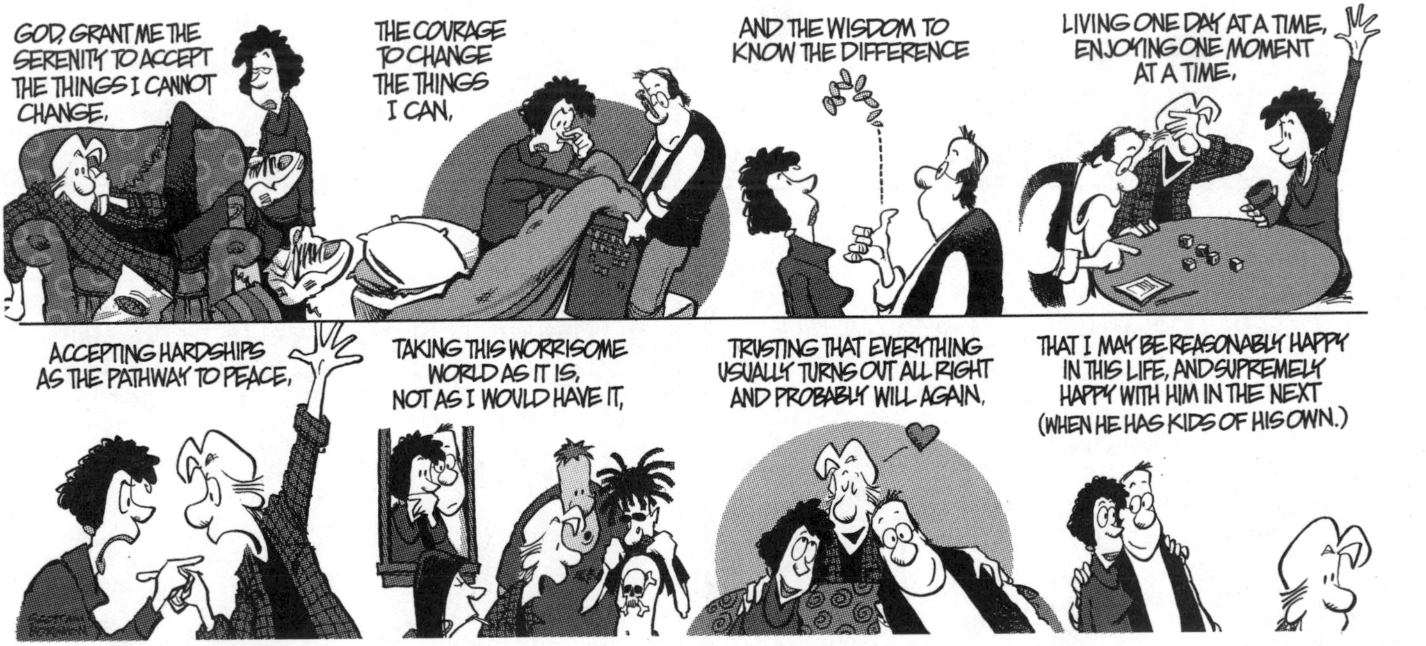
GOD, GRANT ME THE SERENITY TO ACCEPT THE THINGS I CANNOT CHANGE,
THE COURAGE TO CHANGE THE THINGS I CAN,
AND THE WISDOM TO KNOW THE DIFFERENCE
LIVING ONE DAY AT A TIME, ENJOYING ONE MOMENT AT A TIME,
ACCEPTING HARDSHIPS AS THE PATHWAY TO PEACE,
TAKING THIS WORRISOME WORLD AS IT IS, NOT AS I WOULD HAVE IT,
TRUSTING THAT EVERYTHING USUALLY TURNS OUT ALL RIGHT AND PROBABLY WILL AGAIN,
THAT I MAY BE REASONABLY HAPPY IN THIS LIFE, AND SUPREMELY HAPPY WITH HIM IN THE NEXT (WHEN HE HAS KIDS OF HIS OWN.)

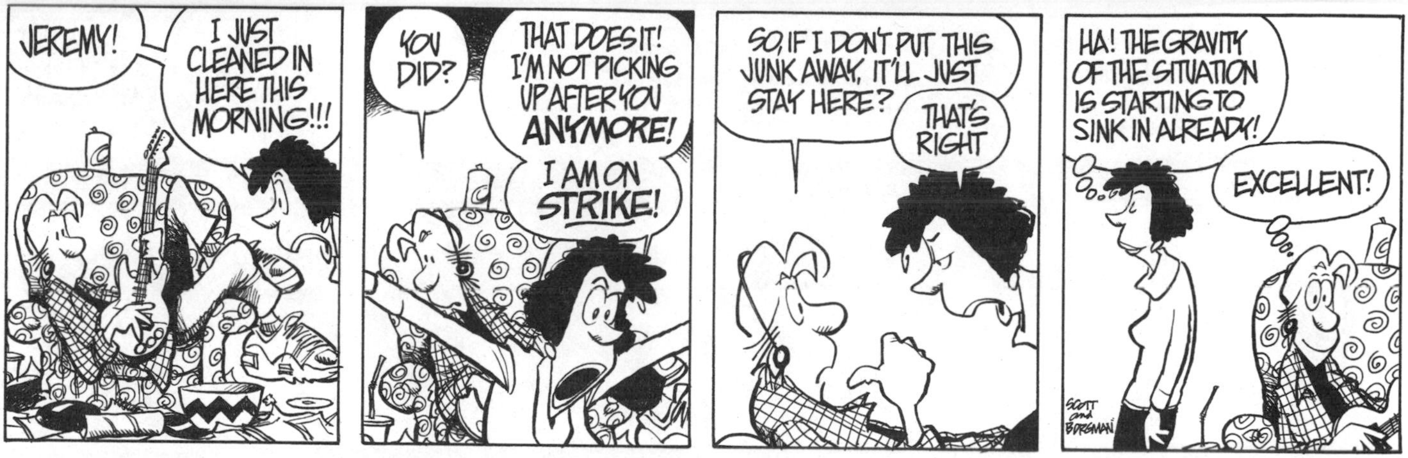
JEREMY!
I JUST CLEANED IN HERE THIS MORNING!!!
YOU DID?
THAT DOES IT! I'M NOT PICKING UP AFTER YOU ANYMORE!
I AM ON STRIKE!
SO, IF I DON'T PUT THIS JUNK AWAY, IT'LL JUST STAY HERE?
THAT'S RIGHT
HA! THE GRAVITY OF THE SITUATION IS STARTING TO SINK IN ALREADY!
EXCELLENT!
SCOTT and BORGMAN

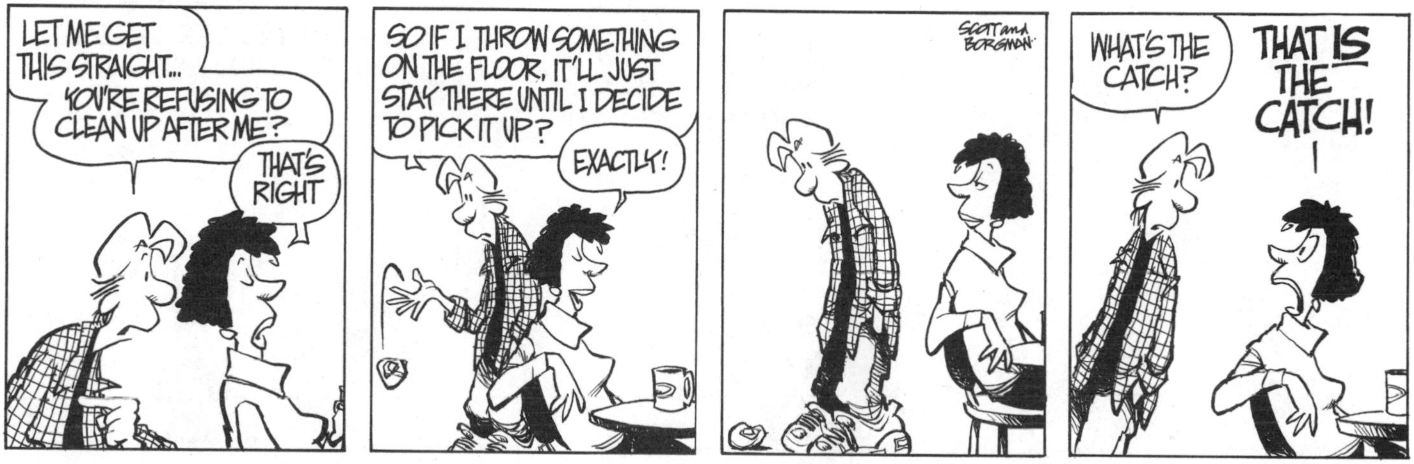
LET ME GET THIS STRAIGHT... YOU'RE REFUSING TO CLEAN UP AFTER ME?
THAT'S RIGHT
SO IF I THROW SOMETHING ON THE FLOOR, IT'LL JUST STAY THERE UNTIL I DECIDE TO PICK IT UP?
EXACTLY!
SCOTT and BORGMAN
WHAT'S THE CATCH?
THAT IS THE CATCH!

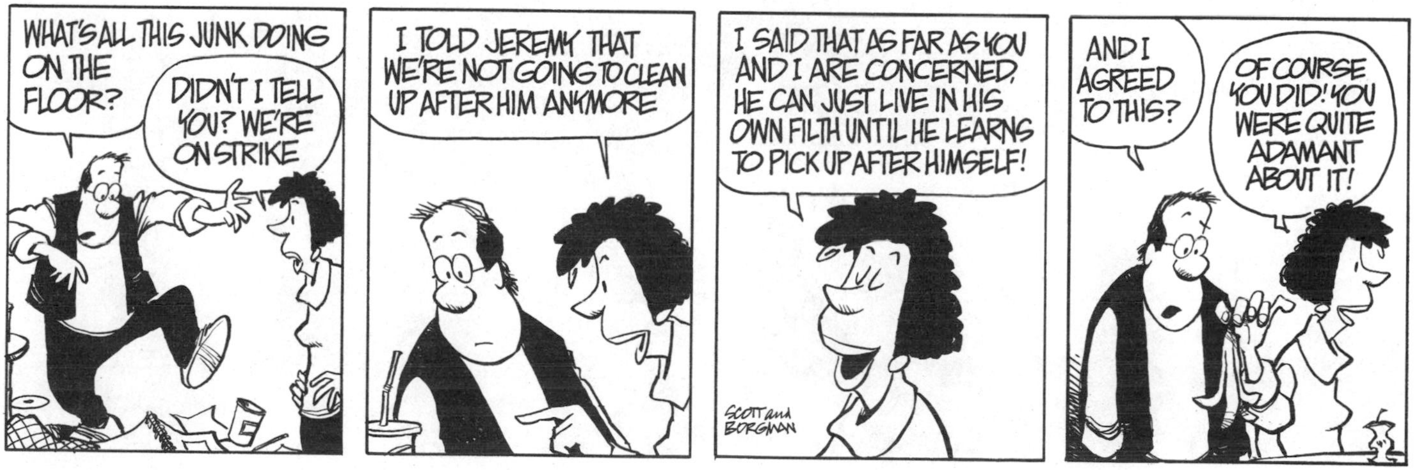
WHAT'S ALL THIS JUNK DOING ON THE FLOOR?
DIDN'T I TELL YOU? WE'RE ON STRIKE
I TOLD JEREMY THAT WE'RE NOT GOING TO CLEAN UP AFTER HIM ANYMORE
I SAID THAT AS FAR AS YOU AND I ARE CONCERNED, HE CAN JUST LIVE IN HIS OWN FILTH UNTIL HE LEARNS TO PICK UP AFTER HIMSELF!
SCOTT and BORGMAN
AND I AGREED TO THIS?
OF COURSE YOU DID! YOU WERE QUITE ADAMANT ABOUT IT!

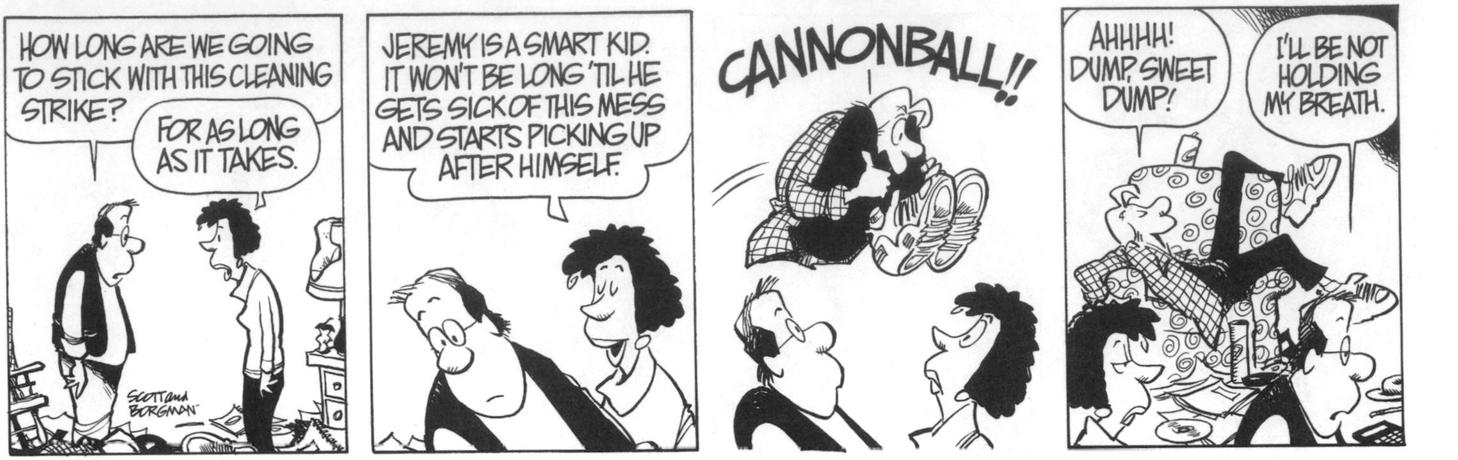
HOW LONG ARE WE GOING TO STICK WITH THIS CLEANING STRIKE?
FOR AS LONG AS IT TAKES.
SCOTT and BORGMAN
JEREMY IS A SMART KID. IT WON'T BE LONG 'TIL HE GETS SICK OF THIS MESS AND STARTS PICKING UP AFTER HIMSELF.
CANNONBALL!!
AHHHH! DUMP, SWEET DUMP!
I'LL BE NOT HOLDING MY BREATH.

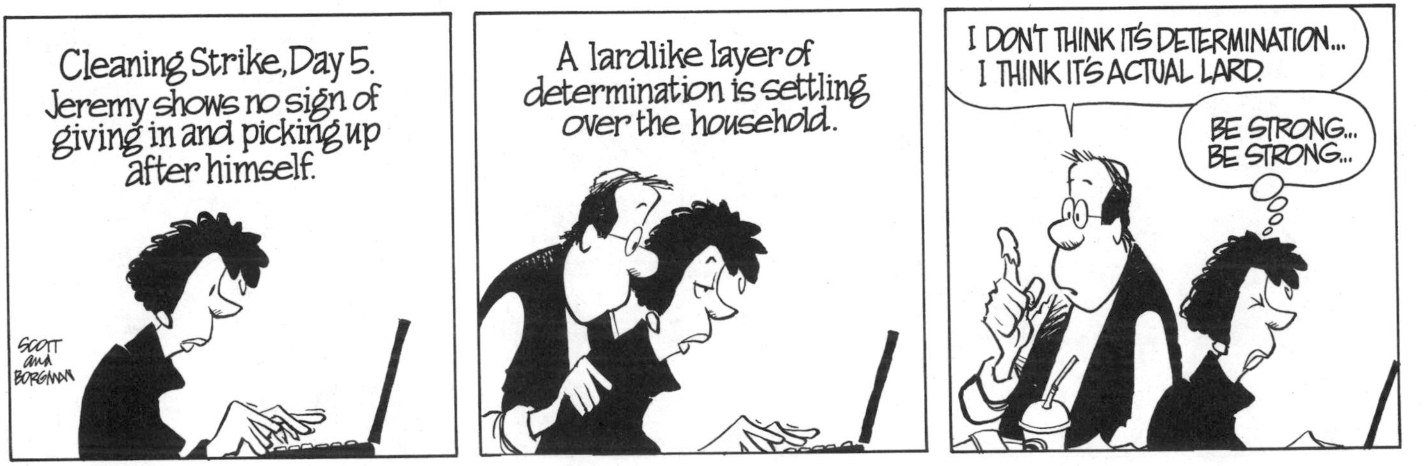
Cleaning Strike, Day 5. Jeremy shows no sign of giving in and picking up after himself.
SCOTT and BORGMAN
A lardlike layer of determination is settling over the household.
I DON'T THINK IT'S DETERMINATION... I THINK IT'S ACTUAL LARD.
BE STRONG... BE STRONG...

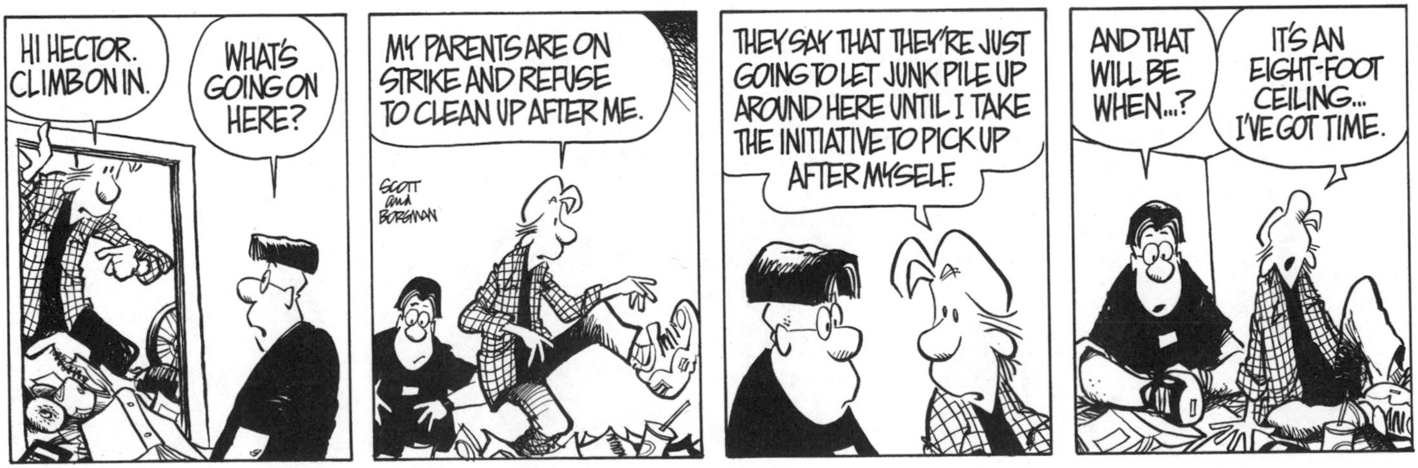
HI HECTOR. CLIMB ON IN.
WHAT'S GOING ON HERE?
MY PARENTS ARE ON STRIKE AND REFUSE TO CLEAN UP AFTER ME.
SCOTT and BORGMAN
THEY SAY THAT THEY'RE JUST GOING TO LET JUNK PILE UP AROUND HERE UNTIL I TAKE THE INITIATIVE TO PICK UP AFTER MYSELF.
AND THAT WILL BE WHEN...?
IT'S AN EIGHT-FOOT CEILING... I'VE GOT TIME.

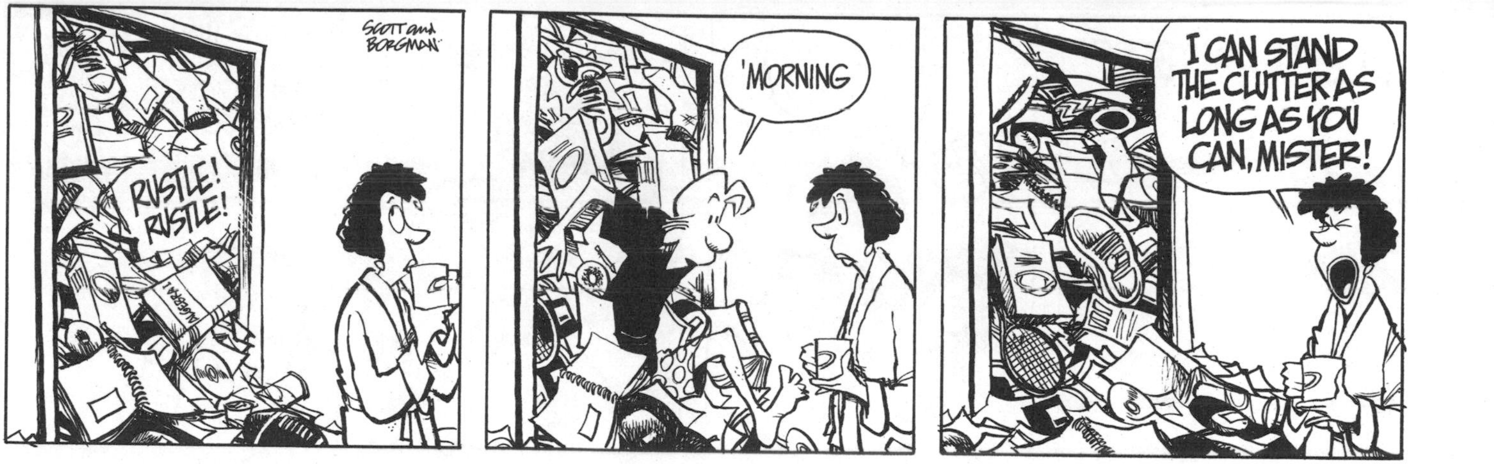
RUSTLE! RUSTLE!
'MORNING
I CAN STAND THE CLUTTER AS LONG AS YOU CAN, MISTER!

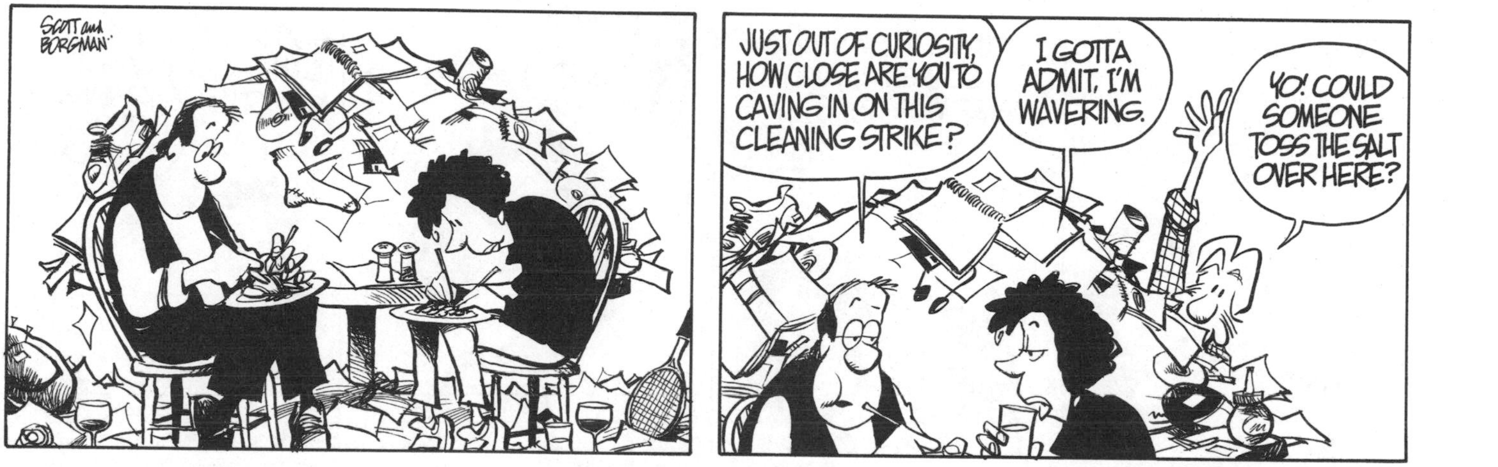
JUST OUT OF CURIOSITY, HOW CLOSE ARE YOU TO CAVING IN ON THIS CLEANING STRIKE?
I GOTTA ADMIT, I'M WAVERING.
YO! COULD SOMEONE TOSS THE SALT OVER HERE?

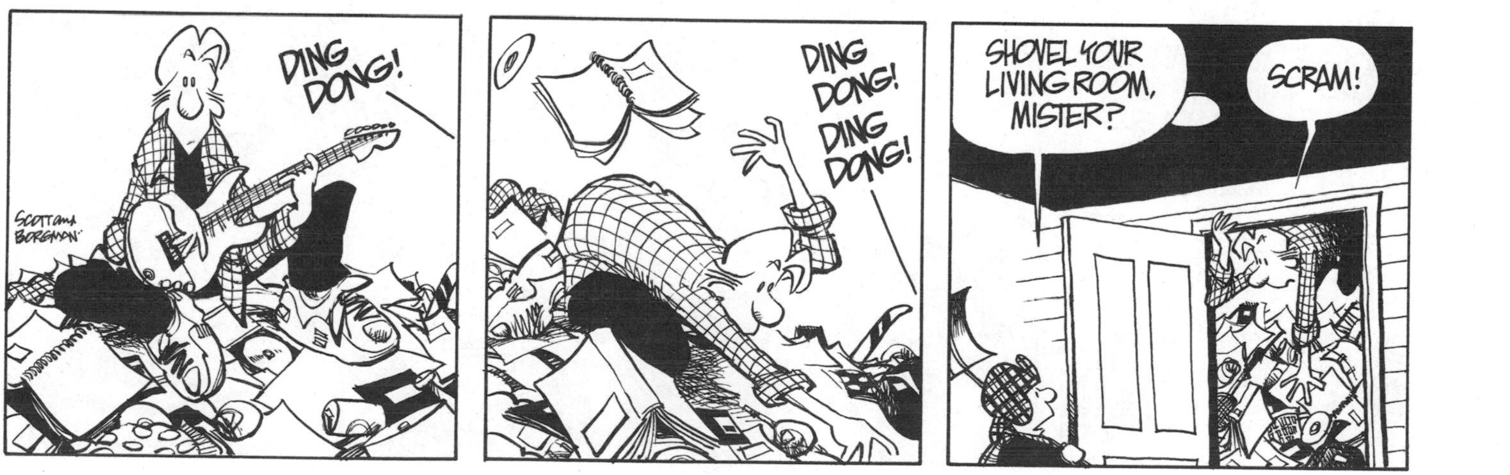
DING DONG!
DING DONG! DING DONG!
SHOVEL YOUR LIVING ROOM, MISTER?
SCRAM!

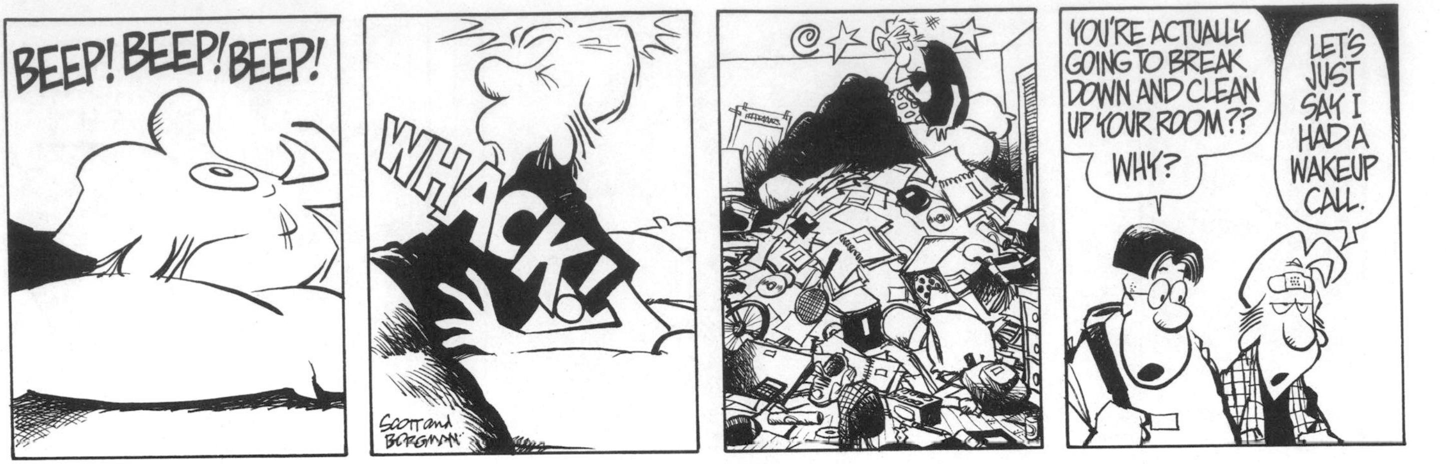
BEEP! BEEP! BEEP!
WHACK!
SCOTT and BORGMAN
YOU'RE ACTUALLY GOING TO BREAK DOWN AND CLEAN UP YOUR ROOM?? WHY?
LET'S JUST SAY I HAD A WAKEUP CALL.

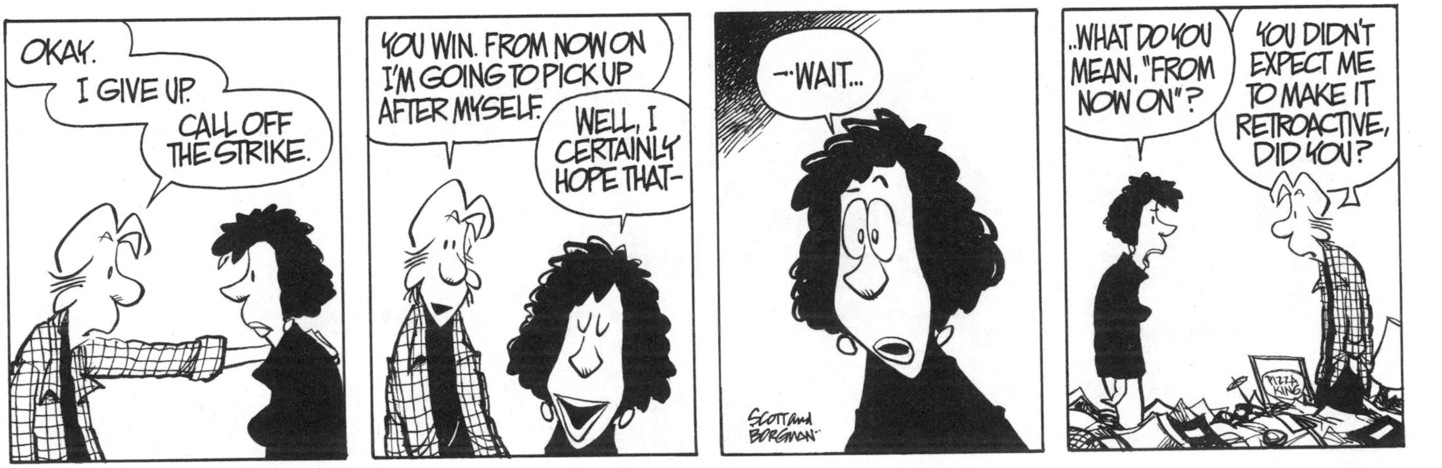
OKAY.
I GIVE UP.
CALL OFF THE STRIKE.
YOU WIN. FROM NOW ON I'M GOING TO PICK UP AFTER MYSELF.
WELL, I CERTAINLY HOPE THAT-
-WAIT...
SCOTT and BORGMAN
..WHAT DO YOU MEAN, "FROM NOW ON"?
YOU DIDN'T EXPECT ME TO MAKE IT RETROACTIVE, DID YOU?
PIZZA KING

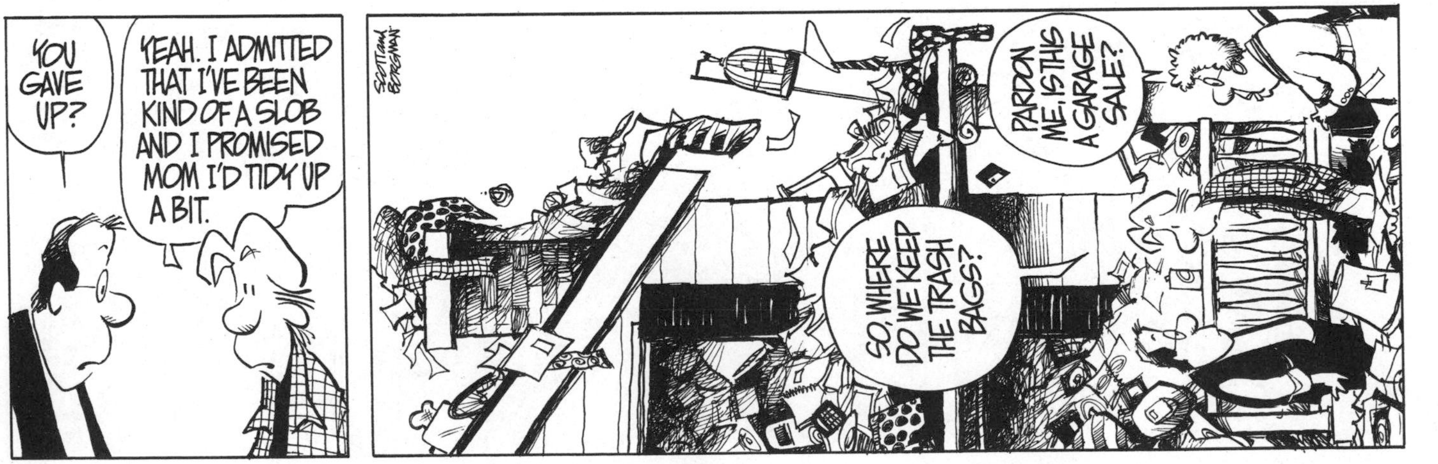
YOU GAVE UP?
YEAH. I ADMITTED THAT I'VE BEEN KIND OF A SLOB AND I PROMISED MOM I'D TIDY UP A BIT.
SCOTT and BORGMAN
PARDON ME, IS THIS A GARAGE SALE?
SO, WHERE DO WE KEEP THE TRASH BAGS?

Zits
by JERRY SCOTT and JIM BORGMAN

JEREMY, I MADE YOU AND YOUR FRIENDS SOME MORE P—
--OPCORN
THANKS
STOP BEING SUCH A PRUDE. THEY'RE JUST GOOD FRIENDS!
I'VE SEEN LITTERS OF PUPPIES THAT MAKE LESS BODY CONTACT!!!
SCOTT and BORGMAN

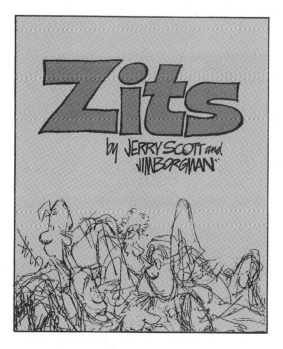

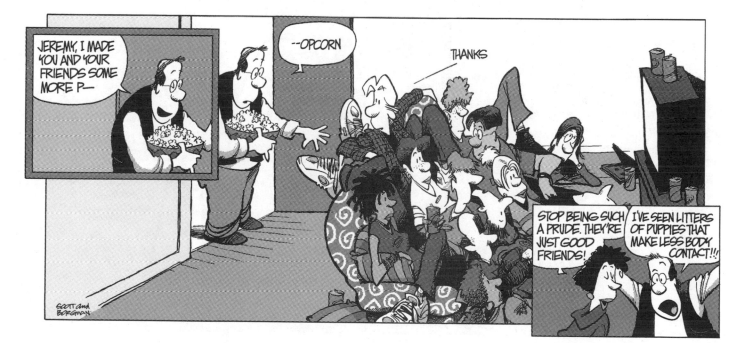

Zits
by JERRY SCOTT and JIM BORGMAN
WHUMP!!!
TAKE ME TO HECTOR'S. I'M LATE FOR PRACTICE.
THANKS FOR THE RIDE, MOM!
THAT WASN'T A RIDE-- IT WAS A CARJACKING!

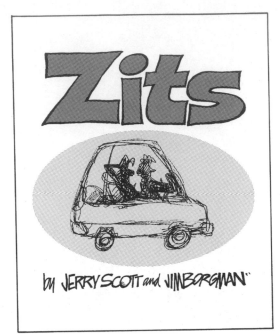

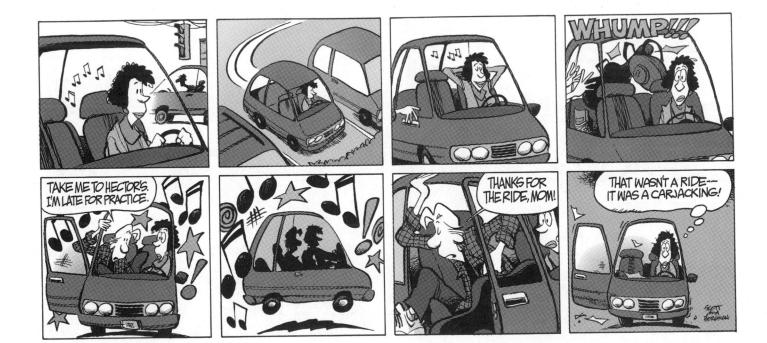

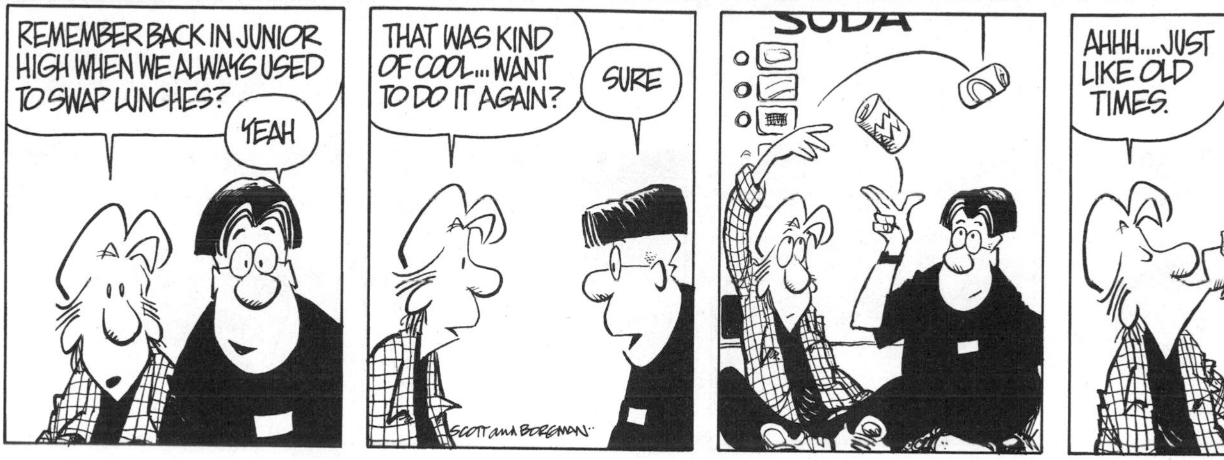
REMEMBER BACK IN JUNIOR HIGH WHEN WE ALWAYS USED TO SWAP LUNCHES?
YEAH
THAT WAS KIND OF COOL... WANT TO DO IT AGAIN?
SURE
SODA
AHHH....JUST LIKE OLD TIMES.
BUT WITH-OUT THE LUNCH-BOXES.

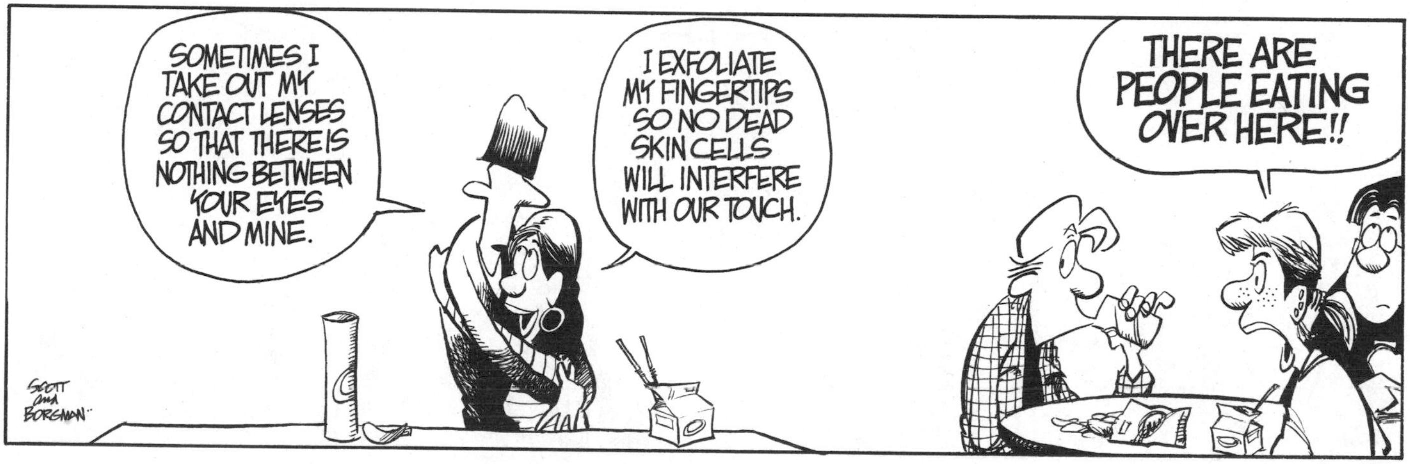
SOMETIMES I TAKE OUT MY CONTACT LENSES SO THAT THERE IS NOTHING BETWEEN YOUR EYES AND MINE.
I EXFOLIATE MY FINGERTIPS SO NO DEAD SKIN CELLS WILL INTERFERE WITH OUR TOUCH.
THERE ARE PEOPLE EATING OVER HERE!!

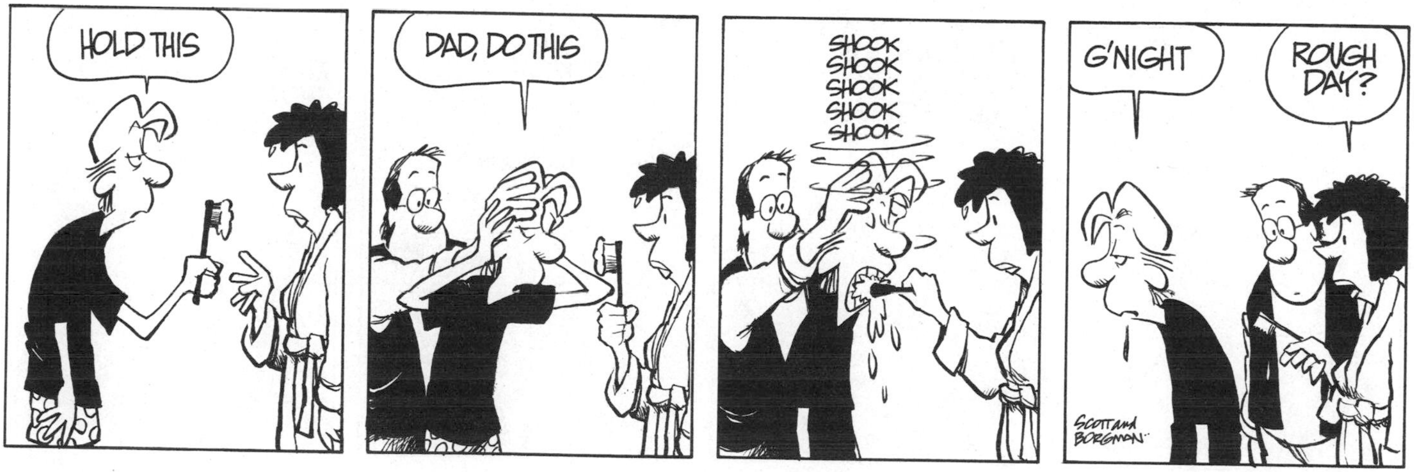
HOLD THIS
DAD, DO THIS
SHOOK SHOOK SHOOK SHOOK SHOOK
G'NIGHT
ROUGH DAY?

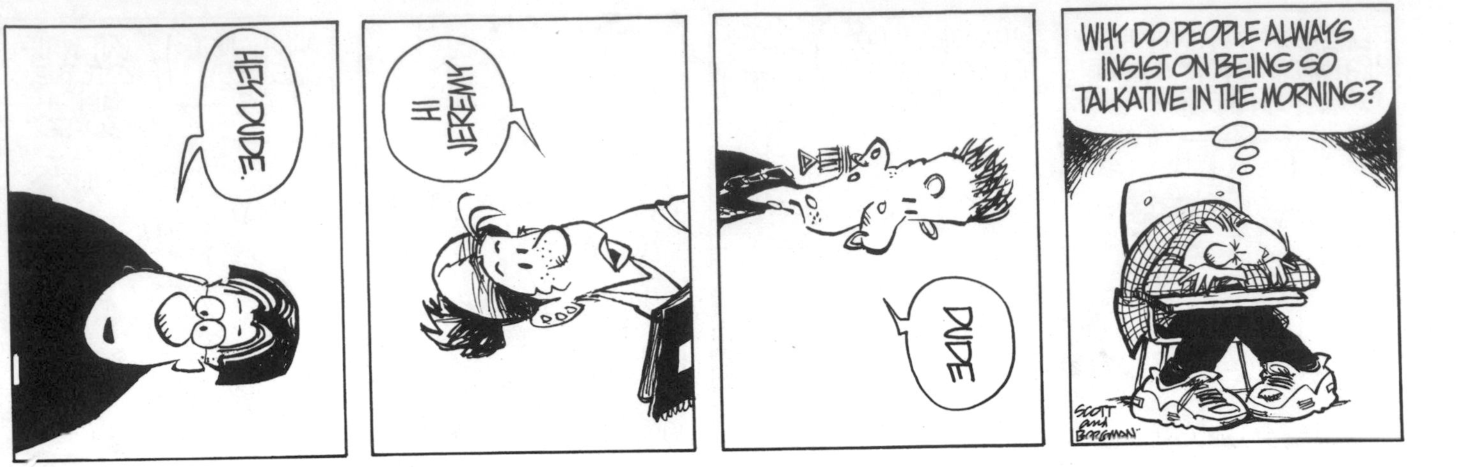
HEY DUDE.
HI JEREMY
DUDE
WHY DO PEOPLE ALWAYS INSIST ON BEING SO TALKATIVE IN THE MORNING?
SCOTT and BORGMAN

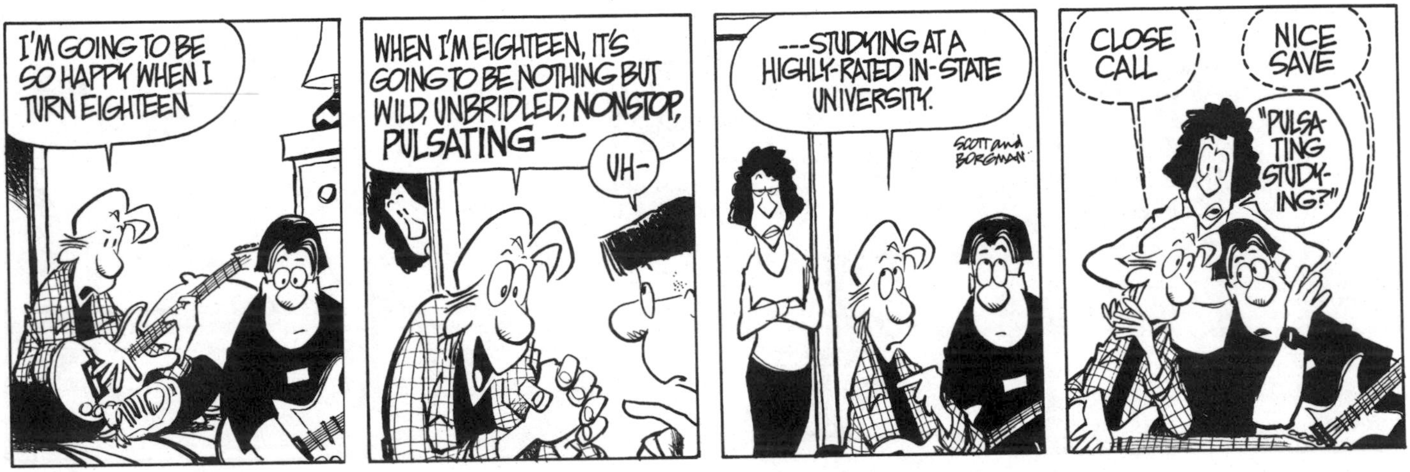
I'M GOING TO BE SO HAPPY WHEN I TURN EIGHTEEN
WHEN I'M EIGHTEEN, IT'S GOING TO BE NOTHING BUT WILD, UNBRIDLED, NONSTOP, PULSATING —
UH-
---STUDYING AT A HIGHLY-RATED IN-STATE UNIVERSITY.
SCOTT and BORGMAN
CLOSE CALL
NICE SAVE
"PULSATING STUDYING?"

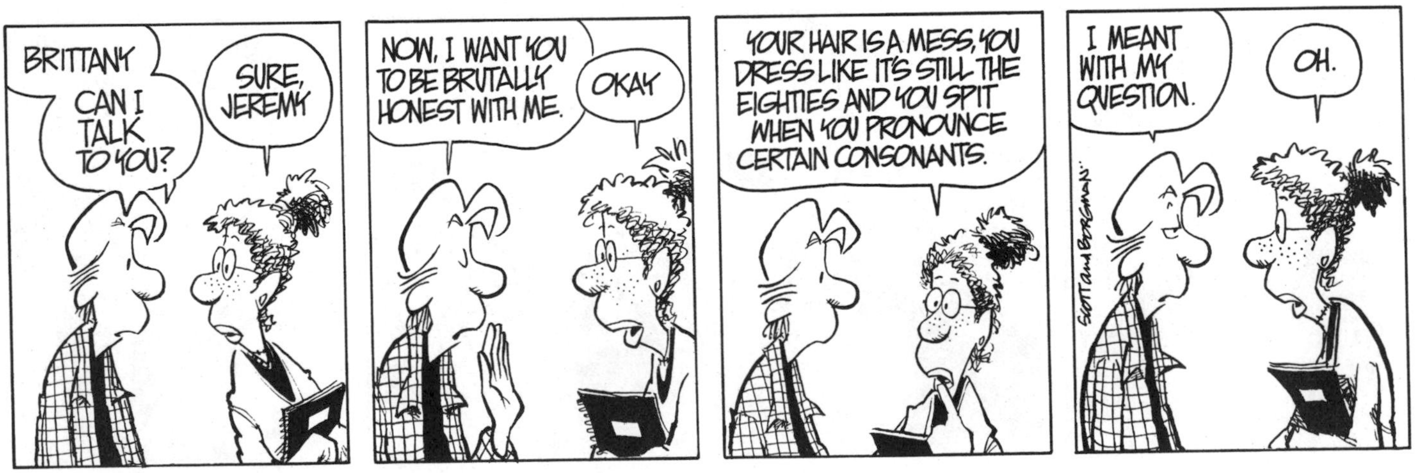
BRITTANY
CAN I TALK TO YOU?
SURE, JEREMY
NOW, I WANT YOU TO BE BRUTALLY HONEST WITH ME.
OKAY
YOUR HAIR IS A MESS, YOU DRESS LIKE IT'S STILL THE EIGHTIES AND YOU SPIT WHEN YOU PRONOUNCE CERTAIN CONSONANTS.
SCOTT and BORGMAN
I MEANT WITH MY QUESTION.
OH.

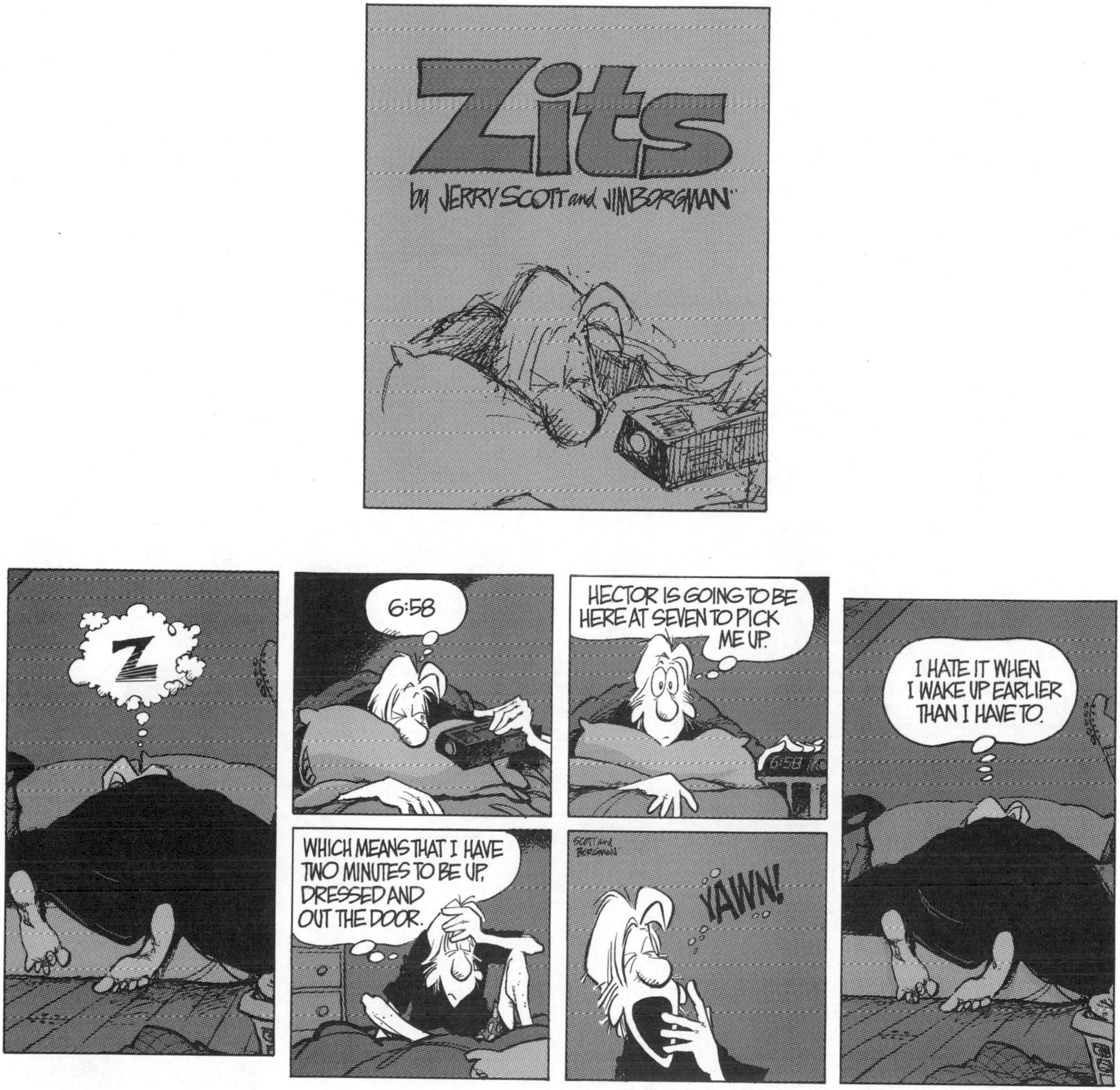
Zits
by JERRY SCOTT and JIM BORGMAN
Z
6:58
HECTOR IS GOING TO BE HERE AT SEVEN TO PICK ME UP.
WHICH MEANS THAT I HAVE TWO MINUTES TO BE UP, DRESSED AND OUT THE DOOR.
YAWN!
I HATE IT WHEN I WAKE UP EARLIER THAN I HAVE TO.

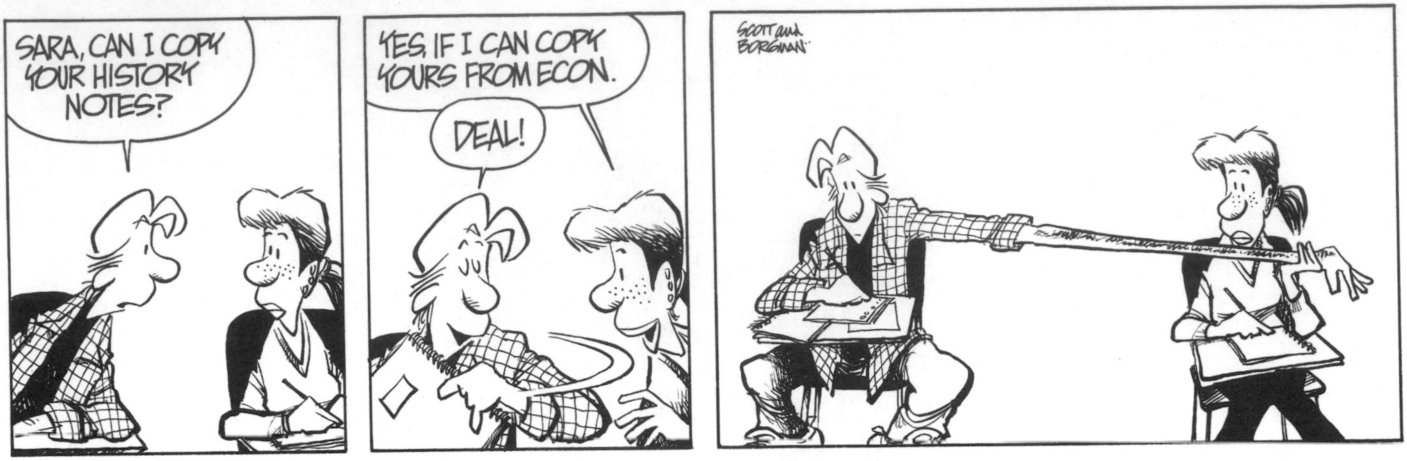
SARA, CAN I COPY YOUR HISTORY NOTES?
YES, IF I CAN COPY YOURS FROM ECON.
DEAL!
SCOTT and BORGMAN

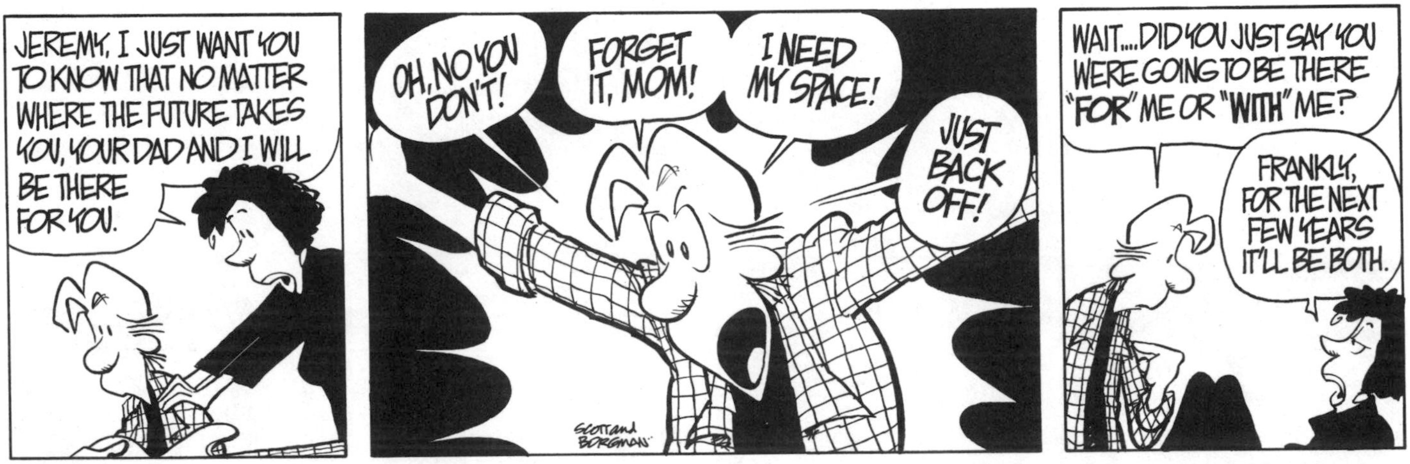
JEREMY, I JUST WANT YOU TO KNOW THAT NO MATTER WHERE THE FUTURE TAKES YOU, YOUR DAD AND I WILL BE THERE FOR YOU.
OH, NO YOU DON'T!
FORGET IT, MOM!
I NEED MY SPACE!
JUST BACK OFF!
SCOTT and BORGMAN
WAIT.... DID YOU JUST SAY YOU WERE GOING TO BE THERE "FOR" ME OR "WITH" ME?
FRANKLY, FOR THE NEXT FEW YEARS IT'LL BE BOTH.

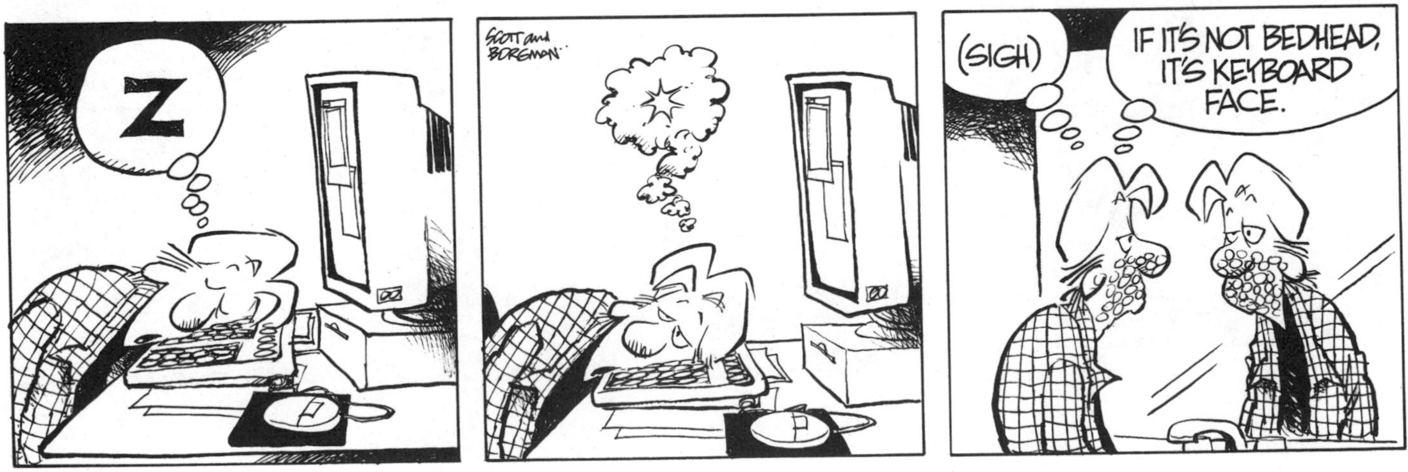
Z
SCOTT and BORGMAN
(SIGH)
IF IT'S NOT BEDHEAD, IT'S KEYBOARD FACE.

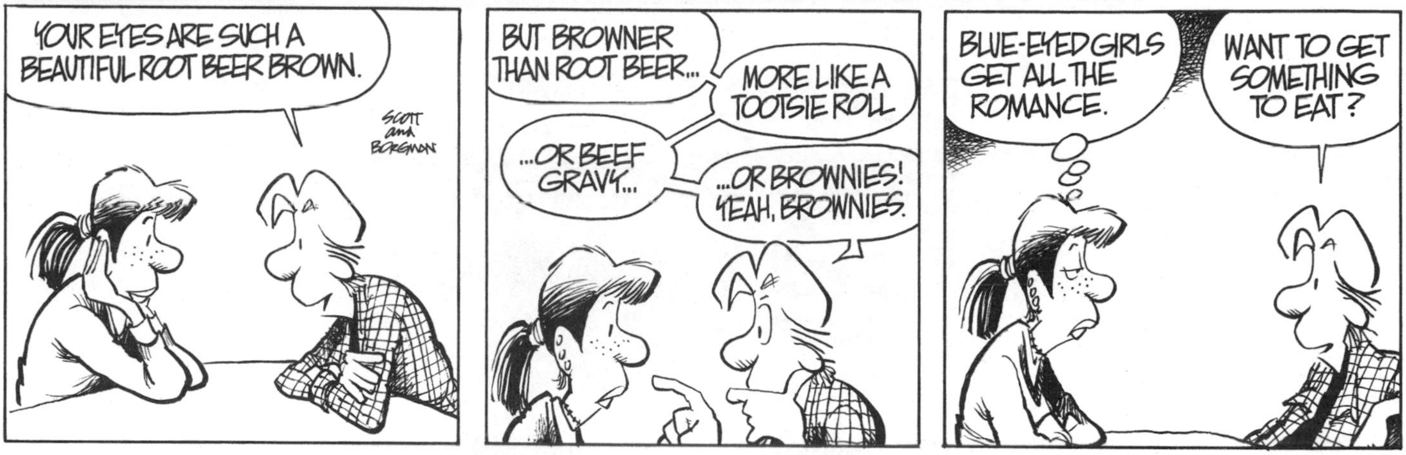
YOUR EYES ARE SUCH A BEAUTIFUL ROOT BEER BROWN.
SCOTT and BORGMAN
BUT BROWNER THAN ROOT BEER...
MORE LIKE A TOOTSIE ROLL
...OR BEEF GRAVY...
...OR BROWNIES! YEAH, BROWNIES.
BLUE-EYED GIRLS GET ALL THE ROMANCE.
WANT TO GET SOMETHING TO EAT?

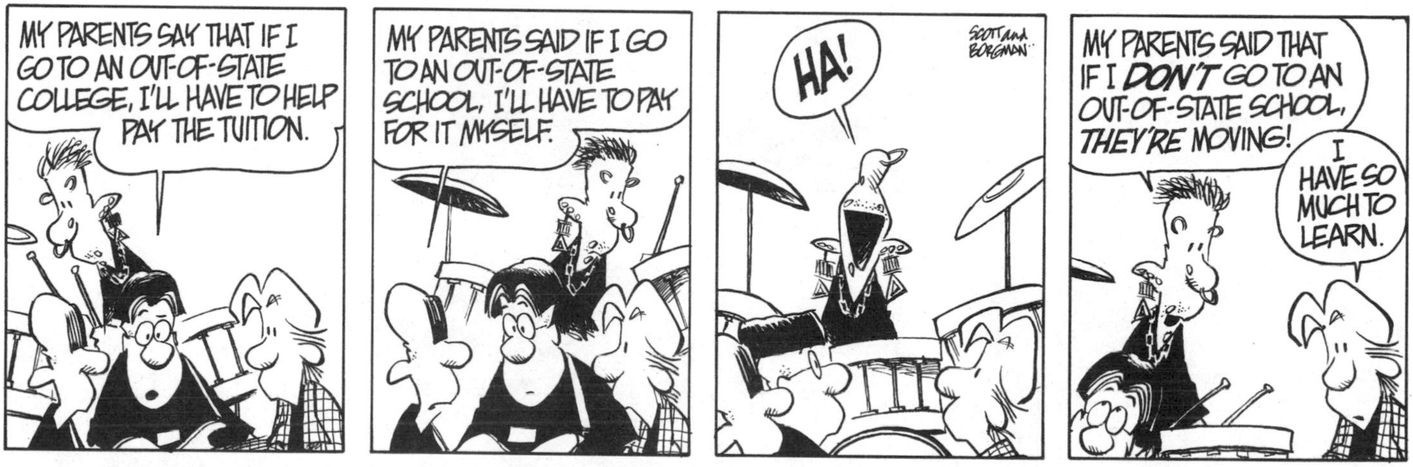
MY PARENTS SAY THAT IF I GO TO AN OUT-OF-STATE COLLEGE, I'LL HAVE TO HELP PAY THE TUITION.
MY PARENTS SAID IF I GO TO AN OUT-OF-STATE SCHOOL, I'LL HAVE TO PAY FOR IT MYSELF.
HA!
SCOTT and BORGMAN
MY PARENTS SAID THAT IF I **DON'T** GO TO AN OUT-OF-STATE SCHOOL, ***THEY'RE*** MOVING!
I HAVE SO MUCH TO LEARN.

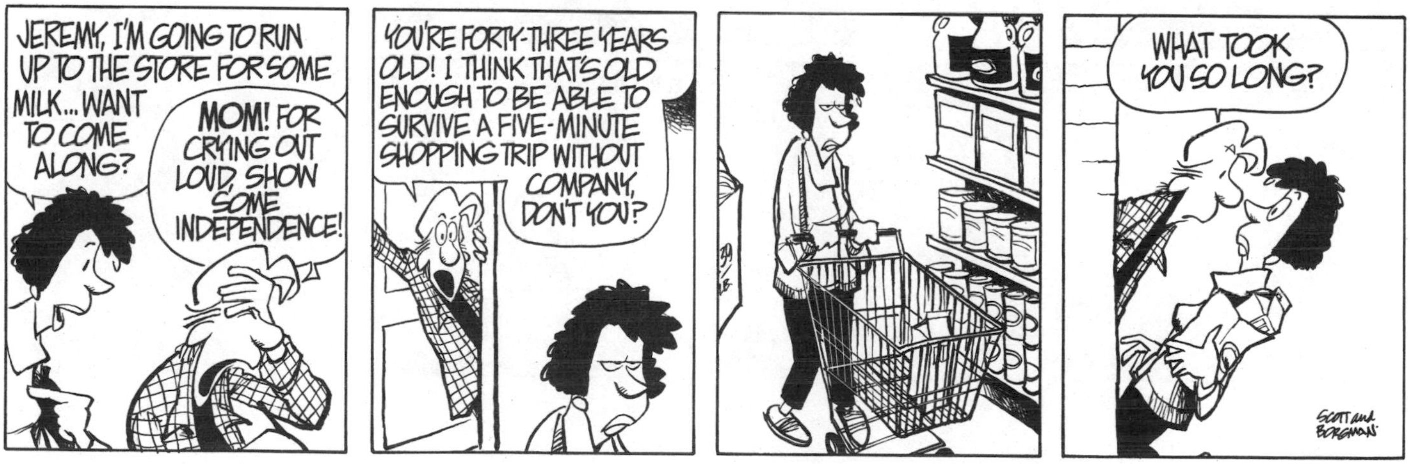
JEREMY, I'M GOING TO RUN UP TO THE STORE FOR SOME MILK... WANT TO COME ALONG?
MOM! FOR CRYING OUT LOUD, SHOW SOME INDEPENDENCE!
YOU'RE FORTY-THREE YEARS OLD! I THINK THAT'S OLD ENOUGH TO BE ABLE TO SURVIVE A FIVE-MINUTE SHOPPING TRIP WITHOUT COMPANY, DON'T YOU?
WHAT TOOK YOU SO LONG?
SCOTT and BORGMAN

Zits
by JERRY SCOTT and JIM BORGMAN
JEREMY! HELP!
JUST HIT 'RESTART,' DAD
IT'S WEIRD. SOMETIMES YOU CAN ALMOST WATCH PARENTS DEVOLVING!
I SHUDDER TO THINK WHAT WILL HAPPEN TO THEM WHEN WE GO AWAY TO COLLEGE.
SCOTT and BORGMAN

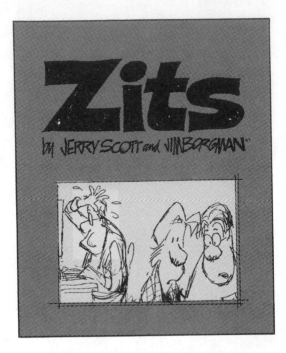

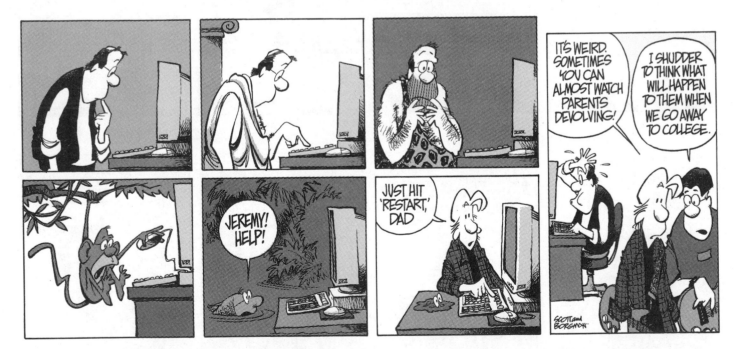

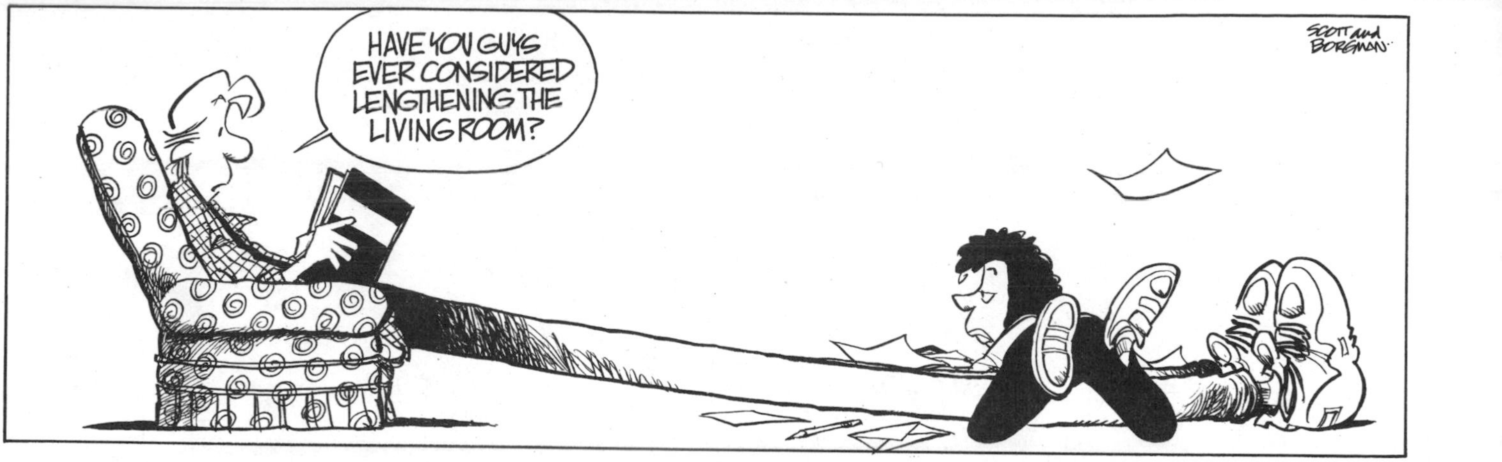
SCOTT AND BORGMAN
HAVE YOU GUYS EVER CONSIDERED LENGTHENING THE LIVING ROOM?

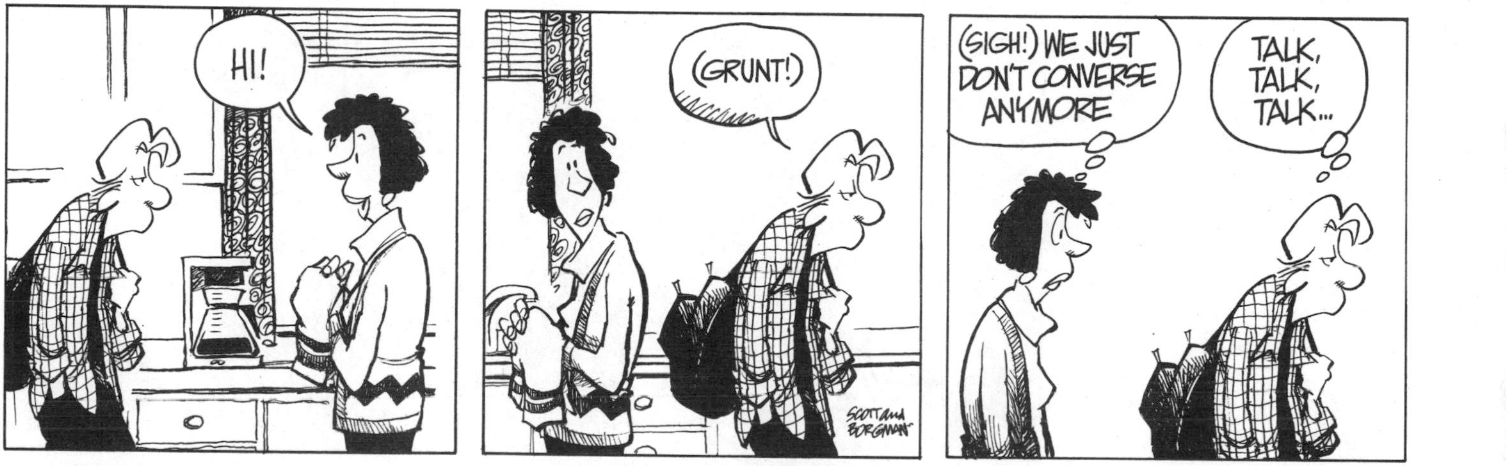
HI!
(GRUNT!)
SCOTT AND BORGMAN
(SIGH!) WE JUST DON'T CONVERSE ANYMORE
TALK, TALK, TALK...

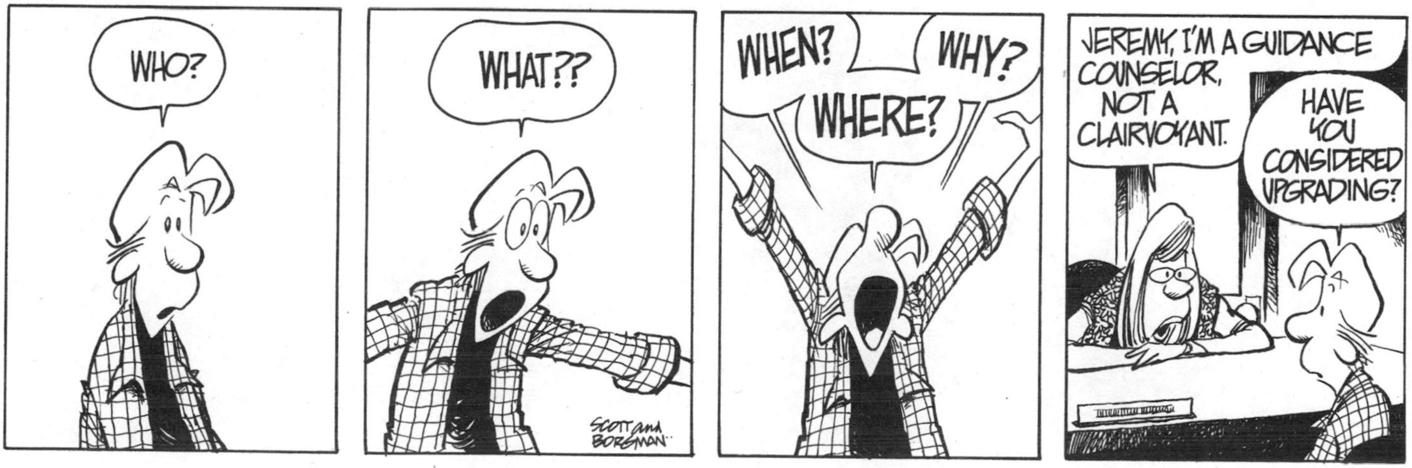
WHO?
WHAT??
SCOTT AND BORGMAN
WHEN?
WHY?
WHERE?
JEREMY, I'M A GUIDANCE COUNSELOR, NOT A CLAIRVOYANT.
HAVE YOU CONSIDERED UPGRADING?

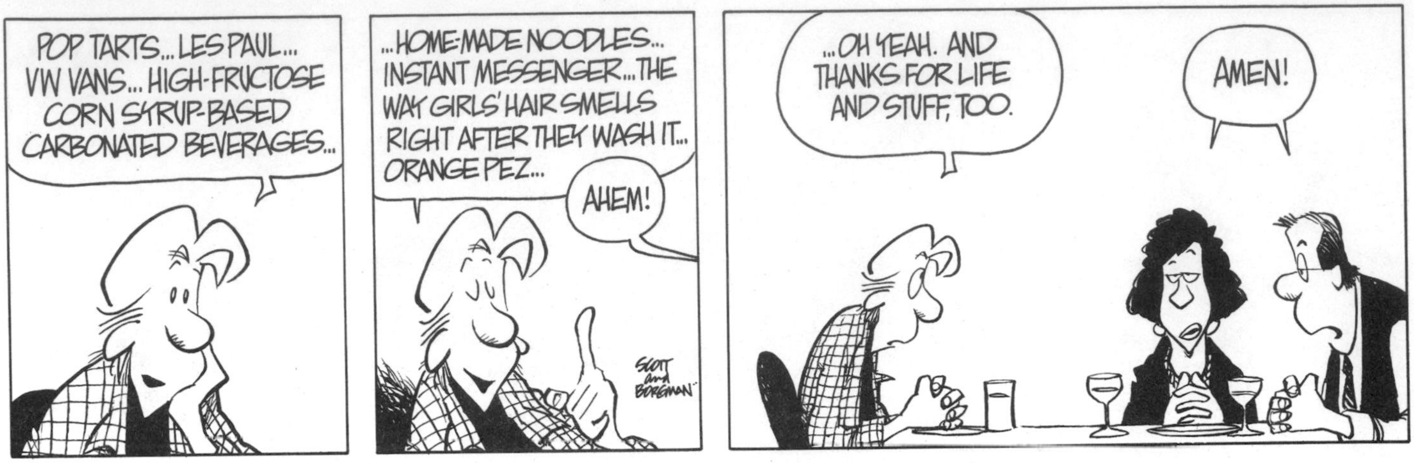
POP TARTS... LES PAUL... VW VANS... HIGH-FRUCTOSE CORN SYRUP-BASED CARBONATED BEVERAGES...
...HOME-MADE NOODLES... INSTANT MESSENGER... THE WAY GIRLS' HAIR SMELLS RIGHT AFTER THEY WASH IT... ORANGE PEZ...
AHEM!
SCOTT and BORGMAN
...OH YEAH. AND THANKS FOR LIFE AND STUFF, TOO.
AMEN!

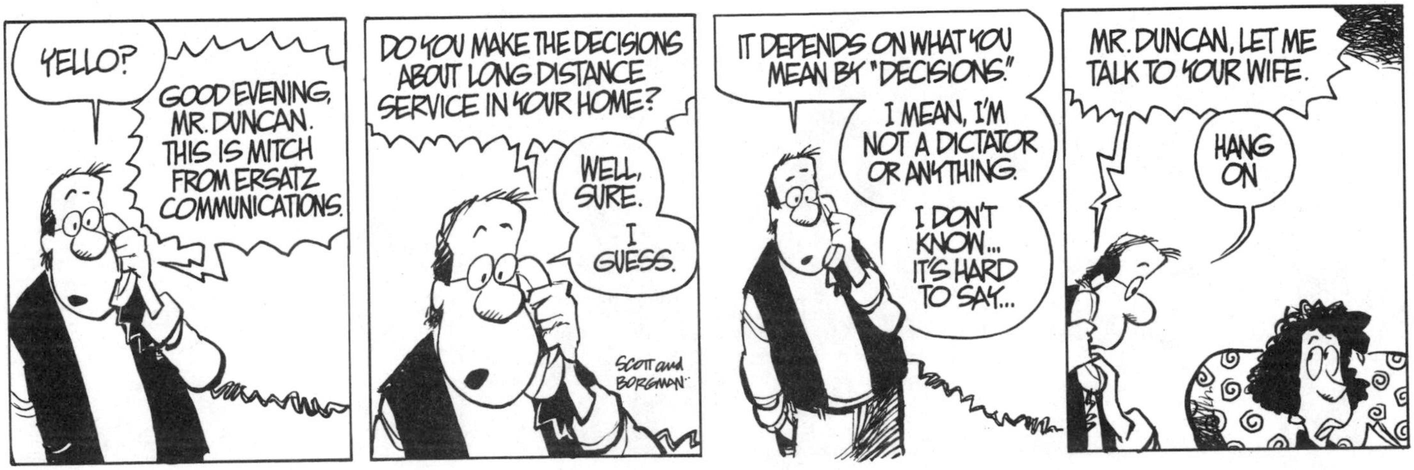
YELLO?
GOOD EVENING, MR. DUNCAN. THIS IS MITCH FROM ERSATZ COMMUNICATIONS.
DO YOU MAKE THE DECISIONS ABOUT LONG DISTANCE SERVICE IN YOUR HOME?
WELL, SURE.
I GUESS.
SCOTT and BORGMAN
IT DEPENDS ON WHAT YOU MEAN BY "DECISIONS."
I MEAN, I'M NOT A DICTATOR OR ANYTHING.
I DON'T KNOW... IT'S HARD TO SAY...
MR. DUNCAN, LET ME TALK TO YOUR WIFE.
HANG ON

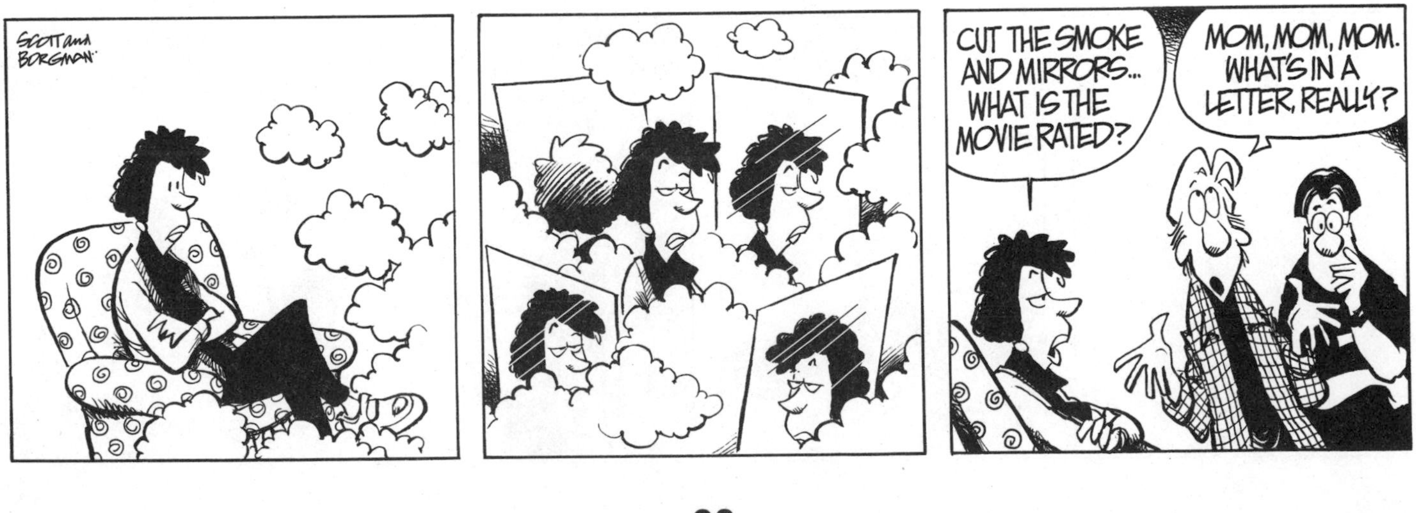
SCOTT and BORGMAN
CUT THE SMOKE AND MIRRORS... WHAT IS THE MOVIE RATED?
MOM, MOM, MOM. WHAT'S IN A LETTER, REALLY?

Zits
by JERRY SCOTT and JIM BORGMAN

WHAT THE–?
1
NO SOLICITORS
WELCOME
DING! DONG!
JUST A MOMENT!
MAY I HELP YOU?
JEREMY, WHAT'S GOING ON HERE? WHERE DID YOU GET A DOOR-BELL AND A—
–COFFEE TABLE?
I FIXED MY ROOM UP LIKE AN APART-MENT.
MOUNTAIN DEW?
OKAY, I GIVE UP. WHAT'S THIS ALL ABOUT?
SELF-SUFFICIENCY.
I'M GOING TO BE OUT ON MY OWN ONE OF THESE DAYS ANYWAY, SO I THOUGHT, WHY NOT START LIVING IN-DEPENDENTLY RIGHT NOW?
SIP!
WITH THAT IN MIND, HERE'S YOUR LAUNDRY AND THE HOMEWORK I CORRECTED FOR YOU.
THANKS. WHAT'S FOR DINNER?
SCOTT AND BORGMAN

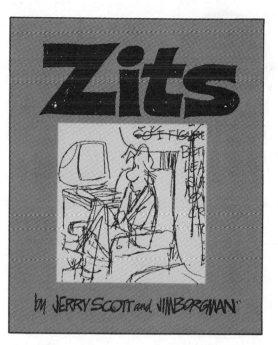

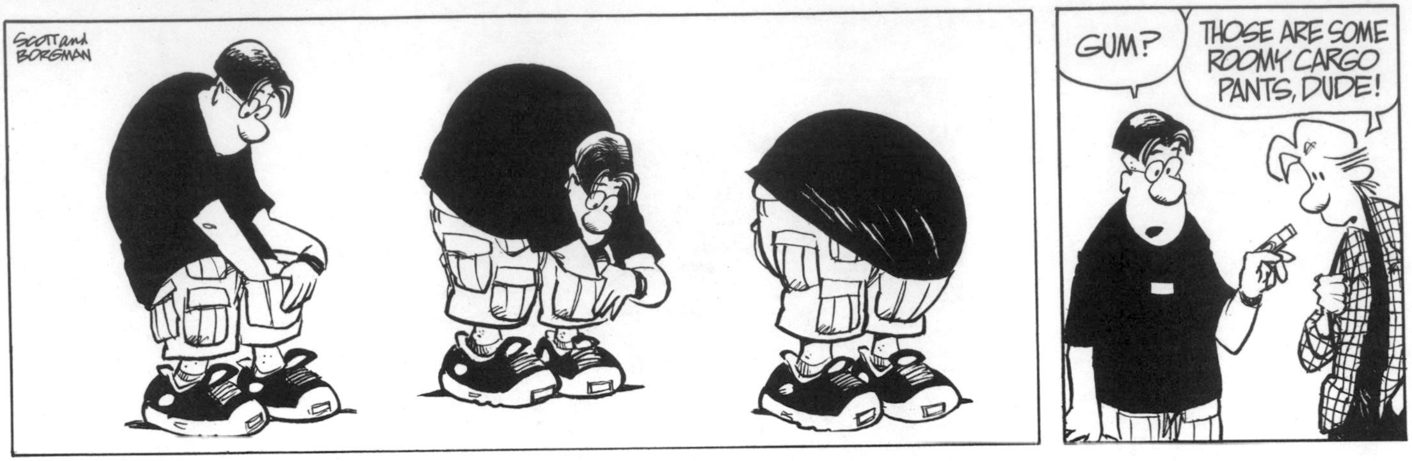
SCOTT and BORGMAN
GUM?
THOSE ARE SOME ROOMY CARGO PANTS, DUDE!

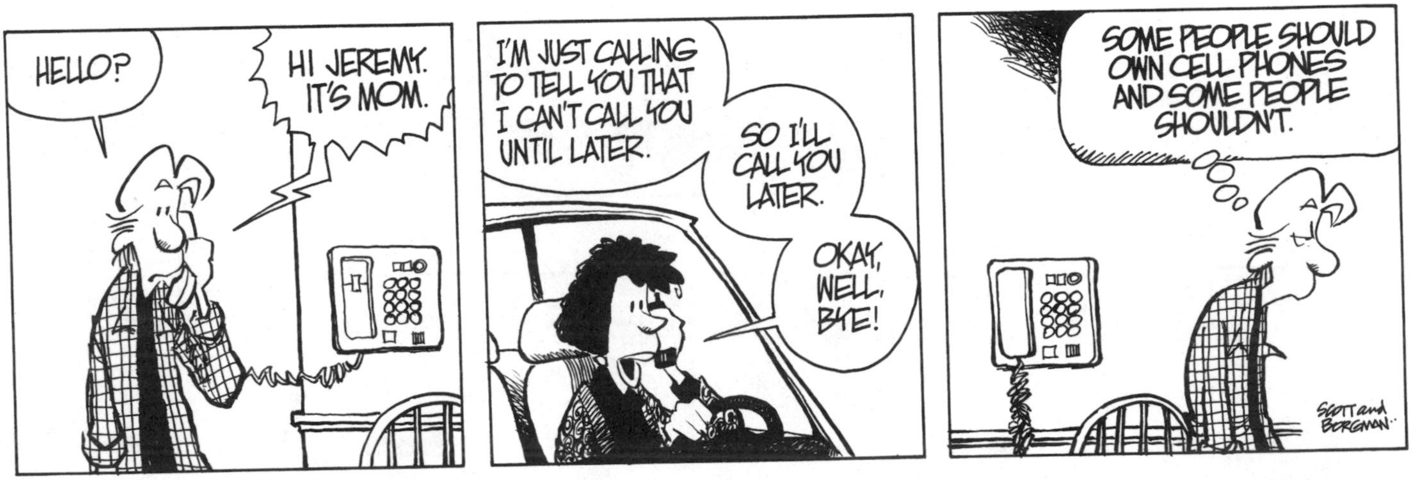
HELLO?
HI JEREMY. IT'S MOM.
I'M JUST CALLING TO TELL YOU THAT I CAN'T CALL YOU UNTIL LATER.
SO I'LL CALL YOU LATER.
OKAY, WELL, BYE!
SOME PEOPLE SHOULD OWN CELL PHONES AND SOME PEOPLE SHOULDN'T.
SCOTT and BORGMAN

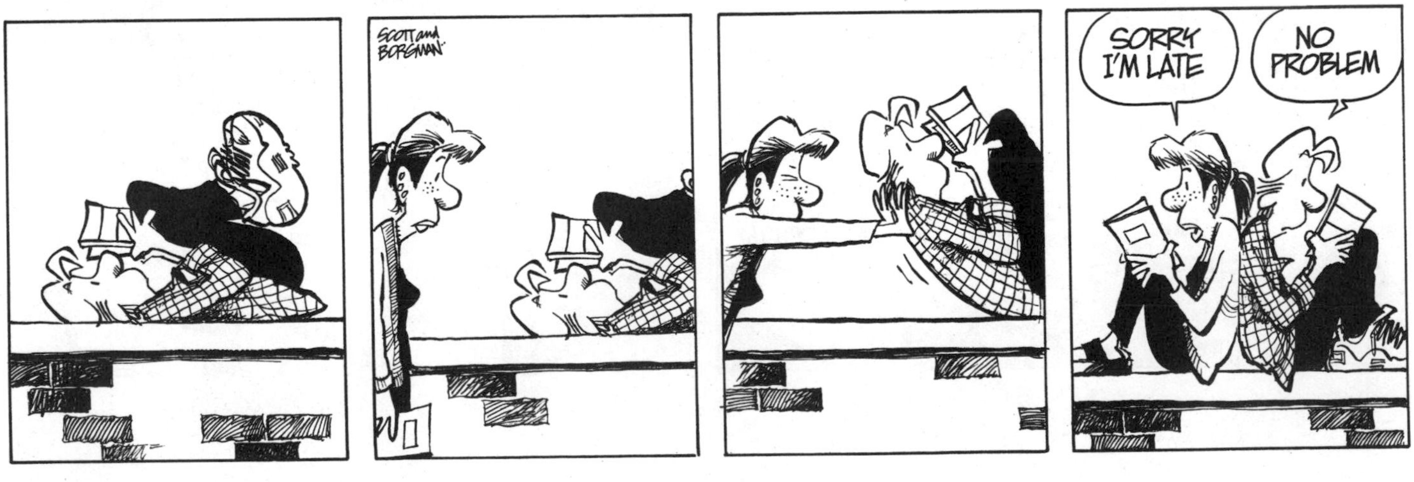
SCOTT and BORGMAN
SORRY I'M LATE
NO PROBLEM

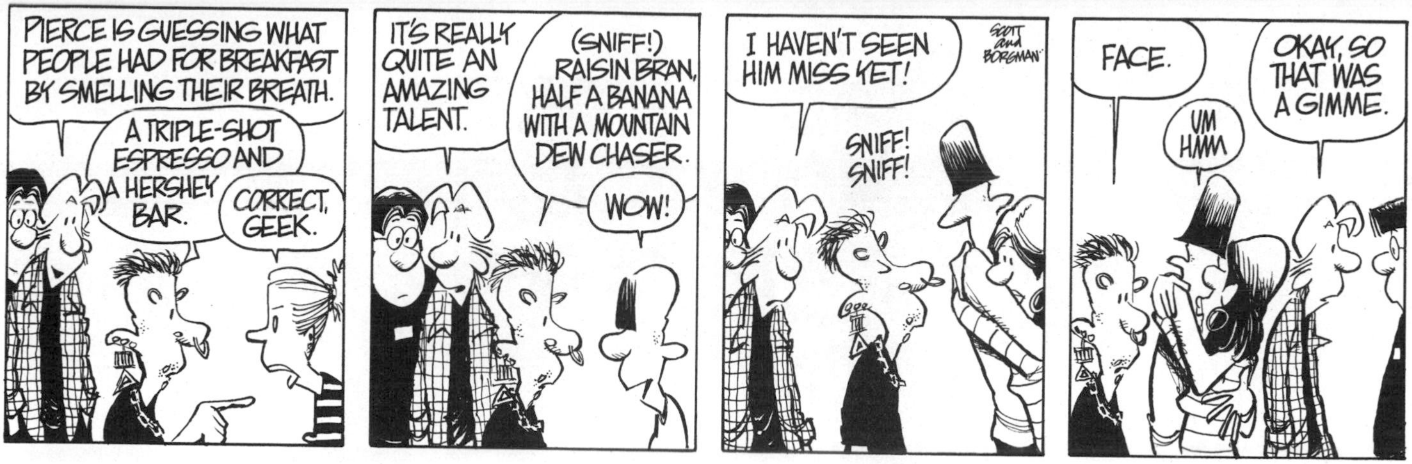
PIERCE IS GUESSING WHAT PEOPLE HAD FOR BREAKFAST BY SMELLING THEIR BREATH.
A TRIPLE-SHOT ESPRESSO AND A HERSHEY BAR.
CORRECT, GEEK.
IT'S REALLY QUITE AN AMAZING TALENT.
(SNIFF!) RAISIN BRAN, HALF A BANANA WITH A MOUNTAIN DEW CHASER.
WOW!
I HAVEN'T SEEN HIM MISS YET!
SCOTT and BORGMAN
SNIFF! SNIFF!
FACE.
UM HMM
OKAY, SO THAT WAS A GIMME.

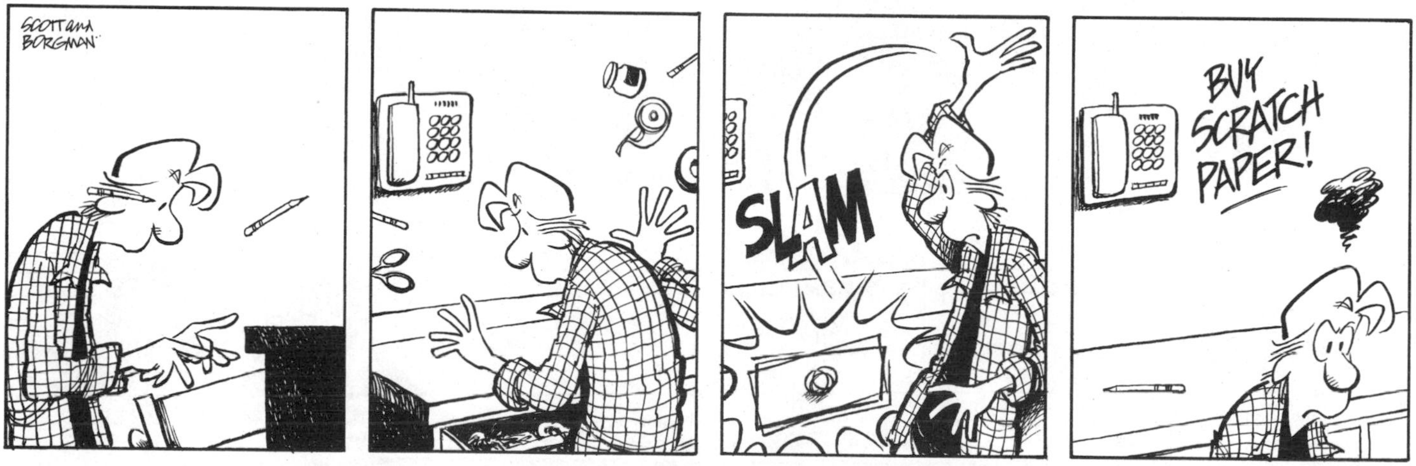
SCOTT and BORGMAN
SLAM
BUY SCRATCH PAPER!

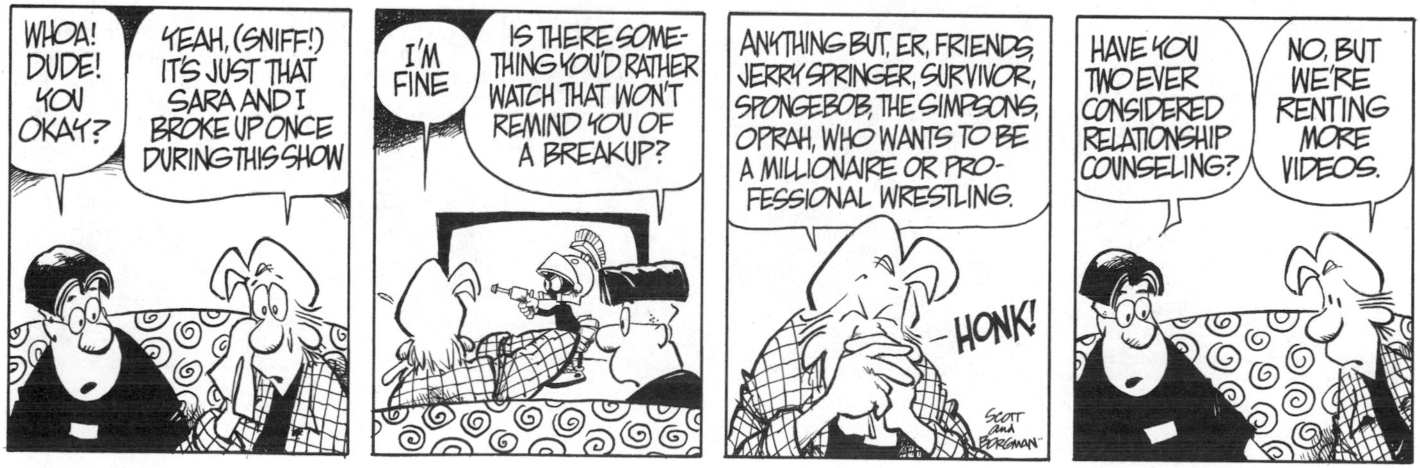
WHOA! DUDE! YOU OKAY?
YEAH, (SNIFF!) IT'S JUST THAT SARA AND I BROKE UP ONCE DURING THIS SHOW
I'M FINE
IS THERE SOMETHING YOU'D RATHER WATCH THAT WON'T REMIND YOU OF A BREAKUP?
ANYTHING BUT, ER, FRIENDS, JERRY SPRINGER, SURVIVOR, SPONGEBOB, THE SIMPSONS, OPRAH, WHO WANTS TO BE A MILLIONAIRE OR PROFESSIONAL WRESTLING.
HONK!
SCOTT and BORGMAN
HAVE YOU TWO EVER CONSIDERED RELATIONSHIP COUNSELING?
NO, BUT WE'RE RENTING MORE VIDEOS.

Zits
BRRRMMMMMMMM
by JERRY SCOTT and JIM BORGMAN

CHIRP! CHIRP!
BRRRMMMMMMMMM
SNIP! SNIP! SNIP! SNIP!
RRRRR!
BEEP!
CHUKKA-TA CHUKKA-TA
BZZZ-ZZZ!
CHK! CHK! CHK! BAM BAM BAM BRRRZZZZZZZ
DO YOU PEOPLE HAVE ANY IDEA WHAT TIME IT IS???
ELEVEN FORTY-THREE
I'VE GOT QUARTER TO TWELVE
'BOUT NOON
LUNCH-TIME
BARBARIANS!
SCOTT and BORGMAN

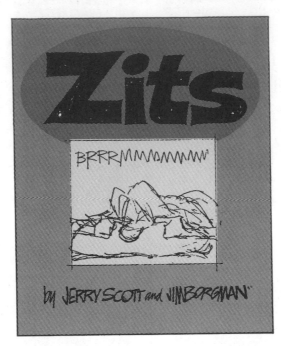

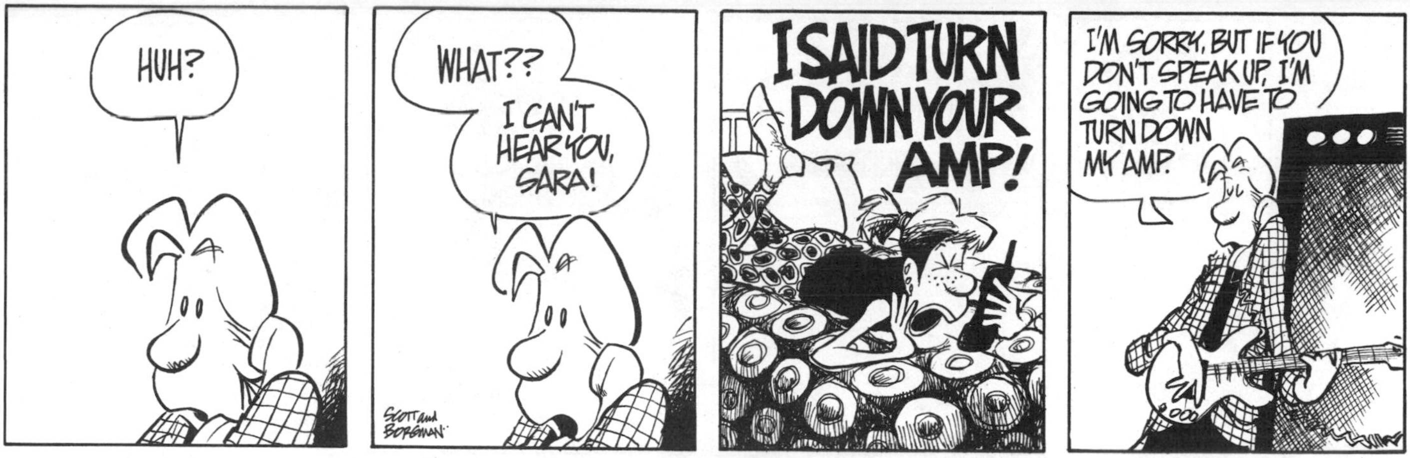
HUH?
WHAT??
I CAN'T HEAR YOU, SARA!
SCOTT AND BORGMAN
I SAID TURN DOWN YOUR AMP!
I'M SORRY, BUT IF YOU DON'T SPEAK UP, I'M GOING TO HAVE TO TURN DOWN MY AMP.

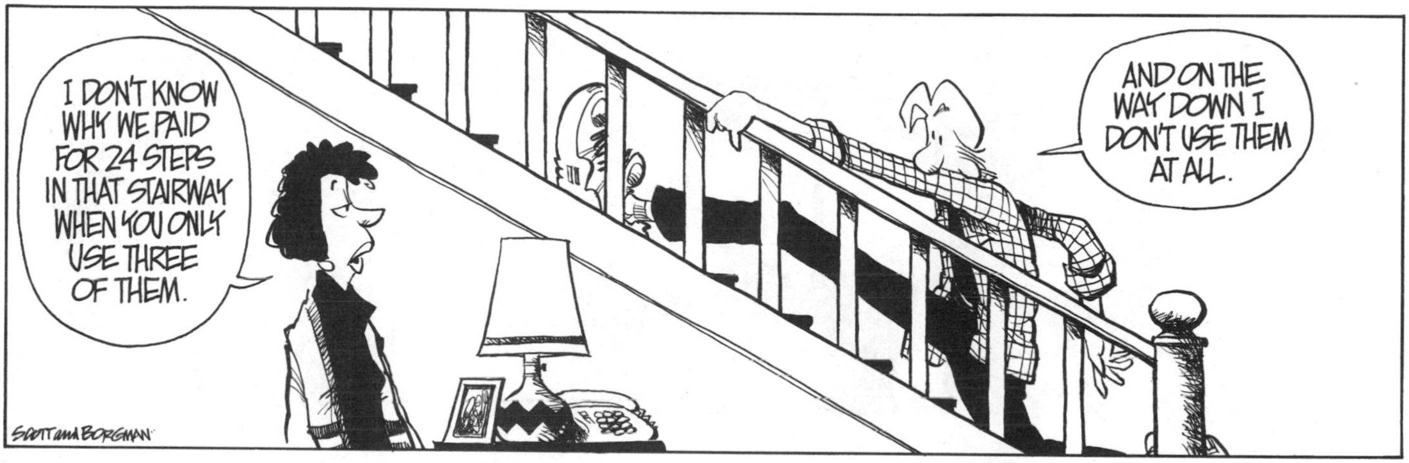
I DON'T KNOW WHY WE PAID FOR 24 STEPS IN THAT STAIRWAY WHEN YOU ONLY USE THREE OF THEM.
AND ON THE WAY DOWN I DON'T USE THEM AT ALL.
SCOTT AND BORGMAN

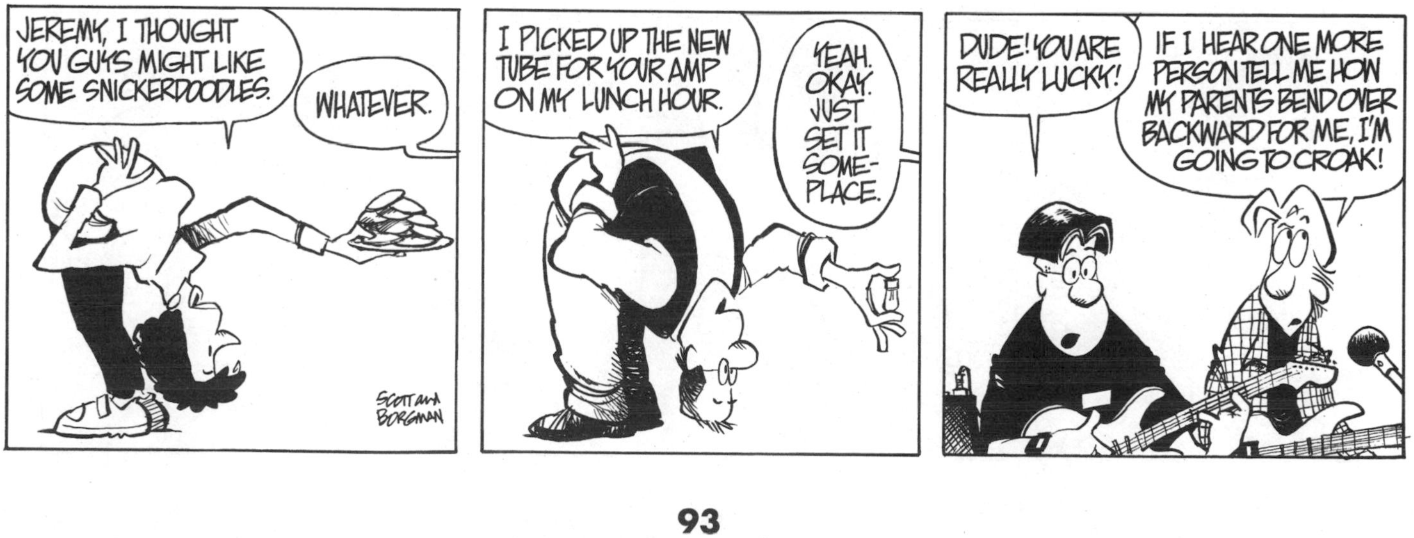
JEREMY, I THOUGHT YOU GUYS MIGHT LIKE SOME SNICKERDOODLES.
WHATEVER.
SCOTT AND BORGMAN
I PICKED UP THE NEW TUBE FOR YOUR AMP ON MY LUNCH HOUR.
YEAH. OKAY. JUST SET IT SOME-PLACE.
DUDE! YOU ARE REALLY LUCKY!
IF I HEAR ONE MORE PERSON TELL ME HOW MY PARENTS BEND OVER BACKWARD FOR ME, I'M GOING TO CROAK!

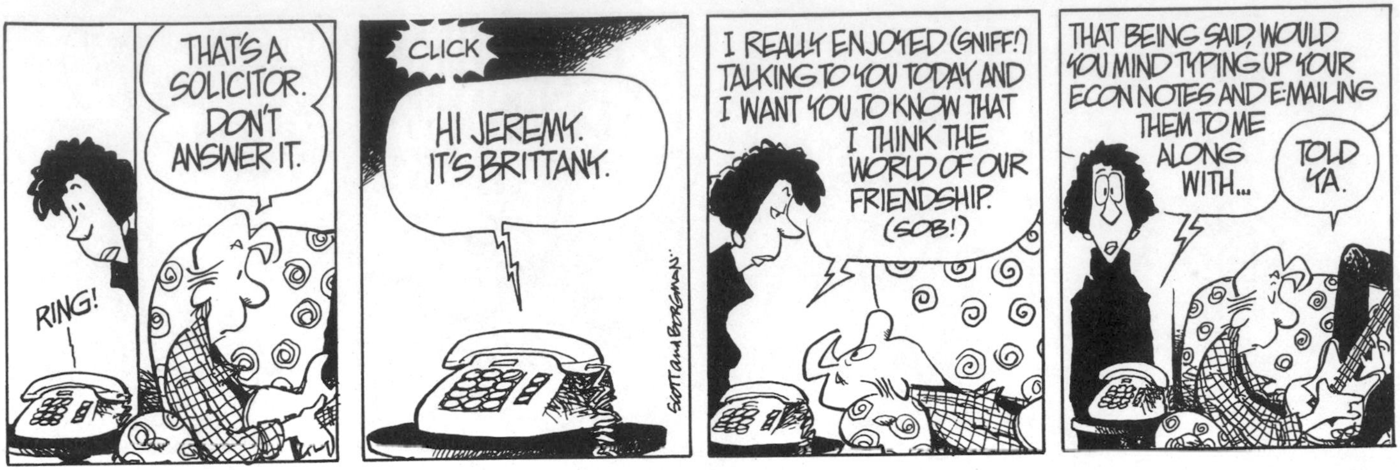
THAT'S A SOLICITOR. DON'T ANSWER IT.
RING!
CLICK
HI JEREMY. IT'S BRITTANY.
SCOTT and BORGMAN
I REALLY ENJOYED (SNIFF!) TALKING TO YOU TODAY AND I WANT YOU TO KNOW THAT I THINK THE WORLD OF OUR FRIENDSHIP. (SOB!)
THAT BEING SAID, WOULD YOU MIND TYPING UP YOUR ECON NOTES AND E-MAILING THEM TO ME ALONG WITH...
TOLD YA.

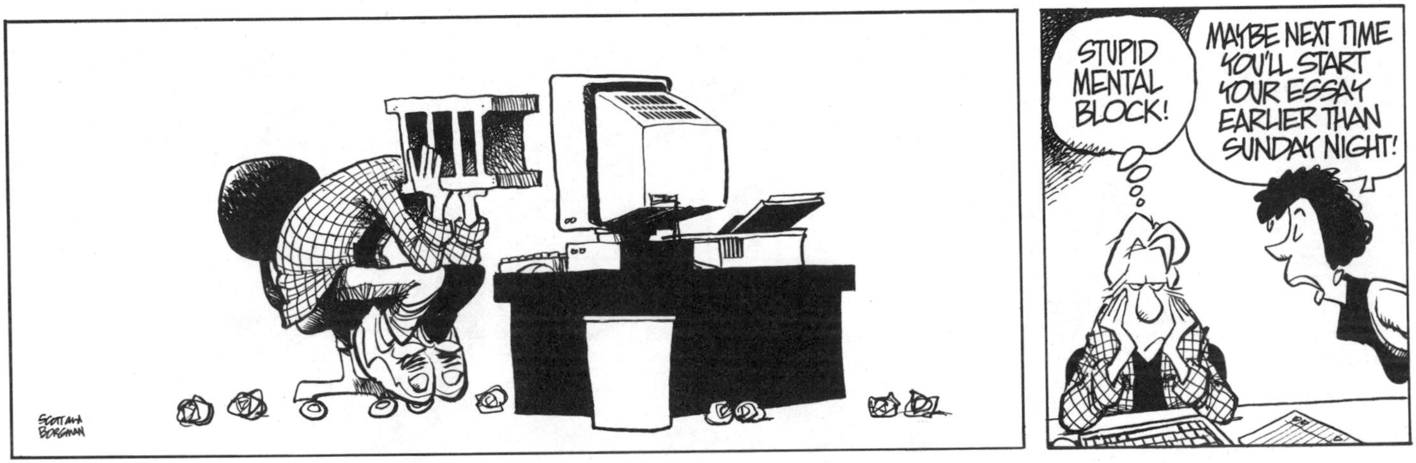
SCOTT and BORGMAN
STUPID MENTAL BLOCK!
MAYBE NEXT TIME YOU'LL START YOUR ESSAY EARLIER THAN SUNDAY NIGHT!

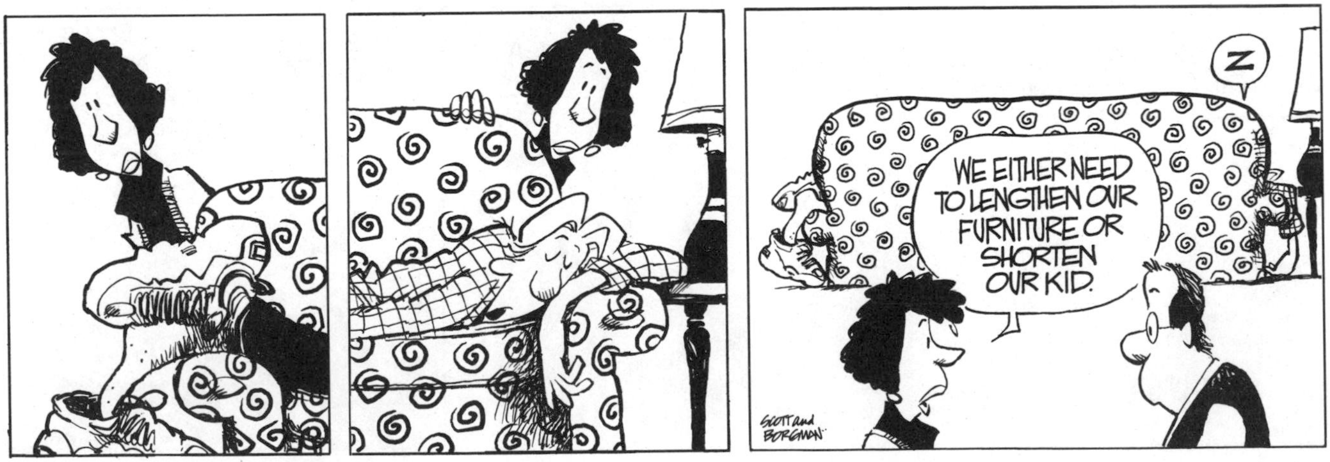
Z
WE EITHER NEED TO LENGTHEN OUR FURNITURE OR SHORTEN OUR KID.
SCOTT and BORGMAN

Zits
by
JERRY SCOTT and
JIM BORGMAN

JEREMY, YOUR MOTHER AND I JUST WANT YOU TO KNOW THAT YOU CAN ALWAYS TALK TO US IF THERE'S EVER ANYTHING ON YOUR MIND.
SEX
DUH!
YOU'LL BE THE FIRST TO KNOW
SEE? I TOLD YOU HE'S FINE.
STILL, I CAN'T HELP BUT WORRY...

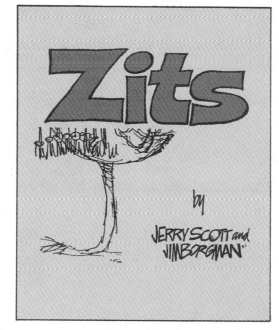

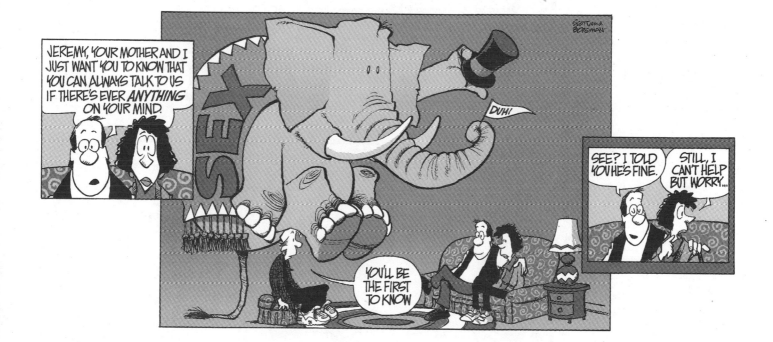

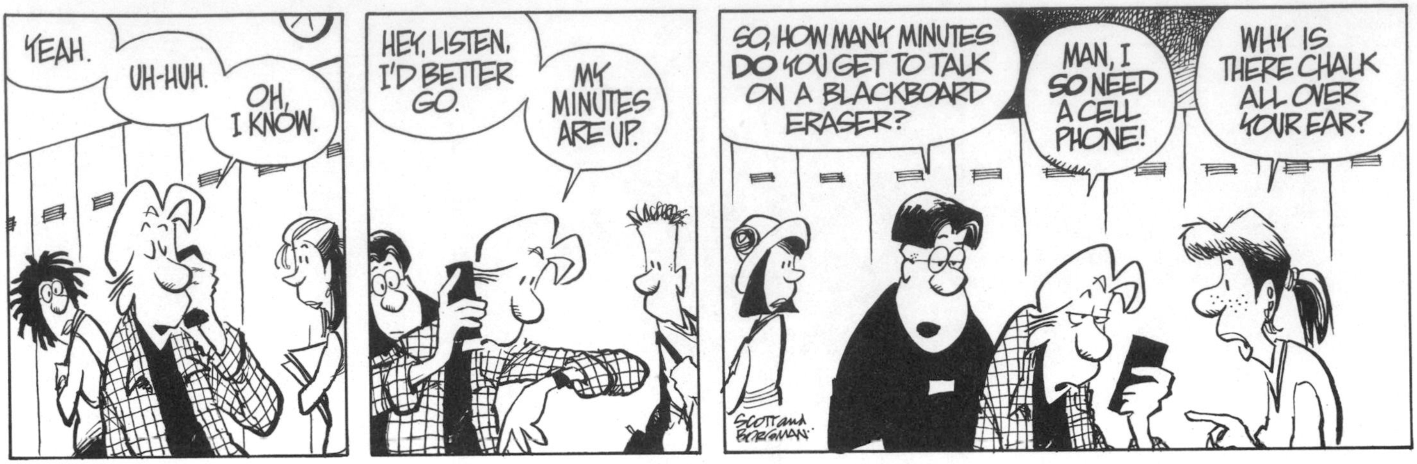
YEAH.
UH-HUH.
OH, I KNOW.
HEY, LISTEN, I'D BETTER GO.
MY MINUTES ARE UP.
SO, HOW MANY MINUTES **DO** YOU GET TO TALK ON A BLACKBOARD ERASER?
MAN, I **SO** NEED A CELL PHONE!
WHY IS THERE CHALK ALL OVER YOUR EAR?
SCOTT and BORGMAN

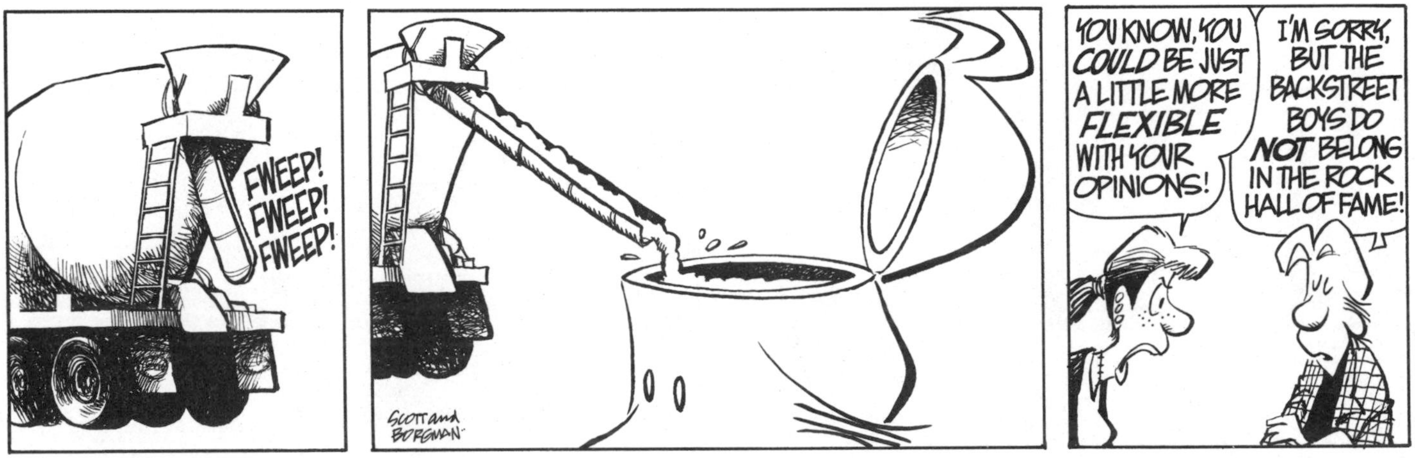
FWEEP! FWEEP! FWEEP!
SCOTT and BORGMAN
YOU KNOW, YOU ***COULD*** BE JUST A LITTLE MORE ***FLEXIBLE*** WITH YOUR OPINIONS!
I'M SORRY, BUT THE BACKSTREET BOYS DO ***NOT*** BELONG IN THE ROCK HALL OF FAME!

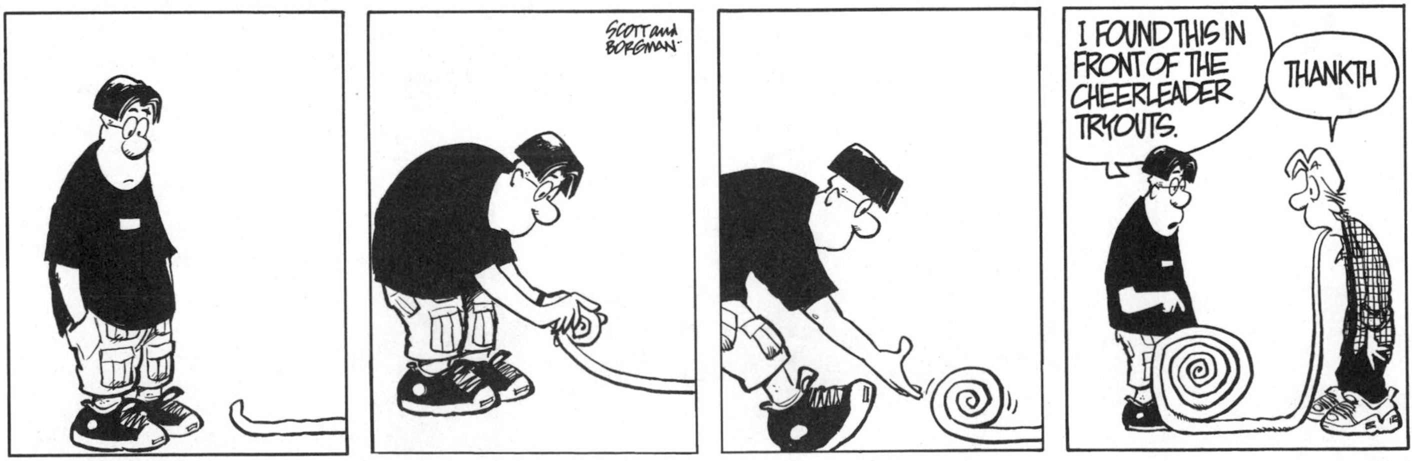
SCOTT and BORGMAN
I FOUND THIS IN FRONT OF THE CHEERLEADER TRYOUTS.
THANKTH

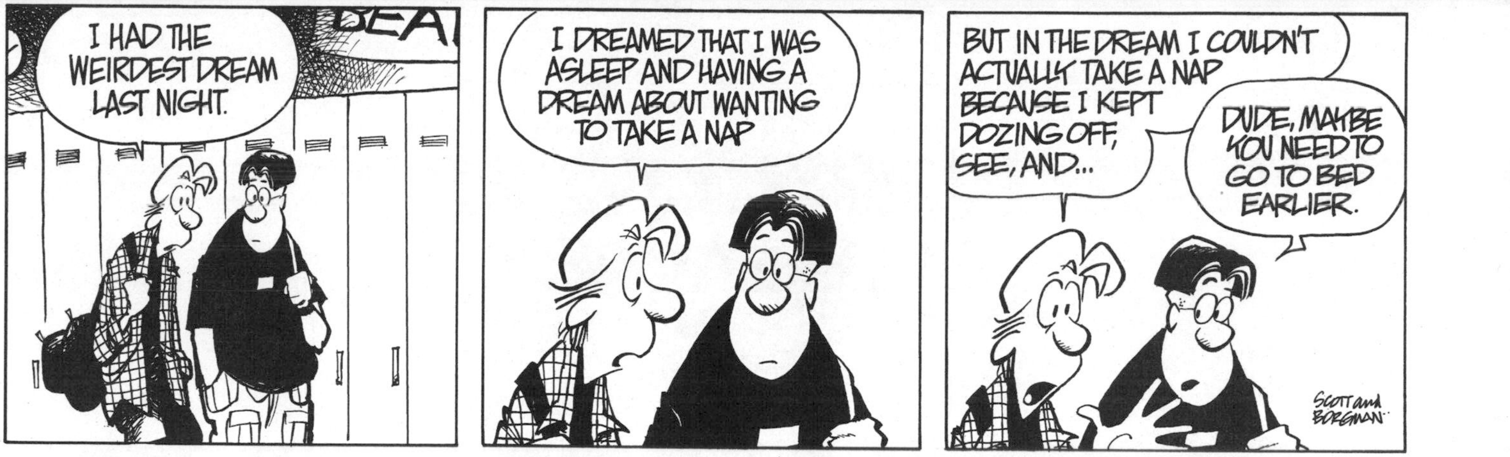
I HAD THE WEIRDEST DREAM LAST NIGHT.
I DREAMED THAT I WAS ASLEEP AND HAVING A DREAM ABOUT WANTING TO TAKE A NAP
BUT IN THE DREAM I COULDN'T ACTUALLY TAKE A NAP BECAUSE I KEPT DOZING OFF, SEE, AND...
DUDE, MAYBE YOU NEED TO GO TO BED EARLIER.
SCOTT AND BORGMAN

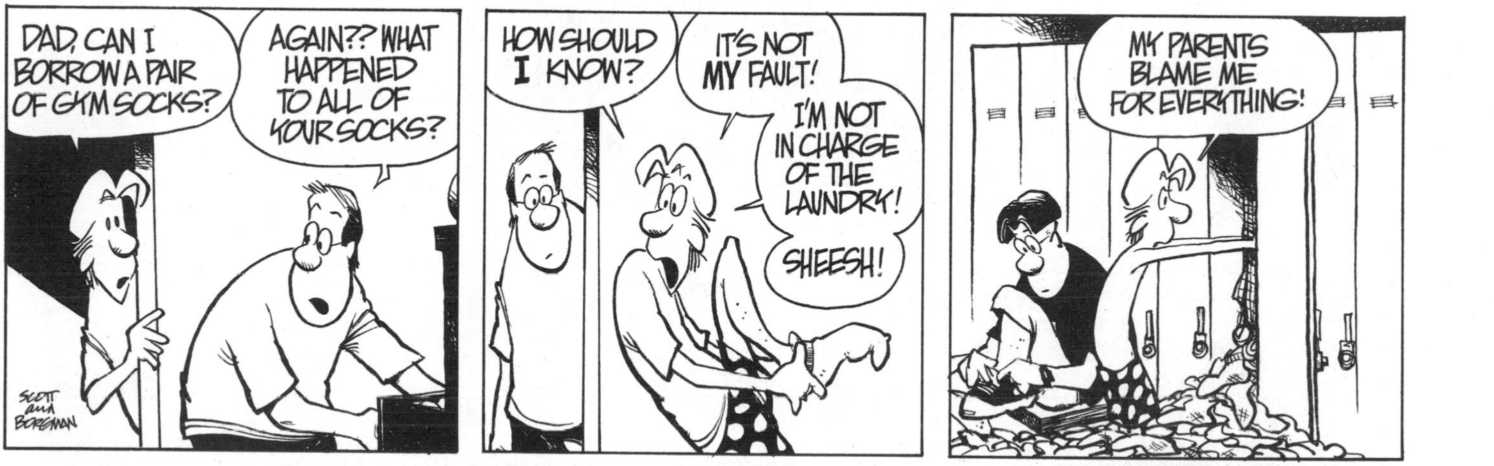
DAD, CAN I BORROW A PAIR OF GYM SOCKS?
AGAIN?? WHAT HAPPENED TO ALL OF YOUR SOCKS?
SCOTT AND BORGMAN
HOW SHOULD I KNOW?
IT'S NOT MY FAULT!
I'M NOT IN CHARGE OF THE LAUNDRY!
SHEESH!
MY PARENTS BLAME ME FOR EVERYTHING!

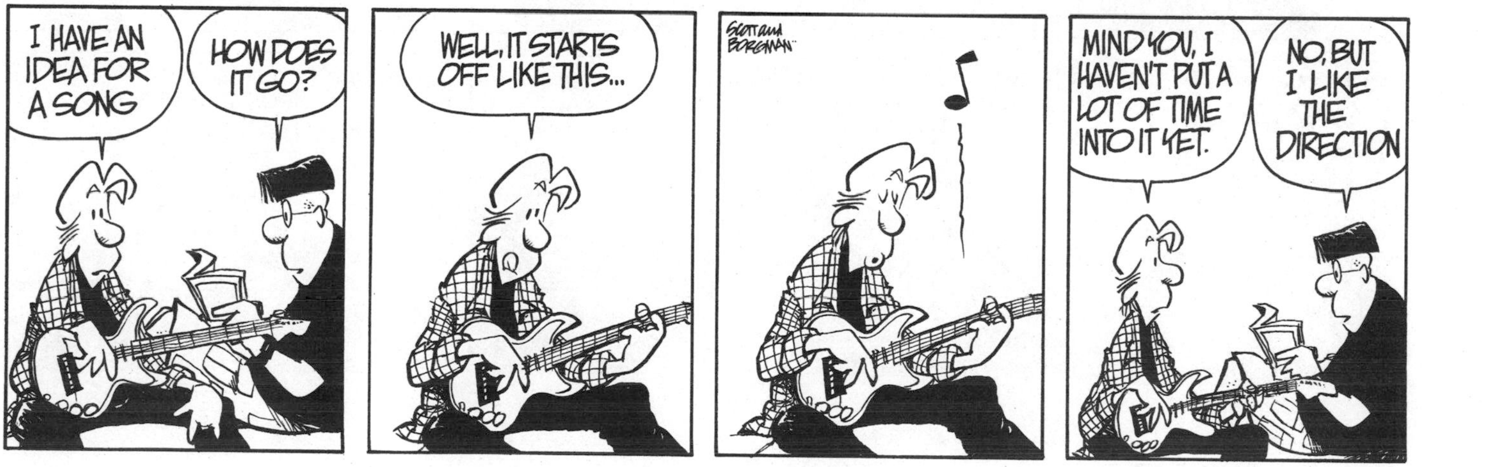
I HAVE AN IDEA FOR A SONG
HOW DOES IT GO?
WELL, IT STARTS OFF LIKE THIS...
SCOTT AND BORGMAN
MIND YOU, I HAVEN'T PUT A LOT OF TIME INTO IT YET.
NO, BUT I LIKE THE DIRECTION

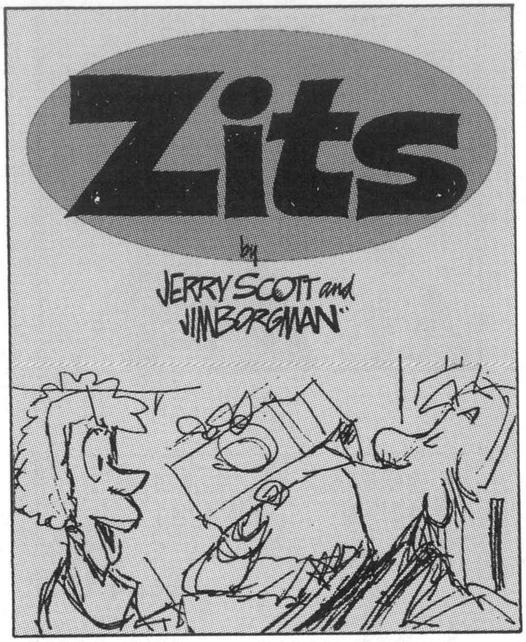
Zits
by
JERRY SCOTT and
JIM BORGMAN

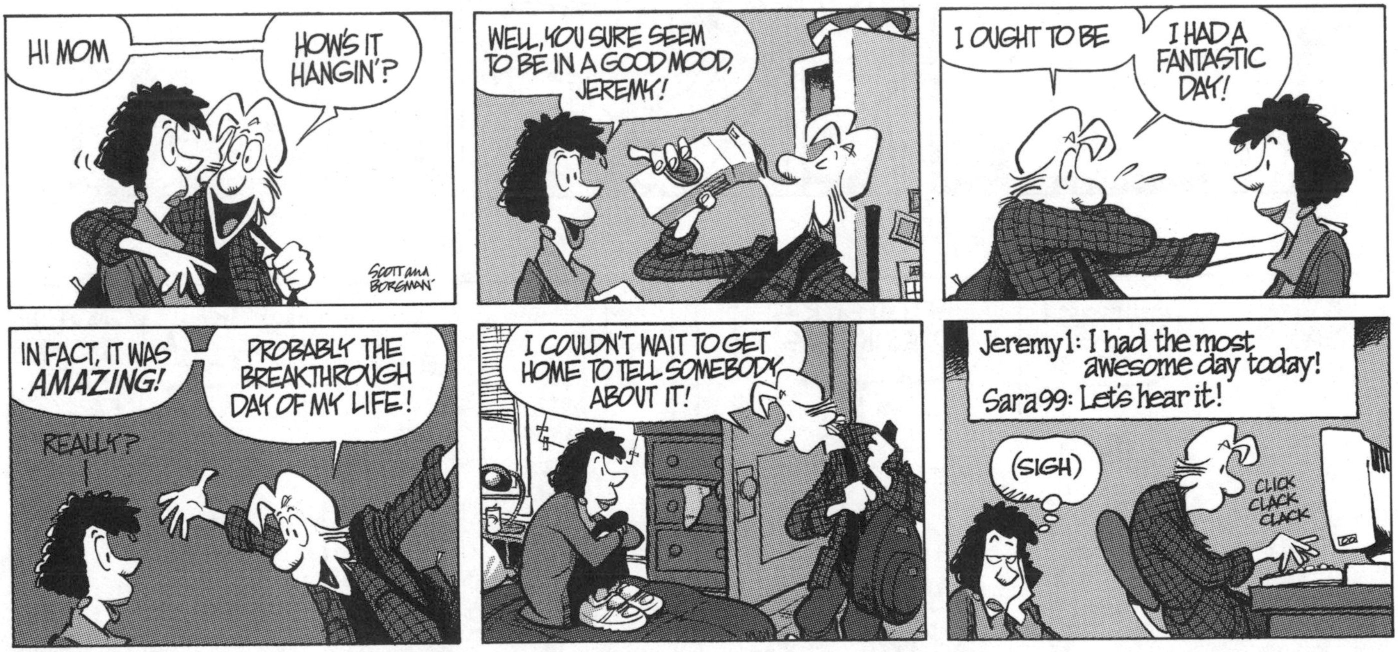
HI MOM
HOW'S IT HANGIN'?
SCOTT and BORGMAN
WELL, YOU SURE SEEM TO BE IN A GOOD MOOD, JEREMY!
I OUGHT TO BE
I HAD A FANTASTIC DAY!
IN FACT, IT WAS AMAZING!
PROBABLY THE BREAKTHROUGH DAY OF MY LIFE!
REALLY?
I COULDN'T WAIT TO GET HOME TO TELL SOMEBODY ABOUT IT!
Jeremy1: I had the most awesome day today!
Sara99: Let's hear it!
(SIGH)
CLICK CLACK CLACK

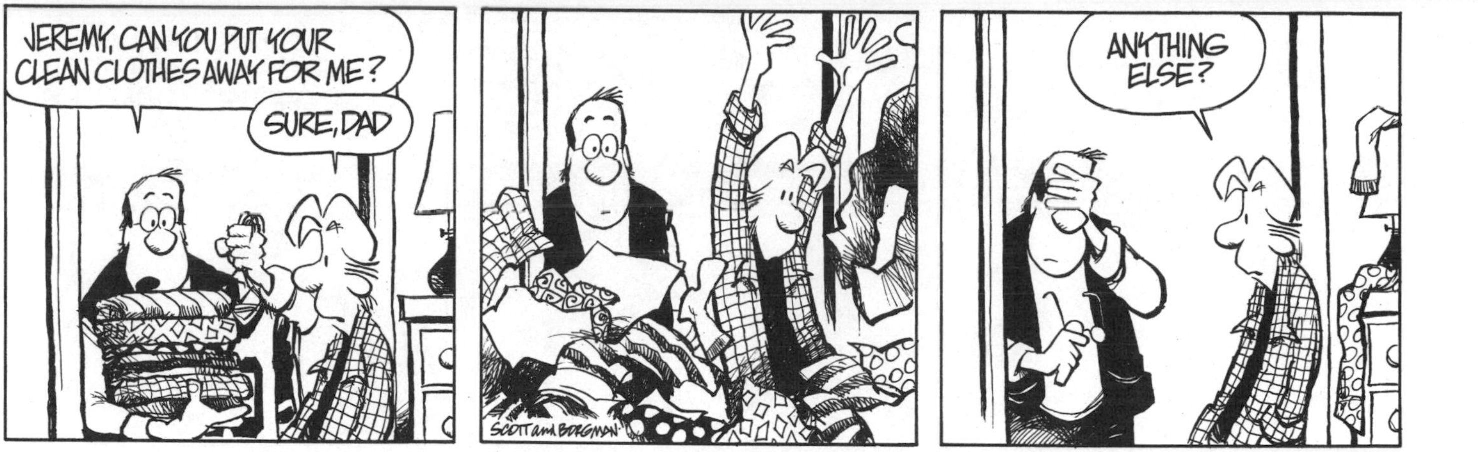

JEREMY, CAN YOU PUT YOUR CLEAN CLOTHES AWAY FOR ME?
SURE, DAD
SCOTT AND BORGMAN
ANYTHING ELSE?

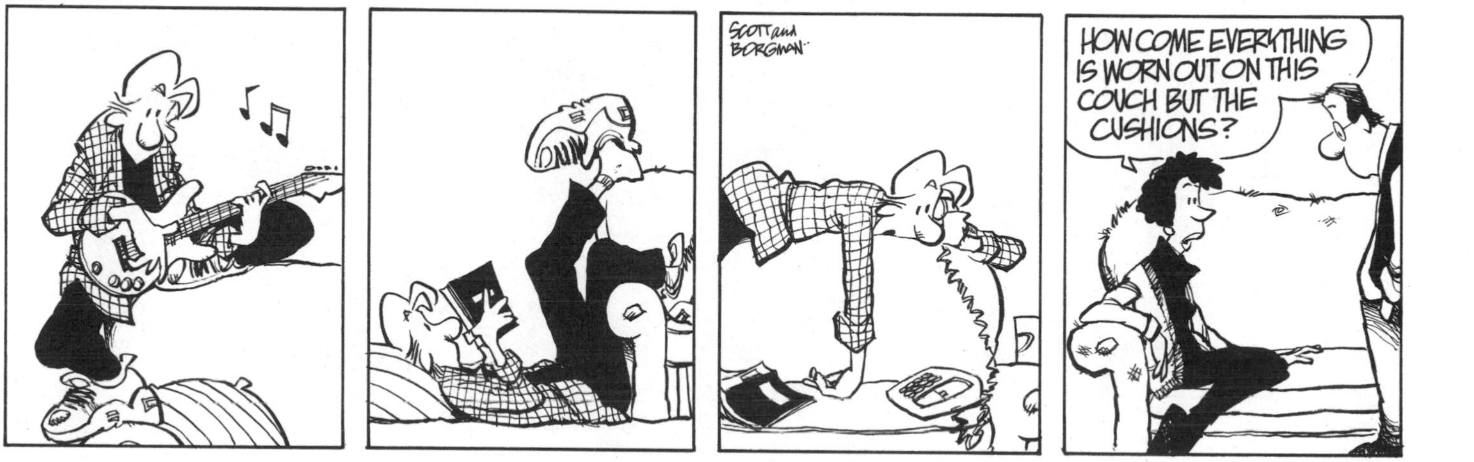

SCOTT AND BORGMAN
HOW COME EVERYTHING IS WORN OUT ON THIS COUCH BUT THE CUSHIONS?

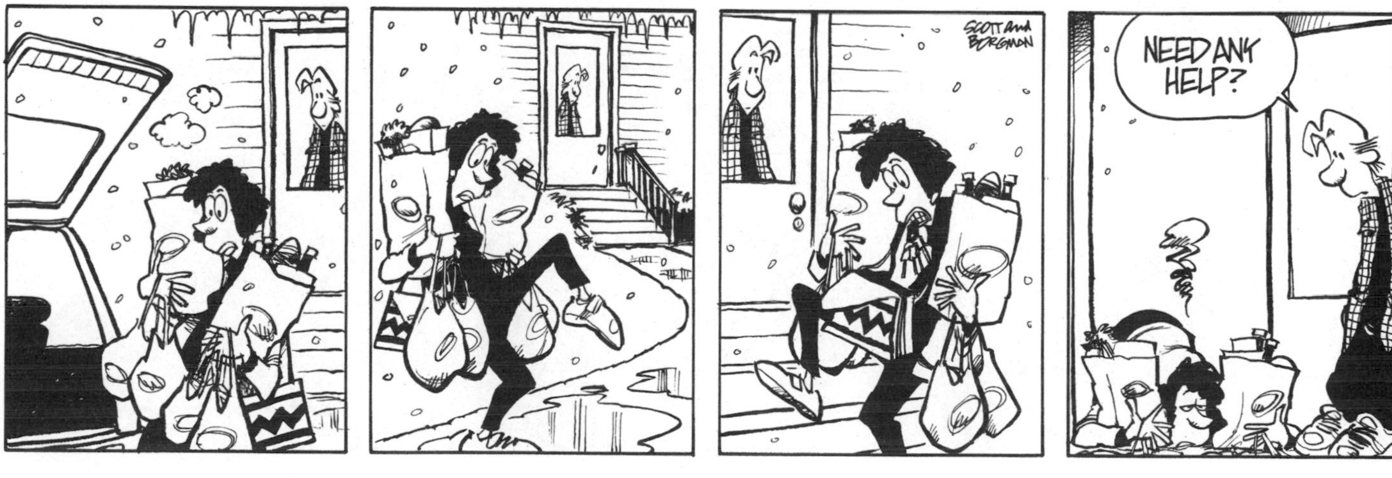

SCOTT AND BORGMAN
NEED ANY HELP?

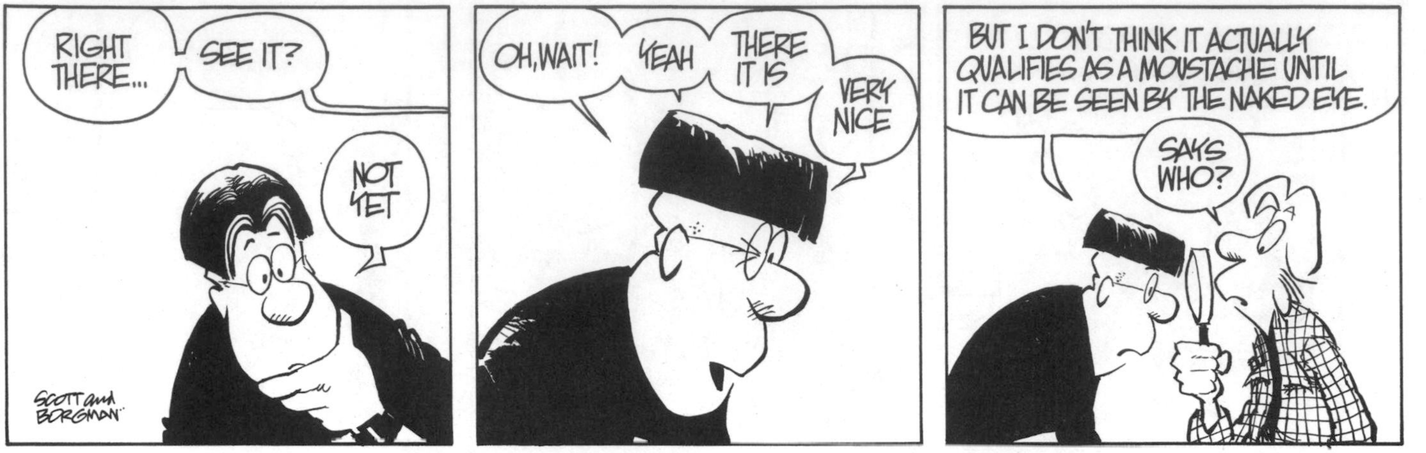
RIGHT THERE...
SEE IT?
NOT YET
OH, WAIT!
YEAH
THERE IT IS
VERY NICE
BUT I DON'T THINK IT ACTUALLY QUALIFIES AS A MOUSTACHE UNTIL IT CAN BE SEEN BY THE NAKED EYE.
SAYS WHO?
SCOTT and BORGMAN

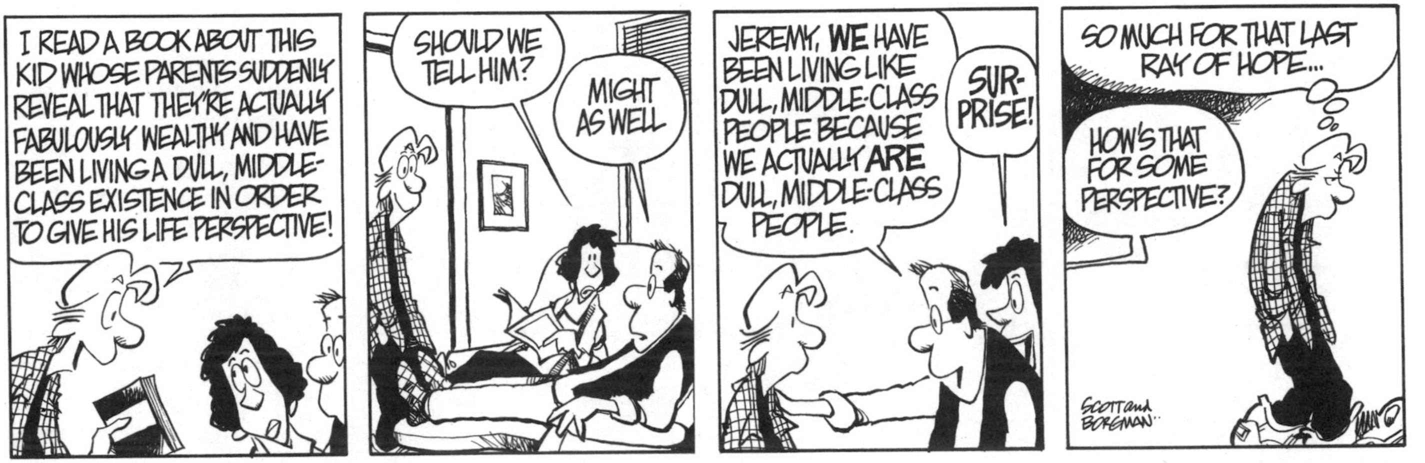
I READ A BOOK ABOUT THIS KID WHOSE PARENTS SUDDENLY REVEAL THAT THEY'RE ACTUALLY FABULOUSLY WEALTHY AND HAVE BEEN LIVING A DULL, MIDDLE-CLASS EXISTENCE IN ORDER TO GIVE HIS LIFE PERSPECTIVE!
SHOULD WE TELL HIM?
MIGHT AS WELL
JEREMY, **WE** HAVE BEEN LIVING LIKE DULL, MIDDLE-CLASS PEOPLE BECAUSE WE ACTUALLY **ARE** DULL, MIDDLE-CLASS PEOPLE.
SUR-PRISE!
SO MUCH FOR THAT LAST RAY OF HOPE...
HOW'S THAT FOR SOME PERSPECTIVE?
SCOTT and BORGMAN

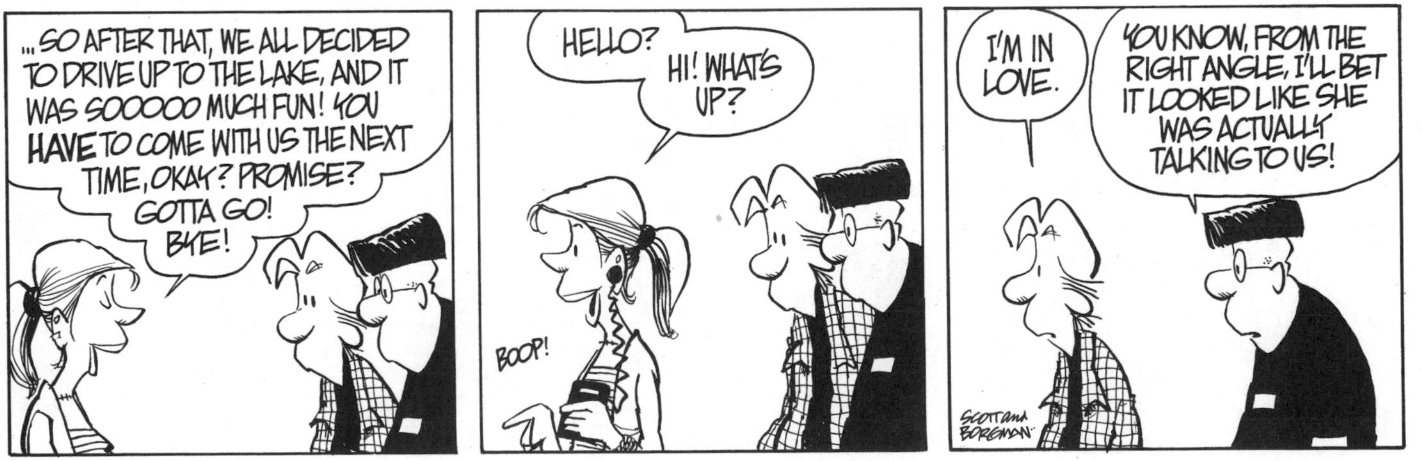
...SO AFTER THAT, WE ALL DECIDED TO DRIVE UP TO THE LAKE, AND IT WAS SOOOOOO MUCH FUN! YOU **HAVE** TO COME WITH US THE NEXT TIME, OKAY? PROMISE? GOTTA GO! BYE!
HELLO?
HI! WHAT'S UP?
BOOP!
I'M IN LOVE.
YOU KNOW, FROM THE RIGHT ANGLE, I'LL BET IT LOOKED LIKE SHE WAS ACTUALLY TALKING TO US!
SCOTT and BORGMAN

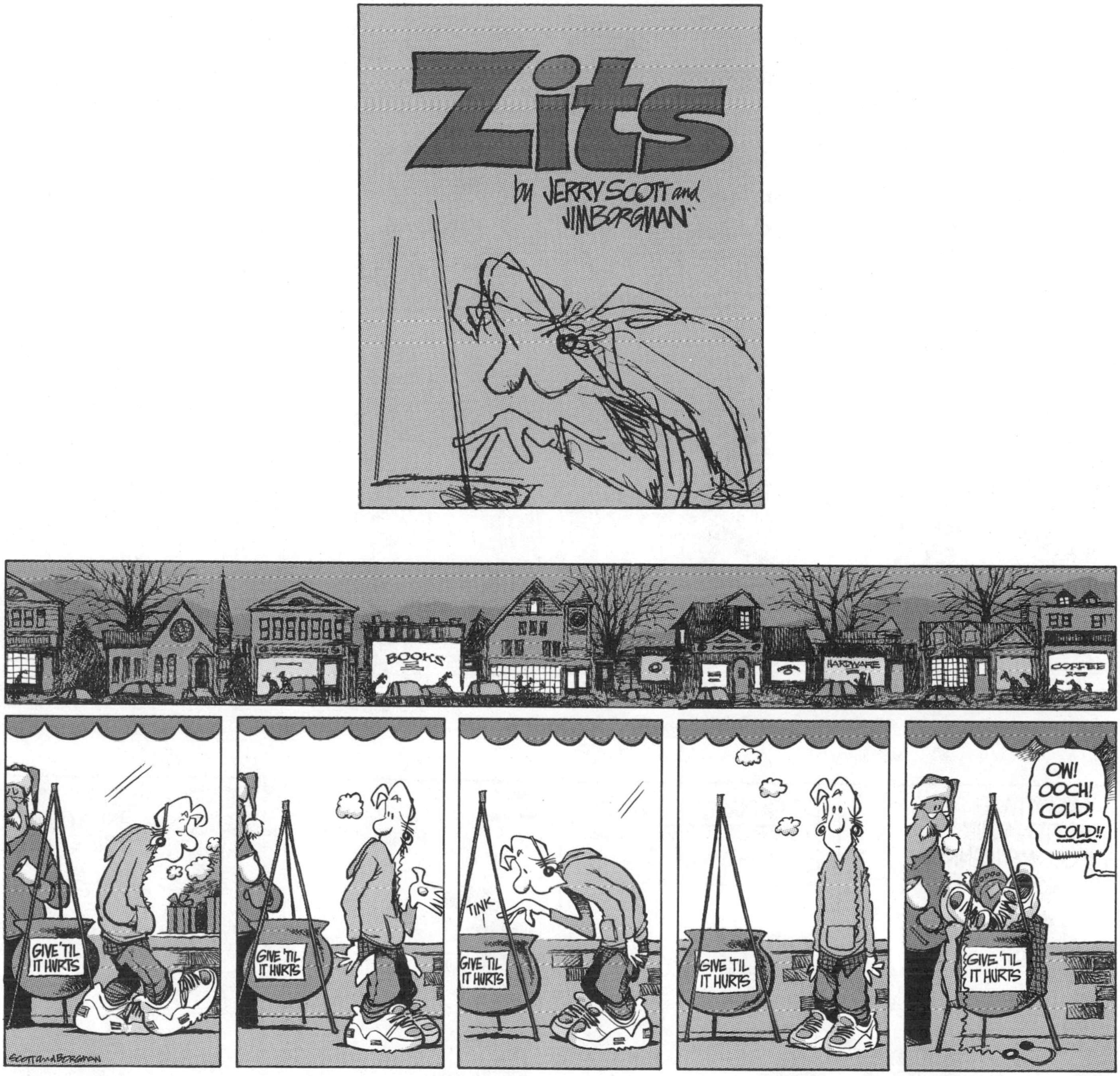
Zits
by JERRY SCOTT and JIM BORGMAN
BOOKS
HARDWARE
COFFEE
GIVE 'TIL IT HURTS
GIVE 'TIL IT HURTS
TINK
GIVE 'TIL IT HURTS
GIVE 'TIL IT HURTS
OW! OOCH! COLD! COLD!!
GIVE 'TIL IT HURTS

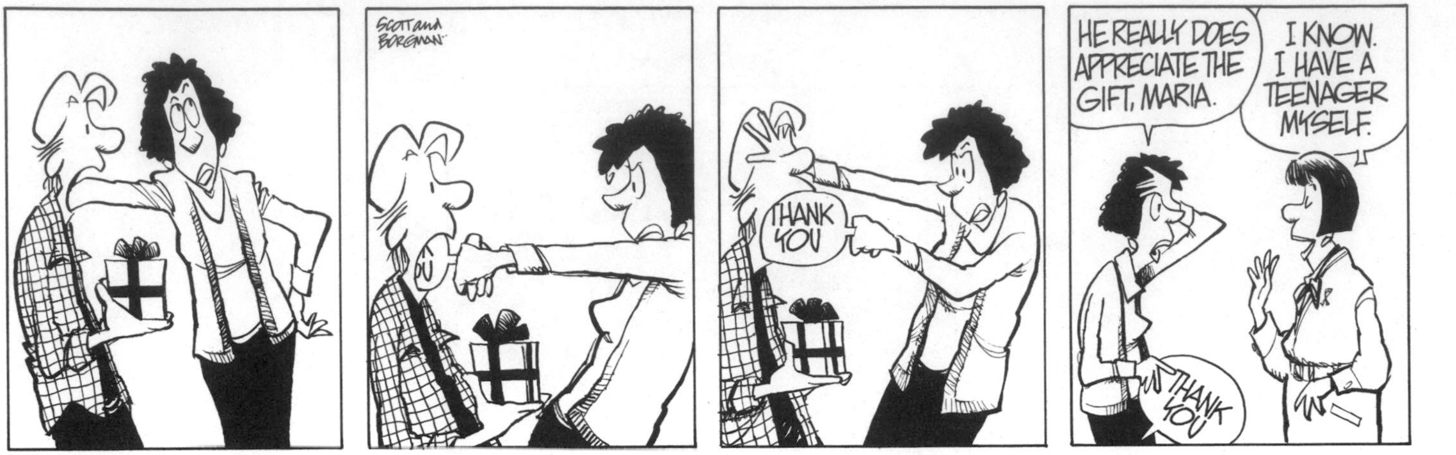
SCOTT and BORGMAN
THANK YOU
HE REALLY DOES APPRECIATE THE GIFT, MARIA.
I KNOW. I HAVE A TEENAGER MYSELF.
THANK YOU

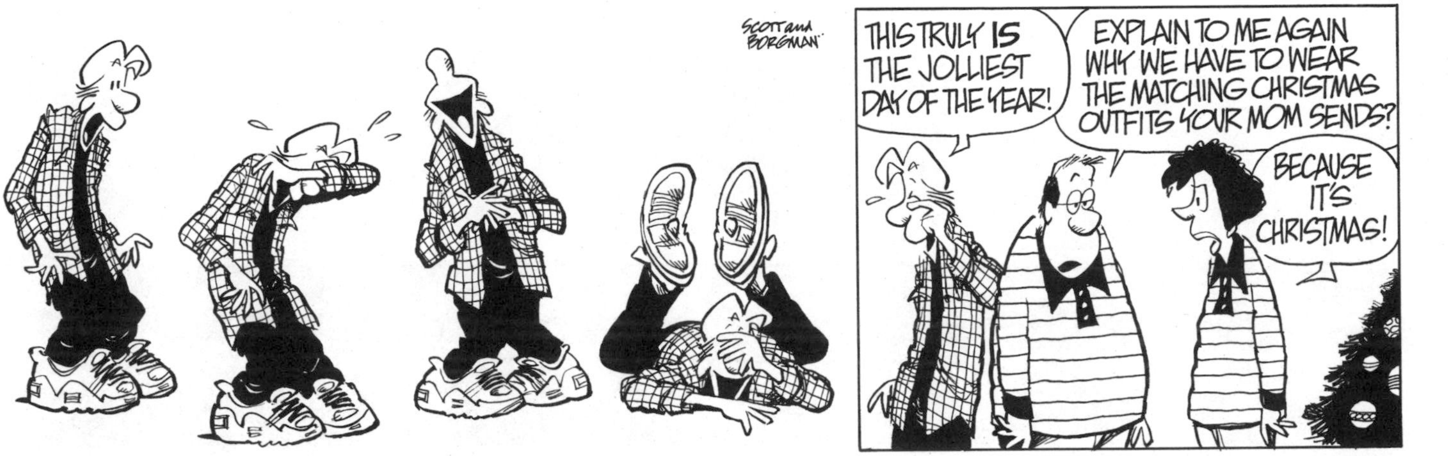
SCOTT and BORGMAN
THIS TRULY IS THE JOLLIEST DAY OF THE YEAR!
EXPLAIN TO ME AGAIN WHY WE HAVE TO WEAR THE MATCHING CHRISTMAS OUTFITS YOUR MOM SENDS?
BECAUSE IT'S CHRISTMAS!

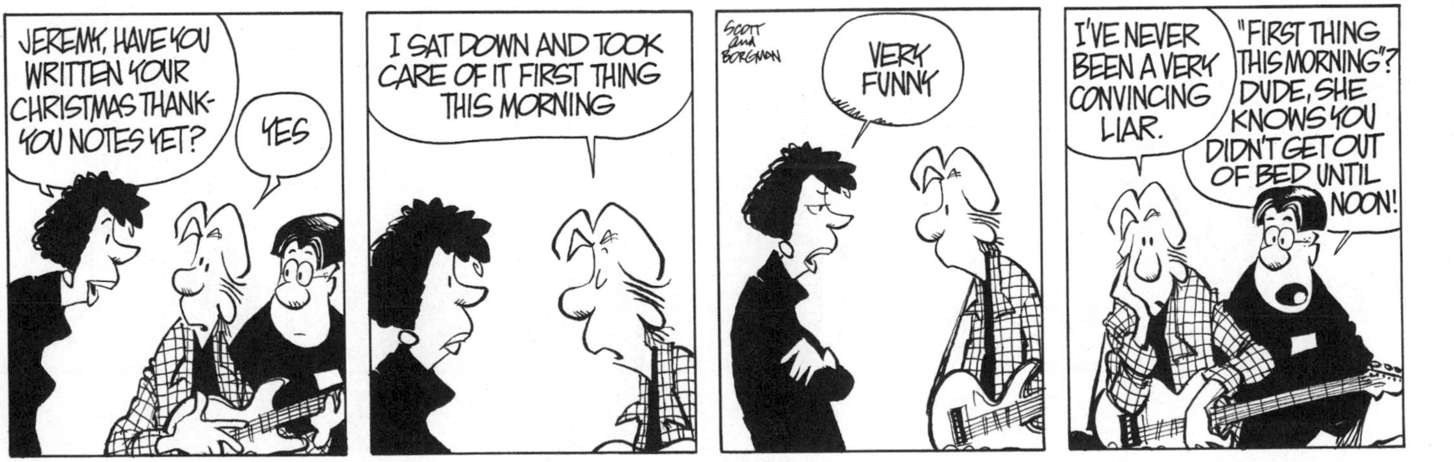
JEREMY, HAVE YOU WRITTEN YOUR CHRISTMAS THANK-YOU NOTES YET?
YES
I SAT DOWN AND TOOK CARE OF IT FIRST THING THIS MORNING
SCOTT and BORGMAN
VERY FUNNY
I'VE NEVER BEEN A VERY CONVINCING LIAR.
"FIRST THING THIS MORNING"? DUDE, SHE KNOWS YOU DIDN'T GET OUT OF BED UNTIL NOON!

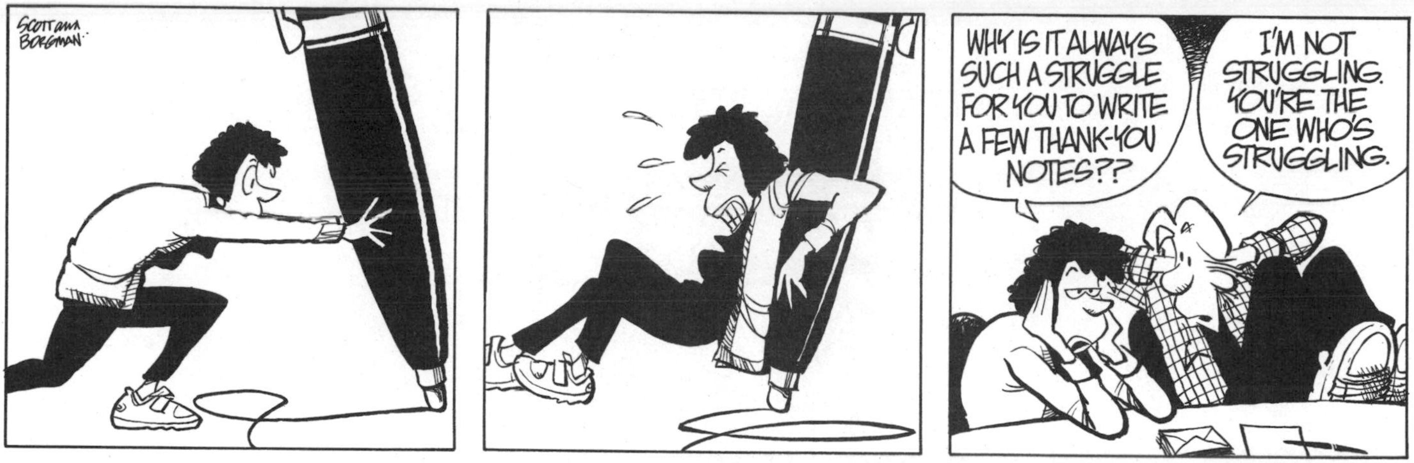
WHY IS IT ALWAYS SUCH A STRUGGLE FOR YOU TO WRITE A FEW THANK-YOU NOTES??
I'M NOT STRUGGLING. YOU'RE THE ONE WHO'S STRUGGLING.

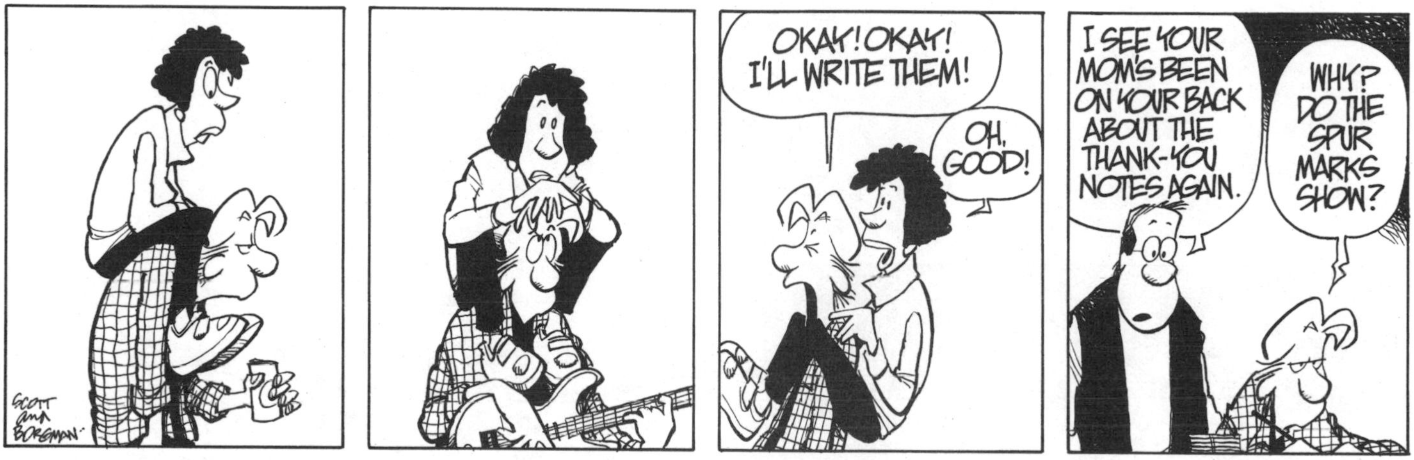
OKAY! OKAY! I'LL WRITE THEM!
OH, GOOD!
I SEE YOUR MOM'S BEEN ON YOUR BACK ABOUT THE THANK-YOU NOTES AGAIN.
WHY? DO THE SPUR MARKS SHOW?

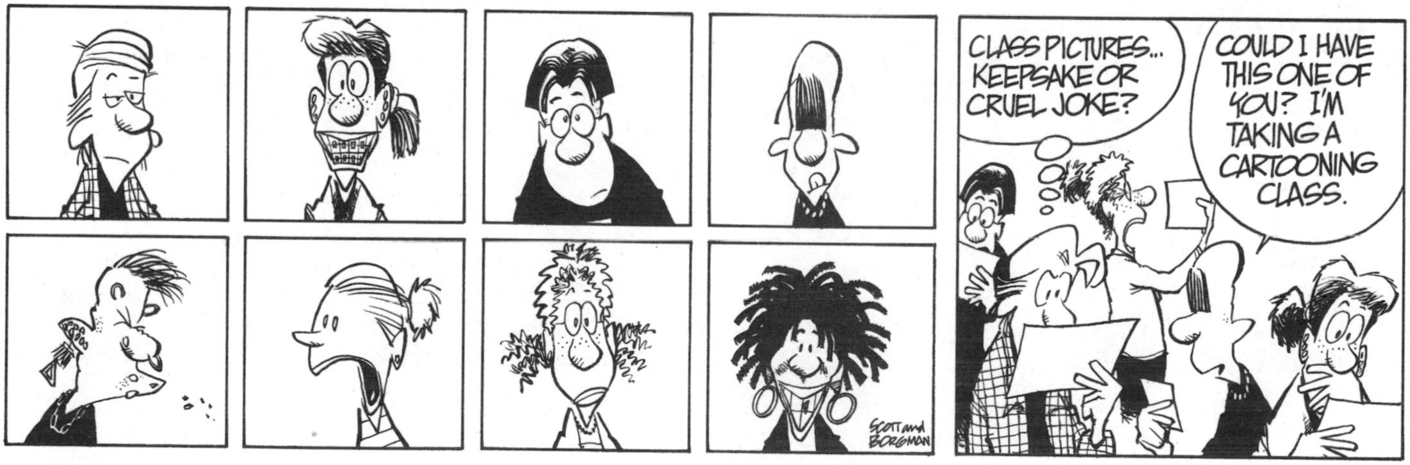
CLASS PICTURES... KEEPSAKE OR CRUEL JOKE?
COULD I HAVE THIS ONE OF YOU? I'M TAKING A CARTOONING CLASS.

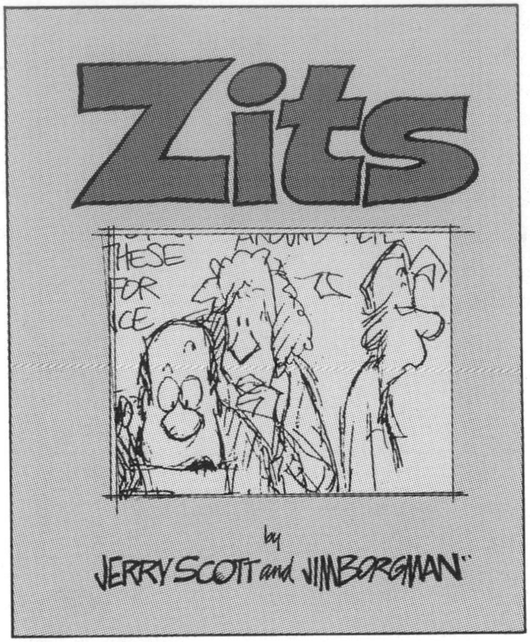
Zits
by
JERRY SCOTT and JIM BORGMAN

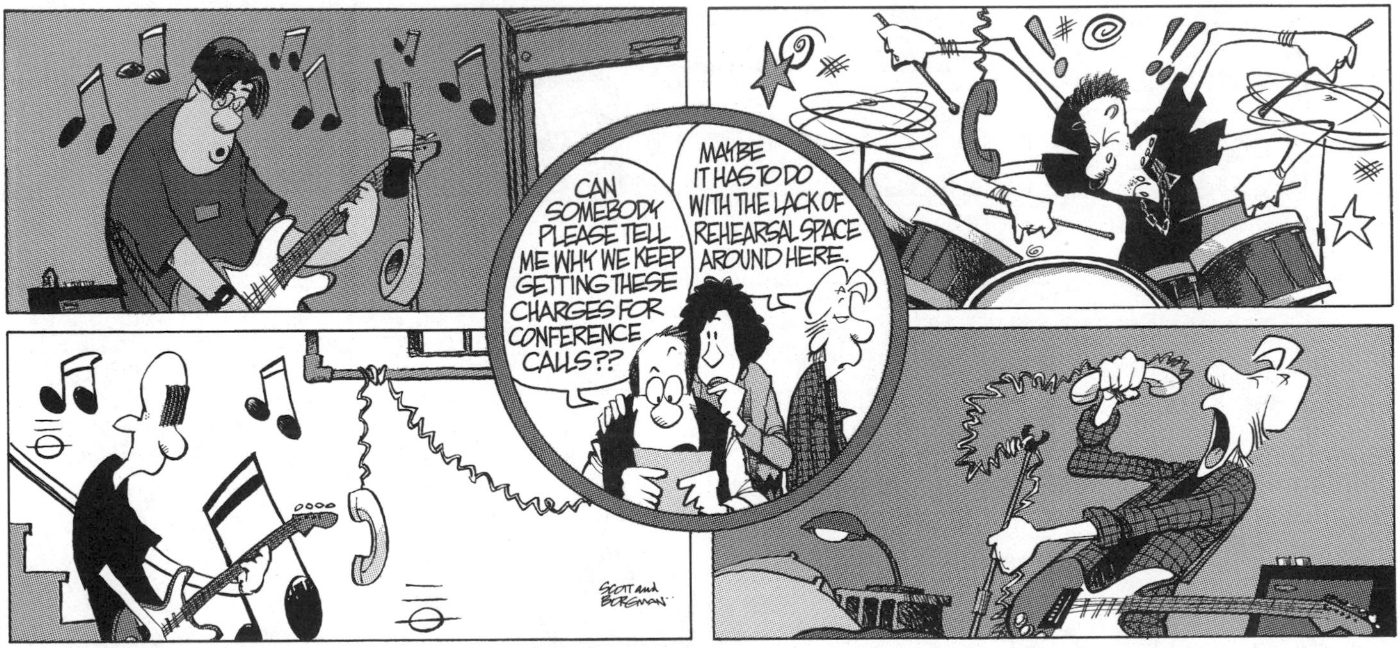
CAN SOMEBODY PLEASE TELL ME WHY WE KEEP GETTING THESE CHARGES FOR CONFERENCE CALLS??
MAYBE IT HAS TO DO WITH THE LACK OF REHEARSAL SPACE AROUND HERE.
SCOTT and BORGMAN

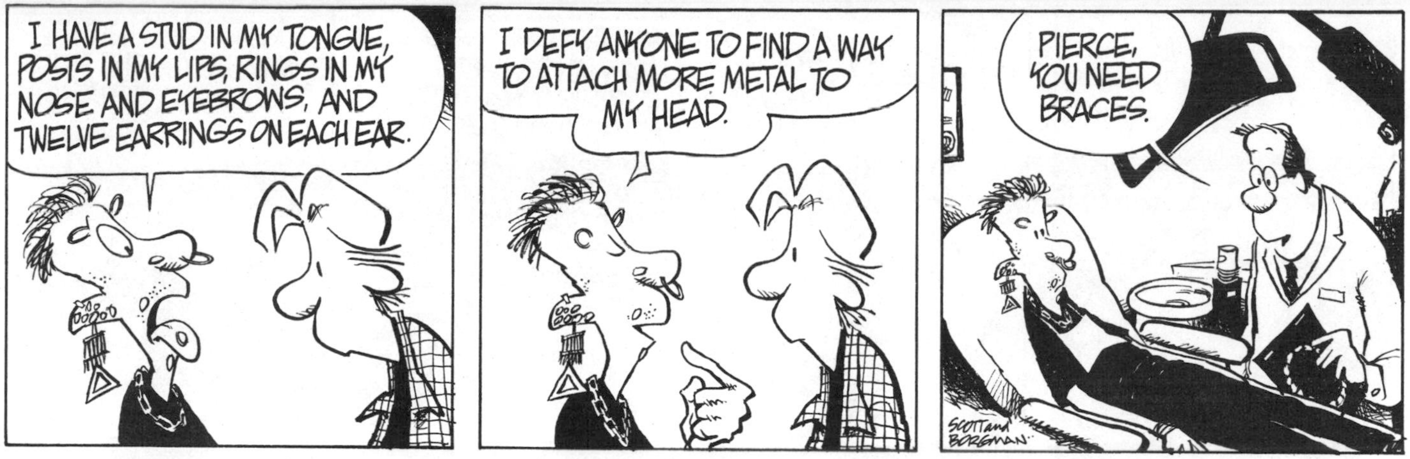
I HAVE A STUD IN MY TONGUE, POSTS IN MY LIPS, RINGS IN MY NOSE AND EYEBROWS, AND TWELVE EARRINGS ON EACH EAR.
I DEFY ANYONE TO FIND A WAY TO ATTACH MORE METAL TO MY HEAD.
PIERCE, YOU NEED BRACES.
SCOTT and BORGMAN

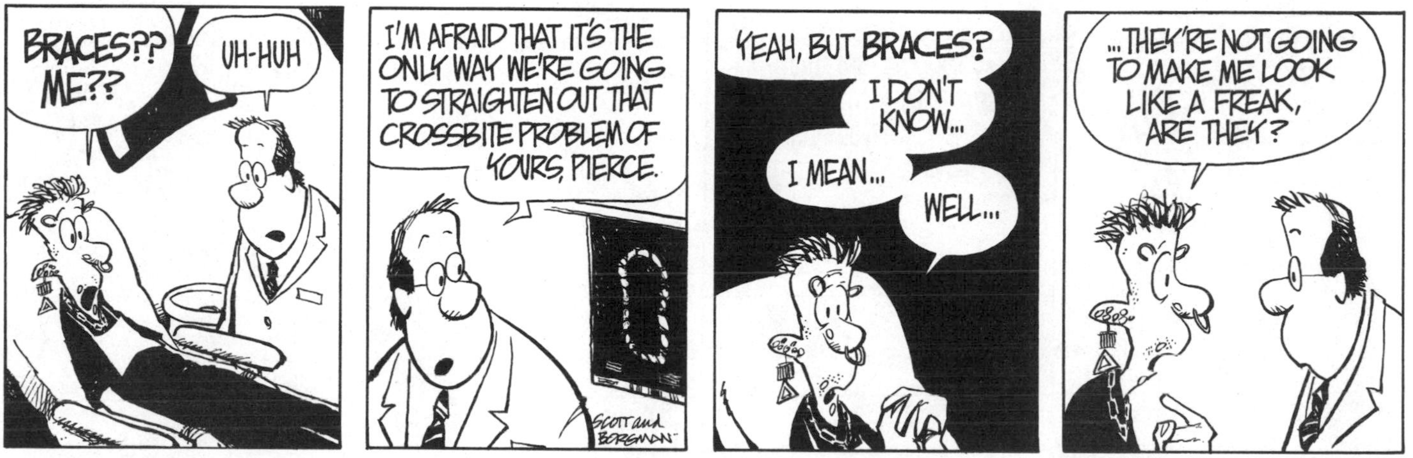
BRACES?? ME??
UH-HUH
I'M AFRAID THAT IT'S THE ONLY WAY WE'RE GOING TO STRAIGHTEN OUT THAT CROSSBITE PROBLEM OF YOURS, PIERCE.
SCOTT and BORGMAN
YEAH, BUT BRACES?
I DON'T KNOW...
I MEAN...
WELL...
...THEY'RE NOT GOING TO MAKE ME LOOK LIKE A FREAK, ARE THEY?

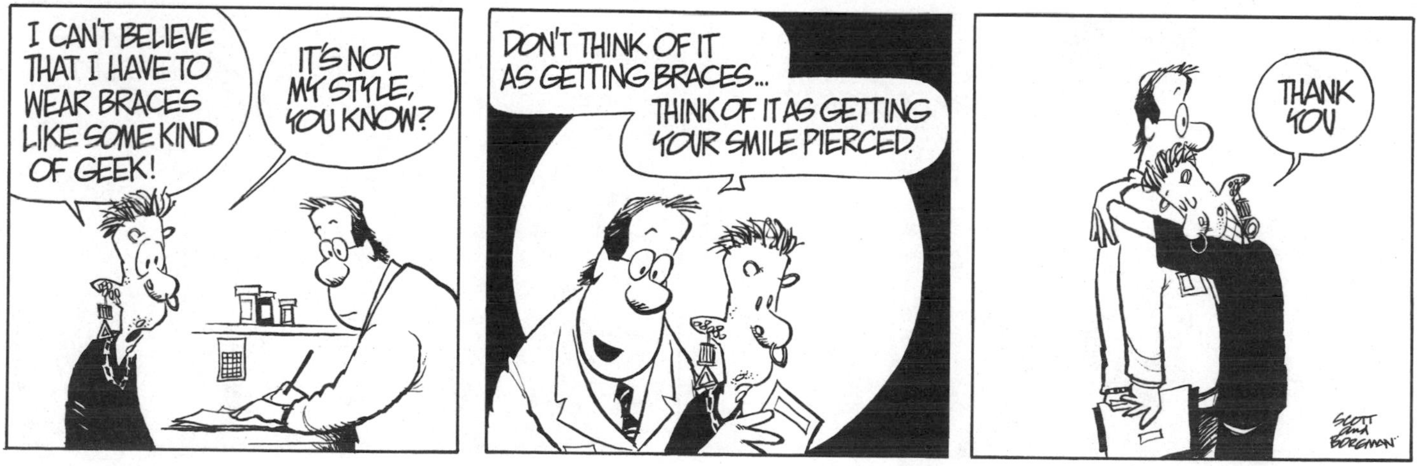
I CAN'T BELIEVE THAT I HAVE TO WEAR BRACES LIKE SOME KIND OF GEEK!
IT'S NOT MY STYLE, YOU KNOW?
DON'T THINK OF IT AS GETTING BRACES...
THINK OF IT AS GETTING YOUR SMILE PIERCED.
THANK YOU
SCOTT and BORGMAN

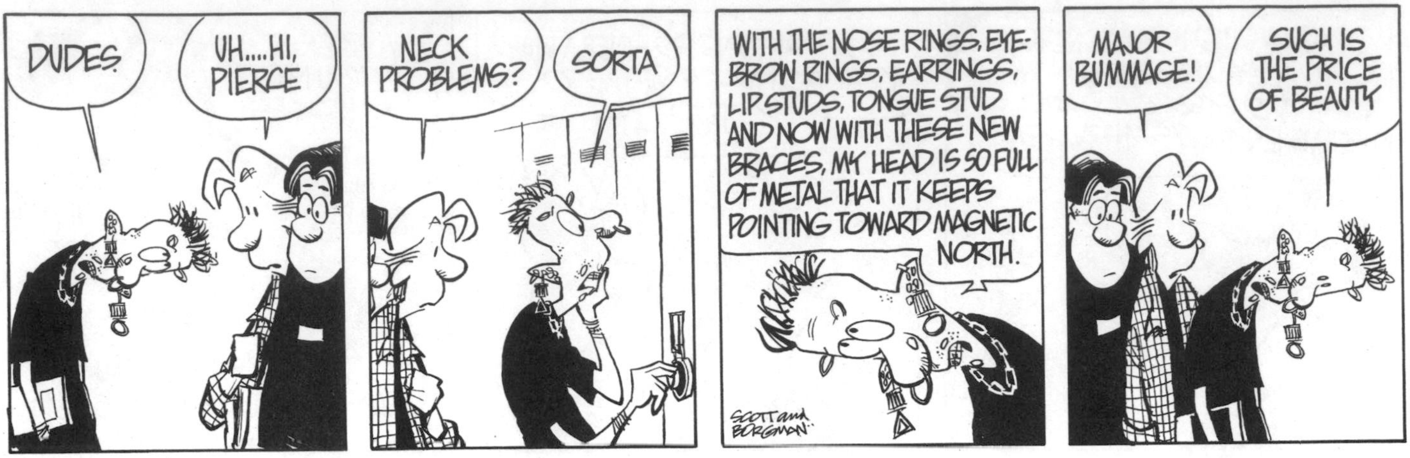
DUDES
UH....HI, PIERCE
NECK PROBLEMS?
SORTA
WITH THE NOSE RINGS, EYEBROW RINGS, EARRINGS, LIP STUDS, TONGUE STUD AND NOW WITH THESE NEW BRACES, MY HEAD IS SO FULL OF METAL THAT IT KEEPS POINTING TOWARD MAGNETIC NORTH.
SCOTT and BORGMAN
MAJOR BUMMAGE!
SUCH IS THE PRICE OF BEAUTY

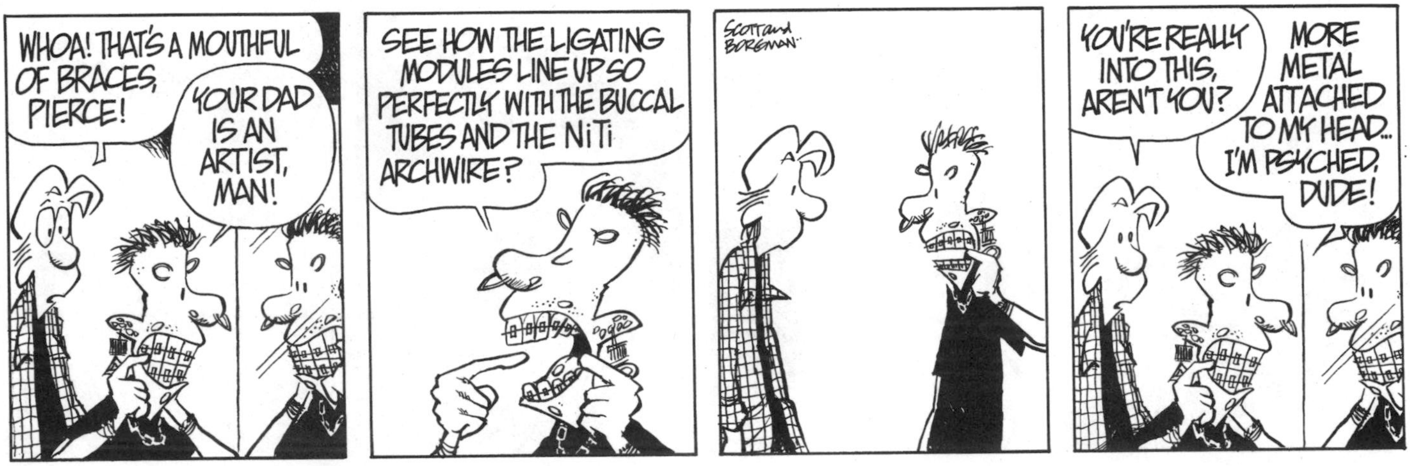
WHOA! THAT'S A MOUTHFUL OF BRACES, PIERCE!
YOUR DAD IS AN ARTIST, MAN!
SEE HOW THE LIGATING MODULES LINE UP SO PERFECTLY WITH THE BUCCAL TUBES AND THE NiTi ARCHWIRE?
SCOTT and BORGMAN
YOU'RE REALLY INTO THIS, AREN'T YOU?
MORE METAL ATTACHED TO MY HEAD... I'M PSYCHED, DUDE!

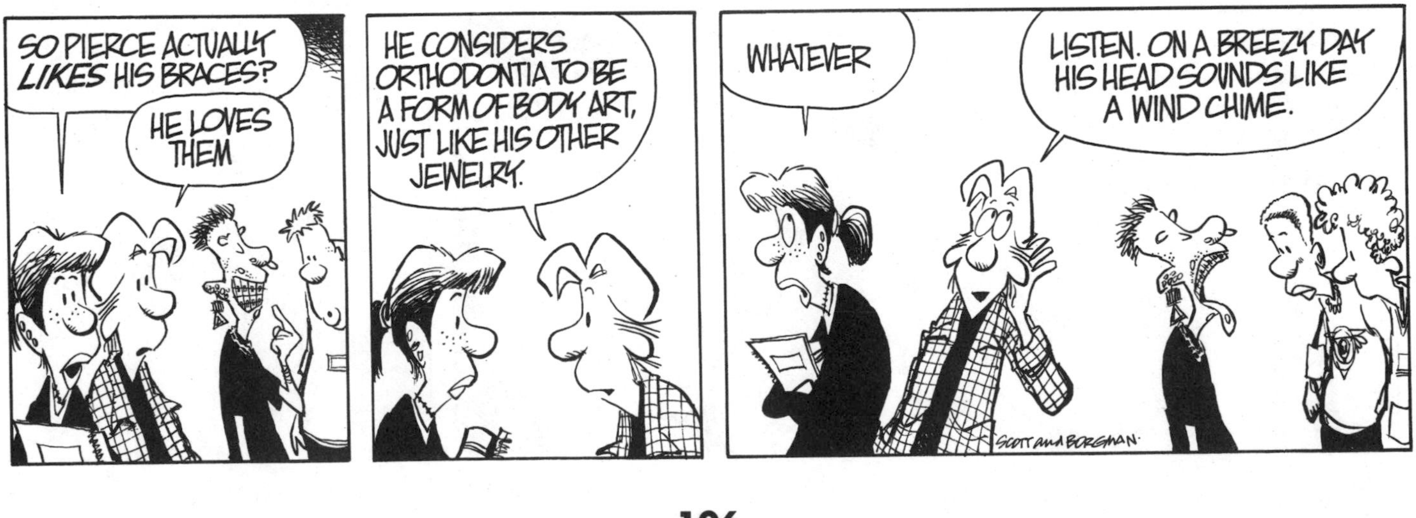
SO PIERCE ACTUALLY LIKES HIS BRACES?
HE LOVES THEM
HE CONSIDERS ORTHODONTIA TO BE A FORM OF BODY ART, JUST LIKE HIS OTHER JEWELRY.
WHATEVER
LISTEN. ON A BREEZY DAY HIS HEAD SOUNDS LIKE A WIND CHIME.
SCOTT and BORGMAN

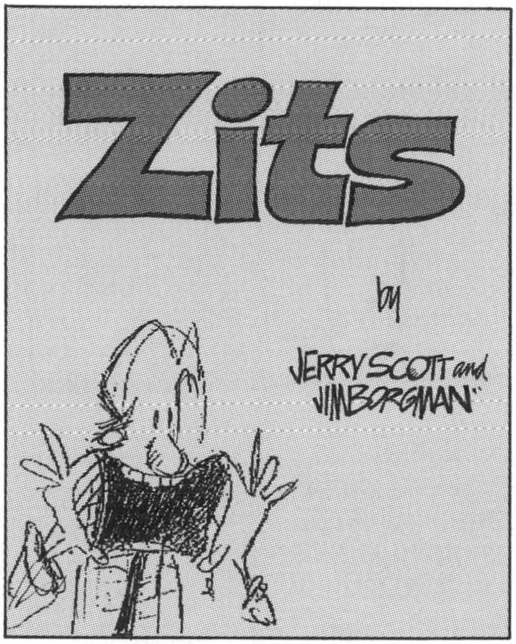
Zits
by
JERRY SCOTT and
JIM BORGMAN

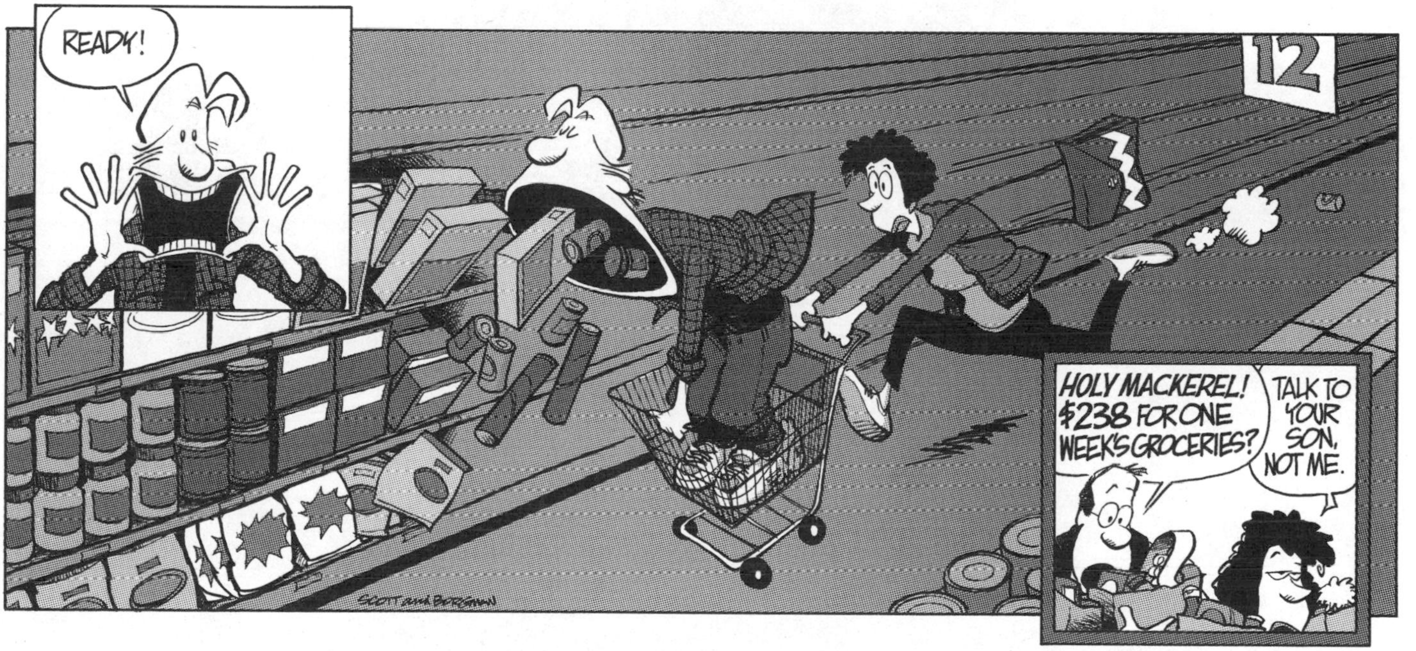
READY!
12
SCOTT and BORGMAN
HOLY MACKEREL! $238 FOR ONE WEEK'S GROCERIES?
TALK TO YOUR SON, NOT ME.

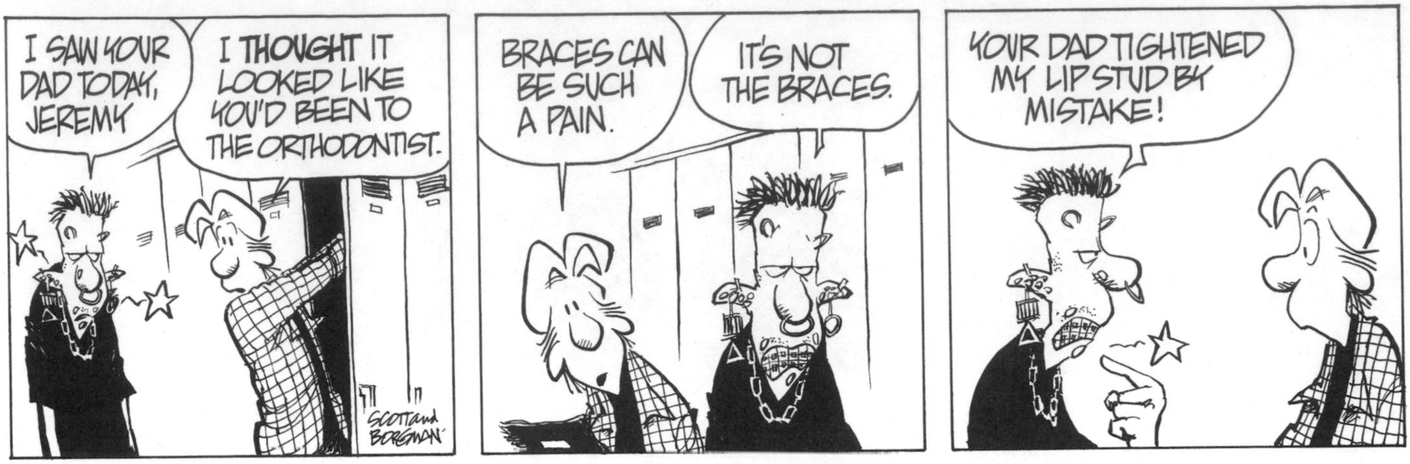
I SAW YOUR DAD TODAY, JEREMY
I THOUGHT IT LOOKED LIKE YOU'D BEEN TO THE ORTHODONTIST.
SCOTT and BORGMAN
BRACES CAN BE SUCH A PAIN.
IT'S NOT THE BRACES.
YOUR DAD TIGHTENED MY LIP STUD BY MISTAKE!

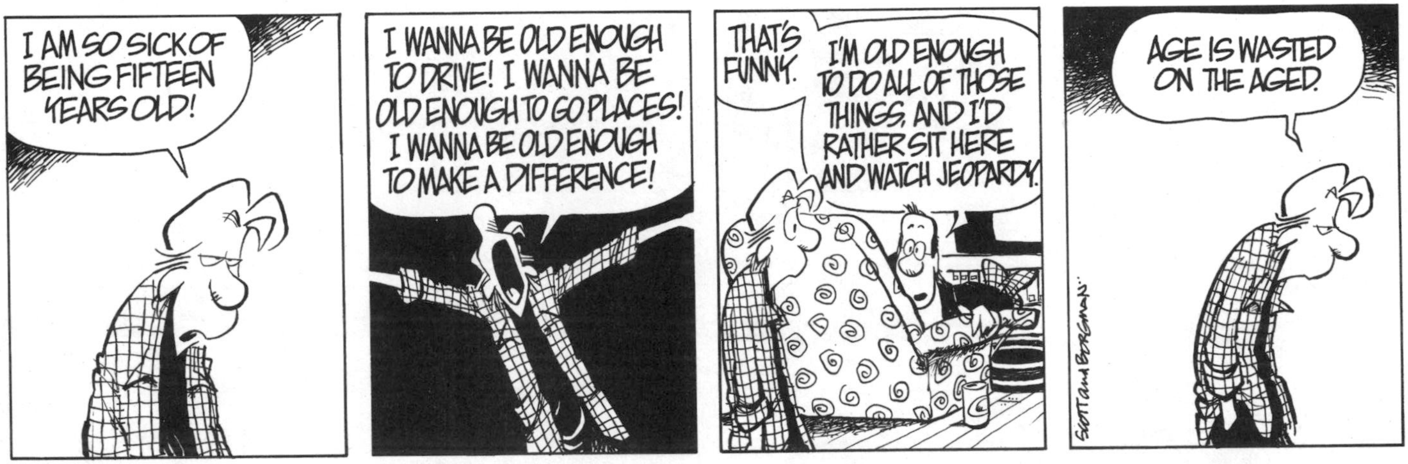
I AM SO SICK OF BEING FIFTEEN YEARS OLD!
I WANNA BE OLD ENOUGH TO DRIVE! I WANNA BE OLD ENOUGH TO GO PLACES! I WANNA BE OLD ENOUGH TO MAKE A DIFFERENCE!
THAT'S FUNNY.
I'M OLD ENOUGH TO DO ALL OF THOSE THINGS, AND I'D RATHER SIT HERE AND WATCH JEOPARDY.
SCOTT and BORGMAN
AGE IS WASTED ON THE AGED.

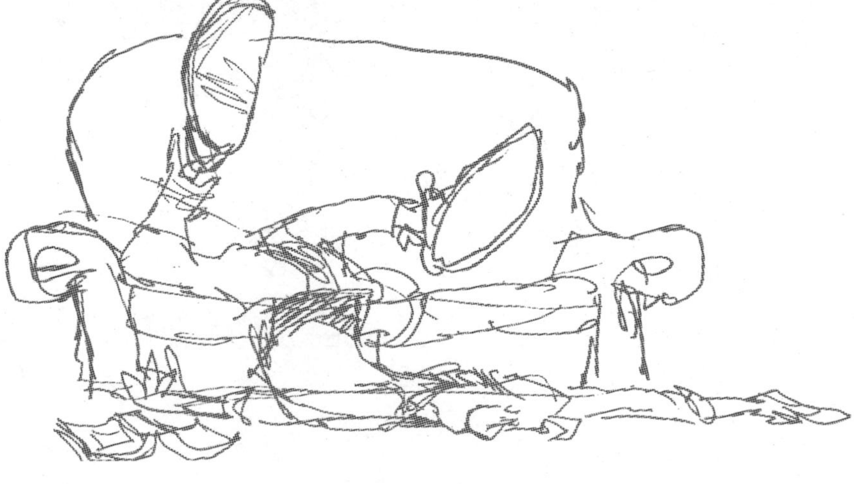

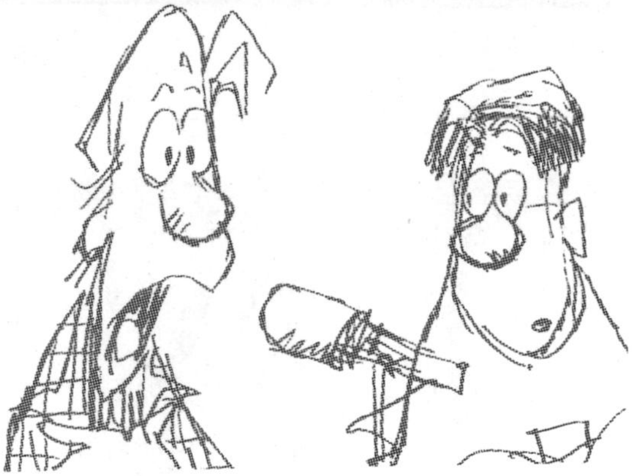

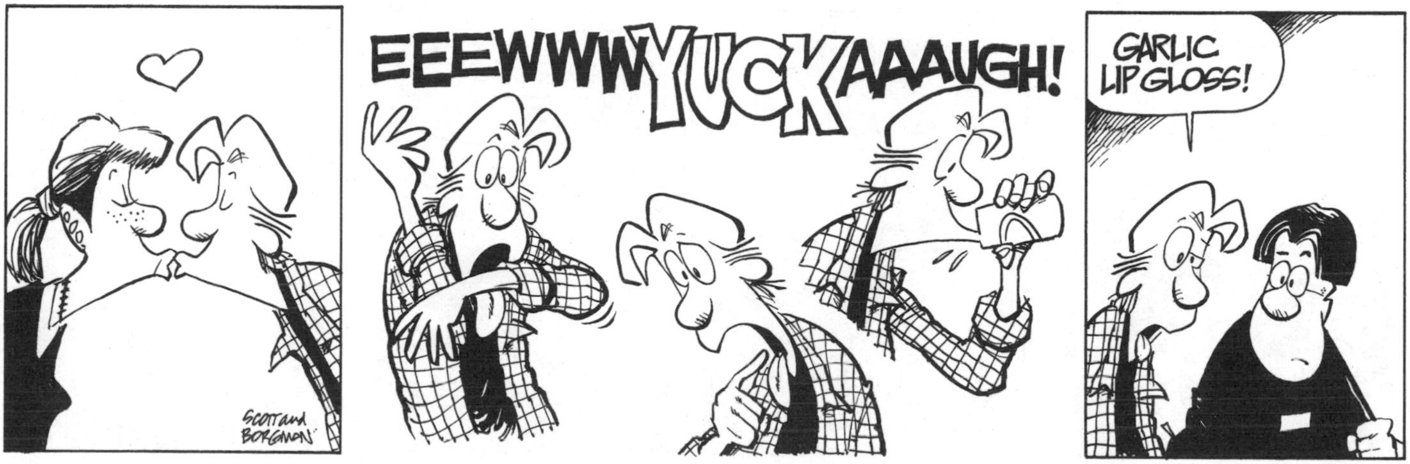
SCOTT AND BORGMAN
EEEWWWYUCKAAAUGH!
GARLIC LIP GLOSS!

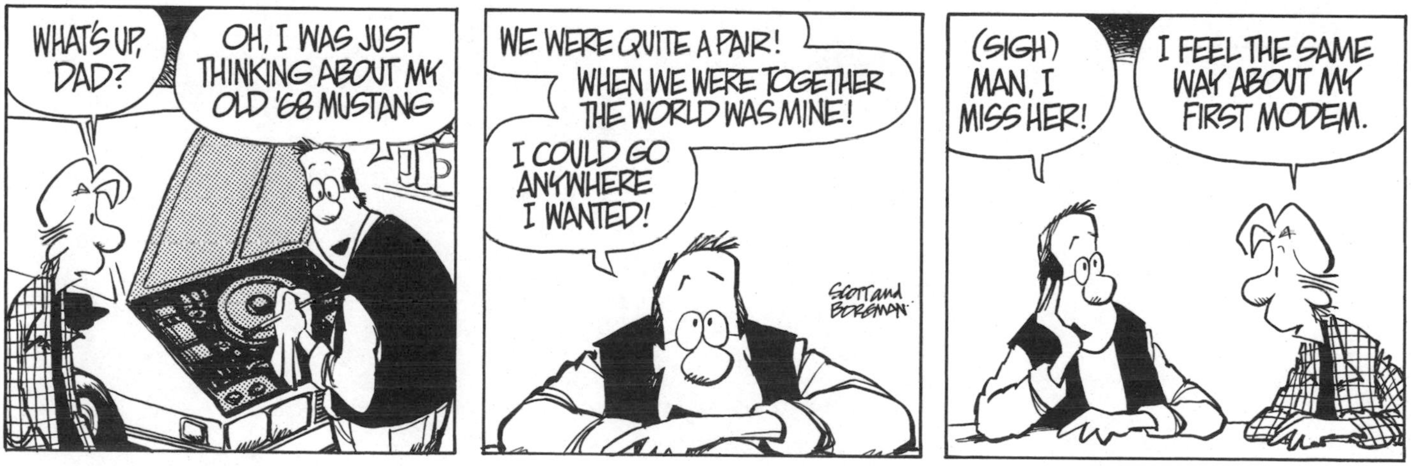
WHAT'S UP, DAD?
OH, I WAS JUST THINKING ABOUT MY OLD '68 MUSTANG
WE WERE QUITE A PAIR!
WHEN WE WERE TOGETHER THE WORLD WAS MINE!
I COULD GO ANYWHERE I WANTED!
SCOTT AND BORGMAN
(SIGH) MAN, I MISS HER!
I FEEL THE SAME WAY ABOUT MY FIRST MODEM.

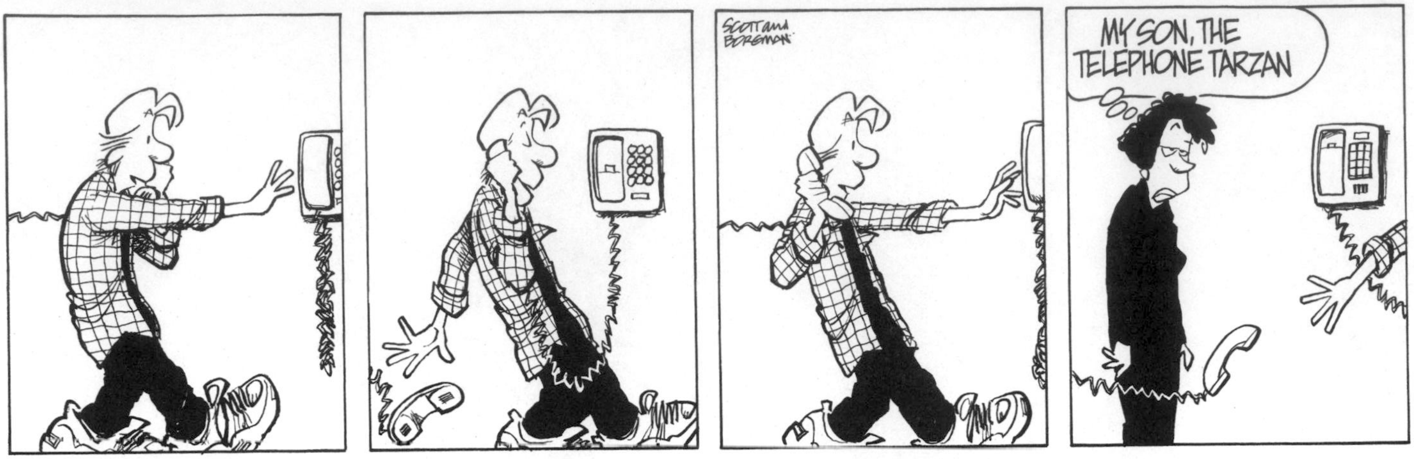
SCOTT and BORGMAN
MY SON, THE TELEPHONE TARZAN

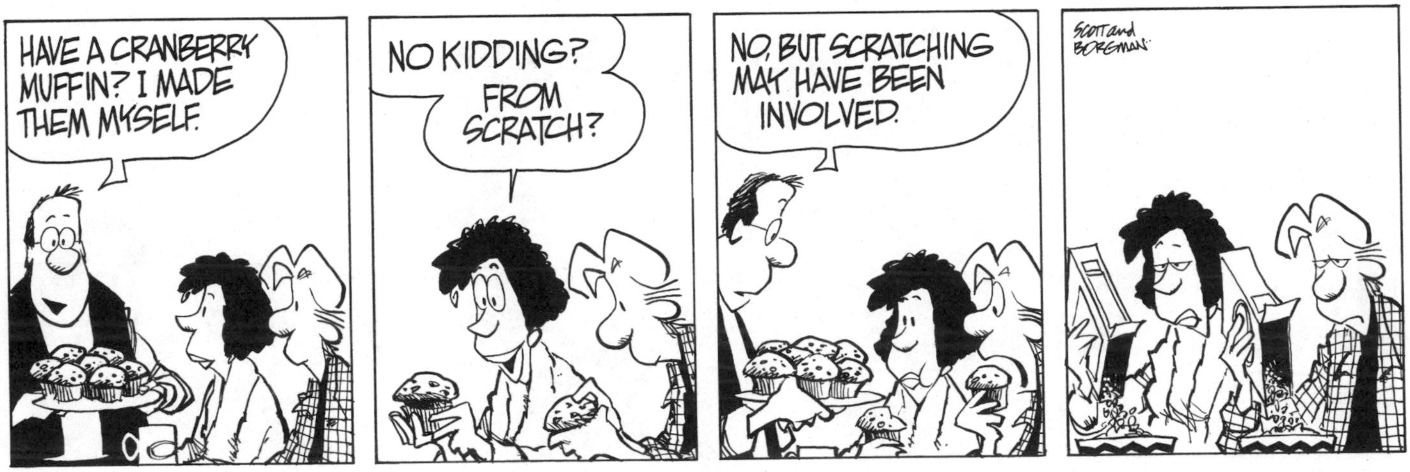
HAVE A CRANBERRY MUFFIN? I MADE THEM MYSELF.
NO KIDDING?
FROM SCRATCH?
NO, BUT SCRATCHING MAY HAVE BEEN INVOLVED.
SCOTT and BORGMAN

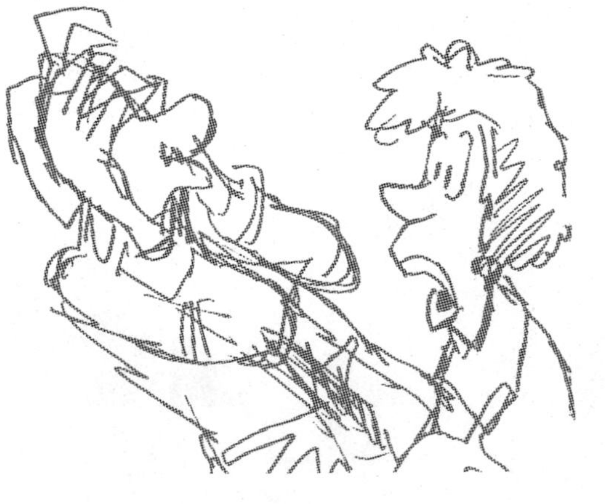

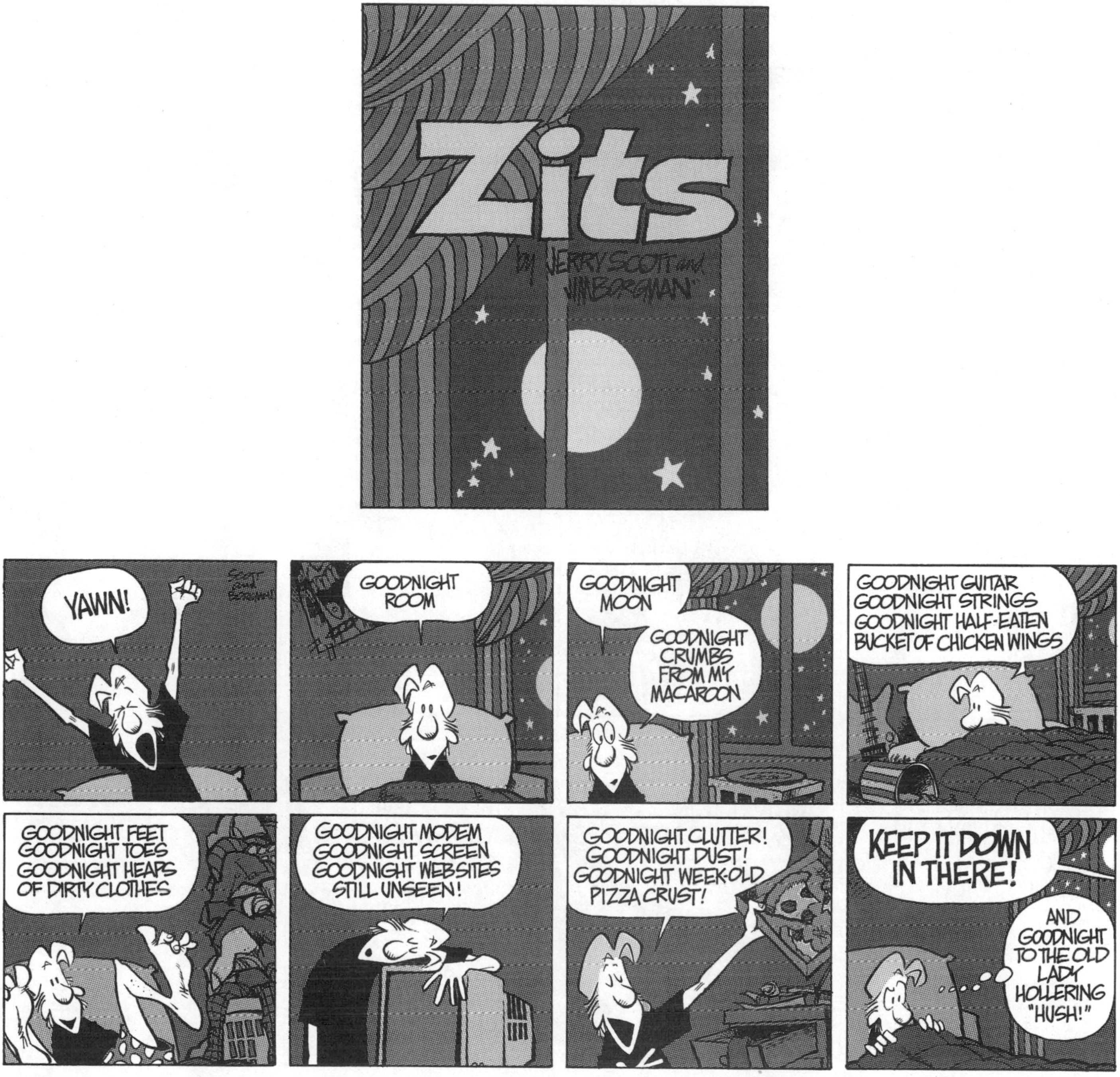
Zits
by JERRY SCOTT and JIM BORGMAN
YAWN!
GOODNIGHT ROOM
GOODNIGHT MOON
GOODNIGHT CRUMBS FROM MY MACAROON
GOODNIGHT GUITAR GOODNIGHT STRINGS GOODNIGHT HALF-EATEN BUCKET OF CHICKEN WINGS
GOODNIGHT FEET GOODNIGHT TOES GOODNIGHT HEAPS OF DIRTY CLOTHES
GOODNIGHT MODEM GOODNIGHT SCREEN GOODNIGHT WEBSITES STILL UNSEEN!
GOODNIGHT CLUTTER! GOODNIGHT DUST! GOODNIGHT WEEK-OLD PIZZA CRUST!
KEEP IT DOWN IN THERE!
AND GOODNIGHT TO THE OLD LADY HOLLERING "HUSH!"

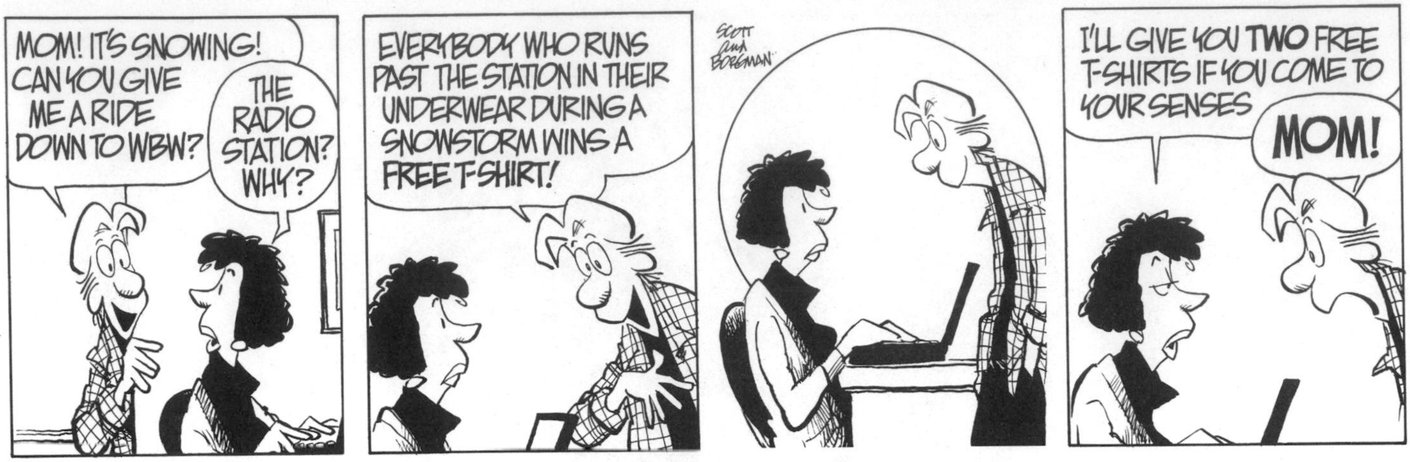
MOM! IT'S SNOWING! CAN YOU GIVE ME A RIDE DOWN TO WBW?
THE RADIO STATION? WHY?
EVERYBODY WHO RUNS PAST THE STATION IN THEIR UNDERWEAR DURING A SNOWSTORM WINS A FREE T-SHIRT!
SCOTT AND BORGMAN
I'LL GIVE YOU TWO FREE T-SHIRTS IF YOU COME TO YOUR SENSES
MOM!

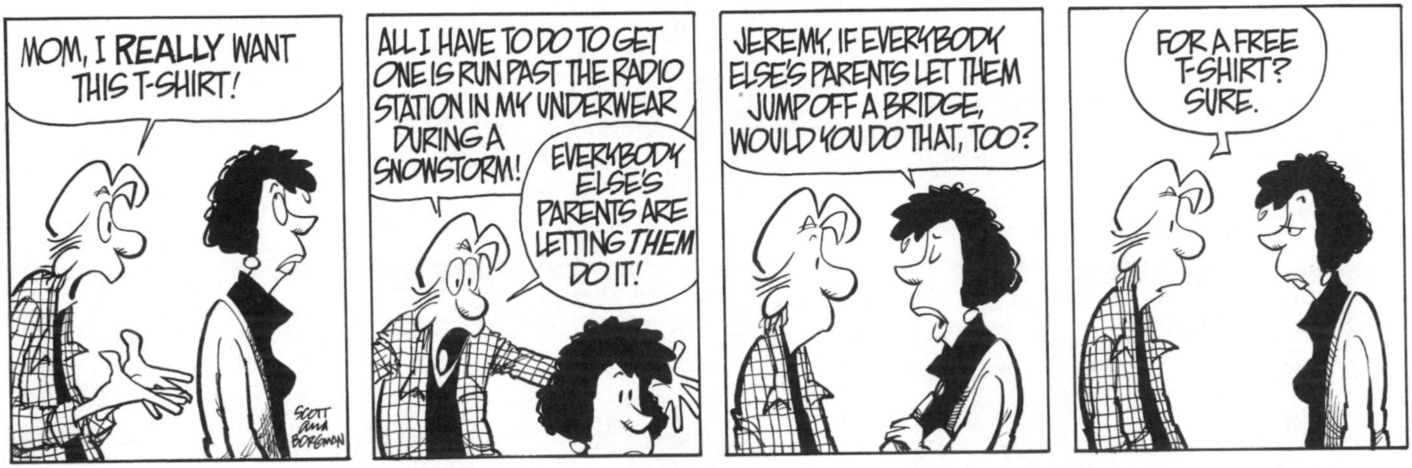
MOM, I REALLY WANT THIS T-SHIRT!
SCOTT AND BORGMAN
ALL I HAVE TO DO TO GET ONE IS RUN PAST THE RADIO STATION IN MY UNDERWEAR DURING A SNOWSTORM!
EVERYBODY ELSE'S PARENTS ARE LETTING THEM DO IT!
JEREMY, IF EVERYBODY ELSE'S PARENTS LET THEM JUMP OFF A BRIDGE, WOULD YOU DO THAT, TOO?
FOR A FREE T-SHIRT? SURE.

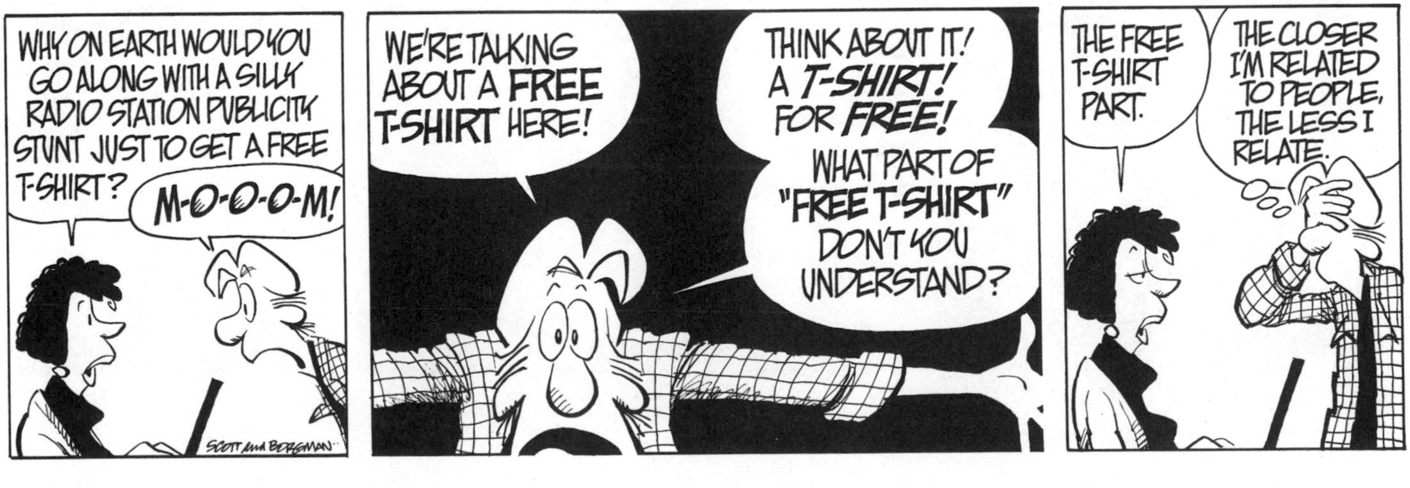
WHY ON EARTH WOULD YOU GO ALONG WITH A SILLY RADIO STATION PUBLICITY STUNT JUST TO GET A FREE T-SHIRT?
M-O-O-O-M!
SCOTT AND BORGMAN
WE'RE TALKING ABOUT A FREE T-SHIRT HERE!
THINK ABOUT IT! A T-SHIRT! FOR FREE!
WHAT PART OF "FREE T-SHIRT" DON'T YOU UNDERSTAND?
THE FREE T-SHIRT PART.
THE CLOSER I'M RELATED TO PEOPLE, THE LESS I RELATE.

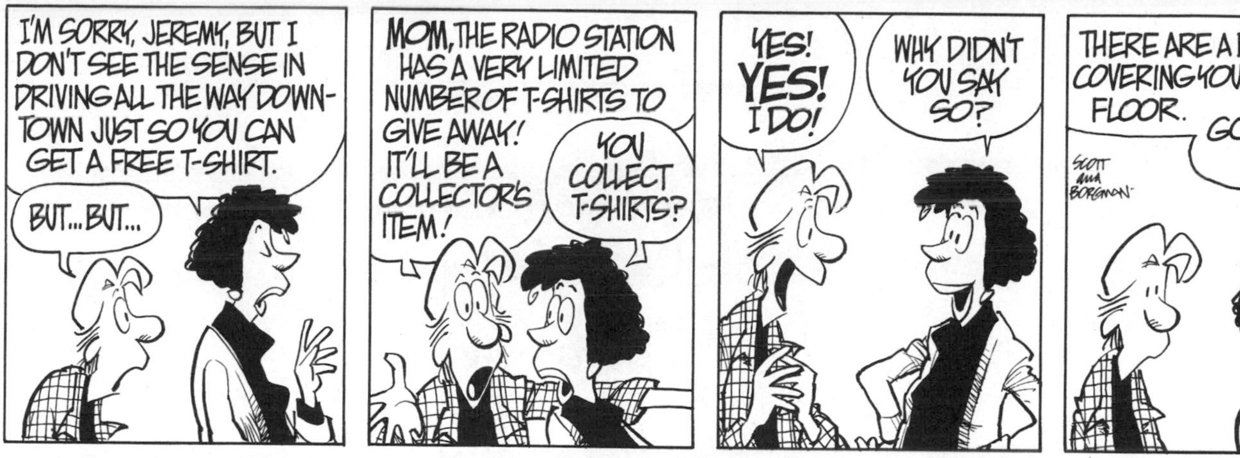
I'M SORRY, JEREMY, BUT I DON'T SEE THE SENSE IN DRIVING ALL THE WAY DOWNTOWN JUST SO YOU CAN GET A FREE T-SHIRT.
BUT...BUT...
MOM, THE RADIO STATION HAS A VERY LIMITED NUMBER OF T-SHIRTS TO GIVE AWAY! IT'LL BE A COLLECTOR'S ITEM!
YOU COLLECT T-SHIRTS?
YES! YES! I DO!
WHY DIDN'T YOU SAY SO?
THERE ARE A DOZEN OF 'EM COVERING YOUR BEDROOM FLOOR.
GO COLLECT THEM.
SCOTT and BORGMAN

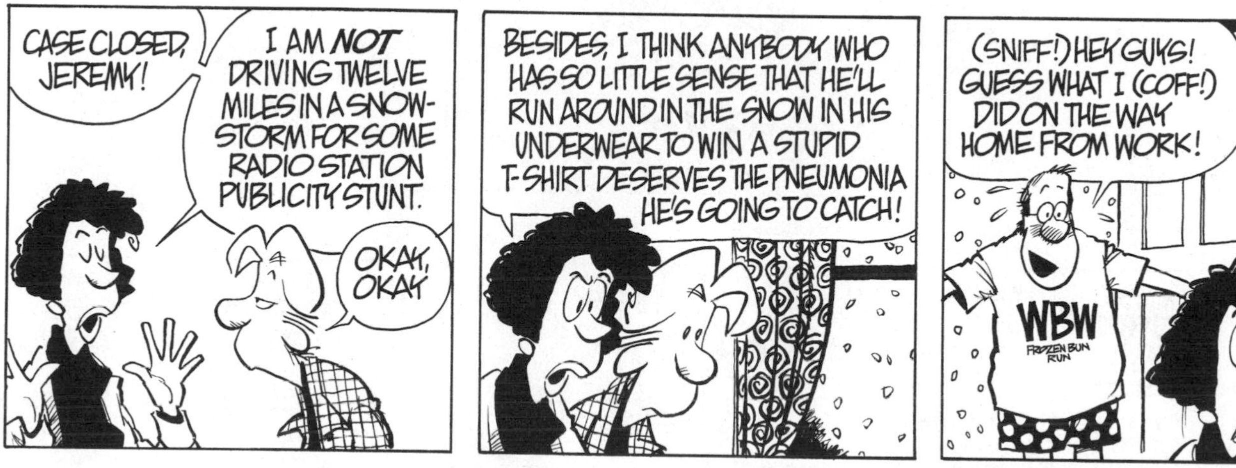
CASE CLOSED, JEREMY!
I AM NOT DRIVING TWELVE MILES IN A SNOWSTORM FOR SOME RADIO STATION PUBLICITY STUNT.
OKAY, OKAY
BESIDES, I THINK ANYBODY WHO HAS SO LITTLE SENSE THAT HE'LL RUN AROUND IN THE SNOW IN HIS UNDERWEAR TO WIN A STUPID T-SHIRT DESERVES THE PNEUMONIA HE'S GOING TO CATCH!
(SNIFF!) HEY GUYS! GUESS WHAT I (COFF!) DID ON THE WAY HOME FROM WORK!
WBW
FROZEN BUN RUN
SCOTT and BORGMAN

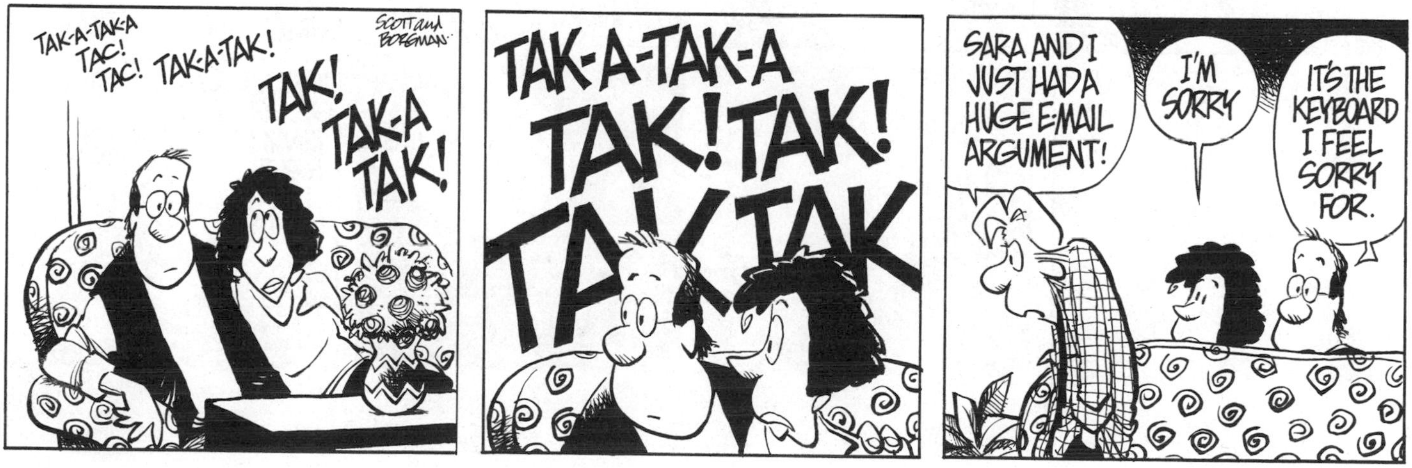
TAK-A-TAK-A TAC! TAC! TAK-A-TAK!
TAK! TAK-A TAK!
SCOTT and BORGMAN
TAK-A-TAK-A TAK! TAK! TAK TAK
SARA AND I JUST HAD A HUGE E-MAIL ARGUMENT!
I'M SORRY
IT'S THE KEYBOARD I FEEL SORRY FOR.

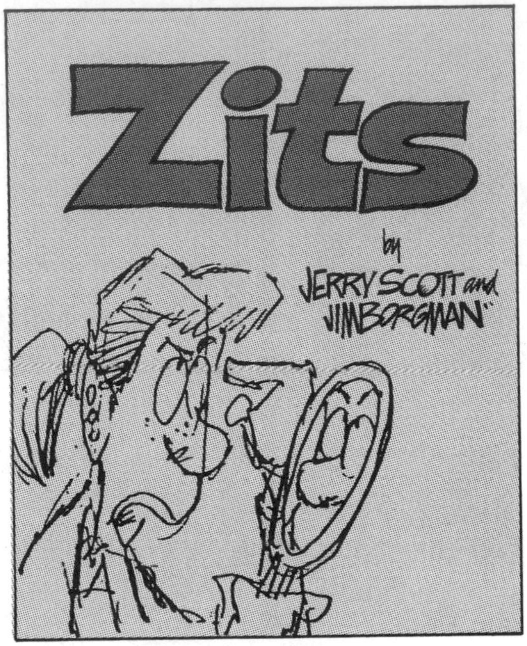
Zits
by
JERRY SCOTT and JIM BORGMAN

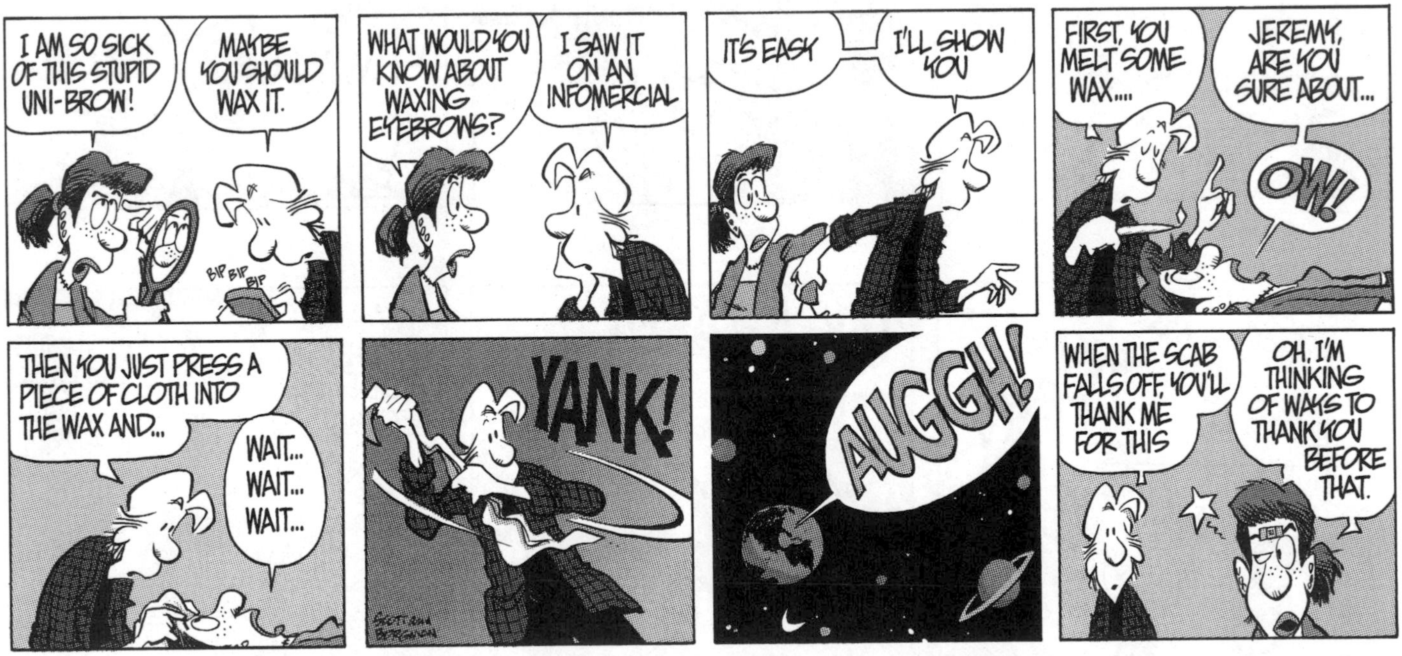
I AM SO SICK OF THIS STUPID UNI-BROW!
MAYBE YOU SHOULD WAX IT.
BIP BIP BIP
WHAT WOULD YOU KNOW ABOUT WAXING EYEBROWS?
I SAW IT ON AN INFOMERCIAL
IT'S EASY
I'LL SHOW YOU
FIRST, YOU MELT SOME WAX....
JEREMY, ARE YOU SURE ABOUT...
OW!
THEN YOU JUST PRESS A PIECE OF CLOTH INTO THE WAX AND...
WAIT... WAIT... WAIT...
YANK!
AUGGH!
WHEN THE SCAB FALLS OFF, YOU'LL THANK ME FOR THIS
OH, I'M THINKING OF WAYS TO THANK YOU BEFORE THAT.

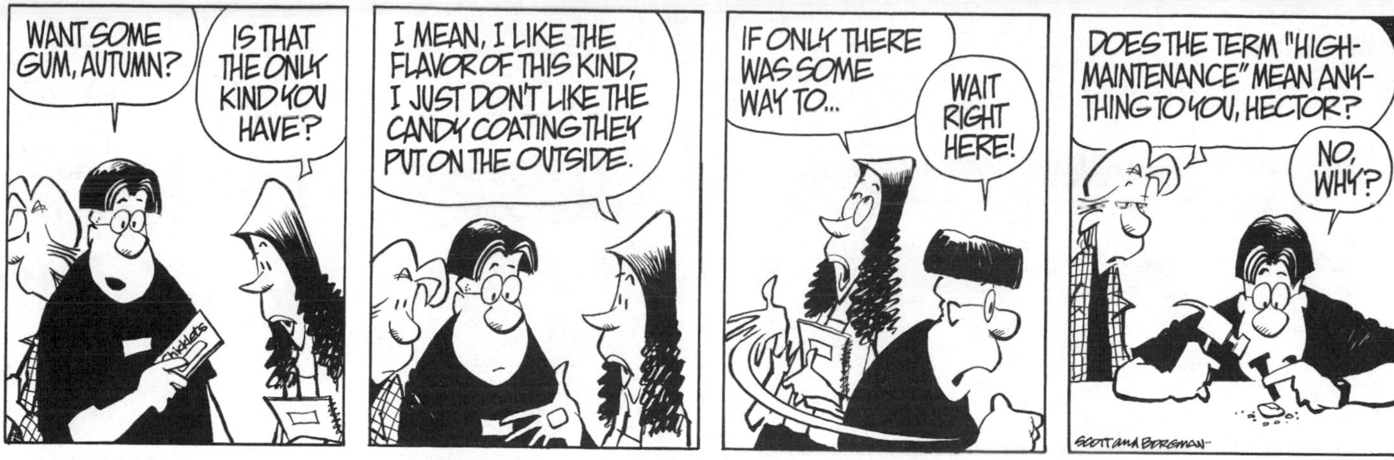
WANT SOME GUM, AUTUMN?
IS THAT THE ONLY KIND YOU HAVE?
I MEAN, I LIKE THE FLAVOR OF THIS KIND, I JUST DON'T LIKE THE CANDY COATING THEY PUT ON THE OUTSIDE.
IF ONLY THERE WAS SOME WAY TO...
WAIT RIGHT HERE!
DOES THE TERM "HIGH-MAINTENANCE" MEAN ANYTHING TO YOU, HECTOR?
NO, WHY?
SCOTT and BORGMAN

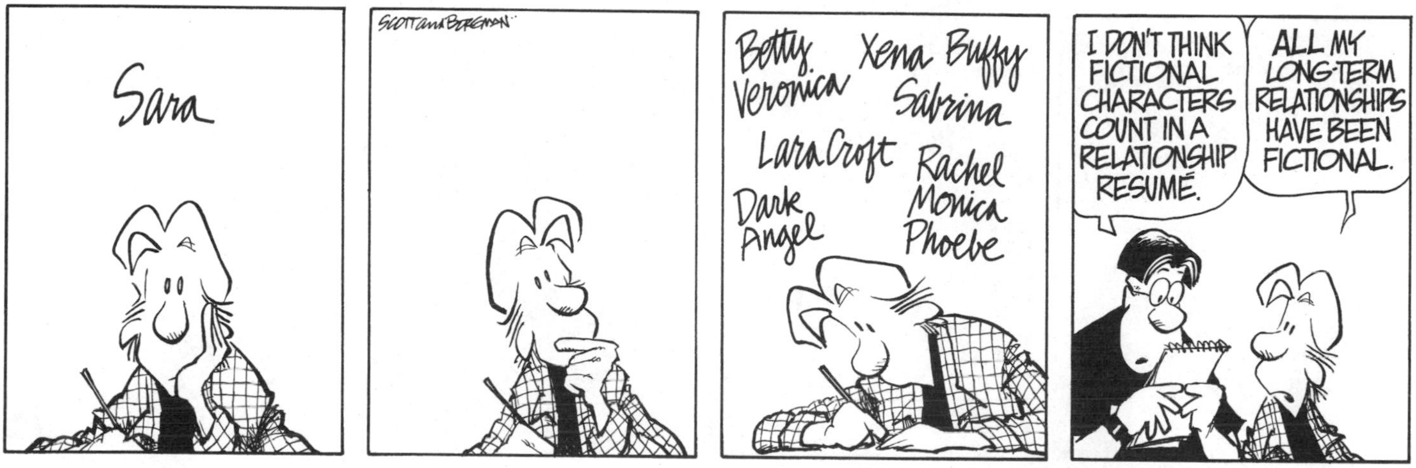
Sara
SCOTT and BORGMAN
Betty Xena Buffy
Veronica Sabrina
Lara Croft Rachel
Dark Angel Monica
Phoebe
I DON'T THINK FICTIONAL CHARACTERS COUNT IN A RELATIONSHIP RESUMÉ.
ALL MY LONG-TERM RELATIONSHIPS HAVE BEEN FICTIONAL.

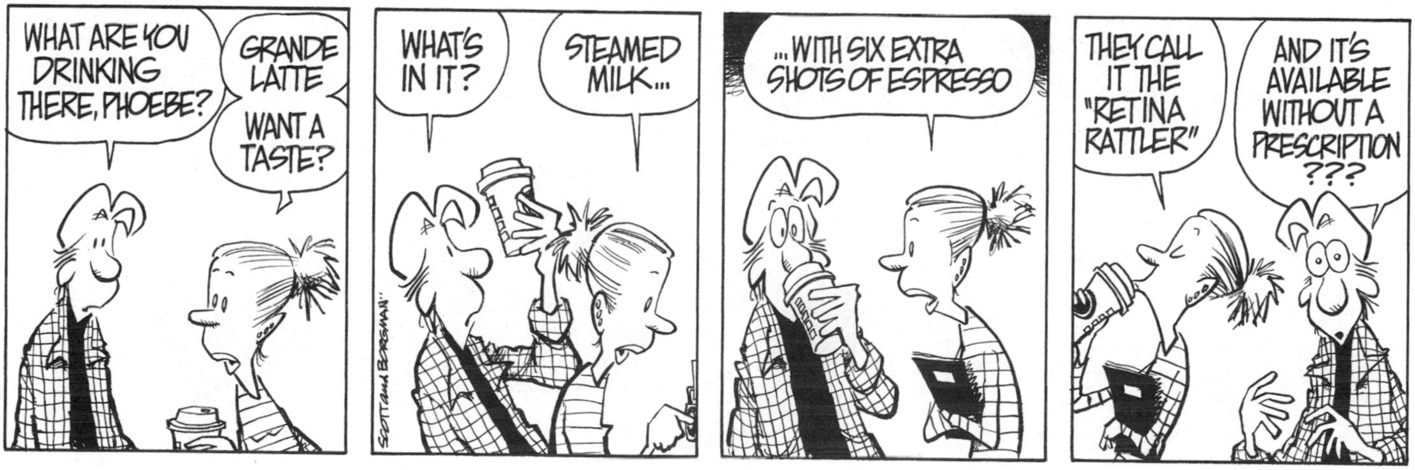
WHAT ARE YOU DRINKING THERE, PHOEBE?
GRANDE LATTE
WANT A TASTE?
WHAT'S IN IT?
STEAMED MILK...
SCOTT and BORGMAN
...WITH SIX EXTRA SHOTS OF ESPRESSO
THEY CALL IT THE "RETINA RATTLER"
AND IT'S AVAILABLE WITHOUT A PRESCRIPTION ???

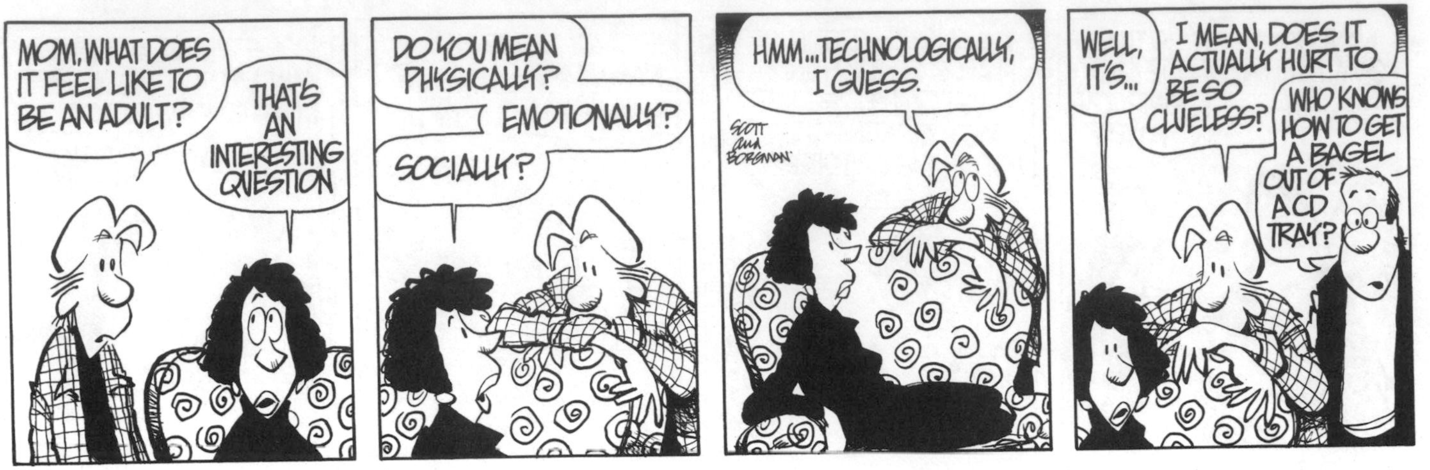
MOM, WHAT DOES IT FEEL LIKE TO BE AN ADULT?
THAT'S AN INTERESTING QUESTION
DO YOU MEAN PHYSICALLY?
EMOTIONALLY?
SOCIALLY?
HMM...TECHNOLOGICALLY, I GUESS.
WELL, IT'S...
I MEAN, DOES IT ACTUALLY HURT TO BE SO CLUELESS?
WHO KNOWS HOW TO GET A BAGEL OUT OF A CD TRAY?

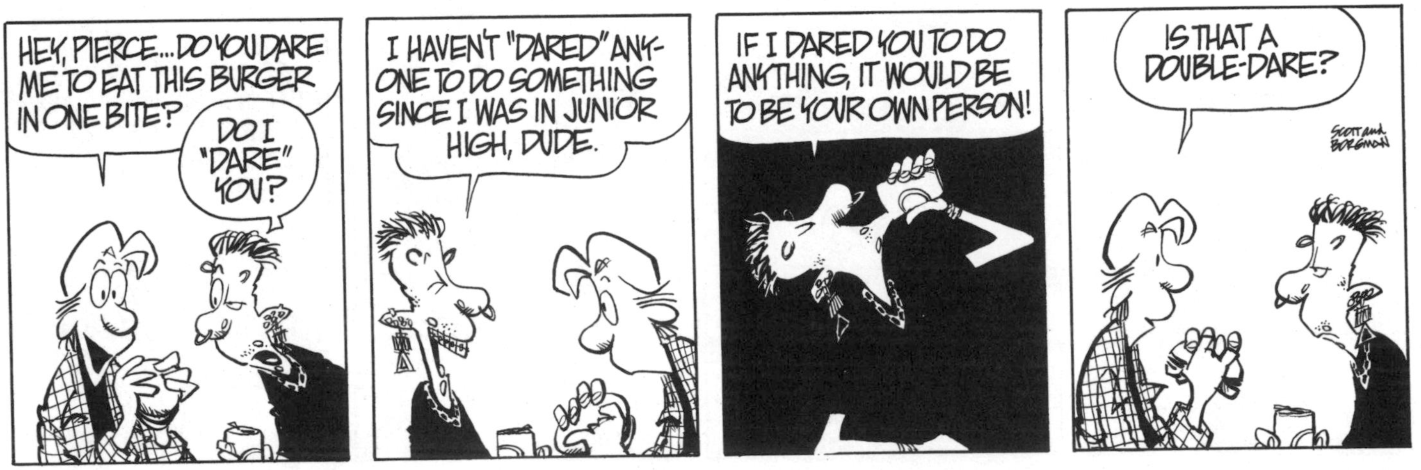
HEY, PIERCE...DO YOU DARE ME TO EAT THIS BURGER IN ONE BITE?
DO I "DARE" YOU?
I HAVEN'T "DARED" ANYONE TO DO SOMETHING SINCE I WAS IN JUNIOR HIGH, DUDE.
IF I DARED YOU TO DO ANYTHING, IT WOULD BE TO BE YOUR OWN PERSON!
IS THAT A DOUBLE-DARE?

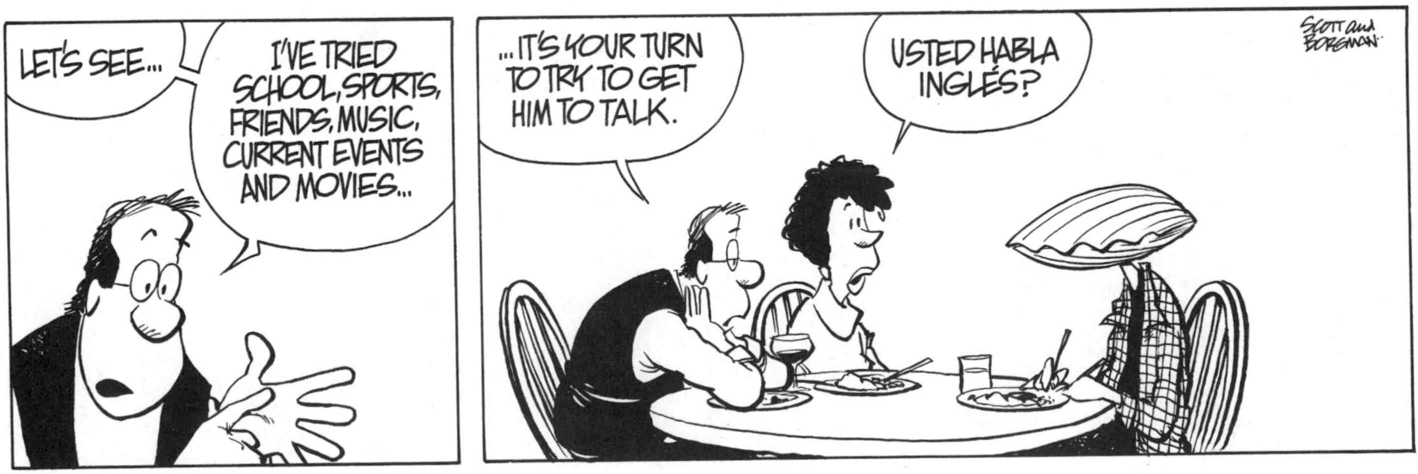
LET'S SEE...
I'VE TRIED SCHOOL, SPORTS, FRIENDS, MUSIC, CURRENT EVENTS AND MOVIES...
...IT'S YOUR TURN TO TRY TO GET HIM TO TALK.
USTED HABLA INGLÉS?

Zits
by JERRY SCOTT and JIM BORGMAN

SCOTT AND BORGMAN
GRAVITY SEEMS PARTICULARLY STRONG ON SUNDAY AFTERNOONS IN JANUARY.
ESPECIALLY WHEN SHAKESPEARE IS INVOLVED.

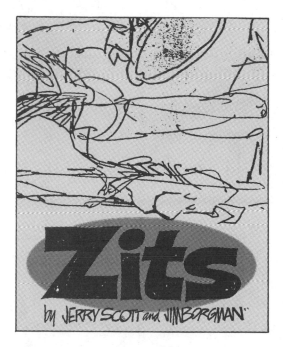

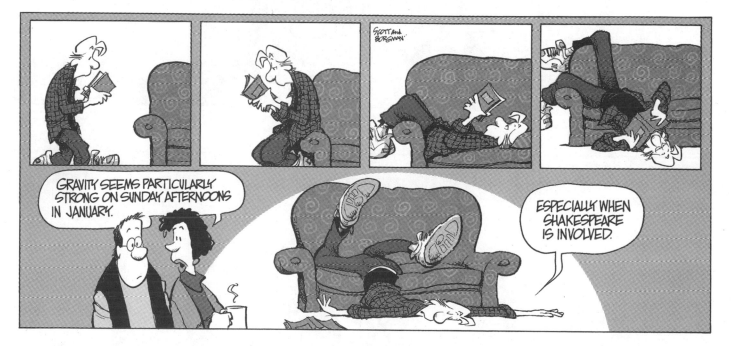

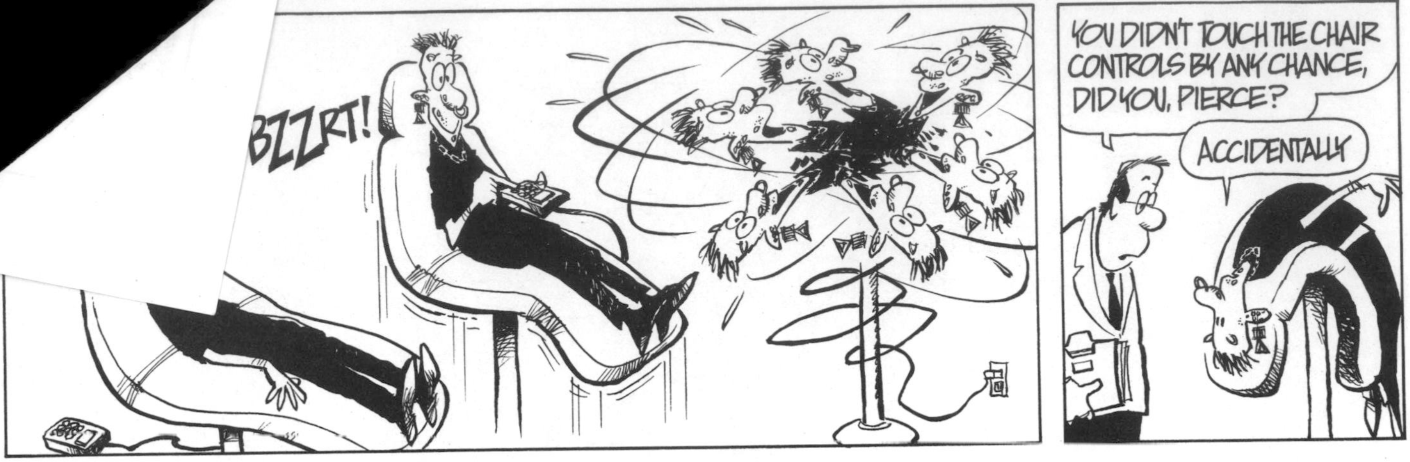
BZZRT!
YOU DIDN'T TOUCH THE CHAIR CONTROLS BY ANY CHANCE, DID YOU, PIERCE?
ACCIDENTALLY

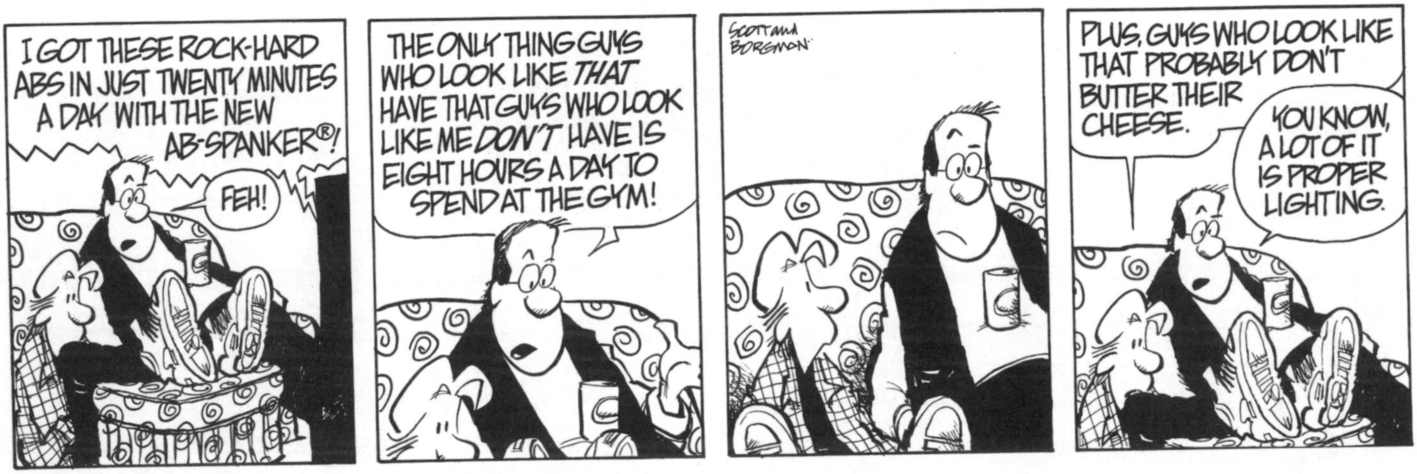
I GOT THESE ROCK-HARD ABS IN JUST TWENTY MINUTES A DAY WITH THE NEW AB-SPANKER®!
FEH!
THE ONLY THING GUYS WHO LOOK LIKE THAT HAVE THAT GUYS WHO LOOK LIKE ME DON'T HAVE IS EIGHT HOURS A DAY TO SPEND AT THE GYM!
SCOTT AND BORGMAN
PLUS, GUYS WHO LOOK LIKE THAT PROBABLY DON'T BUTTER THEIR CHEESE.
YOU KNOW, A LOT OF IT IS PROPER LIGHTING.

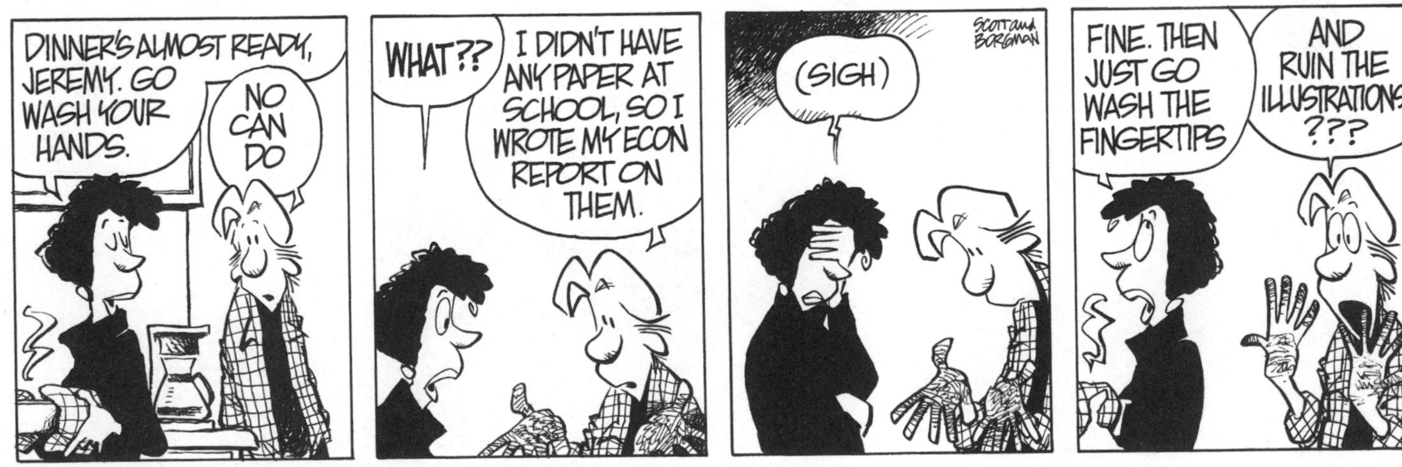
DINNER'S ALMOST READY, JEREMY. GO WASH YOUR HANDS.
NO CAN DO
WHAT??
I DIDN'T HAVE ANY PAPER AT SCHOOL, SO I WROTE MY ECON REPORT ON THEM.
SCOTT AND BORGMAN
(SIGH)
FINE. THEN JUST GO WASH THE FINGERTIPS
AND RUIN THE ILLUSTRATIONS???

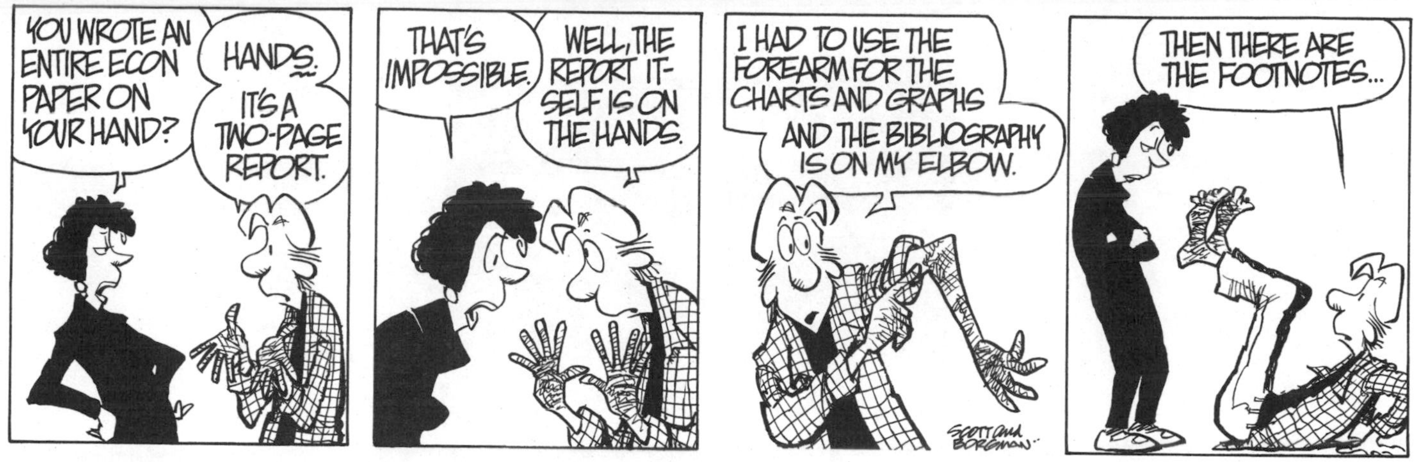
YOU WROTE AN ENTIRE ECON PAPER ON YOUR HAND?
HANDS.
IT'S A TWO-PAGE REPORT.
THAT'S IMPOSSIBLE.
WELL, THE REPORT IT-SELF IS ON THE HANDS.
I HAD TO USE THE FOREARM FOR THE CHARTS AND GRAPHS
AND THE BIBLIOGRAPHY IS ON MY ELBOW.
THEN THERE ARE THE FOOTNOTES...

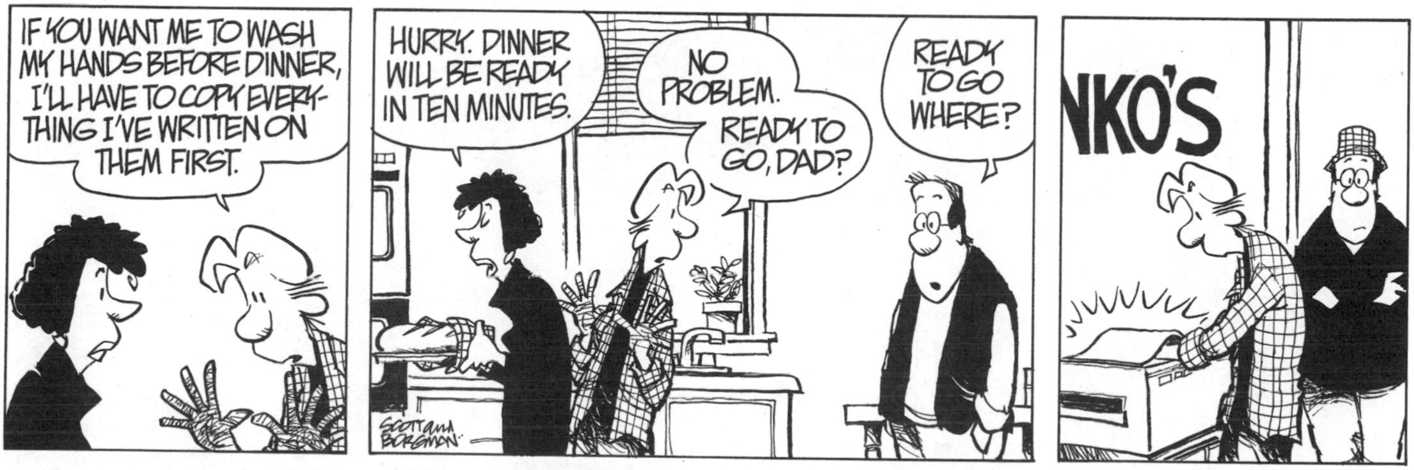
IF YOU WANT ME TO WASH MY HANDS BEFORE DINNER, I'LL HAVE TO COPY EVERY-THING I'VE WRITTEN ON THEM FIRST.
HURRY. DINNER WILL BE READY IN TEN MINUTES.
NO PROBLEM.
READY TO GO, DAD?
READY TO GO WHERE?
NKO'S

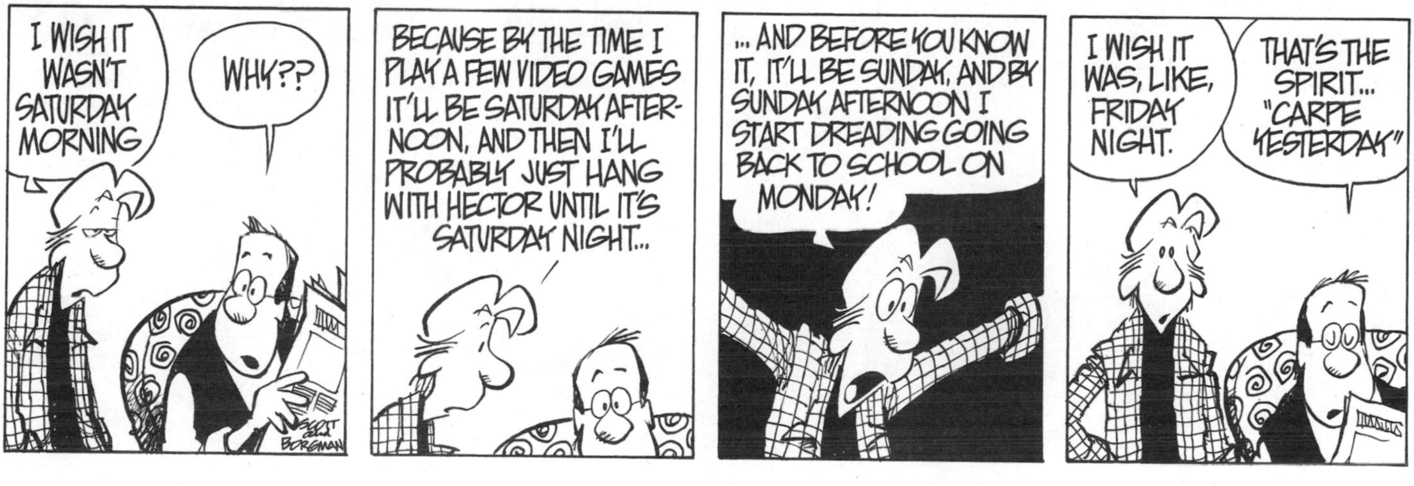
I WISH IT WASN'T SATURDAY MORNING
WHY??
BECAUSE BY THE TIME I PLAY A FEW VIDEO GAMES IT'LL BE SATURDAY AFTER-NOON, AND THEN I'LL PROBABLY JUST HANG WITH HECTOR UNTIL IT'S SATURDAY NIGHT...
... AND BEFORE YOU KNOW IT, IT'LL BE SUNDAY, AND BY SUNDAY AFTERNOON I START DREADING GOING BACK TO SCHOOL ON MONDAY!
I WISH IT WAS, LIKE, FRIDAY NIGHT.
THAT'S THE SPIRIT... "CARPE YESTERDAY"

Zits
by
JERRY SCOTT and JIM BORGMAN

BLIP!
BOOP!
BLEEP! BLEEP!
BLOOP!
SCOTT and BORGMAN
TIKKA TIKKA TAKKA TAK
JEREMY, WHAT ARE YOU DOING?
TAKING OUT THE GARBAGE, LIKE YOU ASKED ME TO.
THAT WAS AT TEN O'CLOCK THIS MORNING!
I GUESS THAT EXPLAINS WHY MY ARM IS ASLEEP AND MY SHIRT IS DAMP....

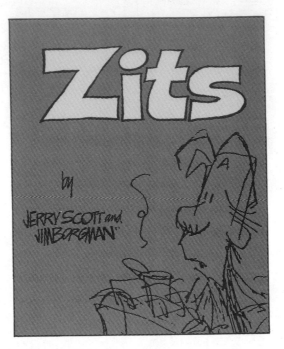

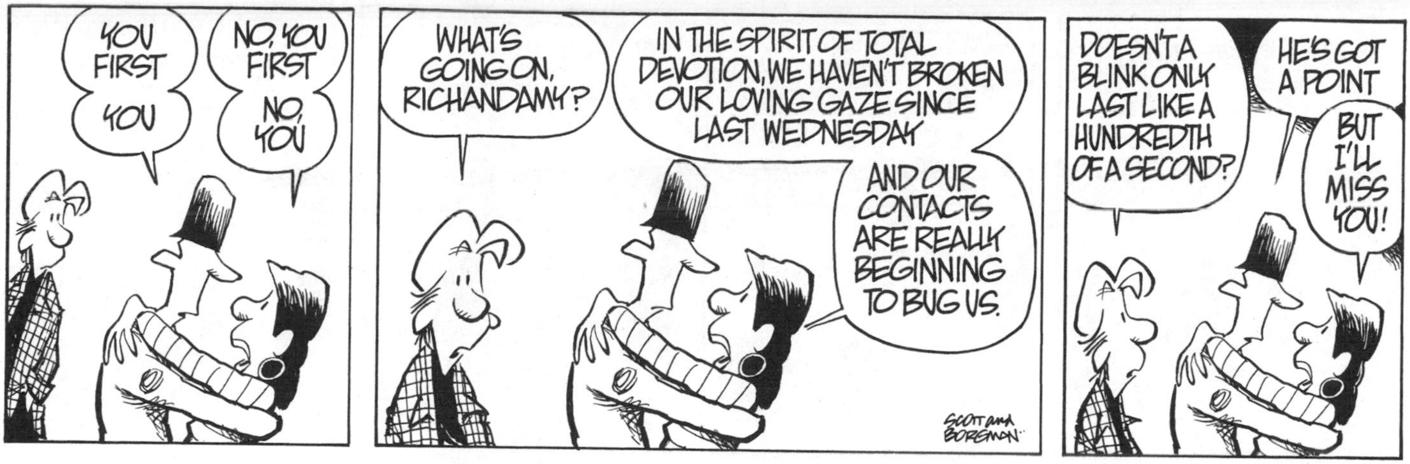
YOU FIRST
NO, YOU FIRST
YOU
NO, YOU
WHAT'S GOING ON, RICHANDAMY?
IN THE SPIRIT OF TOTAL DEVOTION, WE HAVEN'T BROKEN OUR LOVING GAZE SINCE LAST WEDNESDAY
AND OUR CONTACTS ARE REALLY BEGINNING TO BUG US.
SCOTT AND BORGMAN
DOESN'T A BLINK ONLY LAST LIKE A HUNDREDTH OF A SECOND?
HE'S GOT A POINT
BUT I'LL MISS YOU!

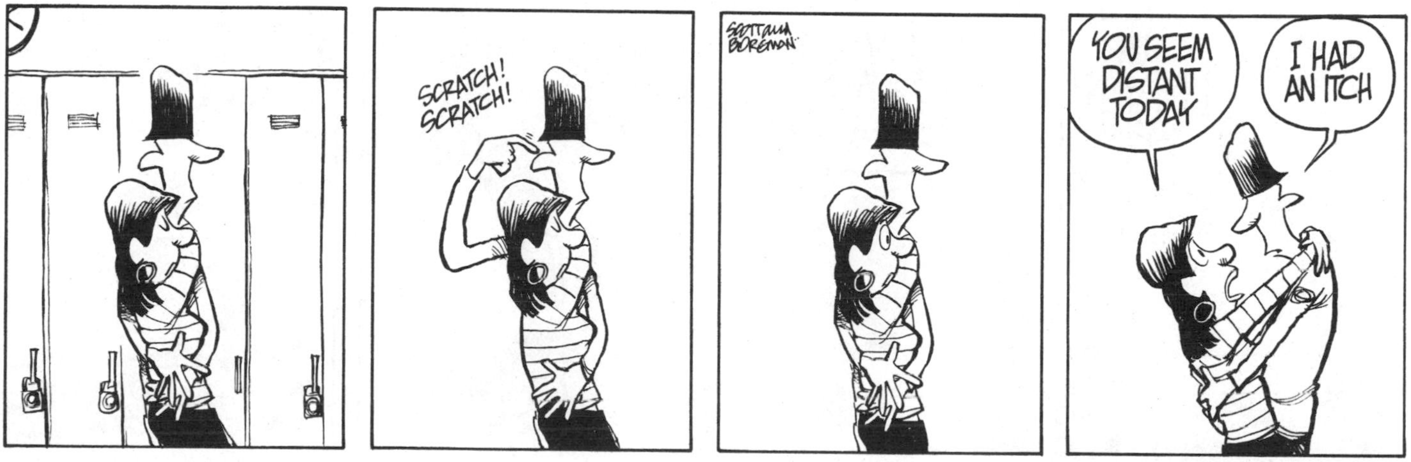
SCRATCH! SCRATCH!
SCOTT AND BORGMAN
YOU SEEM DISTANT TODAY
I HAD AN ITCH

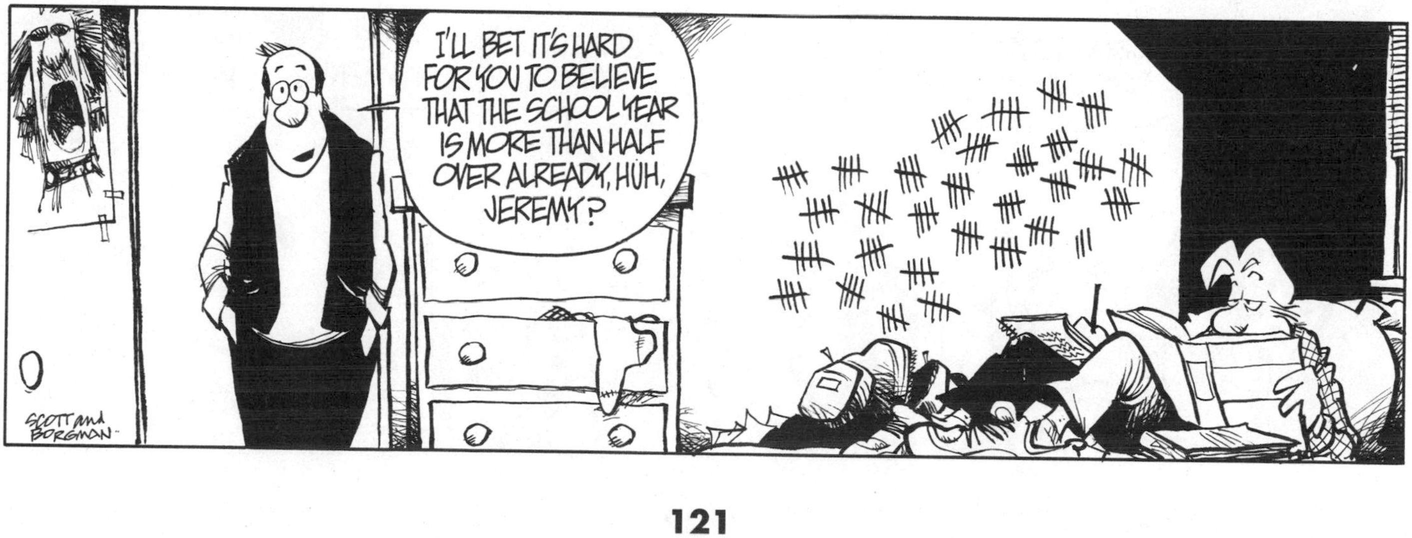
I'LL BET IT'S HARD FOR YOU TO BELIEVE THAT THE SCHOOL YEAR IS MORE THAN HALF OVER ALREADY, HUH, JEREMY?
SCOTT AND BORGMAN

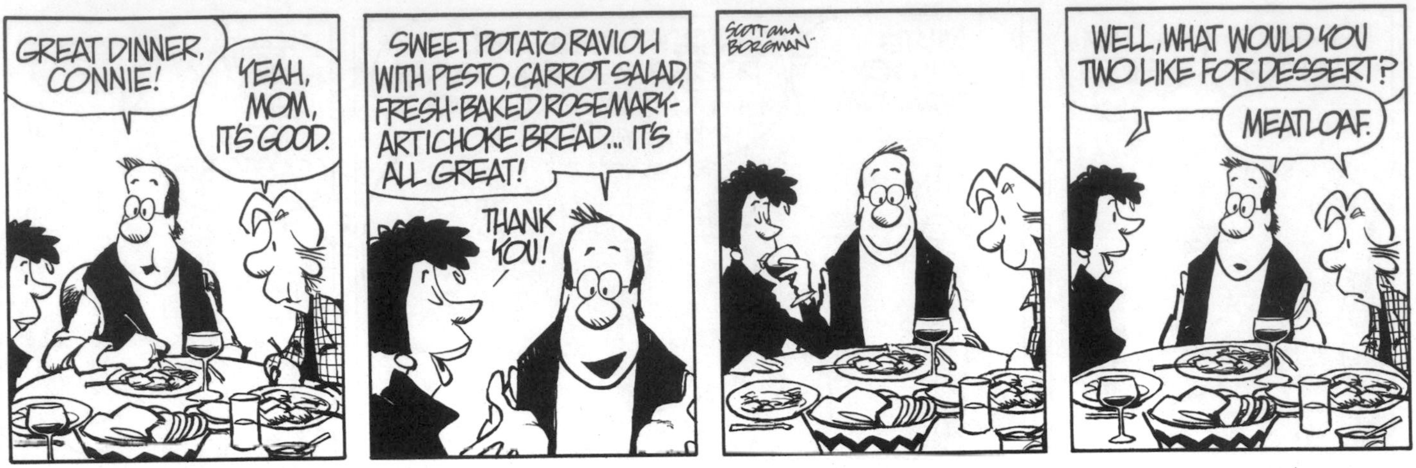
GREAT DINNER, CONNIE!
YEAH, MOM, IT'S GOOD.
SWEET POTATO RAVIOLI WITH PESTO, CARROT SALAD, FRESH-BAKED ROSEMARY-ARTICHOKE BREAD... IT'S ALL GREAT!
THANK YOU!
SCOTT and BORGMAN
WELL, WHAT WOULD YOU TWO LIKE FOR DESSERT?
MEATLOAF.

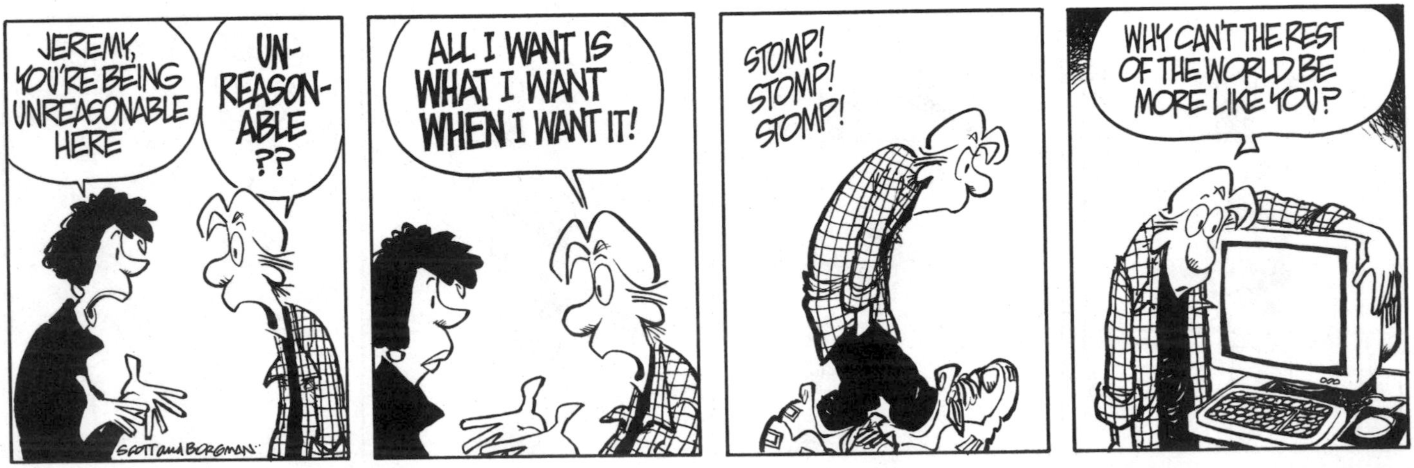
JEREMY, YOU'RE BEING UNREASONABLE HERE
UN-REASON-ABLE ??
SCOTT and BORGMAN
ALL I WANT IS WHAT I WANT WHEN I WANT IT!
STOMP! STOMP! STOMP!
WHY CAN'T THE REST OF THE WORLD BE MORE LIKE YOU?

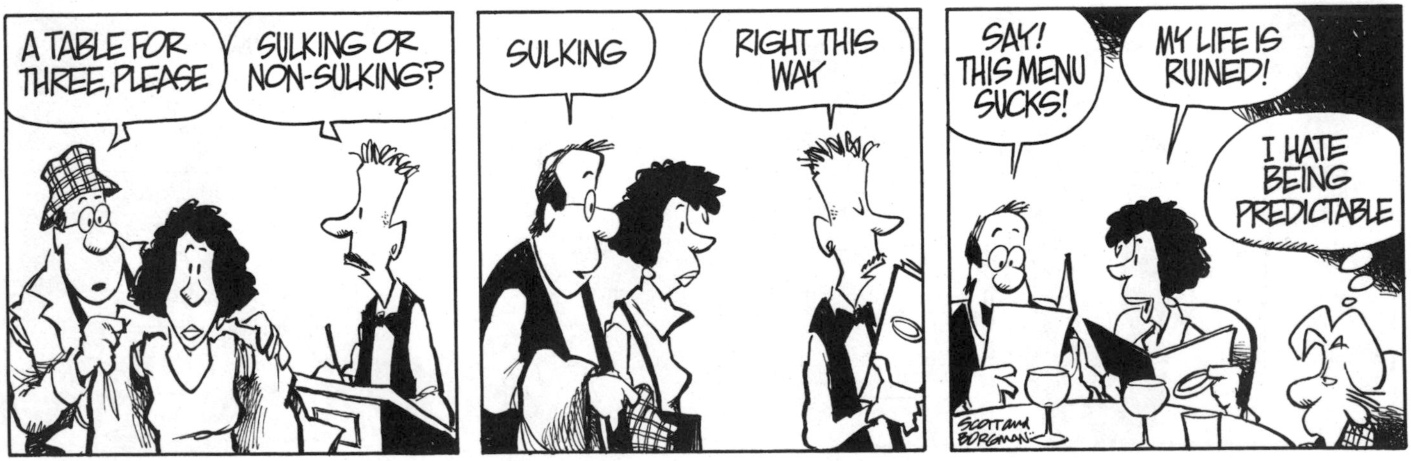
A TABLE FOR THREE, PLEASE
SULKING OR NON-SULKING?
SULKING
RIGHT THIS WAY
SAY! THIS MENU SUCKS!
MY LIFE IS RUINED!
I HATE BEING PREDICTABLE
SCOTT and BORGMAN

Zits
by JERRY SCOTT and JIM BORGMAN

SARA, AM I A GOOD KISSER?
I DON'T KNOW... SURE.
I GUESS
ON A SCALE FROM ONE TO TEN, HOW WOULD YOU RATE ME?
HOW MANY GUYS DO YOU THINK I'VE KISSED??
IT DOESN'T MATTER.
IN THE INTEREST OF SCIENCE,
HOW DO I RATE?
JEREMY, I DON'T THINK--
THIS DOESN'T--
COME ON. GIVE ME A NUMBER.
BE HONEST
OKAY. YOU'RE A SEVEN.
A SEVEN? A SEVEN??
NO WAY! I KNOW FOR A FACT THAT YOU HAVEN'T KISSED VERY MANY GUYS, SO I CHALLENGE YOUR CONCLUSION ON THE BASIS OF INSUFFICIENT DATA!
FINE, NOW YOU'RE A SIX.

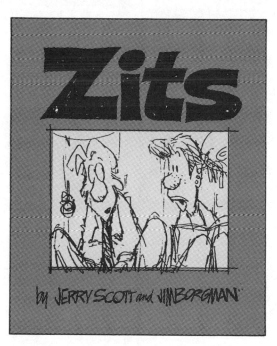

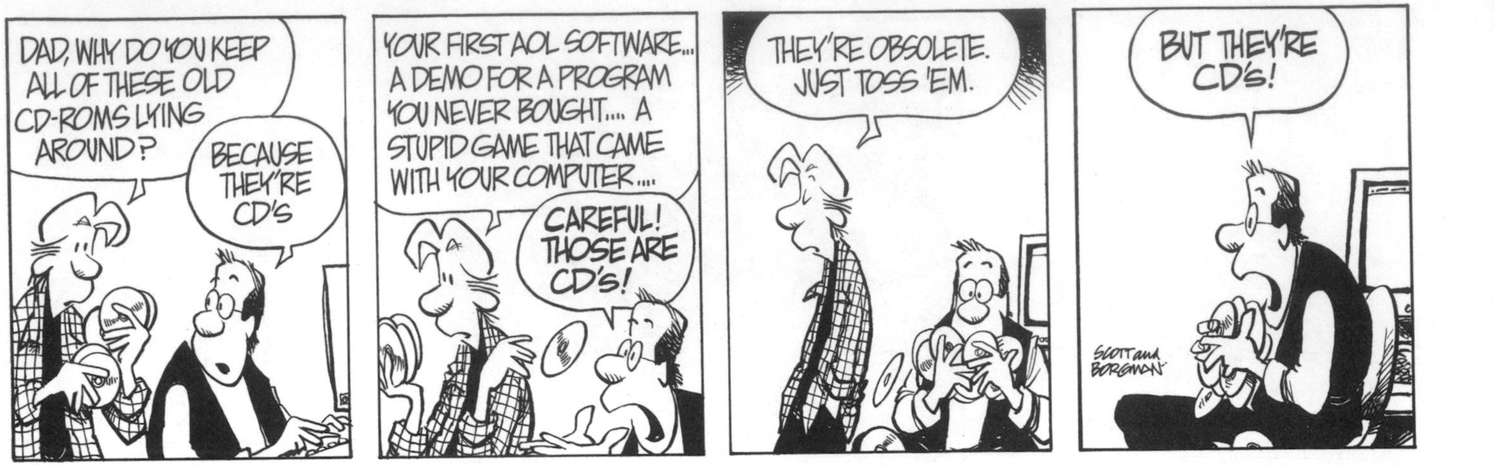
DAD, WHY DO YOU KEEP ALL OF THESE OLD CD-ROMS LYING AROUND?
BECAUSE THEY'RE CD'S
YOUR FIRST AOL SOFTWARE... A DEMO FOR A PROGRAM YOU NEVER BOUGHT.... A STUPID GAME THAT CAME WITH YOUR COMPUTER....
CAREFUL! THOSE ARE CD's!
THEY'RE OBSOLETE. JUST TOSS 'EM.
BUT THEY'RE CD's!
SCOTT and BORGMAN

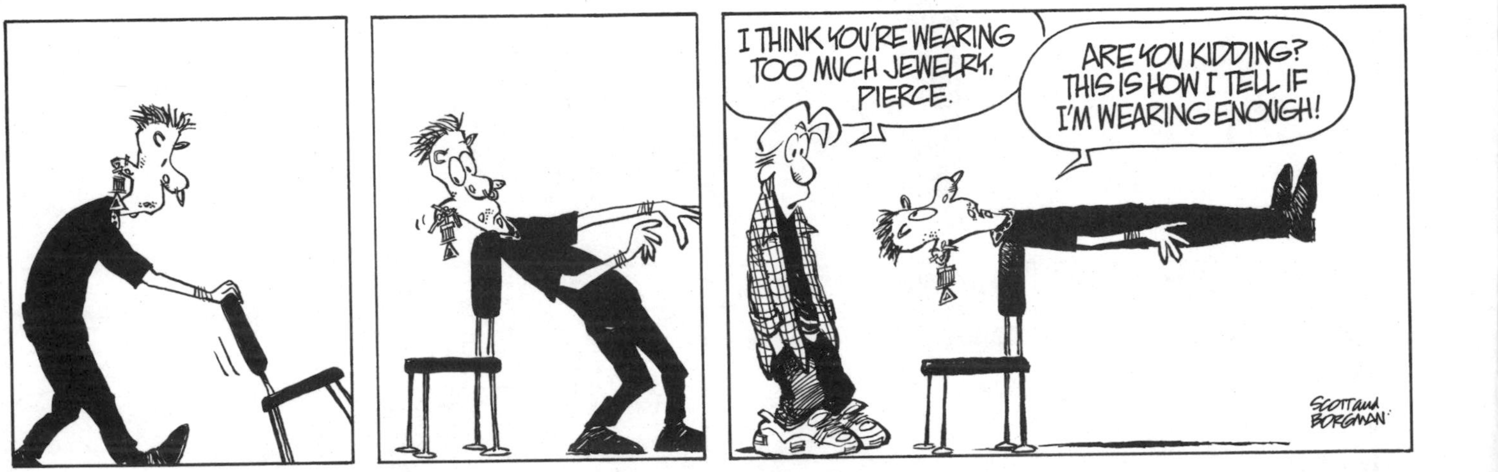
I THINK YOU'RE WEARING TOO MUCH JEWELRY, PIERCE.
ARE YOU KIDDING? THIS IS HOW I TELL IF I'M WEARING ENOUGH!
SCOTT and BORGMAN

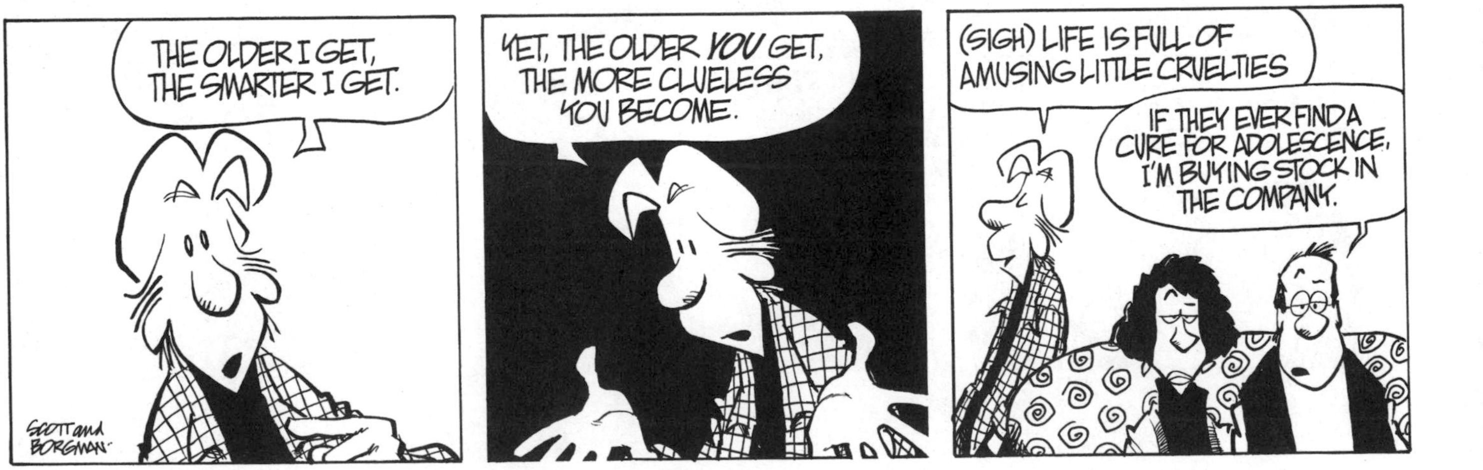
THE OLDER I GET, THE SMARTER I GET.
SCOTT and BORGMAN
YET, THE OLDER YOU GET, THE MORE CLUELESS YOU BECOME.
(SIGH) LIFE IS FULL OF AMUSING LITTLE CRUELTIES
IF THEY EVER FIND A CURE FOR ADOLESCENCE, I'M BUYING STOCK IN THE COMPANY.

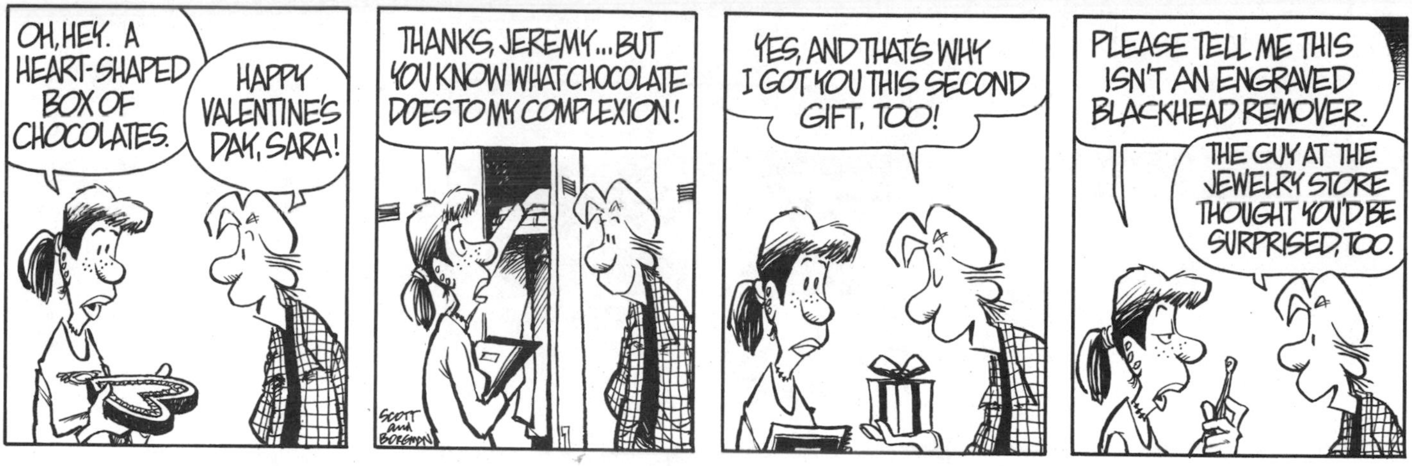
OH, HEY. A HEART-SHAPED BOX OF CHOCOLATES.
HAPPY VALENTINE'S DAY, SARA!
THANKS, JEREMY... BUT YOU KNOW WHAT CHOCOLATE DOES TO MY COMPLEXION!
YES, AND THAT'S WHY I GOT YOU THIS SECOND GIFT, TOO!
PLEASE TELL ME THIS ISN'T AN ENGRAVED BLACKHEAD REMOVER.
THE GUY AT THE JEWELRY STORE THOUGHT YOU'D BE SURPRISED, TOO.

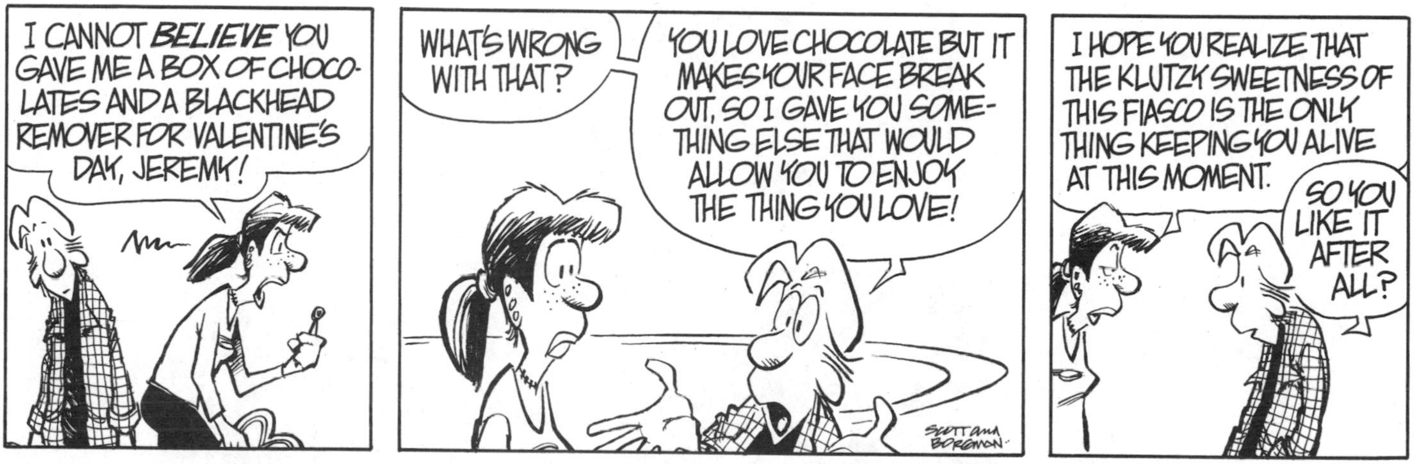
I CANNOT *BELIEVE* YOU GAVE ME A BOX OF CHOCOLATES AND A BLACKHEAD REMOVER FOR VALENTINE'S DAY, JEREMY!
WHAT'S WRONG WITH THAT?
YOU LOVE CHOCOLATE BUT IT MAKES YOUR FACE BREAK OUT, SO I GAVE YOU SOMETHING ELSE THAT WOULD ALLOW YOU TO ENJOY THE THING YOU LOVE!
I HOPE YOU REALIZE THAT THE KLUTZY SWEETNESS OF THIS FIASCO IS THE ONLY THING KEEPING YOU ALIVE AT THIS MOMENT.
SO YOU LIKE IT AFTER ALL?

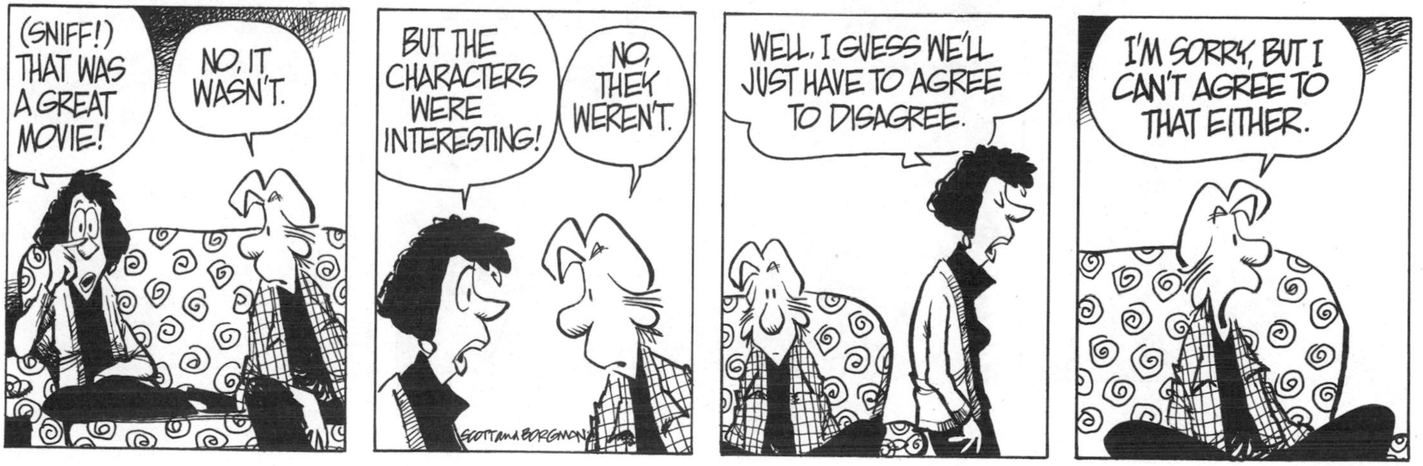
(SNIFF!) THAT WAS A GREAT MOVIE!
NO, IT WASN'T.
BUT THE CHARACTERS WERE INTERESTING!
NO, THEY WEREN'T.
WELL, I GUESS WE'LL JUST HAVE TO AGREE TO DISAGREE.
I'M SORRY, BUT I CAN'T AGREE TO THAT EITHER.

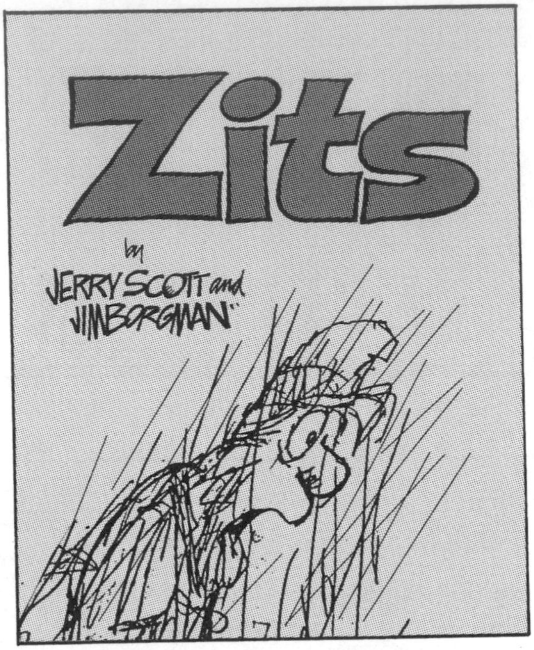
Zits
by
JERRY SCOTT and
JIM BORGMAN

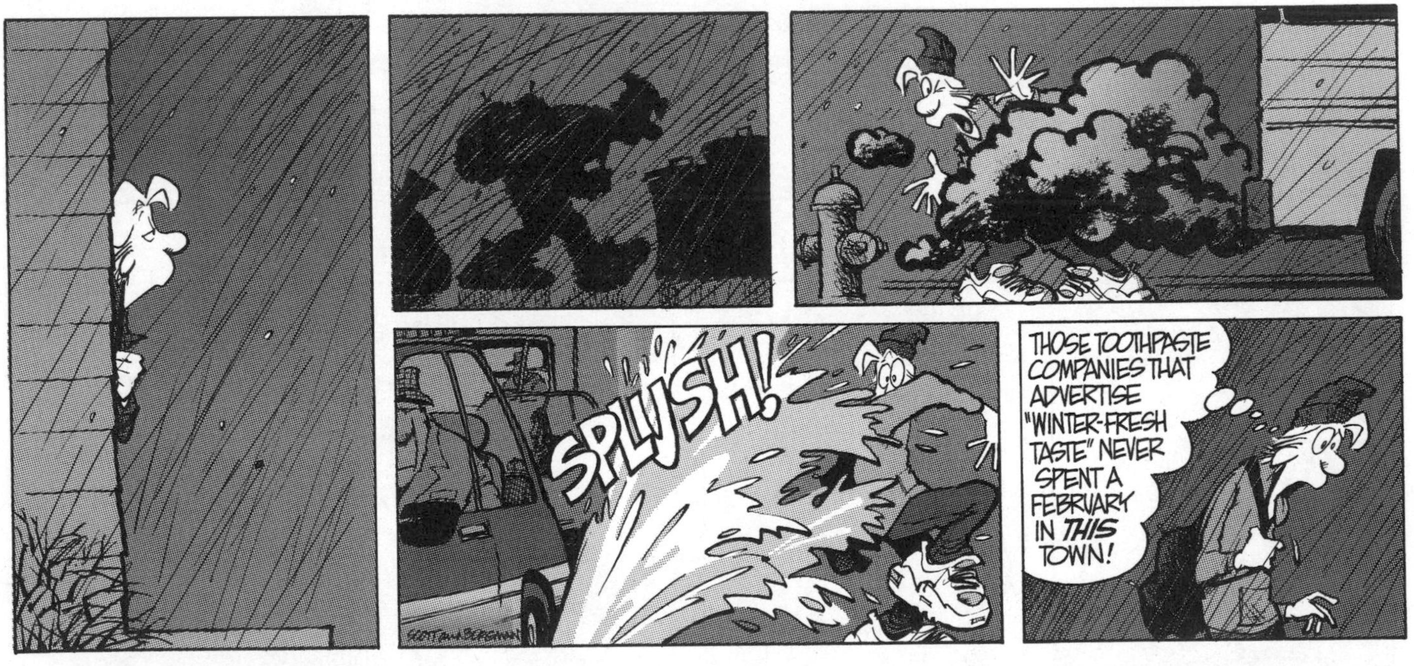
SPLUSH!
SCOTT and BORGMAN
THOSE TOOTHPASTE COMPANIES THAT ADVERTISE "WINTER-FRESH TASTE" NEVER SPENT A FEBRUARY IN *THIS* TOWN!

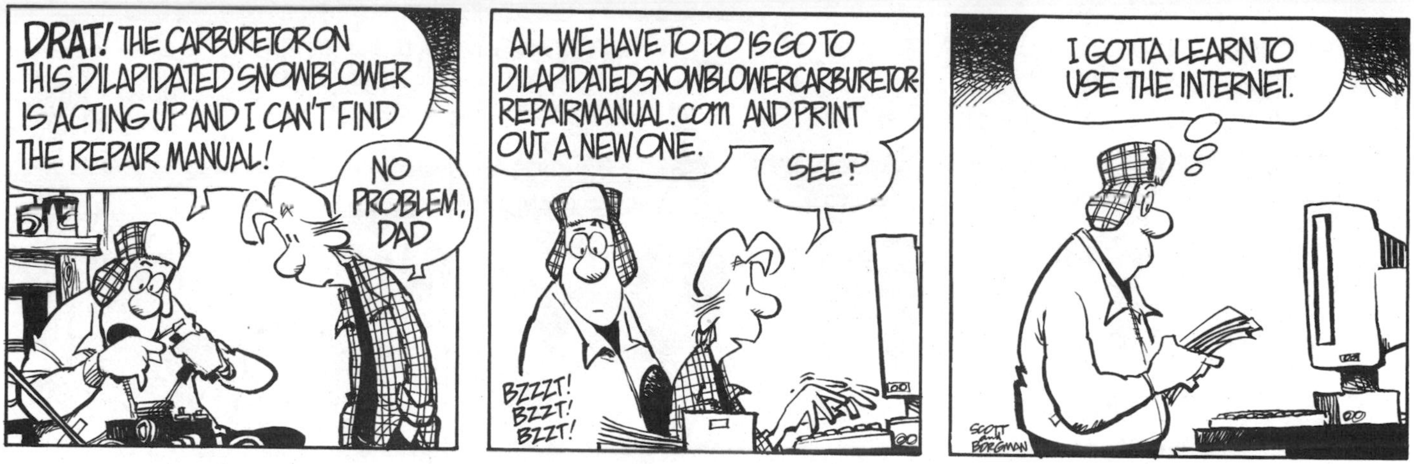
DRAT! THE CARBURETOR ON THIS DILAPIDATED SNOWBLOWER IS ACTING UP AND I CAN'T FIND THE REPAIR MANUAL!
NO PROBLEM, DAD
ALL WE HAVE TO DO IS GO TO DILAPIDATEDSNOWBLOWERCARBURETOR-REPAIRMANUAL.com AND PRINT OUT A NEW ONE.
SEE?
BZZZT! BZZT! BZZT!
I GOTTA LEARN TO USE THE INTERNET.
SCOTT and BORGMAN

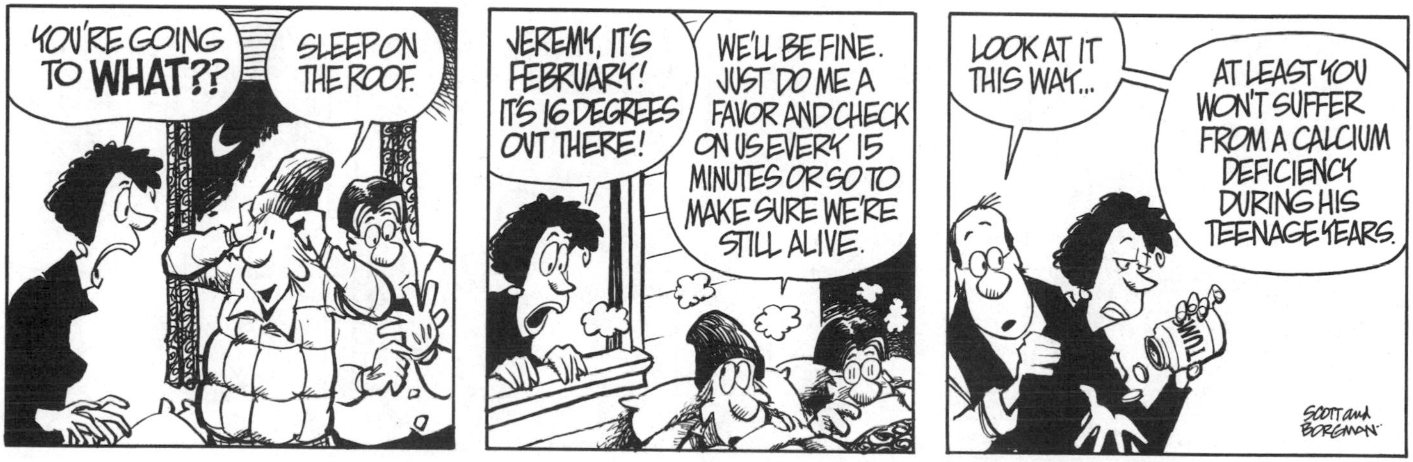
YOU'RE GOING TO WHAT??
SLEEP ON THE ROOF.
JEREMY, IT'S FEBRUARY! IT'S 16 DEGREES OUT THERE!
WE'LL BE FINE. JUST DO ME A FAVOR AND CHECK ON US EVERY 15 MINUTES OR SO TO MAKE SURE WE'RE STILL ALIVE.
LOOK AT IT THIS WAY...
AT LEAST YOU WON'T SUFFER FROM A CALCIUM DEFICIENCY DURING HIS TEENAGE YEARS.
TUMS
SCOTT and BORGMAN

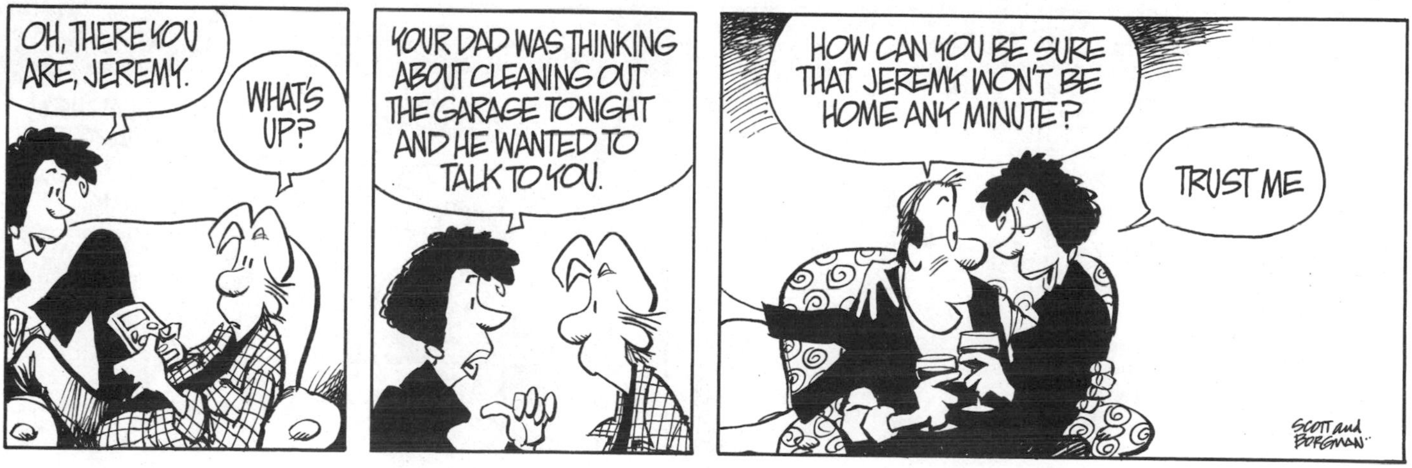
OH, THERE YOU ARE, JEREMY.
WHAT'S UP?
YOUR DAD WAS THINKING ABOUT CLEANING OUT THE GARAGE TONIGHT AND HE WANTED TO TALK TO YOU.
HOW CAN YOU BE SURE THAT JEREMY WON'T BE HOME ANY MINUTE?
TRUST ME
SCOTT and BORGMAN

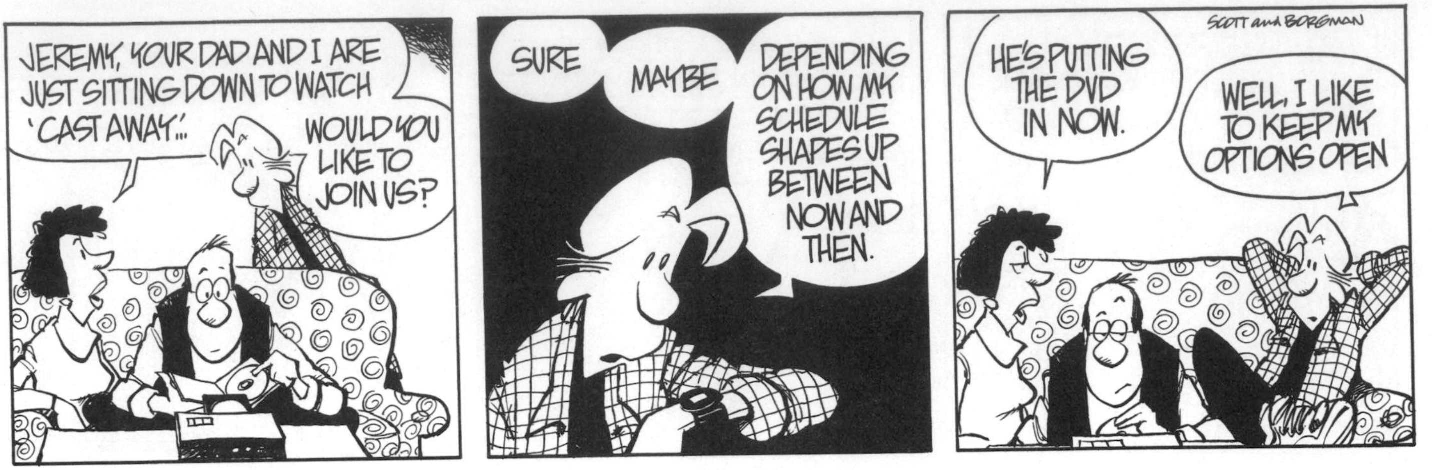
JEREMY, YOUR DAD AND I ARE JUST SITTING DOWN TO WATCH 'CAST AWAY.'...
WOULD YOU LIKE TO JOIN US?
SURE
MAYBE
DEPENDING ON HOW MY SCHEDULE SHAPES UP BETWEEN NOW AND THEN.
SCOTT and BORGMAN
HE'S PUTTING THE DVD IN NOW.
WELL, I LIKE TO KEEP MY OPTIONS OPEN

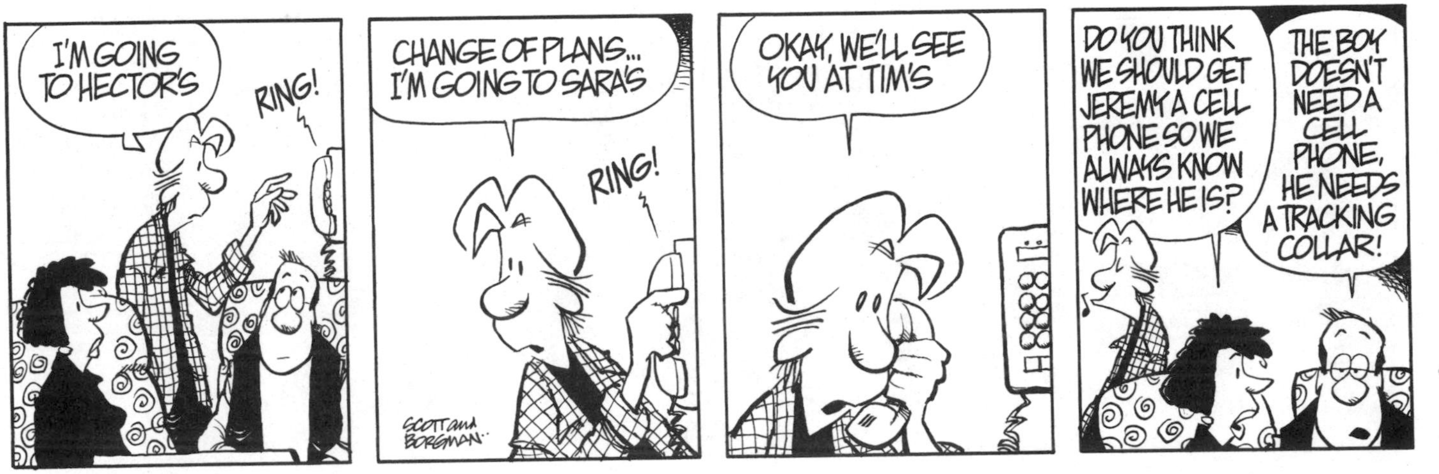
I'M GOING TO HECTOR'S
RING!
CHANGE OF PLANS... I'M GOING TO SARA'S
RING!
SCOTT and BORGMAN
OKAY, WE'LL SEE YOU AT TIM'S
DO YOU THINK WE SHOULD GET JEREMY A CELL PHONE SO WE ALWAYS KNOW WHERE HE IS?
THE BOY DOESN'T NEED A CELL PHONE, HE NEEDS A TRACKING COLLAR!

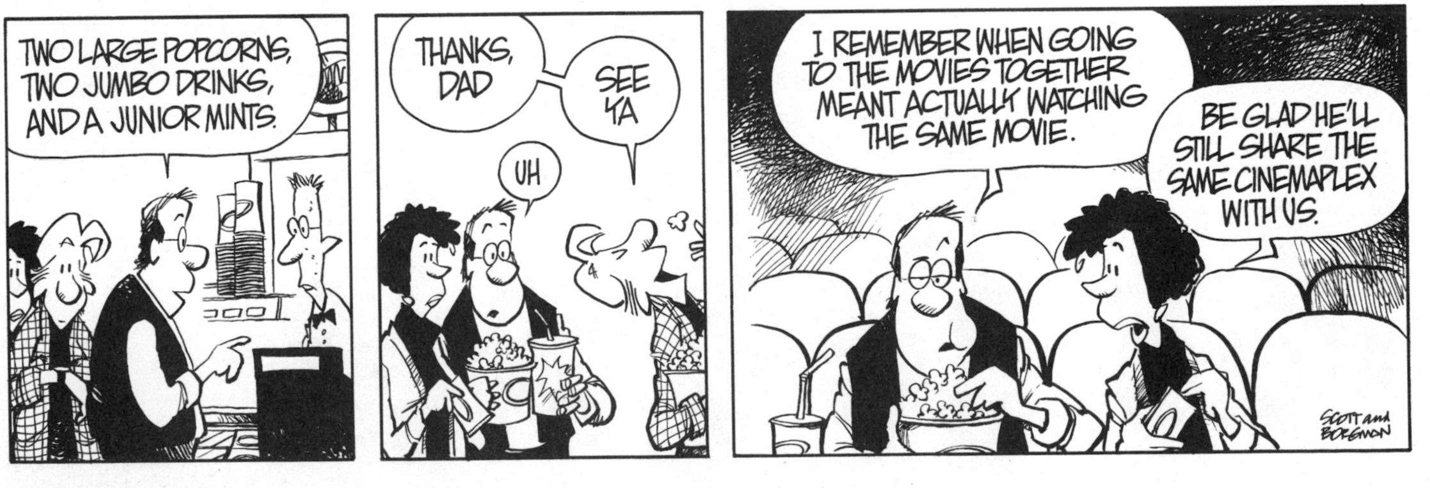
TWO LARGE POPCORNS, TWO JUMBO DRINKS, AND A JUNIOR MINTS.
THANKS, DAD
SEE YA
UH
I REMEMBER WHEN GOING TO THE MOVIES TOGETHER MEANT ACTUALLY WATCHING THE SAME MOVIE.
BE GLAD HE'LL STILL SHARE THE SAME CINEMAPLEX WITH US.
SCOTT and BORGMAN